White Utopias

The publisher and the University of California Press
Foundation gratefully acknowledge the generous support
of the Ahmanson Foundation Endowment Fund in
Humanities.

White Utopias

The Religious Exoticism of Transformational Festivals

Amanda J. Lucia

UNIVERSITY OF CALIFORNIA PRESS

University of California Press
Oakland, California

© 2020 by Amanda J. Lucia

Cataloging-in-Publication Data is on file at the
Library of Congress.

ISBN 978–0-520–37694–6 (cloth : alk. paper)
ISBN 978–0-520–37695–3 (pbk. : alk. paper)
ISBN 978–0-520–97633–7 (ebook)

Manufactured in the United States of America

29 28 27 26 25 24 23 22 21 20
10 9 8 7 6 5 4 3 2 1

For my mother

This has given me the greatest trouble and still does: to realize that what things are called is incomparably more important than what they are. The reputation, name, and appearance, the usual measure and weight of a thing, what it counts for—originally almost always wrong and arbitrary, thrown over things like a dress and altogether foreign to their nature and even to their skin—all this grows from generation unto generation, merely because people believe in it, until it gradually grows to be part of the thing and turns into its very body. What at first was appearance becomes in the end, almost invariably, the essence and is effective as such.

—Friedrich Nietzsche, *The Gay Science*

Contents

List of Illustrations — xi
Acknowledgments — xiii
Author Note — xvii

Introduction — 1

1. Romanticizing the Premodern: The Confluence of Indic and Indigenous Spiritualities — 34
   Interlude: Cultural Possession and Whiteness — 64

2. Anxieties over Authenticity: American Yoga and the Problem of Whiteness — 69
   Interlude: "White People Are on the Journey of Evolution" — 99

3. Deconstructing the Self: At the Limits of Asceticism — 104
   Interlude: Sculpting Bodies and Minds — 137

4. Wonder, Awe, and Peak Experiences: Approaching Mystical Territories — 144
   Interlude: Producing Wonder / Branding Freedom — 175

5. The Cathartic Freedom of Transformational Festivals:
   Neoliberal Escapes and Entrapments   184

   Conclusion   214

Appendix 1: @Instagram Data for Public Figures Cited   227
Appendix 2: Methodology   229
Notes   239
References   273
Index   291

Illustrations

1. Top ten offerings at Shakti Fest, 2012 / 26
2. Top ten offerings at Bhakti Fest, 2013 / 26
3. Top ten offerings at Wanderlust, Oahu, HI, 2014 / 27
4. Top ten offerings at Lightning in a Bottle, 2016 / 27
5. Top ten offerings at Burning Man, 2017 / 28
6. Author portrait, Tea and Turbans tea ceremony, Burning Man, 2017 / 48
7. "From Your Culture to Ours" sign, Burning Man, 2017 / 50
8. Woman in Native headdress, Burning Man Temple, 2016 / 58
9. The Village at Lightning in a Bottle, 2014 / 59
10. Garage Mahal Ganesh Mobile, Burning Man, 2016 / 67
11. Communal altar at Bhakti Fest, 2014 / 79
12. Sunset yoga meditation, Lightning in a Bottle, 2016 / 113
13. Yogic discipline, Wanderlust, Stratton, VT, 2018 / 129
14. Nature church, Wanderlust, Squaw Valley, CA, 2019 / 151
15. *Kīrtan* artists at Prasada Festival, 2018 / 169
16. Jaguar at Shakti Fest, 2016 / 180
17. Dystopian tattoo, Bhakti Fest, 2013 / 192
18. Yoga retreat, Wanderlust, Mont Tremblant, 2018 / 198
19. Galaxia Temple burning, Burning Man, 2018 / 207
20. "HOME" sign, Lightning in a Bottle, 2016 / 216

Acknowledgments

It is somewhat ironic that I write this book from the University of California, Riverside, the home of the Highlanders, which imagines an invented and borrowed Scottish identity based on the idea that the city of Riverside is marginally higher above sea level than the neighboring city of Los Angeles. Despite our student body being comprised of 85 percent non-Anglo-European minorities, at games and graduations, audiences sing songs of Highlander pride and don blue and yellow Scottish tartans. This imagined Scottish Highland is actually the ancestral land of the Cahuilla, Tongva, Luiseño, and Serrano peoples, and UCR is a result of Rupert (Cahuilla) and Jeannette (Eastern Cherokee) Costo's founding vision. I respectfully acknowledge and recognize our responsibility to the original caretakers of the land, water, and air where I live and work. I am also writing as a white faculty member with a degree in the History of Religions and a research specialty in Hinduism, itself a colonial construction. Like the study of Native traditions, the study of Hinduism is rife with contested debates over representation that cannot be extricated from racial power dynamics exacerbated by colonial histories.

I am deeply beholden to UCR as the place where the perspectives of my students and colleagues led me to provincialize myself and my field of study. I am hesitant to name those who challenged my thinking on race and ethnicity in the United States lest I not live up to their high standards, but Daisy Vargas, Josh Little, Leven Kali, Anthea Kraut, Sarita See, Jacqueline Shea Murphy, Jennifer Najera, Michele Raheja, and Dylan Rodriguez each shifted my perspective. Their seeds, even if they didn't know they planted them, altered my perspective and reformulated the ways in which I had been trained to frame the study of religion in the United States. Jonathan Walton once explained that his time at UCR was like earning a second doctorate. Amen. I have been privileged to be supported in such an environment and to learn from and be challenged by students and colleagues alike.

I also recognize my privilege in that this is a post-tenure, second book. This positionality enabled me to research academically marginalized topics outside of the sanction of traditional forms of religion. As one funder exclaimed to me after I presented an early report on my research, "I didn't realize we were paying people to go camping!" Routinely, at least some members of scholarly audiences laughed at my informants and dismissed their practices as New Age silliness. My positionality, including my whiteness, enabled me to feel (mostly) confident in enduring these slights and admonishments. In completing this book, I remain convinced that these populations are more important than the traditionalists realize and that they are actively reshaping our conception of religion in modernity.

This was an expensive book, as it necessitated my keeping up (even in a limited way) with the transformational festival circuit. Considerable funding enabled me to access these networks in difficult but possible ways. This research was supported by grants from UCR's Academic Senate Committee on Research, UCR's Center for Ideas and Society (CIS), a Hellman Fellowship, and a Religion in Diaspora and Global Affairs (RIDAGA) Humanities Studio Award sponsored by the University of California Humanities Research Institute and the Henry Luce Foundation. Two writing retreats, sponsored by the College of Humanities, Arts, and Social Sciences (CHASS) Mid-Career Research Initiative and the Inequities in Health Faculty Commons group, respectively, both funded by CIS, bookended the bulk of my writing. I am grateful to Dana Simmons and Tanya Nieri for facilitating my participation. I thank both CIS's and UCR's administrative staff, particularly Diana Marroquin, for her undying patience and expertise in executing the financial administration that made this book possible.

I thank conference audiences who responded to portions of this work at the American Academy of Religion Annual Conference, South Asian Studies Association Conference, the Race and Yoga Research Working Group at UC Berkeley, the University of Wisconsin-Madison South Asia Conference, and the Society for Pilgrimage Studies Conference. Early presentations of this research at Indiana University and at UCR's Department of Dance colloquium completely transformed the trajectory of my research and my guiding questions, and to these critical audiences I owe an enormous debt of gratitude. I also benefited greatly from the excellent questions asked during my presentations of this research at the Asia Research Institute (ARI) in Singapore; the University of Otago in New Zealand; Middlebury College; California State University, Bakersfield; the University Club in Claremont, California; the Religious Studies department at UCR; the Burning Man and Transformational Event Cultures Symposium at the University of Fribourg, Switzerland; and Yogascapes 2.0 at Kyoto University. I am extraordinarily grateful to Bernardo Brown, Ben Schonthal, E. Burke Rochford, Michael Burroughs, Donna Bernard, Melissa Wilcox, Francois Gauthier, Graham St. John, and Patrick McCartney for their generous invitations to present my research.

With such extensive, multiple, and variegated field sites, this project never would have come to fruition without the dedication and skills of several outstanding research assistants. Jen Aubrecht, Gloria Williams, Larissa Arambula, Jason Cardenas, and Cristina Rosetti were outstanding companions in the field, and their insights and experiences greatly enhanced my own perspective. I am deeply indebted to Anna Beck for her help with transcriptions. She also took an interview on her own that proved exceptionally valuable. I am grateful to Deepak Sarma, Anya Foxen, James Edmonds, Nathan McGovern, Jen Sandler, and Jonas Huffer, as well as two anonymous reviewers for their critical insights in reading and commenting on earlier drafts of this manuscript. I thank Eric Schmidt, Austin Lim, and the editorial board at the University of California Press for their astute suggestions and practical guidance in making this a more legible book. I am also indebted to Dominique Debucquoy-Dodley at Burning Man Project, Karina Mackenzie at Wanderlust, my proofreader Kirsten Janene-Nelson, photographer Scott London, and photo editor Aimée-Linh McCartney for their assistance in the final stages of production.

This book is also entirely dependent on the charity and kindness of my informants in the field. Countless unnamed participants gave me the gift of their time and opened their hearts to intimate conversations with a stranger. Some passed through this ephemeral field and seemingly evaporated into the ether. Some became dear friends. I thank all of the festival producers, yoga teachers, *kīrtan* musicians, and workshop leaders who devote their time and energy to creating rejuvenating environments for weary travelers. In particular, I am grateful to Sridhar Silberfein, Shiva Rea, MC Yogi, DJ Drez, Ana Forrest, Hemalayaa, Brenda Patoine, and

Lorin Roche for fitting our interviews into their demanding schedules. Marian Goodell, Cameron Shayne, Mark Whitwell, Elena Brower, Saul David Raye, Aditi Devi Ma, Michael Brian Baker, Rob Sidon, Maura Malini Hoffman, Prajna Vieira, David Estes, and Seane Corn were also generous in conversation. I thank the participants who used the festival spaces to expose the tenderest parts of their souls, revealing their vulnerable and raw interiors to others. I am deeply grateful, in particular, to Split, Lucifer, Noa, Honoria, Clive, Doug, Dane, Nick, Pixel, Christian, Stone, Meow Meow, Chakra, Buddha, Topanga, Atreyu, Chance, Dao, Luke, Franklin, Wombat, Windflower, Jeremiah, Loco, Bootleg, Dancing Bob, Grace, GunPowder, Firemonk, Foxsicle, Blaine, John, Cafune, Devon, Peter, Chenoya, Tynacity, Chef Dave, Golden Rose, Megan Miller, Megs Rutigliano, Steven Raspa, Josh Lease, Molly Rose, Stuart Mangrum, Caveat Magister, and all the folks in the French Quarter Village, Comfy Cozy Voodoo Lounge, Savage Island, Camp Mystic, and Anahasana Village, and many others for showing me the variety of amazing ways to Burn, the meaning of chosen family, and how to be builders and bakers, movers and shakers. Thank you all.

Lastly, this book has demanded considerable time away from home, and for weathering that, I thank my children, Jonas and Zoe. They have grown up with festival stories in their lives, and through this they have learned to see the world as a place of possibility for adventure, exploration, and wonder. None of this would have been possible without my mother and their father, who managed in my absence everything from my children's first day of first grade to their first day of college. Thank you. Most of all, I am deeply indebted to all of my conversation partners as I worked through my complicated feelings about this research, in particular, my friends and colleagues Sarah Pike, Shreena Gandhi, Christa Kuberry, Anya Foxen, Andrea Jain, Christopher Chapple, Michael Alexander, and most deeply, Matthew King, Jennifer Scheper Hughes, Keith MacGregor, Ingrid Jacobson, Lucas Carmichael, and Jen Sandler. Many of these people weathered this storm and sometimes felt each lash of rain as I did—often before I had taken adequate time to process it. I am in awe of your empathy and generosity. Any and all inadequacies in the forthcoming pages are entirely my own.

Author Note

White Utopias was finalized for publication in June 2020 during long-overdue uprisings for racial justice in the United States and around the globe. I submit this book to readers as my own small contribution to the continued interrogation of whiteness. Several of my informants have been resistant to this centering of whiteness (see Methodology section), and during my research (2011–2019), I rarely heard whites in these fields discuss the Black Lives Matter movement or its concerns. Today, in the midst of marches, protests, organizing, and revolt, many yogis and festival participants are discussing racism in myriad expressions, some in anti-racist ways. I hope that by laying bare the contours, expressions, and controls of whiteness, this project contributes to provincializing its power. No justice, no peace. Black Lives Matter.

NOTE ON LANGUAGE

All of the ethnographic research quoted in this manuscript was conducted in English unless otherwise noted. For Sanskrit terms incorporated into the English language (e.g., guru, ashram, Tantra, mantra, and yoga), I have removed diacritics and italics. When referencing less frequently occurring Sanskrit terms (e.g., *āsana, kīrtan, chaturanga, prāṇām,* and *prāṇāyāma*) and to identify Sanskrit texts (e.g., *Yoga Sūtras*), I have retained italics and diacritics to help readers with pronunciation. I have maintained English pluralization norms (e.g., ashrams, mantras, and *kīrtans*).

Introduction

Shakti Fest, 2015

As the sun crests over the arid desert of Joshua Tree, California, Chandan (Isaiah), a middle-aged white man in the attire of a Hindu priest, sits at a fire pit and leads the assembled crowd in reciting Vedic mantras. A large audience of participants responds with cries of "svāhā!" to each of the hundreds of Sanskrit invocations that he recites as he offers oblations into the fire. There is palpable excitement in the air; the homa *(fire sacrifice) invokes an auspicious beginning of Shakti Fest, a five-day yoga and* kīrtan *(devotional music) festival.* Homas *are ancient Vedic rites traditionally performed by Indian Hindu brahman priests for auspicious occasions. But here in the California desert, whites define, create, and administer the Hindu rituals at Shakti Fest; participants may be serious, dedicated practitioners of Hindu rituals, but they identify as "spiritual, but not religious."*

Several days prior and one hundred yards away, the temple is silent in the Joshua Tree Retreat Center, the home of the Institute of Mentalphysics[1] *and for this weekend, the sacred geography of Shakti Fest. Over the course of the upcoming festival weekend, the temple will bustle with thousands attending lectures, workshops, and yoga classes with some of the leading yogis and* kīrtan *artists in the United States. But this morning, the sacred geometrical architecture of the temple reverberates with a more subtle and calm energy as the famed yoga teacher Eli Gordon intones in a soft lilting voice and invites a small group of dedicated yogis to enter the "waters of consciousness" with a series of deep breaths. He begins this full-day intensive yoga workshop by drawing participants into the heart space that he is creating, weaving together an aura of sacrality with ideas drawn from multiple religious traditions: Hinduism, Buddhism, Zen, Sufism, and Native American*

I

religions. His poetic spiritual tapestries create a narrative that reveals humanity and the earth in crisis: there is a problem with modernity and a dire need for a solution. Like many others before him, he articulates the need in terms of a recovery project: ancient wisdom has been lost, and it needs to be found and revitalized. In his words,

> [Albert] Einstein said very beautifully, "The ancient people seem to have understood something very important that we have lost." And the answer is not of course to go back to the way things were thousands of years ago because that would deny all of what's happened since. This evolutionary wave is coming together which is so beautifully evident here in the desert. All these practices and different tribal members and colors of the rainbow creating a new way. There are certain principles which are so important. And of course, nothing is more important than the Mother, the Earth.[2]

In these few sentences, he weaves together an admiration for science, but also the mourning of the loss of premodern knowledge, a demand for a new evolution, an affirmation of creating a bricolage of practices and people for spiritual innovation, a celebration of the unification of tribes, and a demand for the centrality of ecology. These are the ideals; yoga is the method.

. . .

Burning Man Work Party, Summer 2016

After an hour-long drive wearing my tattered, paint-smeared, get-ready-to-work overalls, I carried my light and somewhat unscathed toolbox through the driveway gate at the Sunland property. In my other hand, I had a cooler, filled with frozen homemade green juice I had pressed for day five of my juice fast. Standing in the courtyard, to my right, was the Blind Mistress, a two-story vision of an art car built out of an old RV, currently languishing in various states of disarray. Looking back, I stood at the precipice between two worlds. For the past five years, I had been inculcated into the world of yogic transformational festivals. I had arrived at this French Quarter Village work party in Los Angeles prepared to learn about the grandfather of these festivals, Burning Man. But instead of continuity, there was difference, which I noted as the cigarettes lit up after the hearty work crew rewarded themselves with a midday meal of loaded pizzas and beers. I longed for all of it, but instead I sipped my green juice—eyes wide open. The collected crew of about ten Burning Man veterans laughed and told stories of life and Burns past. Immediately, I felt at home in this tightly knit and intimately connected established community. When the jokes and stories became marked with silences, it was time to get back to work. I climbed into one of the top-floor sleeping compartments of the Blind Mistress, which was oven hot in the afternoon sun, and I began to wire the outlets.

That morning, when I had first walked in, I had set down my toolbox and cooler of green juice. My presence in the early morning somewhat surprised Sloane and Michael, who were already hard at work. I was a stranger and felt a bit like an intruder, but I explained I was here to help and introduced myself. They exchanged a glance that conveyed a semblance of, "Who is going to take this one?" Sloane stopped what he was doing, looked at me, and said, "What can you do?" I said something like, "I'm fairly handy. I am smart, and I can learn things. I can paint, but I don't do electrical." He paused for a beat and said, "Well—do you want to learn electrical? Because I need an assistant." I learned electrical from Sloane all that day and every weekend for the next month. By the end, I could pull and run wire, wire an outlet with attached switch or stand alone, and climb a twenty-foot ladder safely without being nervous.

From the outset, Sloane was very concerned with teaching me to learn for myself. He would show me and then let me do it. When I was done, I would ask him to check my work, and he would ask: "Do I need to? How do you feel about it? Does it need to be checked?" Several weeks later, on the playa[3] during build week of my first Burning Man (the week before the gates open), I was struggling to throw a heavy cable fifteen feet in the air to him. I tried and failed, repeatedly. A friend walked by, saw my struggle, and threw the cable up to him for me. Sloane laughed, thanked him, and then dropped the cable back down to me, telling him, "I want her to learn to do it." I kept throwing the cable, and eventually, he caught it. While we worked, I learned the basics of how to throw a cable and how to do electrical wiring, but I also learned to recognize that my mental frame had set limitations for my own potential when I had said, "I don't do electrical." At one point during our working banter, Sloane said, "I can't even tell you how many women I have done this for," meaning that he felt he had empowered these women to accomplish tasks they hadn't thought they could do. We might imagine Sloane, over his twenty-year career as a Burner, as an enabler of personal transformation. Burning Man is filled with leaders like him, who actively open avenues for others to exceed their existing sense of self.

. . .

In the four years since that day, that old toolbox fell apart from overuse and I bought a bigger one—and an impact driver. I know more about propane mechanics than I ever thought that I would. I recently told an old friend that I was looking into buying a trailer. He laughed in surprise because a decade ago that idea never would have crossed my mind. Have I been transformed by transformational festivals? Certainly. There is a gallon of homemade green juice in my freezer, and I have a new toolbox. With that said, my decades-long practice of yoga has waned in the course of this fieldwork, as I have focused more explicitly on its global reformulation as a practice for supple bodied, affluent, white women. As a white woman, I moved freely through each of my field sites, and at the close of this research, I am painfully aware of that privilege and the ways in which it, for me, tarnishes the radical potential of these utopias.

There is an ocean of difference between these two transformational festival worlds, and this book does not intend to minimize that fact. But they are also held together by similar utopian visions and a shared commitment to personal and social transformation that is intentionally crafted in the reformulation of everyday practices and perspectives. Both are deeply embedded in much larger interlacing and overlapping networks comprised of organizations, events, literatures, and discourses that echo similar themes. Sloane drew on his experience in other transformational workshops to enable me to reframe and expand beyond what I imagined to be my limitations—for example, "I don't do electrical." Eli Gordon invited us (yoga practitioners) to imagine the world differently, to participate in an "evolutionary wave," and to create a "new way." But Eli Gordon's vision of all of the "different tribal members and colors of the rainbow" coming together to be present in his Shakti Fest yoga class and to actualize that utopian vision doesn't quite match reality. In fact, in the United States, these communities, whether they are made up of yoga practitioners, transformational festival participants, or those involved in metaphysical spirituality, are approximately 85 percent white. This book centralizes this demographic fact and questions why. Especially in a state like California, where whites comprise only 38.8 percent of the population,[4] why do these particular spaces of spiritual seeking remain predominantly white?

White Utopias attempts to unravel this uncomfortable demographic reality in the pages that follow. I argue that while transformational festivals create fecund opportunities for spiritual growth, their dependence on religious exoticism serves as a deterrent to nonwhite potential participants. My ethnographic research reveals that in their critique of the existing status quo, participants turn to Indigenous and Indic[5] religious forms because they imagine them to be expressions of alternative lifeways existing outside of modernity. This fundamental act of distancing and appropriation means that these movements tend to gravitate toward neoromantic forms that stem from nineteenth-century conceptions of the Anglo-European self as civilized and modern while relegating nonwhites to the primitive and premodern.

In his research on the viscosity, or the stickiness, of whiteness in countercultural spaces, Arun Saldanha writes, "It is a commonplace assumption that whites have for a long time been fascinated and transformed by drawing on other people's cultures and landscapes. . . . Yet the fact that white appropriations of otherness were fueled by a conscious effort to transcend the constrains of white society—that European exoticism and primitivism, though intertwined with colonial subjugation, also tell of the self-critique and self-transformation of whites—has seldom been put at the center of theorization."[6] *White Utopias* is an attempt to put this exact notion at the center, engaging the uncomfortable juxtaposition between problematic religious exoticism *and* productive self-critique and self-transformation.

I argue that these populations identify with alterity to forge personal solutions to the struggles of modernity. They identify as "spiritual but not religious" and, as Christopher Driscoll and Monica Miller argue, aim to enact the "decentering or death of whiteness, with 'spiritual' signifying on the manufactured closeness to the 'empirical other.'"[7] In drawing closer to the "other," they destabilize whiteness by rejecting systems of white supremacy in which they are enmeshed, but they do so from within safe spaces of white ethnic homogeneity. At festivals, they speak in self-affirming echo chambers imagined as evolutionary paths to enlightenment and rarely engage with ethnically diverse populations. Because people of color are rarely present as authorities teaching and sharing their own religious and cultural forms, white SBNR adopters and their representations end up reinforcing the logics of white possessivism despite their idealized attempts to decenter whiteness.

My research also reveals that the more yogic the field, the more it is focused on internal self-transformation as the primary agent of social change; as the famed yogi activist Seane Corn writes, "Our evolution *is* the revolution."[8] While some yogis follow Corn's broader call for humanitarian activism, a much larger majority directs attention to personal evolution by engaging with ascetical and mystical modalities. In her analysis of women in the New Age, Karlyn Crowley questions, "Why angels and not activism?"[9] In these fields, with a few notable exceptions, there is a similar focus on spiritual transformation over social engagement.[10] The result is an affective experience of freedom and not the freedom work of building social and political solidarities with the "exotic" populations these communities so deeply admire.

THE AVAILABLE EXOTIC / THE USABLE PRIMITIVE: PLAYING INDIAN

Long before the New Age dawned, Americans turned to religious others when dissatisfied with the dominant culture. As the historian Philip Jenkins explains, "The perennial American interest in Indians grows and shrinks in inverse proportion to satisfaction with mainstream society.... Throughout American history, romantic Indian images are most sought after in eras of alienation and crisis."[11] Americans have engaged with Indigenous and Indic cultural and religious forms in multifarious ways as a means to protest and reject Euro-American culture. By adopting exoticized practices of marginalized religious minorities, they have offered critiques of industrialization, consumerism, rationality, violence, sexual repression, and the devastation of nature. At the turn of the twentieth century, white women flocked to Swami Vivekananda to practice mediation and breathing exercises. Several decades later, South Asian swamis and yogis crisscrossed the United States, drawing large audiences as interested in their mystical personas as in their yogic techniques. Even at that time, whites quickly positioned themselves as representative authorities of yogic traditions. Oom the Omnipotent (Pierre Arnold Bernard from Leon, Iowa), for instance, built his Tantric utopia first in San Francisco and later in the sanctity and seclusion of rural upstate New York. Following the model of white appropriation of Native religions, whites have instrumentalized Indic religious forms to find direction and to craft an outlet for their critique of the existing status quo.[12]

In the wake of World War I, the bohemians of the 1920s flocked to the American Southwest and founded intellectual and artistic communities from which they critiqued assimilationist policies and Christian missionaries; some even argued for the supremacy of Native culture. World War II revealed the fragility and moral failings of European culture, and the subsequent destabilization of Europe called into question Euro-American claims to cultural superiority; subsequently, the 1940s saw a notable popularization of Native American traditions. Similarly, in the 1970s, massive public distrust in government fueled another turn toward Native American traditions. Philip Jenkins's careful historical account of white engagements with Native American religions reveals that one of the primary errors of the 1960s counterculture was to assume that "all previous generations had shared the racist contempt of the early settlers, the dismissal of native religions as crude devil worship."[13] Instead, the 1960s exemplified only the twentieth century's latest expression of a counterculture deeply informed by religious exoticism.

Once again, as a result of dissatisfaction with the status quo, the counterculture of the 1960s was partially constituted by the commonplace practice of modern Anglos "searching for primal authenticity."[14] Employing the modalities of religious exoticism, the leaders of the counterculture embraced symbols and practices extracted from Indic and Indigenous religions. While Frank Waters may have made "the Ganges flow into the Rio Grande" in his writings in the 1950s, as Jenkins suggests, the 1960s counterculture easily blended the Indic and Indigenous, creating a confluence (*sangham*) of distinct cultural rivers. Gary Snyder protested the war in Vietnam by identifying with Native religion and cursing the white man in the *San Francisco Oracle,* penning the famous lines:

As I kill the white man
    the "American"
        in me
And dance out the ghost dance:
To bring back America, the grass and the streams,

To trample your throat in your dreams.

This magic I work, this loving I give
    That my children may flourish

And yours won't live.[15]

The following year, the Beatles sat at the feet of Maharishi Mahesh Yogi in Rishikesh, India, which would lead George Harrison to take the *mahāmantra*[16] of the Hare Krishnas to the number-twelve position on the UK singles chart in 1969 and again in the chorus of the major hit "My Sweet Lord" in 1976. Jimi Hendrix wanted the cover of his 1967 record *Axis: Bold as Love* to reflect his Cherokee heritage, but in an impactful miscommunication, David King, the commissioned cover designer for the Track Records label, misinterpreted his notion of "Indian" and found a mass-produced image of the Hindu deity Vishnu in a London shop and superimposed Hendrix's face (alongside Noel Redding and Mitch Mitchell) over the image. The resulting famous image of Jimi Hendrix in the omnipresent form of the incarnation of the Hindu god Krishna (*virāt puruṣan viśvarupam*) became one of the most iconic album covers in rock history.[17] While centuries had passed since Columbus's infamous error of mistaking Native Americans for Indians, 1960s counterculture blended and sometimes conflated the two seamlessly.

The turn to the exotic is the response of a population seeking a solution to feelings of malaise and dislocation derived from "feeling uprooted from cultural traditions, community belonging, and spiritual meaning."[18] It begins with a salient critique of hegemonic Western modernity, but instead of tackling those challenges through reform, rebellion, or revolution, this population looks to inhabit other social models for alternative solutions, and, more predominantly, to find existential meaning. Its solutions are often therapeutic rather than political, aimed to alleviate the feeling of "rampant alienation that characterizes modernity—the sense of being rootless and adrift, cut off from tradition and history."[19] The exotic other is established as an unsullied premodern subject and diametrically opposed to the "cold conformity and ecological devastation of white America, the 'dead city,'"[20] whose "own cultural heritage of meaningful ritual seems like a well run dry."[21] Religious exoticism romanticizes racialized others as unsullied, exotic, premodern subjects whose cultural products supply practical, therapeutic tools. Exoticism is a mask for utopianism.[22]

This book employs the framework of exoticism as a theoretical tool to define a set of relations between segments of the "spiritual but not religious" populations and those deemed as radically other. As a category, exoticism has been discussed primarily in cultural studies, the arts, and anthropology in reference to the ambivalent portrayal of others as both alluring and repulsive. In her recent work, the French sociologist Véronique Altglas introduces the term *religious exoticism*, which I build upon in this book. She writes,

> [Religious exoticism] suggests an attempt to grasp otherness, yet what is exotic is not an "inherent quality" of particular social groups, places, ideas or practices. Indeed, no one is intrinsically "other." Exoticism is instead relations; it is a "particular mode of aesthetic perception" that emphasizes, and to a certain extent elaborates, the otherness of groups, locations, ideas, and practices (Huggan 2001, 13). Moreover, the exotic is attractive *because* it is seen as being "different" (Todorov 1993, 264); exoticism makes otherness "strangely or unfamiliarly beautiful and enticing" (Figueira 1994, 1). Yet it is less about accounting for cultural differences than formulating an ideal, by dramatizing and even constructing differences.... Furthermore, Todorov (1993, 265) argues that, to elaborate and maintain the representations of idealized others, it is necessary to ignore the "reality" of other peoples and cultures.[23]

Thus, exoticism is a constructed representation of the other in service of the production of the self. In his seminal work on human diversity, Tzvetan Todorov explains that exoticism is the antithesis of nationalism. While nationalists valorize the values of their own country as superior to those of others, exoticists retort that "the country with superior values is a country whose only relevant characteristic is that it is not my own."[24] Its allure is also dependent, at least at the outset, on a lack of knowledge about the other. He writes, "The best candidates for the role of exotic ideal are the peoples and cultures that are most remote from us and least known to us. Now it is not easy to equate unfamiliarity with others, the refusal to see them as they are, with a valorization of these others. It is a decidedly ambiguous compliment to praise others simply because they are different from myself. Knowledge is incompatible with exoticism, but lack of knowledge is in turn irreconcilable with praise of others; yet praise without knowledge is precisely what exoticism aspires to be. This is its constitutive paradox."[25] In the ethnographic fields of transformational festivals discussed in this book, behaviors exhibiting appropriations of the exotic often correlate to the place on the spectrum of knowledge that participants occupy. Those enraptured with the allure of the exotic but holding little knowledge may be seen in exotic costumes playing at inhabiting the imagined identities of radical others. Those who have more experience in proximity to those radical others tend to exhibit a more tempered realism in their dress and behavior. They may still maintain the ideals of exoticism, but they are more serious in their identifications. In the religious field, this identification often takes the form of full lifestyle modifications, conversions in all but name.

Altglas notes that Orientalism, a term introduced famously by Edward Said, follows this same pattern and can be regarded as one example of a larger paradigm of exoticism.[26] The adoption of religious exoticism substantiates claims of a new self, one that is autonomously governed and free from regulatory boundaries and institutional affiliations. As Altglas recounts, "[Pierre] Bourdieu (1984, 370) viewed individuals' involvement in Transcendental Meditation, yoga, Zen, martial arts, holistic and post-psychoanalytic therapies, as well as esotericism, as 'an inventory of thinly disguised expressions of a sort of dream of social flying, a desperate effort to defy the gravity of the social field.'"[27] Bourdieu argued that in their attempt to break free of their finite social station, the petit bourgeoisie perform a "practical utopianism," "which predisposes them to welcome every form of utopia."[28] The turn toward alternative utopias, including the adoption of the practical spiritual wares of religious others, is the result of a therapeutic process of self-definition and class distinction. The petit bourgeoisie engages in religious exoticism to garner distinction in efforts to "detach itself both from the non-cosmopolitan working classes and the conventional fractions of the bourgeoisie." This process employs the domestication of otherness in efforts to "produce an emotionally and culturally competent self."[29]

In this vein, the Dakota scholar and historian Phillip Deloria argues that in postmodern spirituality various codes are reformulated into complex amalgams suited to particular therapeutic desires. The dislocation of codes from their Indigenous cultural context and their amalgamation into a spiritual self becomes an index for an alternative aspiration of wholeness, established in contradistinction to the fragmented self of postmodernity. In fact, in Deloria's view, New Age religion is greatly informed by a crisis of meaning generated by postmodernism, which abolished metanarratives while relativizing claims to truth. He explains, "Heavily based in self-help and personal development therapies, its [New Age's] proponents await a large-scale change in human consciousness and a utopian era of peace and harmony. In New Age identity quests, one can see the long shadows of certain strands of postmodernism: increasing reliance on texts and interpretations, runaway individualism within a rhetoric of community, the distancing of native people, and a gaping disjuncture between a cultural realm of serious play and the power dynamics of social conflict."[30] The New Age further dissociated from real actors in favor of a romanticized imaginary, creating indices more malleable and controllable than their flesh-and-blood referents.

White Utopias argues that the commonplace ideals and practices of religious exoticism are directly related to the overwhelming whiteness of alternative spiritual communities. Although she does not directly address this white majority, Altglas argues that religious exoticism is dependent on feelings of entitlement. She writes that "exotic representations and discourses are overwhelmingly elaborated by the observer, not the observed (Todorov 1993, 264). This presupposes the entitlement and the power to do so (Figueira 1994, 2).... Practicing yoga or meditation, joining Native Americans in a sweat lodge, studying Kabbalah while expressing disdain for Judaism ... are all contemporary practices that unavoidably presuppose a sense of entitlement."[31] As will be discussed in a forthcoming section, this entitlement aligns easily with neocolonial logics of white possessivism.

SPIRITUAL, BUT NOT RELIGIOUS

Twenty-seven percent of the US population identifies as "spiritual, but not religious" (SBNR) according to a 2017 Pew Research study, and that figure is growing exponentially.[32] A similar study, also conducted by the Pew Research Center, identified that just under 20 percent of the US population responds with "none" when questioned about their institutional religious affiliation, and of those, 37 percent identify as SBNR.[33] However, and somewhat surprisingly, only a small percentage of those who respond with "none" identify as nonreligious or antireligious. Instead, a large majority of them say that they believe in God (68 percent) and feel a deep connection with nature and the earth (58 percent), and a significant percentage of them say that they pray every day (21 percent).[34] There is growth in SBNR populations across the various demographic groups in the United States, but the most accelerated growth and the highest numbers emerge from white women who are college educated and vote Democrat. It is no wonder then that American yogis also tend to identify as SBNR, as many of them fall into this very demographic.

There is a broad diversity to the beliefs and practices of people who identify as "spiritual but not religious." The religion scholars Catherine Albanese and Courtney Bender have named *metaphysical religion* as that which draws on long-standing traditions of New Thought, Swedenborgianism, Christian Science, Spiritualism, magic, science, and the occult. Albanese suggests that it stands for "an American religious mentality" that focuses on a preoccupation of mind, a predisposition toward the ancient cosmological theory of correspondence between worlds (as carried out in the esoteric tradition of the West), thinking of the mind and its correspondences in terms of movement and energy, and a yearning for salvation understood as solace, comfort, therapy, and healing.[35] Bender argues that metaphysical religion privileges experience and mysticism and operates through "entangled" networks in an institutional field, in "cultures that catch people in relations to each other."[36] This book envisions transformational festivals as one form of institution wherein SBNR communities congeal and reproduce their common ideologies. It demonstrates how transformational festivals create temporary utopias that invite participants into the celebration of eclectic, bricolage forms of spirituality.

However, I also see a divide in metaphysical religion that has not been thoroughly investigated. One end of the spectrum relies heavily on Christian principles, doctrine, and practice. It is in some sense a creative improvisation in the key of Protestant Christianity as much as it attempts to be "post-Protestant."[37] At the other end of the spectrum are those who turn away from institutional Abrahamic traditions (in the United States, mostly Christianity and Catholicism, but also, to some extent, Judaism) and toward practical tools adopted from non-Abrahamic religions (usually Hinduism, Buddhism, and Indigenous religions, and occasionally Sufism, Kabbalah, and Western esotericism). This subsection of the SBNR population adopts religious exoticism to produce mystical experiences, awakenings of consciousness, and spiritual growth through meditation, yoga, chanting, visualization, dreaming, psychedelics (medicine), and ascetic practices.

Scholars have frequently argued that SBNR populations are defined by unimpeded individual choice that emerges as a result of freedom from religious institutions.[38] Such theories support the notion that today's SBNR populations are creating self-designed bricolage spiritual conglomerations that are personally tailored to their individual preferences. The most famous example of this is Robert Bellah's 1985 account of a woman named Sheila, who described her faith as listening "to my own little voice" and framed her personalized spirituality as "Sheilaism."[39] Bellah, like many sociologists of religion at the time, saw the increase in SBNR populations as a signal for the declining importance of religion in modernity. Many bemoaned the individualism of millions of Sheilas and feared that SBNR populations would not create strong communities. In contrast, *White Utopias* argues that that there is much unrecognized soteriological continuity in these fields and that transformational festivals and yoga classes are two examples of underrecognized institutional communities wherein collective ideals are reproduced and disseminated.

Furthermore, religious exoticism also reveals a historical continuity in the particular cultural ideas and discourses it circulates. In the New Age bookstores of my youth, I found translations of *The Tibetan Book of the Dead* alongside Ram Dass's *Be Here Now*[40] and translations of the *Dao de Ching*, shelved next to Motherpeace tarot cards, statues of Egyptian deities, Native American smudge sticks, and Pagan ritual manuals. This amalgamation was congealed in the religious explorations of the Transcendentalists in the 1840s, renewed at the turn of the twentieth century, revived by the counterculture of the 1960s, and sold in the New Age bookstores of the 1990s—and today, nearly the exact same set of texts and ephemera of religious exoticism continue to inform the spirituality of transformational festivals.

My research uncovers the reasons why Indigenous and Indic religious traditions come to be formulated together as ready materials and instrumentalized in the construction of personalized spiritualities. I also demonstrate the remarkable continuity in SBNR communities and focus on several ways in which that continuity is reproduced. Altglas writes that "the claims of religious freedom made by 'spiritual seekers' are in conformity with a collective discourse, which is encouraged and shaped by their teachers."[41] My research builds on this premise, showing how ideals are codified and repeated in the alternative institutional spaces of yoga classes and workshops in transformational festivals. Chapters 2 and 5 demonstrate how yoga teachers reiterate and reinforce communally supported ideals, sermonizing to somatically receptive audiences during their festival yoga classes. The level of ideological continuity between classes with differently branded teachers and among the intellectually diverse SBNR populations in attendance reveals an underlying ideological commons that binds participants together.

In this way, transformational festivals have the potential to successfully do resistance work by bringing like-minded people together into a *commons*. Silvia Federici positions the commons as a point of resistance, "like the grass in the cracks of the urban pavement, challenging the hegemony of capital and the state and affirming our interdependence and capacity for cooperation. . . . The politics of the *commons are today the expression of this alternative world.*"[42] Federici uses the notion of the commons in the Marxist sense of collective property, as an economic alternative to capitalism: "Lodged halfway between the 'public' and the 'private,' but irreducible to either category, the idea of the commons expresses a broader conception of property, referring to social goods—lands, territories, forests, meadows, and streams, or communicative spaces—that a community, not the state or any individual, collectively owns, manages, and controls."[43] The idea of the commons as neither public nor private matches the liminal space of the transformational festival, as does the notion of creating an alternative world.

Contemporary transformational festivals are an attempt to bring together a community of people united in shared values of alternative ways of being. Burning Man has its 10 Principles; Lightning in a Bottle has its 6 Ways of LIB. At Burning Man, there is an explicitly different social and economic utopia that the organizers and participants seek to establish; it relies on a gift economy (Gifting), and is founded on Radical Self-Reliance and enriched by Radical Self-Expression. At Bhakti and Shakti Fests, focus is on *bhakti* (devotion) and yoga. At Wanderlust festivals, there is a focus on health, vegetarianism, connection with others, personal feelings of harmony, peak experiences, eco-consciousness and environmentalism, spiritual exploration, and personal development. In general, these are spaces that I identify as *ideological commons,* where people come together to share their convictions and critiques with like-minded others.

At both LIB and Burning Man, there are numerous practical and instructional workshops about how to build alternative economies and social networks, whereas at the more explicitly yogic festivals, there are few concrete initiatives aimed at revisioning society. Instead, in these environments, yogis come together to do their "inner work," and they are convinced that their personal transformation will change the world. Their goal is not to directly activate social change through pragmatic forms but rather to lead loving and conscious lives and to spread that vibration through personal connections, by spreading yoga and *bhakti* and by becoming living examples of more evolved ways of being—changing the world one person and one connection at a time. Celebrants exuberantly come together to share ideas and connectivity with like-minded people who unite in their collective critiques of the status quo and their attraction to imagining other ways of being. In this sense, they run the risk of becoming what Federici calls a "gated commons," a utopia "joined by exclusive interests separating them from others."[44] Forebodingly, and as we will see in the next section, the danger with "gated commons," Federici warns, is that they "may even deepen racial and intra-class divisions."[45]

WHITENESS AND WHITE POSSESSIVISM

Each of the transformational festivals in this study is distinct in mission and ethos, but in each case most participants are white. Drawing on my visual perception during my field research in these environments, I observed that the more yoga that festivals incorporated, the whiter they tended to be. According to the 2017 Black Rock City Census, 77.1 percent of Burning Man participants identified as white/Caucasian (non-Hispanic);[46] Lightning in a Bottle has a similar demographic representation. Yoga practice, in general, tends to be even whiter, with approximately 85 percent of American yogis identifying as Caucasian.[47] The transformational festivals that focus on yoga—for example, Wanderlusts—appear to be even whiter than that, with upward of 90 percent of participants presenting as white (though demographic information is not published on these festivals). Bhakti and Shakti Fests, with their explicit focus on the Hindu practice of *bhakti,* appeared to be upward of 95 percent white. Unless explicitly stated otherwise, all informants in this study are white.

National statistics reveal that the United States is still a majority-white nation, with 76.5 percent of the population identifying as white and 60.4 percent identifying as white (non-Hispanic/non-Latino).[48] Thus, one could argue that the ethnic composition of Burning Man and LIB closely mirrors national averages. In contrast, the more yogic festivals (Wanderlust, Bhakti and Shakti Fests) exceed national statistics of white majority by 15 to 20 percent. These figures become more incongruous if one considers the population percentages of non-Hispanic whites; when compared to those statistics, these festivals range from 20 to 45 percent whiter than the national average. The figures become even more stark if one attends to geography a bit more closely. Burning Man and LIB are as white as Oregon (77 percent white [non-Hispanic]), and the more yogic festivals are whiter than Maine (93.7 percent white [non-Hispanic]).⁴⁹ This is despite the fact that many of these transformational festivals either take place in or draw on populations from California, a state where non-Hispanic whites comprise only 38.8 percent of the total population.⁵⁰ For example, nearly 500,000 Indian Americans live in California, 120,000 of them in Los Angeles, but a mere handful of Indian Americans attend Bhakti and Shakti Fests, held just 128 miles from downtown Los Angeles.

When I started to study these festivals, I was most interested to uncover the nuances in the translation processes of globalized yoga and, particularly, its relation to Hinduism. Upon entering the field, I was struck by the significant presence of Native American traditions, and as a result, I began to further explore the soteriological composition of the category of spirituality in these SBNR populations. Importantly, SBNR populations are less white than the transformational festival and yogic communities that this study engages. SBNR populations are still predominantly white (67 percent), but there are growing numbers of African Americans and Latinx Americans who identify as SBNR.⁵¹ Throughout this book, I use the term SBNR as a convenient shorthand, noting throughout that while transformational festival participants largely identify as SBNR, people of color who also identify as such are not represented in these fields.

It is important to mention here at the outset that the intention behind this book was not always centered on whiteness. In honesty, it was only after several years in the field that I focused on the fact that these communities were predominantly, and in some cases entirely, white. Whiteness became a critical theoretical and practical axis around which many of these ideas revolved. Somewhere in the midst of my research, I listened to the African American writer Rich Benjamin speak on NPR about all-white communities that he called Whitopias.⁵² He defined a Whitopia as a community that is "whiter than the nation, its respective region, and its state." It also demonstrates considerable growth from white migrants and has "an ineffable social charisma, a pleasant look and feel."⁵³ Benjamin investigated white exurban communities that attract whites whose anxiety about the insecurities of modernity has sent them in search of strong communities. This overt white flight is usually understood to be the purview of the Right: white evangelicals, Republicans, political conservatives, and white supremacists.

However, my research into transformational festivals and the yogic communities therein demonstrates that these very same factors are at play among populations that are usually understood to be on the Left:

SBNR populations, Democrats, political liberals, and those who would celebrate multiculturalism. Like Benjamin's exurban Whitopias, transformational festivals are also whiter than the nation, the regions, and the states they take place in; demonstrate considerable growth among whites; and are fueled by anxieties about modern forms of precarity that draw participants in search of strong communities. I also agree with Benjamin's conclusion that "Whitopia operates at the level of conscious and unconscious bias. It is possible for people to be in Whitopia not for racist reasons, though it has racist outcomes."[54]

These communities are unlikely bedfellows indeed, and there are many in the SBNR, transformational festival, and yogic communities who would be appalled at any presumed similitude. But this is not an accusation; rather, it is a demographic fact. The solution is not to ignore or suppress this fact but to question the filtering mechanisms in place that create these nearly all-white spaces in the diverse complexity of California, the United States, and the world. Why would so-called conscious, spiritual, and transformational festivals that centralize Hindu devotionalism (Bhakti and Shakti Fests), Indic yoga (Wanderlust), and "Radical Inclusion" (Burning Man) be so white? Where is the "WHITES ONLY" sign hung, and why is it there?

The study of American spirituality and yoga has not yet addressed this pressing question. While there is a significant field of study on New Age religion in the United States, few scholarly inquiries address its ethnic homogeneity beyond a passing mention.[55] Postural yoga is a booming field of academic inquiry, but, with a few notable exceptions, it has a similar blind spot with regard to ethnicity.[56] Similarly, few scholarly works on transformational festivals focus on ethnicity.[57] Among scholars of American religions, in many cases, it is an unacknowledged fact that practitioners of Mesmerism, Spiritualism, New Thought, meditation, and yoga were (and are) white.[58]

In contrast, in Native American studies there is a significant scholarly literature that has centralized the whiteness of the New Age movement and condemned practitioners as false and blasphemous "plastic shamans."[59] Their spirituality is "playing Indian," and their motive is commercial profit, neither of which is deemed to be authentic to Native religions. Their very presence silences Native voices. As Michael Brown explains, "The inequity lies [instead] with appropriators' social capital, which leaves them better positioned than their Indigenous counterparts to reap financial reward."[60] In these analyses, whites flood the spiritual market with their neo-Native pseudoreligion and make-believe shamanism, claiming authenticity to the point that one Onondaga leader argued, "Non-Indians have become so used to all this hype on the part of imposters and liars that when a real Indian spiritual leader tries to offer them useful advice, he is rejected. He isn't Indian enough for all these non-Indian experts on Indian religion."[61] It is a dark irony that love can result in such antipathy; it must be a suffocating love indeed, one deeply intertwined with the fraught ideals of "racial fantasy."[62] For there is no question that the New Agers who immerse themselves in and even embody Native American religions love Native culture. These are whites who sympathize with the religions of racialized others and attempt to act in solidarity through imitation. But as Philip Jenkins explains, "The more white people sympathize with Indians and try to show solidarity with them, the more they do so through forms of imitation that are seen as insensitive profanation rather than sincere flattery."[63] While whites may see imitation as the most sincere form of flattery, many Indigenous activists reject their presumptions of authenticity.

While the discussions of spirituality and yoga have not yet become as vitriolic, there are threads that resemble patterns of what Eric Lott so aptly terms "love and theft" in his seminal study of blackface minstrelsy.[64] The debates over cultural appropriation raging on the Internet show no signs of abating; they have also captured the attention of select scholars.[65] Cultural property and intellectual rights have become an increasingly litigious affair. In the field of yoga, classes have been cancelled in protest of the neocolonialism of whites teaching yoga,[66] websites are dedicated to the project of "decolonizing yoga,"[67] yoga teachers have tried to patent postures and postural sequences,[68] yoga is being revived in India as a form of Hindu nationalism,[69] and whites dominate the public representations of yoga in the United States (and increasingly across the globe) to the exclusion and erasure of Indian voices.[70]

Historically, cultural encounter, whether by trade or warfare, often involves the exchange of cultural forms; many of these moments of cultural exchange occur outside of the context of whiteness. But the notion of cultural appropriation focuses attention on individual white actors and their representative claims of nonwhite cultural and religious forms. Cultural appropriation is an individualized expression of an overarching institutionalized system that expresses white access and ownership. The African American scholar Ta-Nehisi Coates explains: "When you're white in this country [the United States], you're taught that everything belongs to you. You think you have a right to everything. . . . You're conditioned this way. It's not because your hair is a texture or your skin is light. It's the fact that the laws and the culture tell you this. You have a right to go where you want to go, do what you want to do, be however—and people just got to accommodate themselves to you."[71]

Religious exoticism is a white-dominant field, as are its modes of cultural appropriation, Orientalism, minstrelsy, and "playing Indian."[72] It is dependent on the logics of white possessivism, as argued by the Indigenous scholar Aileen Moreton-Robinson in her writing about the settler colonial context of Australia. There, she argues, "signs of white possession are embedded everywhere in the landscape."[73] From the appropriation of Native lands to the institution of slavery, white people have been recognized within the law as "property-owning subjects." Whiteness itself became property, signifying the capacity to possess.[74] At the national level, what George Lipsitz calls the "possessive investment in whiteness" has been institutionalized through colonization, slavery, urban redlining, de facto school segregation, and mass incarceration.[75] One might imagine that religious exoticism's identification with nonwhite religious and cultural forms would result in a rejection of the possessive investment in whiteness. But is there not a similar logic of white possessivism that informs what Deborah Root describes as "cannibal culture," a culture that loves until it devours its lover: black widows in white skins?

Utopian visions of religious exoticism are defined by a particular notion about the other. In its most idyllic form, the other is romanticized as an untouched essence—timeless, pure, and uncorrupted by modernity. The utopian vision of the other must be constructed as such in order to be conceived of as an oppositional solution to the existing order of things. If it were similarly corrupted and corruptible, then it would be no solution at all. It is in recognition of racialized oppression that religious exoticists seek to dissociate themselves from oppressor kinsmen and to adopt the lifeways of their victims. Arun Saldanha highlights Norman Mailer's famed essay "The White Negro" to suggest that in their post–World War II existential crisis, the hippies turned to African American culture for alternative solutions; even the terms *hippie, hip,* and the more modern term *hipster* are derivatives of the Black slang term *hep,* meaning "with it" or "fashionable."[76] In this way, religious exoticism is in essence a project of white identity-making, defining the self through engagement with the other. This fundamental notion is one of the reasons the culture of exoticism tends to attract white youth.

Furthermore, religious exoticism's perseverating focus on the purity, timelessness, and authenticity of the other necessarily dissociates it from the actual communities that practice the religious forms it adopts. Living Native Americans, Indians, or Asians, who are just as embroiled in the multiple systems of modernity, complicate and even render impotent the imagined idealization of these cultures and religions. The complex political realities of the struggles of contemporary Indians and Indigenous peoples, for example, sit in contradistinction to their imagined purity and detachment from modernity. This distance is required because religious exoticism is dependent on "the idealization of religious traditions as being primordial, mystical, and authentic; it aims at dramatizing an opposition to one's own culture and religious background in order to reflect on, criticize, and reclaim the latter through a cultural detour. Religious exoticism is pragmatic and, paradoxically, self-referential. Thus, exotic religious resources are constructed and disseminated on the terms of those who appropriate them."[77] The practitioner of religious exoticism is rendered an introspective dreamer, imagining an alternative, utopian world.

The result is that when confronted with these white self-referential utopian ideals, many people of color feel unrecognized and falsely stereotyped and thus disengage from religious exoticism. Some may not suffer the existential crisis that leads to a "restlessness" and the subsequent "search for the exotic,"[78] likely because many identify within networked religious and cultural communities. For others, put simply, white begets white; that is to say that the optics of a majority-white party serves as a deterrent. This invokes the familiar recognition of the socially demarcated spaces of white property and racialized exclusions that have dominated US history, where the lack of people of color in attendance signals a white-only space. These factors, combined with the financial and vocational surplus necessary to engage in these distant and expensive multiday (sometimes multiweek) "serious leisure"[79] events, constitute significant barricades for would-be nonwhite participants.

However, it is important to remember that in spaces like Burning Man and LIB, just over 20 percent of the participants are nonwhite; this is not an insignificant population (around 14,000 and 5,000 participants, respectively). Furthermore, as these festivals become even more popular and recognized, it appears that they are becoming more diverse. For example, in the 2013–17 Summary Report of the Black Rock City Census, the percentage of white/Caucasian (non-Hispanic) census respondents decreased approximately one percentage point each year, from 82.9 percent in 2013 to 77.1 percent in 2017. In contrast, the transformational festivals that celebrate *bhakti* yoga and postural yoga continue to be over 90 percent white. One reason for this departure may be that the general populace is increasingly attracted to festivals like Burning Man and LIB for the parties, the music, and the art, not to mention the social cachet acquired by attending. In contrast, participants attracted to festivals like Wanderlust and Bhakti and Shakti Fests are explicitly interested in the practice of Indic religious and cultural forms. These figures suggestively lend support to my argument that the greater the index of religious exoticism within a given population, the whiter that population is likely to be. *White Utopias* celebrates the thriving devotion to progressive consciousness expressed in these spiritual communities, but it also argues that the logic of white possessivism lies at their very heart.

THE FIELD(S)
Transformational Festivals

Festivals create imagined utopian worlds. They are a "pragmatic and fantastic space in which to dream and to try another world into being."[80] In the United States, the 1960s countercultural generation became networked through massive public festivals that united the different (and oppositional) factions of the counterculture through the collective shared experience of fun, music, and often drugs. In the political upheaval of the time, festivals were largely depoliticized events aimed at revealing the common purpose of the counterculture through shared experience. Although the Yippies attempted to politicize Woodstock,[81] festivals primarily signified a time to simply *be* together in solidarity (as in the famed 1969 Be-In festival in San Francisco) and, importantly, to be made visible in public spaces together. It is impossible to measure the empowerment and motivation that countercultural activists gained from the images of Woodstock showing 460,000 people spreading expansively over the rural hills of upstate New York. The overwhelming attendance at the festival generated the feeling of a massive movement underfoot, a nation at the cusp of revolution.

Internationally, festival culture also gained traction in Europe and the United Kingdom in the 1950s and 1960s, with massive collectives gathering at "musical mega events,"[82] often with utopian underpinnings. In his historical account of the pop festival, media and cultural studies scholar George McKay writes, "Woodstock (1969, USA), Glastonbury (since 1970, UK), and Nimbin (1973, Australia) are early event markers that point us to the utopian desire of the festival, to the way in which that temporary heightened space-time has the fundamental purpose of envisioning and crafting another, better world."[83] Since the

1960s, festival culture in the United States has continued and expanded, but it has also entered the mainstream. No longer solely a product of the counterculture, the largest festivals in the twenty-first century are music festivals. These festivals appear to be popular with diverse audiences, drawing from multiple aesthetic subcultures—there are country music festivals like Stagecoach, alternative music festivals like Lollapalooza, and EDM festivals like Electric Daisy Carnival. By making the pilgrimage to one of these massive music events, attendees identify with the subculture and its aesthetics.

Festivals as a genre of collective action have also become important for particular identity groups. Andy Bennett and Ian Woodward have shown that "a critical function of the festival is to allow a collective representation, a collective celebration and, in many cases, a collective outpouring of a commonly articulated form of socio-cultural identity."[84] In urban environments, ethnic, cultural, and religious festivals are a developing means by which minority communities assert their social influence. Festivals increase the community's public visibility and demand representation as they transform urban streets, neighborhoods, and districts. City officials regard public festivals as both an opportunity to garner political favor by publicly supporting minority communities residing in their districts and potentially dangerous events that need to be contained and controlled. Festivals of this sort can also be read as control mechanisms administered by the state, which compartmentalize and contain potential sites of social unrest by allowing for tokenized representation in cultural festivals while denying its more concrete forms. As Bennett and Woodward explain, "In a world where notions of culture are becoming increasingly fragmented, the contemporary festival has developed in response to processes of cultural pluralization, mobility, and globalization, while also communicating something meaningful about identity, community, locality and belonging."[85] Festivals are spaces of community and identity production; as urban environments become increasingly diverse, public festivals are increasing, with identity communities vying for visibility, public representation, and in some cases, social dominance.

Transformational festivals are neither music festivals nor a demand for political representation in a multicultural, cosmopolitan society. They are spaces of identity construction through exploration of alternative lifeways and spiritual experiences. Although they are founded on "forms of consumptive engagement [that] are potentially exploitative and based on modes of cultural appropriation," they are simultaneously "motivated by curiosity and a genuine yearning for engagements with alterity."[86] They form one important institutional nexus in the networks of SBNR populations.[87] To describe such nexus points, Hugh Urban employs the notion of "hyphal knots," meaning key intersections that sustain and circulate nutrients through an ecosystem.[88] In New Age spirituality, these hyphal knots have been health food stores, underground newspapers, New Age bookstores, and more recently, yoga studios, meditation centers, and social media platforms. In what follows, I demonstrate that for today's generations, transformational festivals are another hyphal knot, where spiritual knowledge is shared and community connections are forged and solidified. These hyphal knots nourish and sustain SBNR ideals, and they are enlivened in community and strengthened in the assertion of an ideological commons.

The famed French sociologist Emile Durkheim views festivals functionally, as social mechanisms that unite a community around a collectively identified totem and bind its members to each other in the celebratory emotional affect of "collective effervescence."[89] Following Durkheim's reasoning, Roger Caillois argues that festivals transgress the boundaries of mundane reality, opening a space wherein participants become renewed and reemerge prepared, recharged, and ready to reenter society with a zest for everyday life.[90] In this view, the festival is a venting system wherein individuals momentarily break from stasis, and that rupture enables them to return and reinstate the very stasis from which they initially sought reprieve.

In the Renaissance period, the festival was a public-facing social parody, an opportunity for the commons to come together and joust at their beleaguered status only to have it reconfirmed at the close of the festival. The festival broke the monotony of the mundane and inverted social circumstances, with paroxysmal revelry. Caillois and Mikhail Bakhtin argue that the festival event makes mockery and parody of the established social order—of church, of politics, of social hierarchies—in bacchanalian irreverence. Effigies of popes and presidents were hanged and burned, and fake priests flung excrement and urine at the crowd in a parody of incense distribution.[91] They were opportunities for wild hedonistic indulgences, for excess, which stood in stark contrast to the scarcities of daily living. In Caillois's and Bakhtin's analyses, the festival was not a space of social revolution, in fact, it was its antithesis; it was a space that reified existing hierarchies because it supplied a venting mechanism that controlled social outrage.

However, Caillois argues that as the twentieth century proceeded, liberal democracies had ushered in the fusion of the sacred and profane, thereby creating a continuous intermediary zone that is neither sacred nor profane, one that obliterates the potential rupture of the festival.[92] Instead, he argues, with the death of premodern festivals, war had become the socially rejuvenating force that the festival once had been. In modernity, the potential for rupture has been eradicated, and the festival has become the mere simulation; it has been replaced with vacation.[93] The literary critic and scholar Allon White argues that carnivals, the calendrical rituals emblematic of the European social body, were intentionally suppressed between the seventeenth and the mid-nineteenth centuries in efforts to give rise to urban modernity and bourgeois individualism. White argues that the carnivalesque did not simply disappear but rather became diffused "throughout the whole social order of bourgeois life." He writes, "The result was a fantasy bricolage, unanchored in ritual and therefore set adrift from its firm location in the body, in calendar time, and ritual place. Dispersed across the territories of art, fantasy, and style, in flux, no longer bound by the strict timetable of the ritual year, these carnivalesque fragments have formed unstable discursive compounds, sometimes disruptive, sometimes therapeutic, within the very constitution of bourgeois subjectivity."[94] White juxtaposes the death of the carnivalesque with the rise of hysteria, arguing that festivals' celebration of the grotesque and the sexual was displaced from the social body to the individual psyche.

But many in late-capitalist, neoliberal societies are recognizing that holding the entirety of the social order within the individual psyche is exhausting, and for many, it is too much for the individual to bear. In fact, it can result in "hysteria," or what modern psychologists would diagnose as anxiety and depression. Social connectivity is vital for humans, and it is increasingly difficult to sustain in our increasingly isolated and technologically saturated worlds. Recognizing this, creators of transformational festivals have sought innovative ways to bring communities together, to build a collective and unified social body despite current trends of geographical fragmentation and individualistic isolation.

Participants view transformational festivals as opportunities to rejuvenate themselves and to gather strength and sense of purpose in solidarity with community. Introducing his film series on these festivals, Jeet-Kei Leung explains, "Living in a materialist society where the highest value is the maximization of profit has left many feeling a void of meaning and spiritual depth in a world where we are reduced to consumers, customers, servants, and bosses."[95] For the builders and the visionaries, these events are an expression of a larger movement that represents an effort to fill this "void of meaning and spiritual depth." These utopian movements engage with spirituality but also with different economies and socialities; they experiment with alternative ways of being. Leung mourns the disenchantment that modernity has fostered,[96] and he believes transformational festivals begin the processes of reenchantment through the creation of a new commons collectively engaged in building a utopian vision for the future.

During my fieldwork, my interlocutors explained that transformational festivals granted them opportunities to "reset" and "recharge," to "center" themselves, to "remember what's important," to get in touch with nature, to celebrate community, to explore beauty and wonder, and to "reconnect." As such, they echoed Caillois's claim that "it is by being reborn, by reinvigorating himself in this ever-present eternity, as in a fountain of youth with continuously running water, in which he has the chance to rejuvenate himself and to rediscover the plenitude and robustness of life, that the celebrant will be able to brave a new cycle of time."[97]

For many, annual festivals, and more broadly the circuit of transformational festivals, serve as a series of touchstones through which participants cultivate overflowing joie de vivre. The famed yoga teacher Bija Rivers explained her penchant for the festival circuit in the following terms: "I am very committed to the path of realization. . . . I enjoy festivals because I enjoy being around people when they are good hearted . . . I need to be surrounded by, not an artifice of happiness, not an artifice of being kind to each other, but people who live that way as a way of life. I really really really thrive in that way."[98] Transformational festivals invite participants into radically alternative, utopian worlds, wherein they are encouraged to be "good hearted," "kind," and joyous. Fostering a space of openness and connection with others, participants cultivate the self in engagements with alterity, using the festival spaces as loci for the construction of new personal and social identities.

Perhaps those most superficially involved in today's transformational festivals might regard time spent at Wanderlust or Burning Man as merely a vacation. But the majority of my interlocuters viewed transformational festivals as forms of spiritual pilgrimage. They likely would have agreed with Zahir, an African American "spiritual bodyguard," who explained during our interview at Bhakti Fest: "Burning Man, I call it a North American pilgrimage, so it is a very spiritual level place. A lot of people look at it as just the drugs and this and that, but it is actually a really spiritual experience, and that is why people are drawn to it. Every culture, person, needs to go on pilgrimage, you see. It's our birthright. People all over the globe, pilgrims, go to Burning Man, here [Bhakti Fest], lots of places."[99] Such a view represents the dominant perspective, while those who are even more invested aim to create more permanent revolutionary utopias, spaces for self-expression, freedom, and community based in their critique of late-capitalist modernity.

The most dedicated in these environments urge that the principles and practices learned in the festival must be carried into society to become a part of the practice of everyday life. Burning Man Project prefers to dissociate the event from the idea of a temporary festival; and many Burners aim to live according to Burning Man values (10 Principles) year-round.[100] Yoga is also a lived value-system, and is often exported in forms that resemble proselytization.[101] For many at Bhakti and Shakti Fests, the festival is an expression of a deep-seated religious commitment, an opportunity to come together in ecstatic celebration of the divine with a community of fellow *bhaktas* (devotees).[102] Some of the most dedicated participants become yoga teachers, *kīrtan* artists, community leaders, or festival employees, wholly engrossing themselves in actualizing their utopia (and critiquing the existing system [topia]) in creative ways. Some within the transformational festival scene have used the social relationships built through festivals as networks from which to develop permanent communities.[103]

Yoga

The field of transformational festivals is multiple and varied. In approaching Bhakti and Shakti Fests, Wanderlust, and LIB, I focused particularly on yoga as a point of entry. Yoga has become a central practice among SBNR populations, and yoga classes provide a clear view into the soteriological ideals of these communities. Of the festivals I studied, Burning Man accentuates yoga the least, and in that sense, it is somewhat of an outlier to the overt focus on yoga as a point of entry into SBNR populations in this study. Still, yoga ranked among the top ten activities listed in the official program books at each festival (see figures 1–5). At Bhakti and Shakti Fests, yoga ranked as the primary activity. At Wanderlust, it ranked second, bested by athletic activities, like running, hiking, and surfing. At LIB, yoga also ranked second, bested by live music. At Burning Man, yoga ranked ninth, superseded by events such as parties, bar/alcohol related events, sexuality workshops, dances, food-distribution events, games, crafting events, and live music. One can certainly attend any of these festivals, Burning Man in particular, and avoid the practice

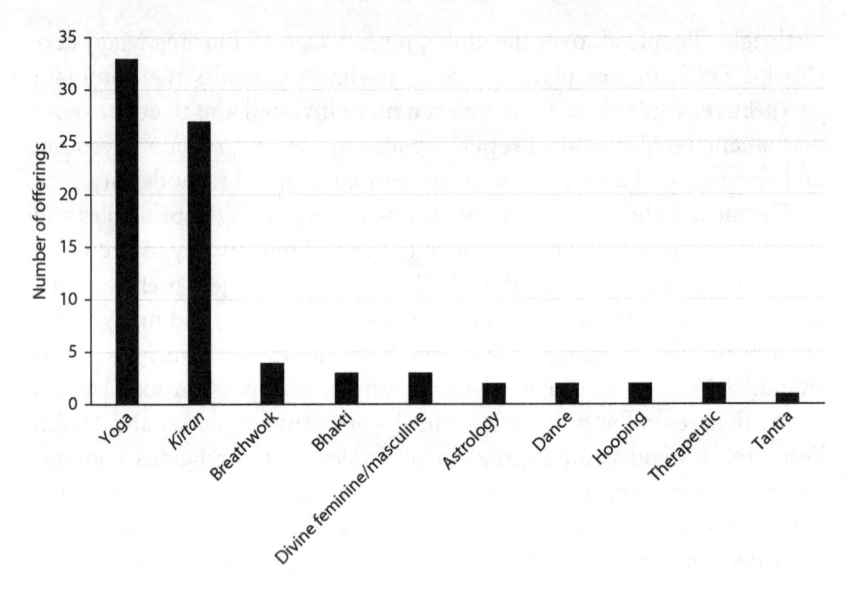

1. Top ten offerings at Shakti Fest, 2012.

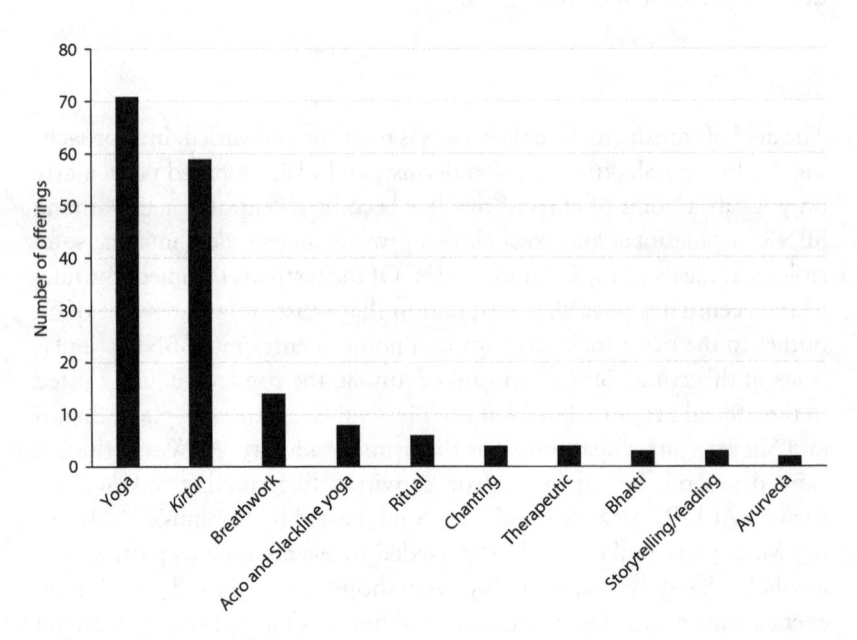

2. Top ten offerings at Bhakti Fest, 2013.

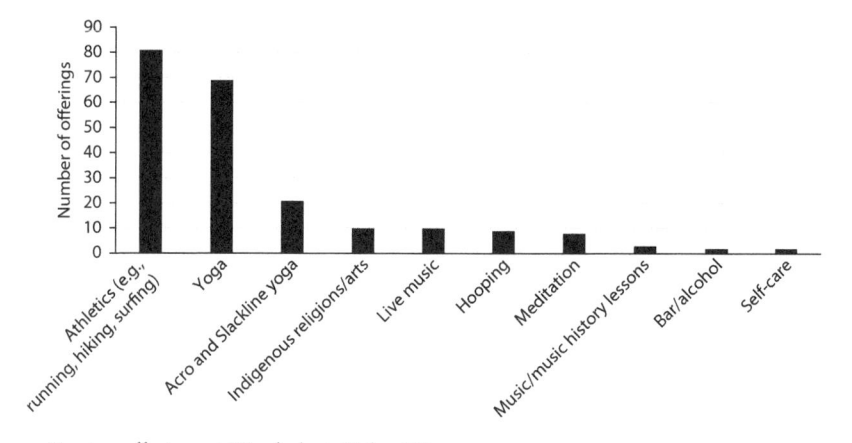

3. Top ten offerings at Wanderlust, Oahu, HI, 2014.

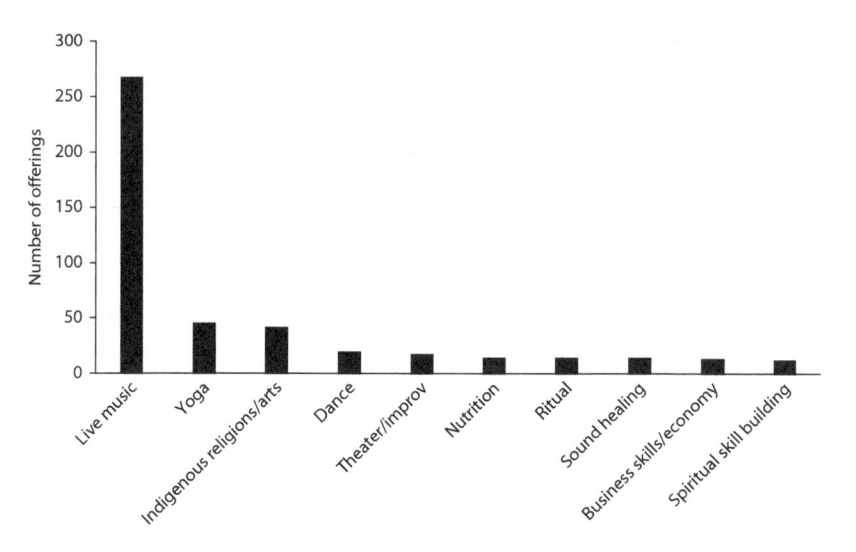

4. Top ten offerings at Lightning in a Bottle, 2016.

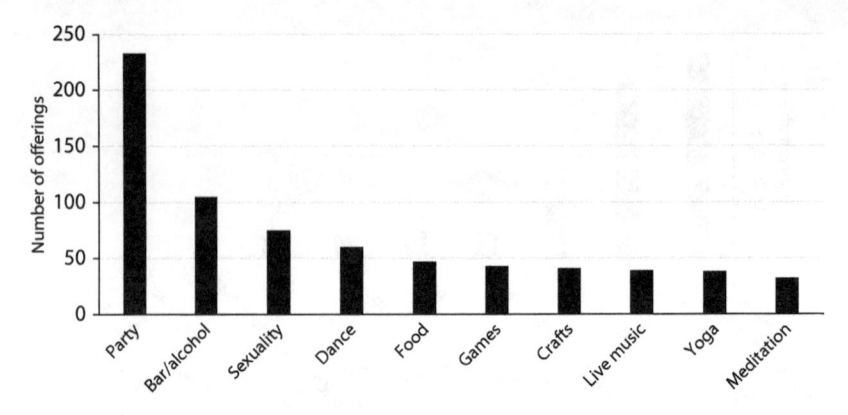

5. Top ten offerings at Burning Man, 2017.

of yoga entirely. Other transformational festivals that are in some ways derivative of Burning Man (such as Symbiosis, Lucidity, Envision, Oregon Eclipse, Earthdance, Global Eclipse, and Faerieworlds) may not focus on yoga, but every one of these festivals includes it. Even at Burning Man, yoga is on the rise. In November 2018, I spoke with Burning Man CEO, Marian Goodell, who lamented that so many of the camp placement applications in recent years cited yoga (and tea service) as their primary interactive communal offerings.[104]

White Utopias spotlights yoga as a primary means to access the ontological and soteriological values of SBNR populations. Yoga is also useful in that it reveals the nuances of religious exoticism as predominantly white populations engage with a South Asian cultural, and often religious, practice. Still, I am under no illusion that yoga is a singular expression. The term *yoga* has many different referents, as it always has. Often translated from the Sanskrit root *yuj,* meaning "yoke" or "union," it can also simply mean "path" in popular Hindi parlance. Like any path, it can take the traveler to many different territories. The fact that one is on a path does not define where one ends up. It is the direction of the path that determines the destination. Foregrounding this colloquial definition perhaps makes it easier to reckon with the extraordinary diversity in contemporary yoga practice.

There are distinctive features to yoga in the United States today that signify seismic shifts from its lengthier and more diverse tradition in South Asia. Coordinated sequences of postures have become central, and the notion that yoga should be practiced because it is good for bodily health has become widely accepted. What has become popular practice in the United States is a "virtual hegemony of a small number of posture-oriented systems in the recent global transmission of yoga, [which] has reinforced a relatively narrow and monochromatic vision of what yoga is and does, especially when viewed against the wide spectrum of practices presented in pre-modern texts."[105] These are particular developments that stem from a host of social and historical conditions that have been widely discussed by scholars of modern postural yoga.[106]

The yogis in this study emerge from a variety of yoga classes, studios, and teacher trainings. However, the very fact that they are participating in transformational festivals means that they are at least nominally interested in the notions of spiritual transformation or raising consciousness. Isolating this intersection between physical and metaphysical aims immediately eliminates the majority of yoga practitioners in the United States, who attend yoga classes online, in their gyms, at Pilates studios, and in physically oriented yoga franchises like CorePower Yoga.[107] There may be some overlap, however. At Shakti Fest, I was once situated behind a man in a yoga class who had a CorePower Yoga tattoo on his right shoulder. Still, it does mean that at this particular juncture in their spiritual journeys or yoga practice, these practitioners are looking for something more.

As will be discussed in detail in the pages that follow, yoga classes offered at transformational festivals, despite the diversity of yogic lineages represented, tend to be more focused on incorporating spiritual or metaphysical concerns. Discourses of this particular strain of yoga, what we might delimit as "soteriological" yoga,[108] attempt to draw yogis into the broader philosophical tradition and extend their interest in the practice beyond its physical effects. The yoga mat is repositioned as a space of self-inquiry and connection to divinity, a sacred space wherein the individual sanctifies a space of introspection through a daily practice. Many of these practitioners are also exposed to Indic yoga traditions through travels to devotional centers in Asia and the reading of Indic scriptures. Usually, this involves exposure to "a small canon of texts, which includes the *Bhagavadgītā,* Patañjali's *Yoga Sūtras,* the *Haṭhapradīpikā* and some Upaniṣads,"[109] which are incorporated into yoga teacher training programs. In particular, Patañjali's *Yoga Sūtras* has been elevated to the position of a canonical urtext for many contemporary yogis, as it is referenced and taught in yoga classes and teacher training at levels far beyond that of any other Indic text.[110] As a result, this study privileges this text above others when analyzing and interpreting how yoga teachers translate Indic philosophical discourses for their students. This methodological decision is not an attempt to justify the elevation of the *Yoga Sūtras* but rather an effort to trace yoga teachers' discourses to the primary interpretive frames that inform them.

In addition to references to religious scriptures, there are other markers that attempt to define yoga performed at transformational festivals as spiritual. Some yoga classes incorporate guided meditations, partner-based spiritual exercises, rituals, prayers, and ecstatic dance accompanied by devotional music. At Bhakti and Shakti Fests, devotional music (*kīrtan*) accompanies nearly all of the yoga classes, drawing on the strengths of the assembled *kīrtan* musicians at the festivals. It is also commonplace to see yogis marking their yoga mats with talismans, *mālās* (prayer beads), Native American ceremonial pipes, *chakra* wands, crystals, and other sacred objects. Some write their intentions and affirmations on pieces of paper and slip them under the mat as they practice, invoking the twenty-first century iteration of the New Thought notion that repeating affirmations attracts "harmonizing vibrations" and eventually makes them become reality.[111] Stepping on someone's yoga mat with outdoor shoes is a faux pas that warrants an apology for the defilement of their designated sacred space. The body-length rectangle of the yoga mat draws boundaries between the sacred and the profane and sanctifies the practice on the yoga mat as distinct and "special,"[112] set apart from actions that occur outside of the mat.

Methodologically, focusing on the practice of yoga was particularly revealing because teachers espoused their spiritual values in lengthy lectures during postural practice. The yoga class provided a means of drawing practitioners into a receptive state wherein teachers could then influence them to adopt a distinct set of values or practices. Yoga classes are an exercise in acquiescence and social (group) influence on individual behavior. Students are told to move their bodies in particular ways, and they are praised for the skill with which they mimetically model the teacher. This builds a relation of receptivity on the part of the student that is bodily, psychological, and somatic. In shaping the body and mind to the teacher's demands, students become mentally and physically supple. Through group yoga practice, they are conditioned to be receptive to a teacher's philosophical interventions.

Exercise-oriented yoga studio spaces are wary of this reality and often restrict what yoga teachers can say outside of directions related to bodily postures. Usually, yoga teachers are under advisement (or contract) not to cross boundaries into religion or philosophy. But in the yogic spaces of transformational festivals, yoga teachers use the opportunity to attract students by espousing their distinctive modes and philosophies. During our interview, Bija Rivers explained: "A festival class is not the city yoga class. The boundaries are expanded so people are more open—like in terms of Bhakti Fest—people are more open to the interior aspects—and in particular, what is *bhakti?* It is unusual for a spiritual tradition to really highlight that, and I think it is really helpful for the yoga tradition, which seems to be, in the mainstream reflections, propelled by people who are curious and get into yoga for physical reasons."[113] Yoga classes are a site of reproduction, wherein the values and practices of SBNR communities are generated and sustained. Attention to these sites of reproduction provides answers to the enduring question of how social values are produced and reproduced in the absence of overt and explicit directives.

As I discuss in chapter 5, my research suggests that these sites of value reproduction/production are surprisingly consistent in their messaging. The core tenets of this ideological commons are iterated in myriad ways, in a variety of vernaculars. But despite their diffusion and transience, the messages promoted and received at transformational festivals and during yoga practice construct institutions of spirituality that bind practitioners in ways that are recognizable and remarkably constant. These consistencies of message are what form an ideological field of continuity. Within these ideological affinities, this ephemeral yet connected anthropological field emerges.

Between 2011 and 2019, I attended twenty-three festivals over a total of approximately 129 days. I have sorted, transcribed, and coded my audio recordings from approximately ninety-seven interviews, fifty-six spiritual workshops and lectures, and sixty-two yoga classes. I also attended related events, such as *kīrtan* gatherings in local yoga studios, yoga classes, Burner meetups, and social gatherings. In most of these environments, I was both a participant and an observer. I participated in *kīrtan,* workshops, guided meditations, and yoga classes. I had my astrological chart read, and I danced, made new friends, and in time, ran into familiar faces and developed lasting friendships. Sometimes I sat in the back of these spaces, recorded, and took notes. In 2015, I was part of the *sevā* (selfless service) team at Shakti Fest and worked several volunteer shifts. In 2017, faced with the retirement of the existing leadership team, I stepped into a leadership role for the French Quarter Black Rock Bakery at Burning Man.[114] This role taught me a tremendous amount about the backstage and production aspects of these experiential spaces, and became a year-round side job in 2018 and 2019.

Because of the extensive time and money required to maintain this ethnographic research, I divided my field research into overlapping stages: from 2011 to 2016, I focused on Bhakti and Shakti Fests; from 2014 to 2016, I attended LIB; from 2014 to 2017, I attended Wanderlust festivals; and from 2016 to 2019, I attended Burning Man. My peak year in the field was 2014, during which I attended LIB, four Wanderlust festivals (in Oahu, Los Angeles, Squaw Valley, and Mont Tremblant), and both Bhakti and Shakti Fests. However, my time commitment exponentially increased beyond that level when I became a part of the leadership team of the French Quarter Village at Burning Man in 2018. Throughout the entire period of research (2011–2019), I kept abreast of new developments in and reactions to each of these transformational festivals and maintained relationships in each field. I discuss in more detail the intricacies of conducting ethnographic work in these ephemeral, multisited fields and the reception of my research among my informants in appendix 2, mostly for ethnographically interested readers.

CHAPTER OUTLINE

How are we to evaluate the ways in which the religious exoticism inherent in spirituality is simultaneously a genuine engagement with alterity, a radically transformative method, and an often exploitative form of cultural appropriation? To this, I answer that it is a complex both/and situation. There is no easy answer here. *White Utopias* grounds this research question sociologically by problematizing religious exoticism and white claims of authority over nonwhite cultural and religious forms juxtaposed against participants' very real experiences of transformation and spiritual evolution resulting from inspirational engagements with alterity. Chapter 1 charts how religious exoticism draws from Indic religious practices and ideas and Indigenous religions, based in problematic imagined and historical divisions between self and other, modern and primitive, civilized and savage. Chapter 2 focuses explicitly on contemporary yoga, demonstrating how the dominant majority of white yoga teachers parse questions of authenticity. In so doing, I invite readers into a microscopic view of the strategies of building authority in the context of cultural appropriation.

At the midway point of the book, the narrative pivots on a particularly salient comment an informant made during our interview at Lightning in a Bottle in 2015. When I asked Niko, an African American DJ, a general question about his impressions of the festival crowd, he immediately began speaking about race. He viewed the religious exoticism of the largely white population as a first step in the gradual evolutionary journey of white people. Many festival participants also believe they are participating in human evolution and spiritual awakening, but Niko's comment suggested that white explorations into alterity can puncture white hegemony and even initiate a politics of friendship based in the recognition of shared humanity.

The second half of the book explores this potential evolution through accounts of personal transformation occurring in transformational festivals. Chapter 3 focuses on the intentional denaturalization of the conventional self through the adoption of ascetical practices. Chapter 4 focuses on unexpected self-transformations catalyzed by encounters with wonder in mystical experiences. Chapter 5 investigates the most common theme that was iterated time and again by my interlocutors across these fields: the expression of affective feelings of freedom. This chapter reveals how these feelings of freedom are not only expressions of release from everyday systems of bondage but are also fostered through empathic human connection generated by the festival. In conclusion, I explain why the commitment to personal transformation generates an ideological commons within festivals while also forming a gated commons that tends to reify ethnic and class boundaries. Ironically, the proclivity toward homogeneity augments affective feelings of freedom and the ubiquitous feeling that participants have "come home." It also fosters feelings of solidarity and supports the feeling of having found one's "tribe." While this may be productive for the largely white population of participants, it also erects boundaries that deter racialized others from participating. In this way, what follows explains why their visions of radical alternative utopias remain, at the present, predominantly *White Utopias*.

I

Romanticizing the Premodern

The Confluence of Indic and Indigenous Spiritualities

Opening Kali fire ceremony with Sundari Lakshmi
  Thursday, May 25, 2014
  Shakti Fest, Joshua Tree, California[1]

Sundari Lakshmi was in the center, her long, natural hair pulled into a low ponytail. She wore a black sari and a microphone headpiece. She was softspoken. She was probably forty-five years old, a Caucasian woman. Her Sanskrit seemed fairly good, though there were times when she accentuated the wrong syllables as she read aloud and defined the hundred names of Kali. To her righthand side, she had a large binder with all of the materials for the pūjā, *which she read from throughout the hour-long ceremony. She was accompanied by three other younger women, whom she called "priestesses." One of these women seemed to be functioning as her assistant, and she seemed more confident than the others because of her Sanskrit and bodily composure. She was also traditionally dressed, wearing a gold brocade sawar-kamiz. She had a long blonde braid that fell to her waist and wore red bangles and ankle bracelets* (payals). *She seemed to be dressed as a proper, married Indian woman. The other two women appeared to be novices, and Sundari Lakshmi guided them on how to hold their* pūjā *articles and their hands, what to do with ritual objects, and so on. There was also a man affiliated with the* pūjā. *He was young, white, and somewhat short, with thickly calloused feet and disheveled hair.*

  The pūjā *was instructive and geared toward novices. Sanskrit was used but then explained in English. At the start, only thirty people or so were there to participate, but by the end it was more like sixty or seventy. The* pūjā *was somewhat traditional, with mantras to Kali, the recitation of her hundred names, and offerings of fire, sandalwood, flowers, clarified butter* (ghi), *and water. Sundari Lakshmi ritually bathed both the self and the goddess in metaphor as she poured offerings into the sacrificial fire. The structure of the fire sacrifice embodied Tantra-reminiscent elements in that practitioners ritually transformed themselves into Kali. After the pouring of oblations into the fire and the ritual transformation of practitioners' bodies into Kali, we were told to choose partners. With our partners, we were instructed in a ritual blessing of the other's body as a living embodiment of Kali. The partnering ritual was intimate, as is frequently expected at Shakti Fest, where participants are actively engaged in therapeutic spiritual work. My partner was a slender, young white woman who wore loose-fitting harem pants, a white T-shirt, and no rings or jewelry. She resonated with a calm and peaceful energy. We were instructed to invoke Kali mantras, and we dutifully repeated the Sanskrit and then followed the instruction to bless each part of the other's body with our hands. Our bodies were knee to knee as we sat cross-legged in lotus posture. First, we were instructed to bless the head, then the throat, heart, eyes, ears, nose, lips, teeth, neck, the nape of neck, back, arms, shoulders, sides, and the "progenitor area." This was the term Sundari Lakshmi used instead of calling the genitals by name. Neither of us touched the other's genitals, but I did glance next to us at a male-female older couple who seemed to share an intimate relationship, and I saw him place his fingertips squarely on either side of her vulva. There was some giggling in the crowd, especially when we were asked to touch each other's teeth. At one point, Sundari Lakshmi exhorted, "Get intimate! You need it. Sometimes we do this* pūjā *sitting in each other's laps!" At this, everyone laughed. Afterward, we were instructed to "close out" our experience with each other and return our attention to the fire while Sundari Lakshmi concluded the* pūjā *with a communal meditation and closing mantras.*

This ritual was performed and practiced at Shakti Fest by white ritual officiants who embodied the ethos of Hindu traditions while drawing on Vedic and Tantric sources. White yogis and spiritual seekers comprised the majority of participants who followed Sundari Lakshmi's instructions to perform the ritual dedicated to the Hindu goddess Kali. Lakshmi claims to be an initiated *yogini*, *pūjāri* (priest), lineage holder, and authorized teacher who has lived and practiced her *sādhana* (spiritual practice) with adepts in Nepal, India, and Tibet. Her practice focuses on the embodiment of the divine feminine in Shakta Tantric lineages; she is serious about her study and her religious practice. According to her website, she is highly educated and has complemented her academic study with decades of practitioner-generated knowledge and numerous traditional Tantric "empowerments and transmissions." Her biography claims that she is an "authorized teacher" based in this knowledge, and she can be found in yoga studios, festivals, and widely on the Internet offering teachings, rituals, *pūjās*, retreats, and online courses.

The example of Sundari Lakshmi introduces a commonplace pattern of embodied white possessivism, and the focus of this chapter will be to unfurl its complexities. In this representational politics, whites not only explore, learn about, and share in cultural and religious forms of racialized others, but also go one step further to embody, possess, extract, and redistribute that alterity as a form of social capital. Their access to alterity, deemed exotic, marks them with distinction in white society. It also identifies them as members of a "tribe"—a tribe defined by an affinity for religious exoticism, comprised of spiritual seekers who have also chosen to identify with radical others as a form of critique of their own culture, society, and ancestral heritage. In Deepak Sarma's words, they imagine that they "can transform from the oppressor to the oppressed, from the colonizer to the colonized. Surely such an imagined transformation is only available to those who are privileged in the first place."[2] Sarma frames the white convert as engaged in either "mimicry or mockery" of Hindu traditions, but this dichotomy belies the ways in which initial acts of mimesis can develop into sincerely held identities. Particularly in the religious field, religious exoticism can be an initial step in a gradual process of self-transformation emerging from engagement with radically different cultures, customs, philosophies, and lifeways. The trouble lies not in the exploration and learning but in the representation, in the white possessivist logics that further economic exploitation and cultural erasure of people of color.

Many scholars have written similar critiques about the politics and ethics of cultural borrowing and appropriation.[3] The Dakota scholar Philip Deloria writes about the history of whites "playing Indian," performing the other in an attempt to cultivate their authentic selves.[4] Laura Donaldson denounces "white shame-ans," whites who appropriate, represent, and exploit Native religion as a form of fetish.[5] Deborah Root writes of "cannibal culture," linking together the commodification of difference and white consumption.[6] But few have analyzed cultural appropriation through the study of religion, which raises particularly perplexing questions about the spectrum between spiritual tourism, cultural appropriation, and conversion.

In what follows, I employ some of the lessons learned from Indigenous studies to think through the appropriative practices of religious exoticism in transformational festivals. In these spaces, many whites adopt and perform aspects of "exotic" cultures and religions as instruments to further their spiritual growth and exploration. In so doing, some even cultivate new selves, as in the example of Sundari Lakshmi. These practitioners participate in religious exoticism as a means to cultivate self-distinction.[7] As Graham St. John has argued, "The essential alterity signified by Amerindians, and the Natives of other regions, speaks of the primitivism that has tactically assisted, and continues to assist, Western desires for completeness and ideologies of progress. It also speaks of the practice of cultural appropriation through which a fantasized and projected otherness is adopted and purposed in the cause of establishing countermodernities, practices that have indeed generated a range of critiques from those exposing dubious claims to authority and indigeneity, 'fakelore,' 'imperialist nostalgia,' a 'salvage paradigm,' 'postmodern neocolonialism,' and entrepreneurial expropriation and commodification."[8] Religious exoticism is not necessarily problematic in its "desire for completeness" or cultural exploration; rather, the issue lies in its "dubious claims to authority and indigeneity."

For example, in the yogic field, white yogic practitioners may align and identify with Indic cultures and traditions as a critique of Western modernity, but as they do, they also flood the yoga market and, more broadly, the New Age market. White yogis not only learn and practice yoga but also become representatives, entrepreneurs, and spokespeople because of their greater access to social capital. As a result, Indian yogis, and Indigenous and Asian spiritual leaders more broadly, are overwhelmed in the cacophony of dominant white voices, or silenced entirely. What began as an act of imagined solidarity becomes yet another tool for their oppression. Debates, often nonproductive ones, ensue regarding cultural appropriation, intellectual and cultural property, intellectual commons, conversion and its impossibility, and so on.

White Utopias focuses explicitly on these dynamics through the practice of yoga in transformational festivals. But here, in this first chapter, I broaden the lens to analyze religious exoticism more generally, and its impact in defining the intellectual fields of those who identify as spiritual but not religious. I argue that religious exoticism entails the turn toward alterity *primarily as a critique of one's own positionality—a search for something else, something beyond the familiar*. Alterity—that is to say, racialized others and their cultural forms—becomes a tool instrumentalized to further self-critique and self-transformation. Religious exoticism engages with a variety of forms of alterity, the sole requirements of which are that they are disidentified with the self and the home culture. For this reason, Indigenous and Indic cultural forms become indexed with alterity, set outside and in contradistinction to Western modernity. Equated as such under the logics of white possessivism, they are easily hybridized and interchanged in the practices of religious exoticism.

THE SPIRITUAL BRICOLAGE OF TRANSFORMATIONAL FESTIVALS

Opportunities for spiritual growth vary widely between different transformational festivals. Each of the festivals discussed herein incorporates yoga into a variety of religious traditions, particularly Hinduism, Buddhism, Tantra, and Indigenous religions. Transformational festivals seamlessly transition between these traditions. In some cases, they are segmented into autonomous workshops and classes on subjects such as Buddhist meditation, Tibetan singing bowls, creating your own *maṇḍala*, Ayahuasca, and Native American ceremony. In other cases, however, instructors blend these traditions together within a singular workshop or class, for example when a yoga teacher splices Buddhist, Tantric, and Native American ideas into one yoga class. Echoing this, some vendors sell products focused particularly on the wares of one tradition (e.g., a shop selling Hindu *murtis* [religious figurines]), while others offer products that amalgamate a variety of Indigenous and Indic religious traditions (e.g., Hindu, Buddhist, Indigenous, and consciousness wares). From an aerial view, transformational festivals are broadly eclectic, exhibiting a variety of practices, worldviews, and products drawn from Indigenous and Indic religious traditions. The aesthetic of festival fashion also embraces Indigenous and Indic motifs blended with expressions of the mystical and magical—from body jewelry to "tribal" body paint, feathered headpieces, *bindis,* and *gopi*[9] skirts.

With a few exceptions related to their more ritualistic and mystical forms, Abrahamic religions (Christianity, Judaism, and, in particular, Islam) are notably absent. Also absent are appropriations of African and African American religious and cultural forms. This is an interesting anomaly particular to the field of religion; in the cultural mainstream, for instance, white appropriations of Black aesthetic, arts, and cultural forms have been particularly ubiquitous.[10] This lack of engagement may signify that the religious exoticism of these subcultures is deeply, if unconsciously, intertwined with legacies of anti-Black racism, as many scholars have argued.[11] It may also signify that appropriations of Black culture are viewed as taboo (politically incorrect) in these predominantly politically liberal communities, while Indic and Indigenous traditions are understood to be more available for white consumption.

It may also be the notion that African Americans are the primary referent of racialized others in the United States and thus cannot fully fulfill the allure of the exotic. Such speculations open fields of potential research but are largely beyond the intended scope of this project.

Predictably, the relationship between transformational festivals and religion is complex. The majority of interlocutors I interviewed identified as "spiritual but not religious" (SBNR). At Burning Man, the only event that hosts a community census and publishes it publicly, 46.4 percent of participants identified as SBNR (24.3 percent identified as atheist, and 15.2 percent identified as agnostic, while only 5.5 percent identified as religious).[12] Events at Burning Man exhibit the most overt rejection of religion; even with the 2017 theme of Radical Ritual, events engaging the parody of religion outnumbered formal religious services advertised on the *playa*[13] three to one. Most participants view LIB and Burning Man as intentional, consciousness-raising, and transformational festivals. They host the highest number of workshops and events focused on religion, meditation, and other spiritual techniques, but the percentage of such offerings in relation to the massive size and scale of these events renders the impact less influential. Bhakti and Shakti Fests are the most overtly devotional, with the most concentrated emphasis on ritual and the majority of events focused on the Hindu ideal of *bhakti* (devotion). Wanderlust festivals are situated as transformational events, and the practice of yoga as a method of reenchantment, a kind of "secular church."

In general, among many participants there is a sense that religions have a pure and beautiful essence and have created practical and efficacious tools with which to access that essence. However, they also feel that religions have become institutionalized, political, and corrupt. As Devanand (Joshua) explained during our early morning interview at Bhakti Fest:

> There are so many different approaches because there are so many different people and types, and what is attractive to one person is definitely not attractive to another. But love, truth, compassion, kindness, generosity, these are all attractive to every human being. And those are all what's at the core of most major religions, and all of these things that they were founded on, these kinds of principles, but then [they] gradually became corrupted systems of control.... Once people have power, they're like, "We want to keep this power, so we've got to control rather than allow its expansion and a flow of consciousness and allow people to believe that they can choose their own life." And that is where they started to separate that there's God out there, over here somewhere among the clouds, and we have to obey, which is quite the opposite of what we are.[14]

Many of my SBNR informants echoed this sentiment, and as a result, the majority had deliberately turned away from institutionalized forms of religion. At Bhakti Fest, Kara explained to me:

> Well, being raised in a Pentecostal, charismatic environment in Indiana in the 1960s and '70s, ... it was like, ... "We don't do that. It's against my religion." ... I have more of an aversion to Jesus than a love for him. ... I hated church, though I felt really deeply moved by so many things, you know, music, art, or love. ... It's taken me a long time to remember how to pray. It's like—how do you pray? Who am I praying to? What am I asking for? And to me, it just comes back to gratitude. As long as I feel gratitude, then that's all. So, I say my religion—I have the religion of common sense.[15]

In addition to having this personalized sense of spiritual communion, the majority of these SBNR participants employed theological universalism as a means to conflate and obfuscate differences between traditions. Even if they practiced a particular religious form, still they maintained that there are any number of possible paths to God, self-realization, and enlightenment. During our interview at Bhakti Fest, Susan explained,

> It does not matter whether you are singing God's name in Qawwali or Sanskrit or in Hindi or what have you. Do you think God cares? Just ask him. No. ... The type of meditation I'm doing, it's a very scientific approach, a very mechanical approach. Yes, it's Sanskrit. Yes, it's a lot easier for me to pull my energy to the eye center if I'm focusing on my teacher's face, which is a devotional aspect of it. And yet, is it necessary? No. It doesn't matter if you're Muslim or Catholic or Lutheran or Jewish or Sikh, it's the same. It's pulling you up, and it's connecting to the divine. And all of the paths can get you there if practiced with diligence.[16]

In this soteriology, one can pick and choose the most effective tools across traditions because, in essence, they all lead to the same goal. This fundamental and widely pervasive belief has led SBNR practitioners to view religious forms as practical tools that can be extracted from the institutional mores and theological cosmologies of their parent traditions.

My interlocutors echo Altglas's research on Kabbalah centers and modern Hindu gurus, wherein she found that "courses, commentaries of the scriptures and writings, and teacher's interviews all associate religion with dogma, constraint, obedience, 'mindless ritual,' lack of consciousness, and lack of fulfillment."[17] Likewise, speaking of the New Age movement's propensity toward religious exoticism, she articulates this same *pragmatic approach* to religion: "Above all, individuals seek practical methods for personal growth in a 'lifelong religious learning,' beyond religious particularities. . . . The imperative of self-improvement constitutes an incentive for not stagnating and endlessly trying new techniques that could hasten this improvement."[18]

Esme, a young female participant at Shakti Fest, self-identified as a "quester" for this "lifelong religious learning" in the following terms: "We're questers, spiritual questers. So we quest for a lot of different areas, and thus in that questing you expose yourself to a lot of different paths, a lot of different experiences, a lot of different thoughts. You know, just allow that which really works for you, and [adopt] the essence as it were. Find the commonality amongst all the paths."[19] Rather than stagnate within a fixed religious identity framed by dogma and institution, these questers search for practical tools that will lead them to pure and ancient essences that are believed to be untainted by the corruptions of modernity.

The result is that even among those who visibly practice meditation, postural yoga, Vedic rituals, or *kīrtan*, few self-identify within the particular religion from which these practices are extracted. As I have written elsewhere, this is commonplace among those who identify as SBNR, many of whom believe in God and routinely practice religion.[20] Very few yogis attending transformational festivals claim to be Hindu or Buddhist, but 95 percent practice meditation, 94 percent practice *āsana*, 90 percent practice *prāṇāyāma*, 74 percent read yogic texts, 67 percent recite mantras, 64 percent sing *kīrtans*, 41 percent read Hindu scriptures, 38 percent read Buddhist scriptures, and 33 percent worship deities (*pūjā*).[21]

There are multiple reasons for this absence of religious self-identification: (1) alternative spirituality is a category established in opposition to religion and formal religious affiliation, which fosters an antiestablishment and anti-institutional constituency; (2) these practitioners are not exclusive to one religious tradition, and this exclusivity is a defining feature of religious belonging;[22] and (3) white SBNR populations are excluded from some of the religions in question because the assumption of a particular ethnic identity is considered a qualification for belonging. This last point is critical; both Hinduism and Native American religious traditions are ethnoreligions, within which there are no standard avenues for formal conversion. Neither is traditionally a proselytizing religion, and both have a history of foregrounding secret rites transmitted through oral traditions along strict hierarchical systems. Both are exclusionary toward outsiders and have established regulatory systems to enact that exclusion (purity and pollution in the context of Hinduism, and earned hereditary knowledge in the context of Native American religions). In fact, their predominance in SBNR communities may have everything to do with their secrecy, because the history of metaphysical religion is deeply intertwined with the quest for esoteric knowledge. Wouter J. Hanegraaff traces the very idea of the birth of a New Age to "modern Theosophical speculation which, in turn, is dependent upon older traditions in Western esotericism."[23]

Yoga, *pūjās, kīrtan,* and *homas* (Hindu fire sacrifices) blended seamlessly with Tai chi, Qi gong, Tibetan singing bowls, and mindfulness meditation at the transformational festivals I studied. Altars combined images of the Buddha and Shiva; Ganesha sat next to the Virgin Mary. They were often erected in beatific natural spaces, such as at the bases of trees and at the top of hills, and included feathers, pine cones, crystals, and sage. Rituals included not only Buddhist and Hindu religious practices but also South American crystal skulls, labyrinth-walking meditations, shaman-led visualizations, Maori storytelling, medicine wheel creation, and Native American drumming, singing, and prayers. This religious behavior extends beyond the boundaries of *benevolent Orientalism*[24] to encapsulate a form of religious exoticism, one that employed a pragmatic approach by valorizing religious forms and practices that were viewed as both exotic and effective spiritual tools.

Wanderlust festivals celebrate a form of *enchanted secularism* that involves sublime experiences engaging with nature, personal introspection through yoga, and spiritual fulfillment in contact with community. In contrast, Bhakti and Shakti Fests cultivate explicitly religious experiences by drawing on the teachings of various Hindu-derived gurus, devotional yoga (*bhakti*), devotional music and chanting (*kīrtan*), *mantra* recitation, Vedic rituals, and postural yoga. They also include the most significant population of white practitioners who identify as Hindu *bhaktas* (devotees). Many of the core facilitators of this community are serious devotees and do not represent the "noncommittal"[25] and superficial, "aesthetic" choices of the New Age,[26] as is often described by scholarly critics. Rather, many were born into the Self-Realization Fellowship (SRF) or the Hare Krishnas (ISKCON), or born into families that were deeply committed to a particular form of Indic spirituality. For example, when I asked Jesse, a young male attendee, when he got involved in the guru-yoga scene, he told me that his grandmother had been on the board of the SRF in the 1940s.[27] When I asked Gopal, a prominent *kīrtan* musician, when he became a Krishna *bhakta,* he told me that he and his bandmates were born into ISKCON families.[28] Some have lived for decades in guru-led communities in the United States or in India, while others make annual pilgrimages to the subcontinent or otherwise divide their lives between East and West. Although these participants are mostly whites who adopt Indic cultural forms, including dress and bodily comportment, they complicate the stereotyped critique of noncommittal and aesthetically based spiritual tourism. Many of the core facilitators of this community are converts in all but name.

In opposition, Burning Man and LIB emphasize spiritual expression and exploration through the creation of *transtraditional spiritual assemblages,* or *bricolage,* rather than religious devotion to any one tradition or teacher. LIB hosts multiple learning environments wherein participants are exposed to workshops focused on everything from conscious business and entrepreneurial skills to permaculture and essential oils. There are opportunities to engage in chanting Hindu mantras, meditating with Tibetan singing bowls, and singing with members of the Native American Church (Peyote Religion). In 2016, the LIB Temple of Consciousness, which ran programming every hour for the entirety of the festival, focused explicitly on Indigenous knowledge; there were over forty different lectures and workshops related to Indigenous traditions and arts. In 2017, LIB festival organizers established a permanent space dedicated to learning about and supporting the spirituality and political activism of Native peoples.[29]

Wanderlust festivals in Great Lake Taupo, New Zealand, in Sunshine Coast, Australia, and in Oahu, Hawaii, opened and closed with ceremonies conducted by Maori, Australian aboriginals, and Hawaiians, respectively. Throughout each Wanderlust festival week, there were special lectures, guided walking tours, meditations, and rituals focused on Indigenous knowledge. These inclusions were the festivals' attempts to raise consciousness of the fact that they occur on settler colonial lands with a fraught history of oppression of Indigenous people. For the initial welcome ceremony of Wanderlust in Great Lake Taupo, the festival's organizers invited a large group of Maori leaders and performers to conduct a Pohiri ritual dramatizing the encounter between different tribes. To do so is a political recognition of the Maori history of New Zealand; indeed, to open a Wanderlust festival in New Zealand without a Maori-led Pohiri ceremony would be a public affront to the history and land rights of the Maori people. Similarly, the 2014 LIB festival began with a collaborative ceremony between multiple Chumash tribal leaders and LIB organizers prior to the formal opening of the festival. Bhakti and Shakti

Fests also acknowledged the Serrano, Cahuilla, Chemehuevi, and Mohave, for whom Joshua Tree, California, is ancestral land. However, organizers addressed this issue by having their own (white) performers lead Pan-Native prayers and invocation of the blessings of the sky, earth, and four directions to begin the festival.[30]

But the importance of Indigenous religions extends beyond public recognition of the Indigenous lands upon which these festivals are conducted through ceremony. My 2014 survey of attendees at a wide variety of yoga festivals asked, "Which traditions have some of the deepest resources for spiritual growth on our planet?" The top five traditions respondents cited were: yoga (86 percent), nature (83 percent), Buddhism (72 percent), Native American traditions (56 percent), and Hinduism (53 percent).[31] In fact, American yoga practitioners valued Native American traditions as containing deeper "resources for spiritual growth" than Hinduism! Certainly, the Hindu American Foundation's Take Back Yoga campaign proffered a subjective (and motivated) interpretation of yoga by claiming it as a Hindu practice,[32] but the practice certainly developed in India, influenced by Hindu, Buddhist, and Jain religions.[33] Hindus in India created modern forms of postural yoga from a foundation in Sāṃkhya-Yoga philosophical ideals, body building, esoteric dance, gymnastics, and Hindu, Buddhist, and Jain religious texts. In the early twentieth century, the founders of modern postural yoga—Shivananda, T.M. Krishnamacharya, and Krishnamacharya's students B.K.S. Iyengar, K. Patthabi Jois, and T.K.V. Desikachar—universalized a system of physical practices and readied them for international export.[34] These modern innovators lived within a religious worldview wherein the term *yoga* referred to a religious path, or more specifically, yoking or binding oneself to Absolute Truth, as in the various yogas (*karma yoga* [the path of action], *bhakti yoga* [the path of devotion], and *jñāna yoga* [the path of knowledge]) in Hindu scriptures, such as the *Bhagavad Gītā*. They also centralized the *Yoga Sūtras*, a Sanskrit text that integrates Hindu, Buddhist, and Jain religious ideas.[35] While these first-generation proselytizing yogis universalized yoga as a new scientific method for health and wellness, they also rooted the tradition with Hindu and Indic texts and India's religious systems.[36] So then why would today's American yogis claiming alliance with these lineages rank Native American traditions as a deeper "resource for spiritual growth" than Hinduism?

In response to this surprising data, I began to look for evidence of Native American traditions in the field. I found yoga teachers invoking the ritual systems of Native American ceremony, calling for a return to ancient Indigenous lifeways, demanding a return to respect for Mother Earth, encouraging their students to find and follow their spirit, and developing alternative epistemologies and ways of inhabiting the body through the philosophical lessons and practical methodologies by combining Indigenous and yogic knowledge. The broader context of these transformational festivals provided attendees with Indigenous-derived experiences, like singing with South American crystal skulls,[37] lectures on Indigenous methods for attaining mystical experiences (including peyote, ayahuasca, and DMT), fire ceremonies, ecological messages, Chakra Village healing sanctuaries (established in teepees), teepees erected in communal spaces, Native American Church sacred singing workshops, and workshop and lecture themes focused on learning from Indigenous knowledge systems.

Several prominent yoga teachers hybridized Indigenous and Indic worldviews in their teaching. For example, Ana Forrest, a revered global yoga teacher who often teaches at Wanderlust festivals,[38] extracts practical spiritual tools from both Indic and Indigenous sources. In her autobiographical book, *Fierce Medicine,* she writes:

> I have no loyalty to concepts that aren't *true* for me. Although I studied Yoga with B. K. S. Iyengar himself, the most important lesson I learned from him was to disobey the dictator if you don't find a man's character congruent with his teachings. . . . I discarded what didn't work from both ancient and modern wisdom traditions and braided in the wisdom from my years as a horse whisperer to create the unique approach I call Forrest Yoga . . . . This book lays out a system of practices founded in Yoga and Native American Medicine. . . . I created Forrest Yoga to do my part in Mending the Hoop of the People. This is my life's calling, my Spirit Pledge.[39]

Throughout the text, Forrest posits Indigenous knowledge as a panacea for the errors of Western modernity. In her view, Native cultures have retained that which has been lost or corrupted in the West. She writes,

> One of the things I prized about my years on the reservation was seeing the initiation ceremonies the people used to hone intuition and the skillfulness in wielding it. Children who grow up with Native American traditions see the importance of developing these skills, of becoming aware of the sensitive, magical part of ourselves that don't yet have outlets. Western culture squashes and invalidates our nature so we don't develop intuition, nor do we know how to use the information from our intuition as a tool for improving the quality of our daily life. I am working to correct that.[40]

Forrest envisions her integration of Native American ceremony and yoga as a means to mend the "Hoop of the People," to teach people how to get back into alignment with their bodies and nature, and then to activate that change into more eco-conscious patterns of action and consumption. In addition to working with Native traditions and yoga, she also studied as an energetic healer. During healing sessions, she summoned the energy of the Hindu goddess Kali to serve as her "healing partner." In Forrest's view, Kali, whom she describes as "one murderous bitch of a goddess," was "exactly what I needed in my healing work."[41]

Eli Gordon, one of the central yoga instructors at Bhakti and Shakti Fests, seamlessly blends environmentalism drawn from Native traditions, rituals of sage and sweat, and Native dances and songs infused with yoga, *bhakti,* and *kīrtan.* Many of his classes began with Native American invocations, and his rhetoric integrated Indigenous ideals of sacrality with *bhakti.* As quoted in the ethnographic vignette at the beginning of the introduction, his message calls for restoration of ancestral wisdom and veneration of the divinity of nature. These incorporations of Native American religious forms into the contemporary yogic landscape reveal the importance of place in the formulation of transnational religion. American yogis have reached across the oceans to adopt Indic rituals and yogic practices, but they are still ensconced in the contextual history of the United States. This history reveals that when white Americans embody religious exoticism, the alternative sacred forms that they imagine to exist outside of Western modernity are geographically localized. Because of the context of settler colonialism, even if white Americans are pursuing yogic and Indic religions, Native American traditions serve as the most proximate others—supplying pragmatic spiritual tools to revision the self and society.

Festival yogis, organizers, and participants focused on Indigenous rituals and ontologies as a means to open a conversation about alternative modes of sociality, economy, and relation to nature. Indigenous ideas and practices provided a bridge to engage with yoga and Indic religions as alternative pathways of being and knowing in the modern world. The presumed ancient essence of Indigenous and Indic knowledge becomes a generative platform from which to create visions of alternative utopias—new futures that do not attempt to fully revert to the ancient past but rather to use its resources as practical tools in order to evolve into a more conscious future. In the racialized global context of white supremacy, whites easily displace Indigenous peoples and Asians as representatives of that knowledge. As Shelby Michaels told her yoga class at Wanderlust in Great Lake Taupo, "*All* people are Indigenous and can find the landmarks that lead straight back to *original spirit.*"[42]

CULTURAL APPROPRIATION AND ITS IMPACT

The Burning Man community has had a tense relationship with issues of cultural appropriation for many years. In 2009, a "Go Native!" Burner party in Oakland devolved into the organizers' tears and apologies when Hopi and Kiowa tribal members shut down the party and spent more than four hours lecturing white Burners about cultural sensitivity.[43] Most recently, in 2016, members of the Burning Man theme camp Red Lightning became embroiled in an Internet-fueled culture war that many participants and camp leaders became aware of only when they emerged from the dust and reconnected to social media. As virtual documentation of the Burn and ethnic diversity on the playa increases, such altercations over cultural boundaries seem likely to impact the way the event is perceived.

In the view of many participants, Burning Man exists as an alternate reality, separated from social conventions, where play and provocation performatively intertwine. In 1990, when participants first entered the Black Rock Desert, they "joined hands and stepped over a line drawn in the desert's surface signifying their collective entry into another zone of experience."[44] That line signified the separation of the playa from conventional social norms and parameters. Today, many Burners seek to maintain that line and challenge critics to leave politics in the default world, retaining the playa as a zone of unrestrained Radical Self-Expression. Many view Burning Man as an artistic space and vigorously defend the right of artists to express themselves without regulation. Ideally, Burning Man Project places regulations on art only when that art is imminently dangerous to participants.[45] However, this utopian vision remains only tenuously detached from the disciplining of cultural boundaries that occurs in the default world. As increasing numbers of people of color attend Burning Man, Radical Self-Expression that they find to be racist may be a deterrent to their involvement, thus limiting the potential for the Radical Inclusion of nonwhite participants; both are listed among Burning Man's 10 Principles.

In 2018 at Burning Man, I participated in a tea ceremony called Tea and Turbans at the Appropriated Dragon camp in the French Quarter Village. I walked up the red stairs of the Chinese-styled pagoda to the top-floor sitting area, where I was greeted by two white women in turbans. They directed me to select a cloth bundle from a table piled high with them in multiple colors and then to find a partner and take a seat at one of the café tables. In time, a Middle Eastern man greeted us, led

48 | Romanticizing the Premodern

6. Author portrait taken during a Tea and Turbans tea ceremony, Burning Man, 2017 (photo by Bootleg).

the small crowd in a lesson on how to wrap our turbans around our heads in Moroccan fashion, and narrated the symbolism of the traditional tea service. We then enjoyed a tea service of three pours each, and I enjoyed an intimate conversation with my new friend Nomad, augmented by the caffeinated accelerations of my sensory perception. It was a magical playa moment of newfound connection and Immediacy (another one of the 10 Principles) as we talked about paranormal events, yoga, travel, Bali, and Maori mythology. I lost track of time as we sat together, and a photographer snapped a picture of me at ease, gazing across the playa in my turban (see figure 6).

When the ceremony was over, we took a group picture of all of us in turbans, and then I went back to the Black Rock Bakery to check on operations. When I entered the bakery, I encountered a group of six or seven of our campers, all of whom were Asian American. Immediately, I made a joke of having "gotten turbaned" and stripped my head of the turban. They all laughed but seemed relieved at my having called to the fore the questionable politics of the Tea and Turbans experience. Later, sitting in front of the bakery during a community meal, I spoke with Kevin, one of our Chinese American campers, who mentioned that initially he had been eating his meal on the steps of the Appropriated Dragon before he had become viscerally aware of the fraught optics of such a scene and had moved over to sit in front of the bakery, which has a traditional French Quarter New Orleans façade. We spoke a bit about the politics of cultural appropriation and the Appropriated Dragon. He thought that the Appropriated Dragon was an interesting idea but was "not smart enough" in its confrontation with the debates concerning cultural appropriation to be an effective performance art piece.[46]

Bacchus, one of the innovators behind the Appropriated Dragon, traces the concept back to his ideal of Burning Man as a city, Black Rock City. He envisioned the great cities of the world as having ethnic neighborhoods and sought to create a kind of Chinatown, which became the Appropriated Dragon. When I asked him about his vision for the Appropriated Dragon and its relation to cultural appropriation, he explained: "I'm all about stealing everything. Steal everything from every culture. It's all about what is tasteful. If it's real and I found it—found objects are fine. That's fine—if it's not a performance like cosplay then I'm not into it because then you're pretending to be something that you're not. If it's a real expression—like, fashion is real because fashion is an expression. But if it's not and you just got it from some costume place, then it's not cool. Then you're just trying to dress up and become something you aren't." He explained that initially he had the idea to have a headdress burn barrel in front of the Appropriated Dragon targeting fashion models wearing headdresses on the playa—those who would strike a pose for Instagram in their warrior bonnet and declare, "I'm so free!"[47]

The Appropriated Dragon aims to be a "cultural exchange zone," but the founders thought that educational materials asserting ethical standards on cultural appropriation would be too "heavy-handed." Instead, Burners enter a Chinese pagoda space with a Chinese Buddhist altar and a placard above the broad staircase to the second floor that boasts the flags of multiple countries and mocks the idea of cultural appropriation with the tag line "From your culture to ours" (see figure 7). Like many performance pieces at Burning Man, the Appropriated Dragon is playing with and parodying a current cultural issue without indoctrinating participants into a specific moral code. It raises a question, provides an experience, and then leaves participants to have independent reactions.

However, there is a fundamental critique at the heart of Bacchus's vision of the Appropriated Dragon. When I spoke with him, he was concerned with the end result of moralistic claims of cultural appropriation. He saw the debate as an authoritarianism of the Left, wherein the liberal Left circles back and conflates with the ideology of the

7. "From Your Culture to Ours" sign, Appropriated Dragon Camp, Burning Man, 2017 (photo by author).

conservative Right. He explained: "The Far Right is obsessed with purity, that we should only fuck white people, eat white food, restore white culture. It's the same idea on the Far Left, with the debates on cultural appropriation. Both have a conviction of ethnic purity, that we should stay within the confines of our own culture—only fuck white people, not eat phở, not cross cultural boundaries. Fuck that. The Appropriated Dragon is a project challenging both of those discourses—attempting to challenge us to think differently."[48]

In contemporary American identity politics, the policers of cultural appropriation seem to maintain the ideal of authentic cultural essences that can be distilled, represented, and stolen. The notion of cultural appropriation reifies the boundaries of cultural insiders and outsiders and depends on the notion of cultural autonomy and even ethnic purity. As such, it risks causing harms of a similar kind of fascist essentialism to which critics are objecting.[49]

However, in society, there are some groups that are bounded, exclusive entities that forbid appropriation of their practices by outsiders. For example, impersonating a police officer, using a service animal if able-bodied, and taking on gay affect if straight are all understood to be cultural "wrongs" that violate boundaries of group membership. Violations have varying implications and consequences. For example, taking on a gay affect may be viewed as in poor taste, but impersonating a police officer is illegal. In Erich Matthes's work, the perceived harm of cultural appropriation is that it "interacts with *dominating systems* so as to *silence* and *speak for* individuals who are already *socially marginalized.*"[50] When whites adopt the religious and cultural forms of marginalized peoples, they occupy spaces of representation that people of color might otherwise hold. They also identify within the historical legacy of the looting of the global South that was justified by imperialism. Those who make a profession from such forms of representation also siphon away financial rewards that people of color might otherwise have earned. Socially, the move toward mimesis performs an impotent form of alliance that obfuscates other means of direct political action that would express solidarity with the forms of injustice and discrimination that racialized others suffer. In cases wherein people of color are discriminated against for representing their cultural forms while whites do so with impunity, religious exoticism becomes an embodied performance of white privilege.

WHITE *BHAKTAS* AND THE POLITICS OF REPRESENTATION

In 2016, Carrie Grossman (Dayashila) was disrupted during her *kīrtan* performance at Brown University by protesters claiming that as a white woman singing *kīrtans,* she was wrongly appropriating elements of Hinduism.[51] The protesters were mostly white and African American students who employed the moral policing strategies of the liberal Left to confront the *kīrtan* artist for her expression of white privilege and her exploitation of Indian Hindu religious forms. Similarly, in 2018, the Bhakti Yoga Club at American University was disbanded after a South Asian student levied an accusation of cultural appropriation. The club had invited a troupe of white Hare Krishnas to host an "India Day" festival and perform the Indian epic the *Rāmāyana*. The student who levied the accusation wrote: "The sponsors of this show and the artists acted as if their actions were acceptable because they have converted to the Hare Krishna sect of Hinduism. The reality of this is that white European dancers will never know my intersectional experience as a Hindu woman, being a brown bodied person and the other aspects of systematic racism that I, as well as other South Asian people, have experienced."[52] This is not the first time that the whiteness of the Hare Krishnas has been critiqued, particularly because the traditional branches of the religion encourage devotees to adopt Indic cultural dress and to proselytize in public spaces.[53]

Importantly, the critique of cultural appropriation is deeply informed by the context of multiculturalism, wherein identity depends on the performance of ethnic and cultural authenticity. Multiculturalism may be an important valorization of diversity, but it also problematically imagines cultures as coherent and uniform wholes to be presented and represented by their members, in what political theorist James Tully has explained as "a desire for cultural uniformity" and "a 'billiard ball' model of cultural diversity."[54] Along these same lines, Charles Taylor has famously argued that the politics of recognition inherent within multiculturalism "acquiesces in a stifling model of the nature of agency and its relationship to culture, or to 'identity' more generally."[55] Multiculturalism demands that minority groups perform authenticity and adhere to fixed standards of cultural, religious, and ethnic identity to be recognized as full subjects. This imagined fixity of autonomous, sovereign, and authentic identities demands culturally specific performances, and essentializes and even solidifies extant cultural stereotypes. In Prema Kurien's phrasing, it is "a multiculturalism that demands a performance of authenticity."[56] This performance confines people of color to localized representations of cultural specificity, whereas whites are free to imagine themselves as universal, global citizens, with rights of property to all cultural and religious forms.

In contrast, in India, where Indian Hindus are the majority, whites performing and adopting Hindu beliefs and practices does not usually pose a significant problem for Indians.[57] In popular Indian tourist centers, whites are sometimes disparaged by locals for their negative environmental impact, criminality, sexual lasciviousness, or participation in black markets, but their religiosity is rarely at the center of popular critique. In India, where Hindu religiosity is valued highly, even white *bhaktas,* if they are serious and devout, command respect from the general populace. One can see this in the veneration given to many of the *swamīs* and *brahmacārīs* of ISKCON—for example, Radhanath Swami, born Richard Slavin in Chicago, Illinois. Many Indian Hindus even take particular pride in their religion when they see foreigners attracted to it. In response to the protests against Dayashila at Brown University, Rajan Zed, the president of the Universal Society of Hinduism, reflected such a view, arguing that the "color of the person should not matter in devotional singing and anybody should be able [to] pay respectful homage to Hindu deities through *kīrtan* or other forms."[58]

But in the United States, anti–cultural appropriation activists aim to guard against cultural exploitation of people of color. They note the racialized disparity between whites—who can embody nonwhite cultural forms while reserving the ability to discard them if and when they become inconvenient or a liability—and nonwhites, who cannot. This cultural policing is based on physical appearances, not intent, education, or experience. For the student critic at American University, it did not matter that the Hare Krishnas identified as converts to Hinduism. In her view, their whiteness and accompanying white privilege prevented them from accessing the religious and cultural forms of ethnically Indian Hindus. In the larger field of Hindu studies, such a view aligns with the Hindu ideologues of the far Right, who have argued in recent decades that Anglo-European outsiders should not represent India, Hinduism, or Sanskrit because of their outsider status, regardless of their intent or knowledge.[59]

In Western academia, many scholars distance themselves from such an authoritarian view of cultural property and justify their engagement with India and Hinduism by citing their accumulated knowledge, educational pedigree, and respect for (or even love for) Indic culture. This view extends beyond judgment based in external physical characteristics and judges validity based on interiority. As Anthony K. Appiah writes, "Cultural borrowing is great; the problem is disrespect."[60] Such a view exempts scholars from critique yet enables them to critique white *bhaktas* and yogis based on the assumption that these communities are superficial in their adoptions of Indic religions. In $elling Spirituality, Jeremy Carrette and Richard King argue, "What is being sold to us as radical, trendy and transformative spirituality in fact produces little in the way of a significant change in one's lifestyle or fundamental behaviour patterns (with the possible exception of motivating the individual to be more efficient and productive at work)."[61] But Carrette and King's assumptions about the content of *kīrtan* and yoga in the West are simply not validated by the teachings of some of the most influential and internationally famous teachers in the festival context. There, many *kīrtan* artists and yogis are highly engaged with South Asian religious traditions. Many are reading texts, attending workshops, and adopting Buddhist and Hindu devotional practices. The festival becomes an educational shared space that provides an opportunity to learn more about the various spiritual peripheries of *kīrtan* and postural yoga. In short, many of these participants are serious.[62]

But the ubiquity of white voices, even serious ones, can still create a crisis of representation wherein people of color are occluded and erased. In this vein, Roopa Singh, an Indian American woman and a founding member of the South Asian American Peoples Yoga Alliance (SAAPYA),[63] addressed a room of white yoga teachers tearfully with the following sentiment: "As you fill that space [of representing yoga], teach in that space, know that there is someone, who looks very much like my mother and looks very much like my father, who is not there, who doesn't feel as confident to integrate, to be in public in this country—just know that you are taking a space that is precious."[64] Singh speaks to the manner in which white bodies travel freely in public, universal spaces, while brown bodies are relegated to the private and the local. Cultural appropriation is, in actuality, a question of representation; it is not the root of the problem but rather an effect of systemic racial injustice.

GOING NATIVE: BECOMING A TRIBE

The very foundations of religious exoticism are deeply intertwined with the adoption and appropriation of nonwhite religious and cultural identities that borrow heavily from Native American traditions. Historically, religious exoticism both idealized and distanced itself from actual Native American peoples. For many, Native ways are a symbolic representation of alternative ways of being and of relating to the self and to the earth. By identifying with Native ways, the counterculture also self-identifies as being critical of discriminatory US governmental policies toward Native Americans. This identification is largely politically impotent and expresses solidarity through the adoption of Native aesthetics and spirituality rather than direct political action or protest. There are moments of attempted political solidarity, but even those can become highly problematic, for participants and witnesses alike.

For example, in 2016–17, members of the Red Lightning Tribe at Burning Man traveled to Standing Rock Reservation in North Dakota to protest in solidarity with Native Americans. They then brought Sioux and Dakota elders to the playa for a global synchronized drum circle in an initiative called the Power of Prayer.[65] In the case of Red Lightning, the village collectively identified with Native ways as a rejection of disenchanted Western modernity and a desire for reenchantment. Leaders sought to sacralize their community, and Burning Man more generally, through the performance of Native rituals.

But Red Lightning Tribe's actions at Burning Man 2017 incited a storm of vitriolic criticism, mostly levied via the Internet. Fundamentally, critics rejected the idea of hosting Native American sacred ceremonies in an environment like Burning Man; others faulted Red Lightning Tribe for allowing drugs and alcohol to infiltrate the ceremonies, though they were disallowed within the camp. Others criticized the camp for being "plug and play" (wealthy, based on a capitalist model) and predominantly white. One critic wrote, "Cultural appropriation in every sense of that word! This camp completely disrespected our ways. You can't just steal someone else's [culture] and bend it and rewrite it to fit into your liking. It was ridiculous. Ceremony's [sic] are sacred, you had drunk acid trippin hippies banging on drums signing the wrong words to my peoples songs, wasicu people there in full head dresses and 'war paint' phony '[Medicine] men' This whole thing is screaming cultural appropriation."[66]

Although Native elders led many of the prayers and ceremonies at Red Lightning's camp, and some camp leaders worked closely with members of the Paiute Nation, some critics claimed that these elders did not have a clear sense of what Burning Man was when they accepted Red Lightning Tribe's invitation to lead the ceremonies. Others accused the Native elders who led the prayers and ceremonies of being "fakes" who were performing ceremonies incorrectly or selling out by performing as entertainment for whites. Others questioned Red Lightning Tribe's intentions and accused them of mocking Native religious traditions.[67] Underlying much of this debate was the central question of cultural property, which encompassed Native ceremonies, prayers, and material culture.[68] The venom of critics was profuse, and the Red Lightning Tribe leadership was largely defensive and uncomprehending of the critiques. In their view, many of them had stood with Native peoples in solidarity at Standing Rock, invited elders to lead sacred ceremonies in their own camp, and acted in admiration and appreciation of Native religious traditions.[69]

Just after the close of Burning Man in 2017, Chase Iron Eyes—a Lakota leader and Standing Rock's attorney who attended Red Lightning's Power of Prayer Global Sunset Drumming Circle—posted an Internet video wherein he cited the negative effects of "appropriation." He explained, "These types of things, they result in Indian mascotry. They result in cultivating kind of a dehumanized, primitive, spiritual ethos that the American Indian is then made to occupy that space in the imagination of the West." But he justified his presence at Burning Man as an attempt to "build bridges" and get signatures to support Standing Rock water protectors. He also defended his statement that "we are all indigenous," a claim that infuriated many Native critics (and notably echoes the yoga teacher Shelby Michaels, referenced earlier):

> By no means are we trying to mitigate or minimize or do anything by way of lessening and taking the focus off of the genocide, the fifty to eighty million Indigenous people, the original Nations of this hemisphere, . . . [but] all human beings, if you go back far enough, descend from the land or the sacred sites. . . . Race is a purely human construct; arguably, so is religion. . . . The Indigenous people have a role to play in guiding those people who now call themselves Americans or Canadians, . . . who were subjected to those same forces of colonization, those same forces of abstraction and separation. When I say that I am talking about a separation—spirit from mind, heart from intellect, and your being from the sacred connection to the cosmos. If you read any religion, any worldview, people are searching for that. They are searching for how to unite, to transcend, to make themselves one with Divine consciousness, and so forth. This is what ceremony does. . . . Colonization is real, and it happened to every human being. The entire globe was secularized. . . . And so some people are searching for those ways on how to connect with the sacred.[70]

The Red Lightning Tribe took a year off from Burning Man in 2018. Red Bear (John St. Dennis), one of the Red Lightning camp leaders, told me during our interview, "It would be very politically incorrect to bring Red Lightning back."[71] But in 2019, it did come back, albeit under a new name—Red Lightning: Blue Thunder.

Despite its external critics, many Burners love the opportunities for communal ritual, education, movement, and spiritual exploration that are offered in Burning Man camps like Red Lightning and Anahasana Village (focused on Tantra and yoga). Chapters 3 and 4 discuss, and even celebrate, the transformational spiritual experiences that explorations with alterity can catalyze. Engagement with ceremony, ritual, yoga, and meditation are all means by which SBNR communities attempt to heal themselves and to alleviate their feelings of disconnection and isolation. There is significant and measurable positive personal transformation that can emerge from spiritual explorations in transformational festivals. However, the story of these SBNR communities is fraught, and while there are many who are serious, religious exoticism easily devolves into cavalier forms of play when it is disseminated and commodified by the masses. The hubris of whiteness, with its presumption of entitlement and possession, enables this smooth transition from serious study to playful (mis)representation.

For example, material culture has been at the center of the visually centric debates on cultural appropriation involving box braids, *bindis,* and Native headdresses. In recent years, wearing Native American headdresses to festivals has become a popular fashion statement for some whites. This is part of a larger fashion trend that celebrates "tribal" cultures through dress, face paint, and body art. This co-option of tribal material culture is a form of exploitation and costuming that cheapens and undermines Indigenous identities. Transformational festivals abound with superficial adoptions of the material cultures of racialized others. At Burning Man and LIB, I encountered each day at least one Native war bonnet used as a fashion accessory, despite the fact that both festivals have issued public statements condemning the practice (see figure 8). Native headdresses have become a touchstone signifying cultural appropriation as violence against already disenfranchised Native populations. Whites wearing headdresses is often singled out because it is one of the most obviously offensive practices in a much more ambiguous and philosophically complex field.

For example, in 2015, on the very same booklet page that LIB highlighted "The Village"—an assemblage of teepees and a yurt wherein village life (and the following year, Indigenous knowledge) would be celebrated (see figure 9)—it included the following statement:

> Cultural Appropriation: Appreciation or Disrespect?
>
> Sporting a headdress, or other imitation accessories, that were not received through cultural rights with permission and the understanding that comes with it, means being a walking representative of 500+ years of colonialism and racism. LIB embraces raw, creative, and authentic self-expression. But by embracing the current tribal trends you aren't asserting yourself as an individual, you are situating yourself comfortably amongst a culture of power that continues to oppress Native peoples.[72]

Though their condemnatory statement against the headdress is unambiguous, paradoxically, their celebration of the teepee in The Village also seems to embrace "the current tribal trends." Their philosophical argument seems to draw a distinction between disrespectful costuming and the appreciation of Native lifeways. In this view, intent matters. The turn to Indigenous cultural and religious forms symbolizes a turn toward alternative relations between self and sociality. In so doing, organizers and participants form a spiritual subculture that envisions itself as a tribe. Part of the reason that transformational festival cultures attract these particular forms of self-expression through tribal attire stems from participants' attempts to set themselves apart with social distinction, to

8. Woman in Native headdress, Burning Man Temple, 2016 (photo by author; photo edits by Aimée-Linh McCartney).

situate themselves as a part of a community, as members of a tribe. The Indigenous symbolism of The Village creates the affective feeling of community and tribe, but extended fully, it also ambivalently supports white possession and performance of Native identities.

The cultivation and communal reiteration of this shared notion of "tribe" is founded on an agreed-upon mythic past, a critique of the present, and a projected vision of a utopian future. In an interview, Arthur compared Bhakti Fest to other festivals and concluded with a

9. The Village at Lightning in a Bottle, 2014 (photo by author).

sense that he had found his "tribe," meaning other like-minded people who shared his values and ethics: "This one [Bhakti Fest] is just coming home. This is my tribe. Like, we're my tribe."[73] As this is iterated and reiterated in the festival, it serves to distinguish the festival community as a utopian space, distinct from the external world.[74] Michel Maffesoli's work on postmodern tribalism suggests that tribalism is a process of reenchantment of the world, in which the fundamental feature of tribalism is a "shared sensibility or emotion."[75] In Festival Fire's 2017–18 schedule of transformational festivals, festivals such as Lucidity, Earthdance, Unifer, Project Earth, and Elements all called participants to join their "tribe," to participate in "tribal revival," and to come together in "tribal" and "tribal consciousness" gatherings.[76]

The notion of the tribe mirrors one of the fundamental purposes of religion, which is to locate people in time and space and to foster a sense of shared communal identity. Certainly, Native and Indigenous peoples in settler colonial nations do not own the language of tribe; the term was used biblically to refer to the tribes of Israel, in a variety of African contexts, and even in contemporary Christian new religious movements. However, when SBNR communities refer to themselves as a tribe, the Native American context often provides the substantive referent. Problematically, the material and visual practices that accompany this self-identification often recreate essentialized notions of tribal identity, whether in the overt form of donning headdresses or in the more subtle forms of wearing long feather earrings and tribal body paint.[77]

In the 1960s and 1970s counterculture, groups identified as "tribes" as a way to set their collectives against mainstream white culture and the communal distinctions of mainstream religious identity.[78] When the Human Be-In was first announced on the cover of the *San Francisco Oracle*, the title read: "A Gathering of the Tribes for a Human Be-In." The Human Be-In is one of the most important antecedents to today's transformational festivals. When the Human Be-In was held on January 14, 1967, in San Francisco's Golden Gate Park, twenty to thirty thousand people showed up to hear from spiritually eclectic leaders, including Timothy Leary, Allen Ginsberg, Baba Ram Dass (who still went by Richard Alpert at the time), and Alan Watts, and to listen to popular music of the day, such as Jefferson Airplane, Big Brother and the Holding Company, and the Grateful Dead, among others. The event was a unique combination of popular music and psychedelic culture, interlaced with the alternative worldviews of Asian religions, which were reframed, interpreted, and distributed by white American men. Researcher and author Helen Swick Perry wrote, "Afterwards I knew there was an actual day, January 14, 1967, on which I was initiated into this new society, this new religion, as surely as if I had been initiated into the Ghost-Dance Religion of the American Indians."[79] The gathering was framed as a gathering of tribes and centralized Asian religious practices, without actual Native American or Asian American representation.

Similarly, more than twenty thousand people attended the first Rainbow Gathering of the Tribes (aka the Rainbow Tribe, Rainbow Family, the Rainbow Nation) in Colorado in 1972.[80] The Rainbow Family is held together by a romantic vision founded on an adaptation of the Hopi prophecy, "When the Earth shall be ill and the humans will have forgotten who they are, then, members from every race of the planet will unite and form one Tribe. It will save humanity and clean what is to be cleaned. The persons constituting this Tribe will be Rainbow warriors."[81]

Michael Niman traces the privileging of tribalism to an anti-modernist strain of the American counterculture: "By the late twentieth century, the American 'antimodern' revulsion against nineteenth-century industrial capitalism had taken the form of idealizing 'primitives' celebrated by Mormonism and anthropology (e.g., Coates 1987, Dentan

1983). Recasting the medieval Golden Age as a Native American idyll fits this tradition."[82] Even at today's Rainbow Gatherings, Native American spirituality informs the environmental consciousness of the gathering by framing the earth as sacred, and "talk of the universal spirit and oneness are common," even if Native religions are "not well understood."[83] The very foundations of American countercultural spirituality are deeply intertwined with the adoption and appropriation of Native tribal identities.

CONCLUSION

Without explicit avenues for conversion, participants in SBNR communities express a variety of levels of engagement and commitment. Critics who condemn "New Age" spirituality rarely recognize this wide spectrum of commitment and instead find comfort in the easy condemnation of ignorant consumerism, exploitation, and cultural appropriation.[84] These critiques capture low-hanging fruit and evade the more complex (and interesting) questions of the intersections of identity politics and religion. It is easy to condemn outrageous commodifications of postural yoga, drunk white teens wearing Native headdresses at music festivals, and non-Indigenous/Indian entrepreneurs exploiting cultural resources for profit. But in the easy condemnation of cultural appropriation, there are hidden commitments to the impractical ideal of bounded autonomous cultures to which one belongs and thus owns as a commodity. Instead, Michael Brown reminds us of what anthropology has long known: "Many—perhaps most—elements of culture do not answer to a logic of possession and control, to a vision of hermetically sealed social units realizing their destiny in compete autonomy."[85] Furthermore, critics of cultural appropriation condemn whites for adopting the material culture of racialized others (e.g., wearing feathers, beadwork, hoop earrings, and dreadlocks), but they ultimately distract from the larger politics of representation—the systemic racism that makes these cultural appropriations so offensive.

For more serious engagements with religious exoticism, there are deeper roots that far surpass fashion. In a response to critiques of Lucidity Festival's use of the term *tribe* and a totem pole, one of its producers, Jonah Haas, wrote,

> What we see in the transformational festival culture is individuals beginning to awaken from the societal sleep they've been lulled into and are often, for the first time, engaging in a journey of personal discovery. As a mixed-blood

of European descent who has been disconnected from his own cultural roots, I can say that I have indeed experienced a yearning for the primordial embrace of my own indigeneity, the knowledge of which was lost long before I was even born. I am sympathetic to the yearning of a connection to tribe and community, and so when I see (and have engaged in) the grasping for symbols of such things, I understand that we're dealing with cases of misunderstood intentions and misdirected desire for connectivity.[86]

It is easy to empathize with Haas's personal feelings of disconnect and loss of cultural roots; this personally felt, emotional experience cannot be denied. Religious exoticists' questing for authenticity, existential meaning, and connection to a tribe stems from a similar, if not the same, origin. However, such a yearning also brings to mind Renato Rosaldo's notion of imperialist nostalgia, which he defines as "a particular kind of nostalgia, often found under imperialism, where people mourn the passing of what they themselves have transformed. . . . In any of its versions, imperialist nostalgia uses a pose of 'innocent yearning' both to capture people's imaginations and to conceal its complicity with often brutal domination."[87] Religious exoticism depends on nostalgia for the imagined worlds of the "noble savage,"[88] those who have been murdered, colonized, and confined to reservations and museums at the hands of white imperialism.

In the context of largely white transformational festivals, religious exoticism easily elides into whites performing stereotypes and fragments of other cultures. Entire ethnic groups or religious communities are envisioned as authentic remedies to the crisis of modernity. This positioning necessarily relegates people of color to an existence outside of modernity and obfuscates the lived realities, political struggles, and continued oppression of the colonized in the present.[89] In Philip Jenkins's description of ethnic tourism in the American Southwest in the early twentieth century, he explains, "As so often in American history, the romantic image of the Indian counted far more than the living, breathing individual."[90] Instead of turning toward "living, breathing" Native peoples, the exoticist turns toward the imagined authenticity and "magical holism" of the colonized as an antidote to the fragmented self, entrapped within modern systems of alienation and social isolation.[91] As a result, it operates within and revivifies Orientalist and colonial frameworks that reinforce whiteness as the principal progressive, scientific, modern subjectivity.

The recognition of contemporary Indians (both East Indians and Native Americans) complicates, and even renders impotent, these processes of romanticization. Native American struggles against poverty, substance abuse, and domestic violence and their resistance to continued colonial oppression sit uncomfortably within the nostalgia for magical holism. Similarly, the nuclearization of India, its environmental degradation, and the co-option of yoga into the various militances of Hindu nationalism problematize the notion of Indic religiosity as an unsullied alternative to rationalized and industrialized modernity. Instead of furthering the political fight to remake society in solidarity with Indigenous and Asian peoples, the turn toward religious exoticism depoliticizes the critique into a quest for personal development and therapeutic experience.

White embodiments, adoptions, and performances of Indigenous and Indic cultural forms represent a globally ubiquitous form of cultural contact and exchange. But they also enact a particular form of white possessivism. Even the minstrel shows of the nineteenth century were successful in introducing cultures to each other;[92] but they too were dependent on the ambivalences of white attractions to the exotic other. As Eric Lott writes in the afterword to the twentieth anniversary edition of *Love and Theft,* "Fairly soon, 'love and theft' became a kind of shorthand for the dialectic of white racial attraction and repulsion, cultural expropriation born of cross-racial desire, that first arose in public commercial terms in the antebellum minstrel show but is plain today wherever you look."[93] Discussions of cultural appropriation run warp and woof through online forums, college campuses, and art museums in the English-speaking West. Practices of cultural appropriation are most frequently criticized when whites appropriate the culture of the oppressed and thereby profit from it.[94] In William Crane's bald summation, "Appropriation of culture never happens without a corresponding appropriation of labor and human lives."[95]

How might it be different if the affection, and even love, expressed through religious exoticism echoed the sense of what Leela Gandhi refers to as an "affective community," meaning an unlikely community of affinity based in a tentative ideological proximity to the other? Religious exoticism, which is dependent, at least at the outset, on a lack of knowledge about the other, cannot accomplish the political solidarities of what she refers to as "the politics of friendship," if friendship is, as Aristotle says, "the bond that holds communities together," which I will discuss in the next section.[96] In fact, in many cases, religious exoticism seems to create disaffection from members of the appropriated culture. It simultaneously creates relatively homogenous communities of whites, who build solidarities primarily among themselves in their shared affinities for religious exoticism.

Interlude

Cultural Possession and Whiteness

Taking Stuart Hall's definition as a starting point, "Language is one of the 'media' through which thoughts, ideas, and feelings are represented in a culture. Representation through language[1] is therefore central to the process by which meaning is produced."[2] The battles over the notion of cultural appropriation foreground a question of representation conjoined with a concern about power. If a cultural group is in a position of power, say, a dominant majority, they tend to worry very little about nonpowerful people being represented in their culture. This is why the white *kīrtan* musicians are embraced for their beautiful melodies and their devotion on the *ghats* (a flight of steps leading down to a river) of the Ganges in Rishikesh, India, where Indian Hindus are the dominant population. In contrast, in the context of settler colonialism and white supremacy in the United States, those same white *kīrtan* musicians are likely to be critiqued for cultural appropriation and even, as the Brown University incident discussed in the previous chapter reveals, protested against for their usurpations of Indian Hindu minority voices. The difference lies in the power differential and its impacts on security of representation, which is related to sovereignty and self-determination.

Contestations over representation must be understood as products of the racialized power structures in the social and historical contexts from which they emerge. Taking this as a starting point, then, one would presume that we would see increasing contestations over representation when these power structures are in processes of disruption. If the dominant group were fully hegemonic, the oppressed would have no (recognized) voice with which to object. Viewed in this light, contestations over representation can be viewed positively, as the growing pains and stretch marks of a multicultural society. They signify the upsetting of white supremacy and a challenge to the logic of white possessivism that accompanies it.

But contestations over representation also signify an enduring violence, a continual usurpation of the rights of people of color to represent themselves and their own cultures. This violence is the legacy of institutions and systems that privilege white voices while erasing others. Who can possess, and who is possessed by others? Who can represent themselves, and who is represented by others? These are fraught questions that bleed through the academic fields of ethnic studies, cultural studies, museum studies, history, and anthropology. They also bleed outside of academic territories, into the public reaction to curated museum displays, into fashion, into music. Even dance moves (e.g., twerking) have become cultural property flashpoints, spiraling seemingly out of control with viral speed, sparking vitriolic debates in the circulatory networks of the Internet.[3] Bleeding is an apt metaphor, for in critics' eyes, this is a violence. It is a continuation of the bloodshed of the colonial project, a neocolonialism that is accepted only under the auspices of white supremacy.

The specter of white possessivism haunts American society—in the unearthed yearbooks of white politicians wearing blackface, in the stadium crowds wielding foam tomahawks at baseball games, and in the 2019 scheduled retirement of the Cleveland Indians' Chief Wahoo. It is present in public events, like when Kanye West interrupted Taylor Swift's Video Music Awards acceptance speech to announce that Beyoncé deserved the award,[4] or when he pretended to do it again in 2015 when Beck won the Grammy for Album of the Year, again over Beyoncé.[5] It is in the rapper J. Cole's "Fire Squad" lyrics: "History repeats itself and that's just how it goes . . . / While silly n***** argue over who gone snatch the crown / Look around my n***** white people have snatched the sound."[6]

The commonality in each of these events is the contestation over representation. The unfortunate side effect of these eruptions is that public discourse becomes embroiled in the particularities of fashion choices, logos, mascots, and patents and is wholly distracted from the project of dismantling the systemic and institutionalized context of white supremacy from which they arise. Social revolution is derailed by discussions of hoop earrings and dreadlocks, Kanye West and Taylor Swift. We have lost the forest for the trees.

In *kīrtan* and yoga, South Asian cultural erasure has become so complete that one commenter on Facebook wrote, "when i was in india one year, a white kirtan couple came to perform for our group and he said, i am going to sing kirtan, invented by krishna das."[7] For readers who may be unfamiliar with Krishna Das, he is a *kīrtan* vocalist who was born Jeffrey Kagel in Long Island, New York. He is a serious *bhakta* who has been singing *kīrtan* for decades, was nominated for a 2013 Grammy Award, and performs at Bhakti and Shakti Fests regularly. But despite his many accolades, Krishna Das did not invent Hindu *kīrtan,* which can be traced to the medieval *bhakti* tradition, if not considerably further back in Indic history.[8] Similarly, Marisa, an inexperienced new yoga teacher, told me that in her teacher training, she read a Hindu text: "Something about a *fajita,*" she told me as she laughed at her failure to recall the name of the Hindu scripture, the *Bhagavad Gītā.*[9] It is the increasing modifications of yoga practice in the West that have led Indian grandmothers and yogis alike to exclaim, "That is not yoga. That is only exercise."[10]

If we think self-reflexively about academia, contests of representation are also vivified in the challenges to white academics holding a scholarly monopoly in teaching Hinduism.[11] They are in the Hindu attempts to control the historical narrative and the representations of Hinduism in textbooks. In popular culture, they are in the use of images of the Hindu gods and goddess on lunch boxes, socks, toilet seats, and even Burning Man art cars (see figure 10).[12] I could continue.

When I asked Omkara (Jeffrey Goldman), one of the founders of Bhakti and Shakti Fests, about whether the festivals were trying to include Indian Hindus, he explained:

> There's a half a dozen motels [around here] that are owned by the Indians. And we support them two times a year. We fill them up [*snaps his fingers*] in one second. We put them on our website. Super 8, Travelodge, High Desert— in ten minutes, they're booked up. And they love us for that. And we let them come. So, the first year we did it, in 2009, they said, "What do *you* [white *bhaktas*] know about *kīrtan* and yoga?" [And we countered:] "*You* [Indians] don't know anything about *kīrtan* and yoga." Saraswati becomes Sarah, Krishna becomes Ken; they don't even use their own names. We're more spiritual than they are. When I go to India or I speak to people about India—I've been going since 1980 every single year—I live there, two to three months a year. I'm leaving [to go there] in a couple of weeks. They speak to me about different parts of India, I can tell them exactly where to go, what to say, how to act, like that.[13]

I sometimes hear a similar rhetoric among academics and yogis as they lament that Indians vie to represent their heritage but are not

10. Garage Mahal Ganesh Mobile, Burning Man, 2016 (photo by author).

knowledgeable enough to do so.[14] Such a claim not only denies the possibility of South Asian cultural expertise but also enacts a paternalistic and colonialist stewardship argument in its suggestion that whites are better suited to govern and represent because of the assumed intellectual inadequacies of racialized others. Because Indians in the United States "don't even use their own names," we (whites) can "tell them exactly where to go, what to say, [and] how to act."

In the diasporic context, such a claim is also wildly blind to US history, wherein racist policies and practices demanded assimilation that intentionally severed knowledge transmission across generations. Furthermore, post-1965 US immigration policies targeting skilled professionals resulted in more Indian American doctors and engineers migrating to the United States than yogis, philosophers, and religious studies scholars. It is true that some Indian Americans who demand to represent their cultural and religious heritage are not experts in cultural, philosophical, and religious traditions. But that does not mean that inherited knowledge does not exist globally, nor does it justify the erasure of Indian self-representation entirely. What hubris to stand on the legacies of colonialism and racism and assert that because a people has been severed from its heritage, the subsequent void justifies white projects to revive, dominate, and steward its legacy. A restorative justice model would instead seek to reconstruct those connections where they have been severed and to highlight the voices of the significant population of existing scholars and knowledge bearers.

In the field of Hindu studies, in some ways, the Hindutvadis (Hindu nationalists) have poisoned the well with their demands that only Indian Hindus can represent Hindu culture. This ethnonationalism is equally troubling and signifies a deleterious rise in Hindu communalism, as evidenced in the 2019 student protests at Banaras Hindu University over the appointment of a Muslim scholar to teach Sanskrit.[15] The demand that only Indian Hindus teach, practice, and represent Indic culture is not only potentially fascist but also detrimental to the intellectual project of deepening global knowledge of Indic traditions.

White Utopias reveals a structural problem, and my argument suggests inherently that self-awareness of that problem is an important beginning. As for identifying more constructive modes, I leave that for the most part to other practitioners and scholars who may be better equipped to design and implement structural changes and build their own utopias—in their yoga studios, transformational festivals, and academic institutions. However, in my musings, I find myself returning to Leela Gandhi's previously referenced discussion of friendship as a measure of sociality that holds communities together. It is an invitation of alterity, a risk that opens the possibility of intimacy that may produce both sorrow and joy.[16] Therein, affective resonance between unlike persons translates into an "improvisational politics" that builds solidarities in collaborative partnership, based in practices of respect and mutual recognition of common humanity and connection: as Jean-Luc Nancy writes, "Simply: *you shares me* [*toi partage moi*]."[17] Friendship is an invitation to collaboration, open to the inevitable unpredictability of confrontation with alterity and without the pretense of control. In the field of anthropology, Clifford Geertz famously argued that "man is an animal suspended in webs of significance he himself has spun, [and] I take culture to be those webs."[18] There is no denying that we are suspended in these fraught and contested webs of signification, and if we aim for change or, dare I say, transformation, then we must weave in different ways.

2

Anxieties over Authenticity

American Yoga and the Problem of Whiteness

The fields of SBNR discourses and practices are far too broad to be captured in any single research study. Even if one were to narrow one's scope to a specific set of transformational festivals, as I have done, there are still hundreds of different lectures, workshops, rituals, practices, and paths, all of which might be traced to a larger tradition. For example, one might select a Bhakti Fest workshop on the meditative effects of Tibetan singing bowls and then trace those practitioners to a vibrant community of sound healers. Or one might select a Lightning in a Bottle workshop on the ceremonial songs of the Native American Church and then trace those practitioners to a wide network of peyote ritual participants. Or one might select a Wanderlust workshop on the powers of barefoot earth walking and then trace those practitioners to the multiple and varied networks of nature religionists. But of the many and varied spiritual practices at transformational festivals, yoga is the only practice that proliferates in each.

Shakti Fest offered thirty-three yoga classes in 2012; Bhakti Fest offered seventy-one yoga classes in 2013. Both of these festivals have the same production company and have continued to grow and offer even more yoga classes for participants. In 2014, Wanderlust Oahu offered sixty-nine yoga classes, and that is dwarfed by the number of yoga classes offered at Wanderlust Squaw Valley each year. Though primarily music oriented, LIB offered forty-six different yoga classes over the course of the five-day festival in 2016. Even Burning Man, with its reputation for debauchery, sex, and drugs, included twenty-seven different camps that offered multiple yoga classes each day and thirty-eight (one-time event) yoga classes in 2017. These figures are based on the listings in the 2017 "What Where When" schedule booklet and do not include unlisted yoga programming offered at camps that emphasize yoga. For example, Anahasana Village, Chakralicious Camp, Camp Mystic, HeeBeeGeeBee Healers, and Sacred Spaces all offered a variety of unlisted yoga classes multiple times each day.

While the varieties of intentional spiritual experiences are many and varied in these environments, yoga has become an important access point that reveals how knowledge is transferred in these important institutions of unchurched spirituality. Attending carefully to the discourses offered during yoga classes reveals much about SBNR values and how those values are conveyed and reproduced. In a field consisting mostly of adopters,[1] how are knowledge claims justified? How are discourses of intellectual property, cultural appropriation, and authenticity unfurling? However, even such a focused inquiry can easily become diffuse. For example, one might look at Bikram yoga and the attempts of its creator, Bikram Choudhury, to copyright a series of poses in India; the Indian government's nationalist claims to celebrate yoga as India's gift to the world; or the Hindu American Foundation's Take Back Yoga campaign. Instead, I focus specifically on contemporary yoga practitioners and teachers in the transformational festival scene.

As I observed and analyzed their discourses, I found that yogis and their students seemed to be wholly consumed with questions of authenticity. That preoccupation has everything to do with their nostalgic longing for the purity of the uncorrupted premodern, as discussed in the previous chapters. Following Jean Jacques Rousseau, "the inventor of authenticity," the corruptions of modernity were to be remedied by the emulation of both the "noble savage" and innocent children and society rejuvenated in the celebration of "great symbolic festivals where participation in the milling crowd would work its solidifying magic."[2] But the desire for authenticity in yoga also speaks to the proliferation of yoga in the global market, which results in struggles for control and authority over the practice. This chapter will show how identity politics influences these discourses by revealing the strategies these American yogis (nearly all of whom are white) use to justify their authority as spokespeople for an Indic tradition. I argue that discourses of authenticity are in fact about authority and that they are perseverated upon explicitly because of anxieties derived from the racialized context of religious exoticism.

AUTHENTICITY AND AUTHORITY

Questions about authenticity are in actuality questions about authority and origins. The term *authority* and its related term *author* both derive from the Latin *augere,* meaning to increase, originate, or promote. The quest for authenticity is a "deep structure within the development of modernity in the Western world," as Russell Cobb explains.[3] In fact, he continues, "the very word 'authenticity' is only a few linguistic paces removed from the word 'authoritarian,' and both words conjure up the idea of a single authority who imposes a master narrative of meaning."[4] Who has the ability to speak, to represent, and to claim authority? Such questions permeate the landscape of modernity in a variety of different fields. They are rooted in the displacements of modernity and globalization. Modernity, or "the condition of living among strangers" intensifies desires for authenticity.[5] When economies were localized in premodern times, authority was much more highly controlled and regulated through social hierarchies and cultural networks. Charles Lindholm writes, "This stable world was transformed utterly by the breakup of the feudal system and the massive movement of individuals out of the countryside and into mixed urban environments. Henceforth, people were no longer quite sure where they belonged, what their futures held for them, or who their neighbors were."[6] Questions of authenticity arose in the transition from a secure, stable, and deterministic social order to one consisting of expansion, dislocation, and a multiplicity of unknown variables. The prospect of the unknown and unverifiable within social relations, products, ideas, and their representations in the public sphere activates fears of inauthenticity. Is it snake oil or penicillin? Is it counterfeit or real? The desire for authenticity is intricately connected to the dislocations and unknowns of a globalized world.

That is largely because confidence in an entity's authenticity is directly related to knowledge of its origins. Conversely, concerns about authenticity and inauthenticity percolate in globalized environments. Lindholm argues that the pervasive desire for authenticity is a consequence of a modern loss of faith and meaning. In it, people seek a sense of belonging, one that is inherently challenged in the globalized postmodern condition. He writes that "there are two overlapping modes for characterizing any entity as authentic: genealogical or historical (*origin*) and identity or correspondence (*content*). Authentic objects, persons, and collectives are original, real, and pure; they are what they purport to be, their roots are known and verified, their essence and appearance are one."[7]

In fact, the socially ordained organizations of authenticity were intimately related to the presence of religion. As Richard Handler elaborates, "In the medieval world view the cosmic order was understood as ordained and encompassed by God, as a hierarchical whole in which humans and all other features of the natural world are subordinate parts whose ultimate reality has been assigned to them by God, and depends upon their relationship to the other parts of the whole. By contrast, individualism allows people to locate ultimate reality within themselves."[8]

One of the most seminal theorists of authenticity, Lionel Trilling, marks the increased centrality of the individual in modernity to a concern with existence, an existential crisis of authenticity; "to thine own self be true," wrote Shakespeare. As Trilling explains, "That the word [*authenticity*] has become part of the moral slang of our day points to the peculiar nature of our fallen condition, our anxiety over the credibility of existence and of individual existences."[9] Roy Rappaport tempers this narrative of a nearly Christocentric fall from grace: "Although the problem of certainty may have become increasingly serious, problematic and even desperate as humanity has evolved socially and culturally, I take it to be *intrinsic to the human condition,* that is, the condition of a species that lives, and can only live, by meanings and understandings it itself must construct in a world devoid of intrinsic meaning but subject to causal laws, not all of which are known."[10]

The idea, then, is that while personal experience has always, to some extent, validated truth claims, its comprehensive function as an evaluative tool has become exacerbated in modernity, wherein we must repeatedly validate our existence by "incorporating that magical proof of existence into what we call our 'personal experience.'"[11] Personal experience becomes the barometer of authenticity and the justification for claims to authority. In its absence, the consumption of the experiences of others becomes the nucleus of authentic experience. As Handler quips, "For those who cannot stomach art, or afford it, there is always the ethnic restaurant, where we can physically ingest the authenticity of others in order to renew our own."[12] While Handler writes this with tongue in cheek, many other scholars extend his point without humor.

David Grazian's excellent study of the search for authenticity in the blues scene in Chicago provides an important foundation to any discussion of authenticity, reminding readers that authenticity, like all representations, is a performance. He writes, "The search for authenticity is always a failing prospect.... Authenticity, therefore, is always manufactured: like life itself, it is a grand performance, and while some performances may be more convincing than others, its status as a contrivance hardly changes as a result." Most relevant to our discussion, he goes on to point out that "the search for authenticity incorrectly presumes that people typically observe highly predictable, customary patterns of behavior—a conceit that tricks us into thinking that cultural worlds other than our own are homogenous and unchanging, rather than complex and contradictory. As a result, we encounter the world with a set of stereotypical ideas about how these worlds should look and feel, and we are surprised when the reality fails to conform to our expectations. Like other kinds of stereotypes, images of authenticity are idealized representation of reality, and are therefore little more than collectively produced fictions."[13]

Similarly, yogic claims to, battles over, and quests for authenticity prove to have an elusive end. The projects inevitably fail, and if they claim to have succeeded, they reproduce stereotypes of imagined yogic and Indic worlds. Claims of authenticity quickly become solipsistic, either encased within the self and verified by personal experience or directed toward the other by performed ideals of a yogic sensibility, usually ensconced within imagined and essentialized constructions of Indianness.

Authenticity is performed publicly as much as it is desired to be obtained internally, but its performative aspect does not preclude it from being consequential and influential in social worlds. As Grazian argues, "While authenticity may be little more than an idealized representation of reality, it hardly means that it ceases to exist as a social fact."[14] In focusing on the discourses of modern yoga, this chapter questions how the adoption of yoga becomes a vehicle for conveying and portraying an authentic self. What are the discursive authorizing strategies used to convey authenticity? How is Indianness used as a barometer of authenticity, and how is it so successfully usurped by whites? To be clear, I am not interested in the project of determining actual authenticity, if there is such a thing. Rather, I am suggesting that the discursive and practical strategies employed to convey authenticity reveal much about yogic fields and racial relations within them. As Laura Christine Graham suggests, in modern postural yoga, "authenticity often becomes an authorizing discourse for particular representations or practices rather than a verifiable fact."[15]

WHY AUTHENTICITY? ESCHEWING THE VERY NOTION OF ESSENCES

Seminal scholars of modern postural yoga have recognized that it is an invention of the twentieth century.[16] As Geoffrey Samuel writes,

"[Modern yoga] should be judged in its own terms, not in terms of its closeness to some presumably more authentic Indian practice."[17] Andrea Jain expresses concern that any attempt to locate essences of modern postural yoga may unjustly canonize or even Protestantize the complex and multifarious yogic tradition. She quotes Samuel, who cautions that the attempt to identify a set of canonical texts reflects a tendency to privilege a Protestant template for religion, as defined and contained within scripture.[18]

Authenticity in modern yoga is not only conveyed through language. As a bodily practice, the corporeal form that conveys the movement also holds considerable significance, notably in terms of class, girth, and pigmentation. Amara Miller's recent research focuses particularly on the authentic yoga body, creating a genealogy of different constructions of authenticity throughout the expansion of yoga into the West. She explains,

> In our current moment, the dominant construction of the "authentic" yoga body is not just visibly thin, affluent, white, female and capable of biomechanically complex postures, but also a body that is toned, firm, and graceful, with particular eating habits and fashion choices. It is constructed as a higher-class body that is contained and that does not fart or burp in public, even during postures that promote better digestion. The voice of the "authentic" yoga body is soothing, calm, and measured—an expectation so many new teachers feel pressured to adopt that trainers in certification programs often explicitly warn against inadvertently changing one's vocal styles.[19]

Miller's research focuses explicitly on the institutionalization of particular constructions of authentic yogic bodies, with a "particular interest in the standpoints of those subjects who tend to disappear from dominant representations of yoga."[20] Complementing this work, I concentrate on the discourses of some of the most famed global yoga teachers in transformational festival circuits, showing how particular "constructions of the 'authentic' yoga body [and the 'authentic' yogi] get legitimated and prioritized [and] often reflect relationships of power in the practice."[21] A growing body of scholarship is raising similar concerns, showing how lithe, white, graceful, and upper-class female bodies are relatively recent signifiers of yogic authenticity.[22]

In these fields, there are two primary strategies for conveying yogic authenticity: one that claims yogic essences, and one that rejects yogic essences. The divide we see in this active debate (in scholarship and among yogis) can be best understood as a debate over intellectual property between two different epistemological paradigms. What is somewhat surprising, which Jain also articulates, is the unlikely bedfellows that such epistemological affinities create.[23] The epistemological divide is between *universal knowledge* and *local knowledge*. On the side of universal knowledge, we find the majority of scholars, Hindu proselytizers, and millions of yogis who have an expansive vision of yoga as a global form of knowledge and practice that is available to everyone. This side also encompasses the Google yogis, YouTube yogis, Instagram yogis, and those who practice what Theodora Wildcroft has termed "post-lineage yoga."[24] But this category also includes scholars who are so wary of the potential authoritarianism of essences that they would rather tolerate wild variations and misinformation in yoga than issue epistemological ordinances. On the other side, the side of local knowledge, we find Hindu nationalists, Christian fundamentalists, Romantic Orientalists,[25] and Indian advocates for intellectual and cultural property, all of whom are convinced of the authority and importance of tradition, lineage, gurus, and origins. Such unlikely alliances result in strange pairings, such as when Prajna Vieira, a white *bhakta* and *kīrtan* artist, recommended the writings of the famed Hindu nationalist Rajiv Malhotra during her Decolonizing Bhakti Yoga workshop at Bhakti Fest.[26] As Bacchus explained in the previous chapter, the ideals of the radical Left circle around and conflate with the conservative Right.

Although there have been white and Indian advocates for both universal and local knowledge, today the most dominant voices on either side are often divided by ethnicity: white universalists and Indian localizers.[27] Whites dominate media representations of modern postural yoga in the West and largely represent yoga as a universal knowledge available to everyone. Indians dominate claims that yoga has Indian (often Hindu) origins and often demand intellectual and cultural property rights over it. As such, we might construct the field as the universalizing, appropriating impulses of white neocolonialism and postcolonial resistance articulated through subaltern demands for representation. In the United States, this is very much the way in which the debate about cultural appropriation often plays out in the popular media and among online yogis.

But the divide between universal and local knowledge is not always ethnically determined. The Indian founders of modern postural yoga (Krishnamacharya, Iyengar, Jois, and Desikachar) represented yoga as a universal good that would be beneficial for the world—a quintessentially universalistic view. I have written elsewhere how later generations of white yogis have emulated these early yogic missionaries in their efforts to represent yoga practice as a universal good.[28] Similarly, although Indian Hindu nationalists may be the most vocal proponents claiming that yoga is India's intellectual and cultural property, white *bhaktas* in the yoga community have a comparable tendency to valorize yoga's ancient, spiritual Indic roots. Other white yogis rely heavily on traditional lineage claims to Indian teachers to garner and maintain yogic authenticity—a local knowledge strategy. Even if they are representing yogic traditions as white yogis, thus usurping Indic authority by their very existence, their authenticity derives in part from the spiritual acumen and traditional lineages of their Indian teachers.

Despite the ethnic fluidity on both sides of the universalist versus localist debate, whiteness has become a central factor in the spread of modern postural yoga. In the United States, and elsewhere, as critical race theorists have long been aware, structures of white supremacy continue to impact human lives. Practically, this means simply that the majority of whites have consistent, institutionalized, generational access to wealth and power that is unavailable to nonwhites. The effect of this access—that is to say, privilege—is that whites have been able to appropriate nonwhite cultural forms and become successful as their primary spokespeople and promoters, while the nonwhite founders of these forms have limited scope and influence. Due to our culture's broad-scale assumption of white normativity, white embodiments of cultural forms are able to become universal, while nonwhite embodiments remain culturally particular, localized.

In many different fields, whites serve as mass-market translators, who popularize and globalize local cultural forms through their transnational networks of access, wealth, and power. This is broadly evident in the fields of traditional African American arts, like jazz and blues. As is well known, Elvis became a sensation who popularized local blues forms into a universal rock and roll. He catapulted to fame partly because of his exceptional talent but also because of the social capital carried by his whiteness. Scholars in dance and ethnomusicology have long problematized these cross-sections of race and artistic innovation.[29] Critical dance studies scholar Anthea Kraut argues that "the history of dance in the United States is also the history of white 'borrowing' from racially subjugated communities, almost always without credit or compensation."[30] Considering the fluid and shared territories between yoga and dance, one might presume that yoga is subject to a similar history of white "borrowing." Recent research has shown this to be the case, whether in relation to yogic borrowings in the world of dance, as in the movements of Ruth St. Denis and Martha Graham, or in complete adoptions of the character of the yogi, as with William Walker Atkinson (Yogi Ramacharaka) and Pierre Bernard (the Omnipotent Oom).[31] The fact that whites have taken over the localized Indian cultural form of yoga and are now its primary representations in American popular culture, and, arguably in the global sphere, reveals the continuing cultural effects and structural influences of white normativity and white supremacy.

Scholars cannot examine globalization and the processes by which ideas spread into the global networks of flows of information and capital, what Arjun Appadurai famously termed "-scapes,"[32] without situating them in the context of existing power relations. As Saldanha argues, "Whites have been squarely in the business of producing and rearranging racial difference, whether it was through relatively benign exoticism and adventurous anthropology or state-sponsored genocide and apartheid laws. . . . The fact of whiteness to a very large extent determined the shape of today's globalization, and most of globalization's injustices cannot be examined separately from it."[33] As Indic yoga has become instantiated and redefined outside of India, moving in the flows of various globalized scapes, it too cannot be examined separately from what has become its predominant whiteness.

Transformational festivals were particularly fruitful environments in which to witness yoga teachers and practitioners representing their personalized understandings of the practice and justifying their authority to do so through discourses of authenticity. In the festival tent, yoga teachers felt free to expand upon their yogic philosophies and sermonize to crowds of attentive yogis, novices, and other teachers. Yoga classes at these festivals were educational spaces, wherein yoga teachers had to introduce and situate themselves within the field for their mixed audiences. In so doing, their particular philosophies, practices, and means of authorizing their various brands of modern yoga were rendered transparent. All but a few of the yoga teachers in these environments identified as white; as such, their authenticating strategies were deeply embedded in the contemporary debates of ethnic identity and cultural appropriation.

LOCAL KNOWLEDGE

Privileging local knowledge in yoga means focusing on India and Indic religious concepts as the primary source of yoga. Yoga teachers who authenticate their teachings with claims of local knowledge often identify yogic lineages or their Indian yoga teacher as the primary source of their authority and authenticity. One might imagine that this attention to the local would privilege Indian teachers and Indian representations of yoga, but that is not the case. Instead, whites dominate the transmission and representation of yoga while legitimating their authority through a localized Indic context. In this field, whites become representatives and translators of Indic traditions. Many famed yoga teachers—including Henry Stevenson, Bija Rivers, Bill Canter, and Zachary Ellis, all of whom were influential teachers at my field sites—draw their authority primarily and overtly from their experiences, studies, teachers, and time spent in India.

These yoga teachers have directly experienced the Indic standard of religious education and present themselves as participants in the guru-disciple relationship, though they sometimes identify with multiple lineages. The most popular postural yoga gurus that these senior American yogis cite as their teachers are T. Krishnamacharya and his student K. Pattabhi Jois, although B.K.S. Iyengar's influence looms large as well. Henry Stevenson (who teaches at LIB and Bhakti and Shakti Fests) directly employs the language of developing an authentic yoga practice when speaking with his students by foregrounding his more than twenty years of study with T. Krishnamacharya and his son T.K.V. Desikachar. Bija Rivers (who teaches at Wanderlusts, Bhakti and Shakti Fests, LIB, and Burning Man) has developed her persona to reflect her unique vision of adventure, innovation, and personal transformation, but she too situates her teaching in Krishnamacharya's lineage, with influences of Tantra and *bhakti,* to legitimate her practice. She wrote a master's thesis on *haṭha* yoga and routinely travels to India to further her practice and to expose her students to the diversity of Indic yoga techniques. Bill Canter teaches at Bhakti and Shakti Fests, and his bio explains that he has been teaching Ashtanga yoga for over thirty years and was the first American certified to teach by Pattabhi Jois. Zachary Ellis teaches at Wanderlust and has developed his own unique brand of yoga, but still he authenticates his teaching through alliances to famed Indic yogic lineages, referencing his more than thirty years of study in India with internationally renowned yoga masters, including Yogi Master Kavi Yogiraj Mani Finger and his son Yogiraj Alan Finger.

The authenticating strategy of lineage is common among many famous American yoga teachers; it also draws on traditional Indic patterns of authority transmission. For example, one yoga institute's website reads, "Vinyasa Krama Yoga is the technique practiced and taught by legendary yogi Sri Krishnamacharya. At Kaivalya Maui we represent and teach what he shared with his longest standing students Srivatsa

11. Communal altar at Bhakti Fest, 2014 (photo by author).

Ramaswami (author of *The Complete Book of Vinyasa Yoga*) and Sri T. K. Sribhashyam (Krishnamacharya's son). We are dedicated to keeping Yoga real, *authentic* and untainted as handed down to us by the Sages of yore."[34] In this example, Indian yogis living in diaspora on Maui, Hawaii, use their cultural heritage to attract students through claims of Indic lineage authority.

Separate from those who garner authority from lineage claims, some American yogis valorize India and often Hinduism as the seat of yogic authenticity. Where there is *bhakti*, it is often accompanied by the invocation of a yogic heart of sacred India. In practice, these yogic *bhaktas* often adorn themselves in Indic apparel; employ chants, mantras, and prayers to Hindu deities; read Hindu scriptures; contextualize yogic concepts within Indic philosophies; build allegiances to Indian Hindu gurus (see figure 11); and valorize the position of India (usually ancient India) as a bountiful progenitor of resources for spiritual growth. Many of these teachers make pilgrimages to India regularly, often with students in tow.

Some teachers are more imbued with *bhakti* sensibilities than others are. Prem Das and Shakti Devi (who teach at Bhakti and Shakti Fests, LIB, and Wanderlust), own a popular *bhakti* and *haṭha* yoga studio where they host *kīrtans* several nights each week and a weekly *kīrtan* tutorial for aspirational *bhaktas*. They express their *bhakti* through their adoption of Hindu names, their devotion to their guru, the active altars to Hindu deities in their yoga space, and their commitment to the traditional yogic practices of India. They also lead annual pilgrimages to the sacred sites of India (*yātrās*). Unsurprisingly, Bhakti and Shakti Fests are *bhakti* oriented, and those festivals thus tend to identify primarily with this form of authority. Bhakti Fest also hosts *yātrās*, and the 2014 Bhakti Yātra advertisement read: "Yearning to go to the Motherland of Yoga? India imbibes the essence of Bhakti—it is a place where people dedicate their lives to the Divine in its many forms. India is a playground that does not just please the senses, but satisfies the soul. . . . [Bhakti Fest offers] a spiritual pilgrimage through India: a land where the streets pulse with spirituality and its people dedicate their lives to the divine in its many forms."[35] This is a romantic and spiritualized reading that relies on an Orientalist understanding of India. India is the "motherland of yoga." It is *bhakti*. Its very streets radiate spirituality. Indians are devoted. Most importantly, it is a place suited to "spiritual pilgrimage," and it is a "playground" for Westerners. In 2018, Bhakti Fest rebranded itself as the Bhakti Fest Group and expanded to formally include Bhakti Tours to India in addition to the festivals.

Kīrtan artists and *bhakti*-oriented yoga instructors tend to intersect more with contemporary India than more mainstream non-*bhakti*-oriented yoga teachers do. Much of their authority is based in presenting an Indic aesthetic bodily comportment, sharing Indian Hindu religious knowledge, demonstrating connections to Indian religious exemplars, and returning to India for repeated visits. In many mainstream yoga studios, teachers are required to eliminate devotional worship from their classes. But in festivals, Bija Rivers felt free to open her classes by shouting, "Greeting to all the crazy 'God people'!" and she routinely expresses that *bhakti* yoga festivals give her "inner *bhakta*" the chance to "come out of the closet."[36] She opened her yoga class at Wanderlust Mont Tremblant in 2014 by telling her students about her most recent trip to India to learn a particular technique. She warned, "There will be aspects of this *sādhana* [practice] that [you should] please share with anybody—starting this evening or tomorrow—and then there are aspects of this *sādhana* that if you would like to learn or to teach, it is something that is connected to this ancient form. . . . It is where I have been going . . . [in] India and the reason why I want to share some of this with you is that it really awakens our instinctual body, and when we practice, ... we practice on the raw earth.... You don't want to feel any barrier between our body and the earth ... roots!"[37] With this, Bija Rivers invited her students into the yoga practice, engaging an earthy, rooted vision of core movements aimed at vitalizing primal, instinctual energies.

Bija Rivers, Prem Das, Shakti Devi, Eli Gordon, and other *bhaktas* are determined to emphasize *bhakti*, the path of devotion, within the yogic field. For these teachers, India and its religious traditions are often framed within the binaries of the materialist West and the spiritual East, the intellectual West and the heart-centered East, the modern West and the ancient East. These binaries easily reflect straightforward Romantic Orientalist reasoning that is as commonplace here as it was in the writings of Sir William Jones in the eighteenth century or in the speeches of Swami Vivekananda in the late nineteenth century. Critique of the West resides at the core of these Romantic Orientalist dispositions, the belief being that the West has lost its way in modernity and needs Eastern spirituality to rectify the imbalance. Graham's research analyzing the popular yoga publication, *Yoga Journal,* reveals that for many contemporary yogis the East itself signifies authenticity and the West inauthenticity. As a result, yogas produced solely "within Western, modern cultures [are] inauthentic *because those cultures are inauthentic themselves.*"[38]

This view equates Western cultures with modernity and thus deems them inauthentic. Indic culture remains authentic, and thus gets positioned as premodern or ancient. This assignment of alternate existences within time erects colonial views wherein the civilized West marches into the future, fulfilling a Hegelian linear narrative of history.[39] In contrast, the Indian had no conception of history and thus lived in the mythic past or in Eliadian ideas of cyclical time, generating and regenerating society through myth and ritual, but never with the destiny of progress.[40] In contemporary American yoga, this romantic view looks to Indic others to build "ancient-futures." In so doing, white yogis celebrate the pre-modern histories of the colonized without destabilizing their own positionality as self-proclaimed champions of progressivist futures.

Lineage yogis and *bhaktas* are the most common advocates of local knowledge in transformational festivals; in their view, yoga is Indian, and India is a source of ancient wisdom. Some novice yogis seek out particular teachers as representatives of authentic yogic lineages and traditions, and sometimes the dividing lines between yogic styles, approaches, and techniques are stark and divisive. While some of the local knowledge proponents may fall prey to unrealistic romantic imaginings of India, they are also some of the most serious yoga practitioners. Many use the authorizing strategies of lineage and local knowledge to distinguish themselves from the teachings of other yoga practitioners, teachings they view as erroneous, superficial, or fleeting. Within this subfield, one is likely to come across Ashtanga yogis who have been practicing seriously for decades, Indiaphiles who have spent decades studying with specific teachers in India, and Hindu *bhaktas* who identify as converts. As such, they are not to be dismissed lightly, and their commitment raises difficult questions about the ease of condemning cultural appropriation. Although the majority of these practitioners are white, they are nonetheless serious students and teachers.

The yogic field is filled with Indiaphiles—those who have traveled to India, learned from Indian spiritual masters, studied Indic languages, practiced Indic religious forms, and adopted Indic behaviors. A significant majority of these Indiaphiles are white for a great variety of reasons, including economic privilege, personal interest, access, and colonial legacies that positioned the exotic and its capture as a form of social distinction. After decades of investment, many of these Indiaphiles are well versed in Indian cultures and religions. Many are respectful students and not that different from Indologists, who devote their lives to studying the literatures, religions, philosophies, and social economies of India. For example, when Gwyneth Paltrow came to University of Chicago to film *Proof* (2005), she surprised my Sanskrit class by reciting portions of the *Yoga Sūtras* in Sanskrit from memory. At the time, Paltrow was the frequent target of cultural appropriation criticisms and a media exemplar of celebrities who were superficially dabbling in India, and she was chastised alongside Madonna,[41] Sting,[42] and Julia Roberts. But Madonna still includes yoga in her daily workout routine,[43] Sting continues to maintain a serious yoga practice, Julia Roberts is a devotee of Neem Karoli Baba,[44] and Paltrow can recite the *Yoga Sūtras* in Sanskrit. So then, what exactly is the critique beyond their whiteness? When the logic of cultural appropriation critiques is taken to its fullest extent, the ethnic isolationism at its heart becomes readily apparent. Are Indian knowledge and cultural forms for Indians only? Take, for example, the Indian nationalist campaigns that have attempted to dethrone scholars who have devoted their lives to the study of India, like Sheldon Pollock and Wendy Doniger. These scholars are critiqued for their particular views but also for their racialized positionality as non-Indian and non-Hindu outsiders.[45] As Doniger puts it, "Should we all just go home? ... Should we not try to learn about other cultures?"[46]

These are the questions of cultural appreciators who wish to distinguish themselves from cultural appropriators. If a white yogi studies seriously with an Indian master, conducts herself with humility and devotion, cites her lineage, and reveres India, then what is the problem? Or, in the field of scholarship, if a white academic becomes one of the most accomplished scholars of Hinduism or Sanskrit in the world, should he be condemned or chastised because he is white? Of course not. But it must be acknowledged that the singular white yogi, white scholar of Hinduism, or white Sanskritist is a hypothetical fiction. Instead, as scholars of religion Christopher Driscoll and Monica Miller have argued, "Race may be far more fundamental to the academic study of religion than contemporary scholars would wish to admit, emerging in and through the category of religion. As such, analysis of one necessitates analysis of the other."[47] In the current situation, wherein whites dominate each of these fields, we must question why whites are overrepresented in these spaces, often to the exclusion of those whose heritage they study. Aided and abetted by structures of white supremacy, these white-predominant environs simultaneously erase, disenfranchise, and revere South Asian yogis and scholars.[48]

It is because of white dominance, stemming from racialized power and privilege, that some people of color elect to separate into nonwhite spaces. These spaces become places to share common experiences, build solidarities, release tension, and be fully accepted among people who are subject to similar forms of racialized exclusion and discrimination. There are several successful camps at Burning Man dedicated to particular minority identities—for example, Camp Beaverton (for women), POC camp (for people of color), and Milk + Honey (previously Sukkat Shalom, for Jews). In 2019, the Black Burner Project sponsored meetups for African American Burners on the playa that were well received and eagerly supported.[49] A similar logic operates in the numerous spaces our society provides for women, such as Junior Leagues, Women's Fellowships, the Red Tent movement, Women & Power Conferences, and Womyn's festivals. There has been little protest against these kinds of spaces.[50] In contrast, in the yoga world, there has been considerable vitriol among whites when their access is restricted. In 2015, a Seattle yoga studio was placed in the spotlight when it advertised its POC Yoga class. The Seattle studio had established the class in an effort to create a safe space for people of color and in response to the overwhelming whiteness of the majority of Seattle's yoga studios.[51] There was outrage as a result of the class, which critics called racist, and both the teacher of the class and the studio's owner were subject to "malicious harassment" and received death threats. Proponents of the class likened it to prenatal yoga or women-only swimming hours at the local community center.

Aileen Moreton-Robertson argues that part of the privilege of whiteness is the assumption of access and ownership.[52] She traces this assumption of possession to the colonial enterprise, wherein whites assumed ownership of inhabited lands based on presumptions of white supremacy. She argues that this premise continues today.[53] She writes, "The possessive logics of patriarchal white sovereignty restrict the availability of the modern world for Indigenous embodied ontologies."[54] People of color exist in a world of restricted access because of their racialized identities, but white privilege allows whites access to all things in all places. If white supremacy and the entitlements of white possessivism mean that white yogis and scholars can create all-white spaces without Indian representation, then likely, yes, in the teaching of Indian cultural and religious forms, some whites should "go home," and avenues should be created for diverse representation.

But why and for whom is this a problem? First, there is a representational politics at stake. Self-representation (Sixth Amendment, US Bill of Rights) and self-determination (Article 1 of the Charter of the United Nations) are considered inalienable rights of all peoples; this language was weaponized to dismantle colonialism in the twentieth century. Thus, when people of color are erased from representing their own cultural forms and their traditions are defined for them by whites, it is a neocolonial act of aggression. Furthermore, religion is the attempt to locate oneself in place and time. As the late Jonathan Z. Smith reminds us, "Religion is the quest, within the bounds of the human, historical condition, for the power to manipulate and negotiate one's 'situation' so as to have 'space' in which to meaningfully dwell."[55] Erasing South Asian forms of self-representation not only challenges these communities' capacity for self-determination but also strikes foundationally at their ability to construct cultural and religious identities.[56]

Second, when there are homogenous white spaces, then distortions, essentializations, romanticizations, and various inaccuracies are more likely to travel unrestrained. To support this point, unfortunately, I can list dozens of examples from my field research of things that wouldn't have been said if there had been nonwhites present. "Indians are so spiritual" would not be as easy to say if there were Indian engineers and atheists present, whose very existence refutes the stereotype. Late one night at Burning Man, a group of whites discussed how it was just fine to say $n*****$, and how it was ridiculous that they couldn't. Had an African American person been present, or even another person of color, perhaps this group of friends may have spoken differently—and, more importantly, been challenged to think differently. The numerous folks who wore headdresses at LIB and Burning Man may have felt differently about their fashion choices had they been confronted by Native people about their offensive behavior. The same is true in the academic world. Orientalist scholarship, which had been conducted by generations of whites with colonial connections, changed radically when scholars from formerly colonized nations—Franz Fanon, Edward Said, Dipesh Chakrabarty, Homi Bhabha, Jacques Derrida, and so on—joined the conversation. Their postcolonial perspectives shifted the conversation in fundamental ways, though there is still much work to be done. Diversity must not demand that people of color take on the labor of preventing whites from being racist; whites must do the work. But diversity insures the presence of multiple perspectives, and thus challenges structures of white supremacy.

Claims of authority based in local knowledge are thus significant for their attempt to build solidarity with India. But if they are constructed in homogenic white communities, then they are prone toward ahistorical, essentialist, unrealistic, and benevolent forms of Orientalism. Citing lineage is an important validation and barometer of authenticity for many yoga practitioners, but it does not correct the problem of representation. What would yoga look like today if American yoga practitioners were sharing space with contemporary Indian yogis? For such a demographic shift to occur, the power structures governing contemporary yoga would have to be dismantled to celebrate the expressions of nonwhite bodies. Nonwhite yogic bodies would need to be aspirational for novices, and thus would need to be featured in yogic publications. The narrative of exotic India (produced by both non-Indians and Indians) would need to be displaced and substituted with one as multifaceted and complex as the lived realities of Indians. In short, Indian yogis would need to be considered (and to represent themselves) as full subjects, with embodied ontologies compatible with the modern world. There would need to be a politics of friendship, discussed in the previous chapter, and shared platforms of representation.

UNIVERSAL KNOWLEDGE

In opposition to the previous discussion of authority attributed to external sources, wellness spirituality most commonly locates authority within the self. Paul Heelas suggests that *authority* is a keyword in what he calls the "spiritualities of life." He explains the locus of this important framing of truth: "Authority is primarily taken to lie within the realm which can be most directly, immediately, experienced—the depths of one's nature. So long as relationships are egalitarian, the spiritually informed authority of others or of the natural world as a whole are also important, but generally not so important as the unmediated source. And finally, thinking of truth, the authority of experience—most critically, spiritually suffused experience—is the key."[57]

This notion describes a secondary strain of authenticating strategies in the field of modern postural yoga. In this view, traditional lineage authority may be important, but it is secondary to the intuitive experience of the individual practitioner. These practitioners may see yoga as India's gift to the world, but now that the gift has been given, they consider it to be a universal knowledge form that can be disconnected from its Indian roots. For example, at Bhakti Fest, Michael Blaine, a one-time studio owner and a yoga teacher in Los Angeles, explained:

> Yeah, I would think the Westerners who are getting into yoga now—just so many, millions of people are jumping on—they're more moved by, you know, if someone says they've studied or anything about India. Or if an Indian teacher comes over from India here, the Westerners are so ready to just do anything. And here's the interesting part, like Bikram, for example, an Indian man—there's a lot of others, but he's the most famous—they have capitalized on that somewhat ignorance of the white man so tremendously, and they're not stopping. $8,000 for a teacher training, $10,000 for a teacher training, and they get that because their last name is Indian or because they're Indian. Foolish. It's foolish. It's about the person's heart. It should be about the teacher's heart and their caring and their knowledge and wisdom. But that doesn't come from India. It could come from anybody who's done vision quests or whatever. You could go around the corner and sit in an alley and sit all day and discover a hell of a lot.[58]

Michael notes the underlying *benevolent racism*[59] behind such logics of Indic authenticity, with a bit of thinly veiled jealousy. As a white male who once owned a yoga studio before financial hardship forced him to sell it, he asserted personal, intuitive experience as a viable means to attain knowledge and yogic authority.

During our interview, the famed meditation instructor Asher Grayson spoke cynically about the distractions inherent in spiritual searching in India:

> There is a tremendous hunger for experience, and people are utterly sincere in my experience. People want to know how to meditate. They want to know how to go inside. They're utterly sincere, and for better or worse, we're still in the beginning stages. . . . [They] are in the midst of profound experiences, they just aren't labeled as such. Whereas the people that preserve the tradition tend to be little boys [who] never experienced anything—and so they go to Indialand. It's just like Disneyland. "I'll go see this guru. I'll take this ride and that ride." And their path is very different. The monk or nun path is very different. And when we apply monk thinking to people on the path to intimacy [gṛhastha/family life], it is denigrating, and I think it is even damaging, because you don't acknowledge and recognize how profound their inner experiences are.[60]

In Grayson's view, there are dangers involved in accepting Indian ascetical traditions carte blanche without leveraging innovation and adaptation to make them relevant to the domestic context. The foreign practice operates discordantly, in particular because householders have different needs and abilities than ascetic communities. Grayson's reference to "Indialand" as Disneyland also alludes to his view that such searching is mere simulacra for the substantive inquiry that is already present internally.[61]

Recent scholarship has revealed that the founders of modern yoga were actively inventing yoga in conjunction with influences from European esoteric gymnastics and dance, as well as Indic martial forms of physical culture.[62] This has emboldened some contemporary yoga teachers to take significant license with their own postural yogic innovations. At Wanderlust Mont Tremblant in 2014, Jordan Light explained to his students,

> If you see things like Revolved Archer, and you say, "I don't know that," that's because I made it up—and I make things up all the time, I make it all up. Because a lot of you are like, "You can't make up yoga," but it's all made-up. You get that, right? Every part of yoga is made-up. Somebody went, "I think I'll call that Warrior II." So you don't get stuck in this idea that yoga was made like a product and it can be passed down like a product. It was a process—just like art is, like rock and roll. It is a process, and it just keeps evolving and changing and growing. That's what it is. Yeah, so I make shit up all the time—so there you go.[63]

In a recent article, Light writes that the guru is dead and that seeking outside of your own experience, intelligence, and intuition for answers is an illusion. In Light's philosophy, one can easily see the effects of Mark Singleton's research, which have led to the radical resolution that if all of yoga was made-up by somebody, then anyone has the license to innovate on their own terms, not through the mentoring of a guru but rather through the investigation of one's own authentic experience.

In short, for these yogis, experience-authenticity undermines lineage-authenticity. Reliance on the authenticity of the self has largely replaced the guru devotionalism of 1960s and 1970s countercultural spirituality.[64] The rapid innovations in modern postural yoga, and even the rampant branding of personalized yogic techniques, suggests that the field is ripe with inventions and modifications that have little to do with authenticating strategies derived from localized knowledge. While the yoga purists or the somewhat derogatively termed "yoga fundamentalists" are often found balking at and decrying such innovations in the public sphere, there are no signs that innovative American yogis are becoming tempered in deference to the annals of tradition.

The positioning of this or that authorizing discourse as authentic yoga is intricately intertwined with the desire to form an authentic self. These two desires are not only intertwined but also dependent on one another, with authentic yoga practice giving rise to the authentic presence of self, stripping away external and emotional corrosion to reveal the open heart and pure consciousness within. Modern American yogis strive for both of these authenticities through practice, imagining that yogic discipline will transform not only their bodies but also their hearts, minds, and souls. In my interviews with yoga practitioners, they consistently iterated how yoga enables them to "find my truth," to become "open-hearted," to "be more conscious," and to discover a "deep truth [within] our own bodies." Brandon, a yoga practitioner and a one-time resident of a Canadian ashram, explained, "It really all starts there, with each person finding a way into themselves at a deeper level and really discovering who they are."[65] Often the revelation of the authentic self includes a devotional aspect, as Helena Blake eloquently invoked during her yoga class at Wanderlust Oahu in 2014: "May we shift our resistance into surrender. May we transform our fear into faith. And may that faith carry us forward on our path and open us to our *authenticity* and to our infinite capacity for love."[66] Similarly, Lucas, a Los Angeles based yoga teacher at Bhakti Fest, gave a definition frequently espoused by the more devotionally inclined, namely that "yoga is about us finding it [God] in our own heart," no matter the terms ascribed to that divinity.[67]

In these sentiments, these yogis speak of a central core to human existence that they often describe in metaphysical terms: love, light, truth, God, presence, and so on. Many of them described how the world of everyday life serves to mask, cover, and veil the reality of this underlying authentic self. In their views, the veils that obscure the reality of the self create the illusion of separateness, and as a result contribute to religious disagreements, social conflict, and violence in modernity. Despite their denial of lineage, these sentiments echo the Advaita Vedantic ideal that the true nature of existence is veiled by illusion (*māyā*). In this view, one must remove the veils of *māyā* in order to recognize that the true essence of self (*Ātman*) consists of the same substance as the cosmic essence of the universe (*Brahman*). Some yoga teachers draw on Buddhist ideas of the existence of no-self, similarly veiled by the illusion of the conventional self.

Outside of Indic philosophy, other yogis rely on a postmodernist notion of perspectival, relative truth that privileges personal experience as the revelatory tool to access the authentic self. For example, Jordan Light told his yoga students,

> No person can know truth. No individual can actually say the truth, because the truth is ever changing and completely subjective. So you might say something and say, "This is the truth"—if it is absolutely true for you, then it is the truth. The only thing that we can do in our lives is embody truth. We can embody truth, but we cannot know or intellectualize truth. We can write down what we think is truth until the end of time, but truth can only be captured in a moment, in this beautiful moment of all parts of you and everything coming together in that moment and being expressed. That is truth for that moment, and that changes.[68]

In his yoga classes, Light encourages his students to discover their own "inner truth," to find what is true for them in each given moment, and to separate themselves from social mores and conventions that would attempt to dictate their truth for them.

In Light's framing, there is neither universal truth nor a universal ethic, and each yoga practitioner (or individual, for that matter) must decipher his or her own personal truth and personal ethic. Thus, life experiences are a set of scientific experiments whereby individuals must discover what is true and what is ethical for themselves. Inherent therein is not only a radical individualism but also a radical relativism—not only cultural relativism, in the most common sense of the term, but a radical form of subjective relativism. Those whom Light calls "yoga fundamentalists" have ferociously critiqued him for what they view as the dangerous territories to which his subjectivism logically leads.

Such subjective relativism even saturates what one might imagine to be fixed facts. In July 2014, at Wanderlust Squaw Valley, prominent yoga teacher Heather Hancock gave a lecture on the history of yoga. As she talked, she began to refer to the *Ṛg Veda* and the *ṛṣis* of ancient India. She explained that the *ṛ* is actually a retroflex *r*, and *ṛṣis* is thus pronounced "ershi." She suggested that if you want to sound like a pretentious yogi, the correct pronunciations are "ershi" and "ergveda." I raised my hand and told her that, in fact, the *r* sound is a *ṛ* (rĭ) sound in the Sanskrit alphabet. Affronted and flustered, she replied, "Well, the way I learned it, it is a retroflex *r*. So there you go. That is exactly the point. Anywhere you go, when it comes to a language that is that old, you will have a lot of people who have learned it different ways. So she [me] is saying that it is a 'rĭ,' and I have learned it that it is an 'er.' So they are both right."[69] Here, in her effort to avoid conflict, Hancock justifies these opposing ideas with the concept of multiple truths—not so far distant from Light's ideal of truth as that which is true for the individual at a particular moment. Hancock is correct that there are multiple variations of the vocalic *ṛ*, depending on geographical location, but her relativism is the more interesting theoretical point: even the alphabet is a subjective truth that is dependent on one's own experience and positionality.

The philosophical underpinnings of this subjectivism also flow into the direction of bodily comportment in many yoga classes in festival environments. Students are encouraged to "listen to your body," to "only do what feels right for you in this moment," to feel free to "create your own practice" designed especially for your body, and to do what "feels good to you in this moment." This individuated rhetoric protects teachers from liability in the event of potential student injury. But it is also an integral part of the customized individual experience of self-nourishment that yogis have come to expect from their teachers. Some yoga teachers have made a name for themselves precisely by fostering the student-generated creativity of free-style yoga, such as Erich Schiffman's Freeform Yoga.[70] In these environs, individuals govern that which is right and true for them and dictate the confines and contours of yogic movement according to their personal desires and motivations. Freeform and creative free-style yoga challenge the movement structures and bodily regulations of classical yoga postures, questioning the very assertion that there is one "right" way of yogic expression. Yogis are free to create both reality and yogic flows according to their own authentic understandings based on their dispositions in the moment.

There are many such vibrant innovations within the yoga community that derive their authority from claims to a relativistic sense of personal authenticity. As Charles Taylor suggests, "Authenticity is itself an idea of freedom; it involves my finding the design of my life myself, against the demands of external conformity." But despite this celebratory language, Taylor also issues a warning, explaining that "self-determining freedom is in part the default solution of the culture of authenticity, while at the same time it is its bane, since it further intensifies anthropocentrism. This sets up a vicious circle that heads us towards a point where our major remaining value is choice itself. . . . [This] deeply subverts both the ideal of authenticity and the associated ethic of recognizing difference."[71]

Philosophically, this leads back to the ideal that if it is true for me at this moment, then it is true. Taylor calls this a slide into a radically flattened world of "subjectivism" that only further atomizes society.[72] Extended to its furthest degree, this kind of postmodernist perspectivalism counteracts the authority of tradition. If knowledge is subjective, then claims of intellectual property cannot exist outside of the individual. According to this view, Indians don't own yoga, and one cannot do yoga wrong. Anyone can "do yoga" in any way that "feels good" to them; individual experience determines authenticity. If it feels right for you, then it is right.

There are several problems that arise from such a worldview. First, unwittingly or not, it functions to justify white privilege and white supremacy. Erasing authoritative claims to lineage and India enables whites to represent Indic culture. It is a strategy of appropriation. Considering the racialized hierarchies of our societies, it is no surprise that whites end up supplanting Indian minorities and representing yoga globally. Second, it creates an explosion of innovation, which also threatens tradition. Both misinformation and innovation proliferate to the extent that the cultural form ceases to signify a fixed referent. One is lost in the play of endless signifiers with no fixed center, strung together loosely through traces of similitude.[73] The effects of this are the proliferation of a wide variety of knowledge claims and an ignorant public easily duped by endlessly multiplied claims of authenticity and authority.

ON TRANSLATION, DOMESTIFICATION, AND APPROPRIATION

The yogic world places such emphasis on questions of authenticity and authority because of its underlying anxiety about the fact that contemporary global yogis are engaged in new acts of translation and representation. As yoga moves across transnational spaces, teachers translate this foreign practice to make it intelligible through domestic sensibilities and interests. This is a process that actively domesticates the foreign, whether in obeisance to or in rejection of its source tradition. In the final section of this chapter, I consider how translation theories can provide insights to the processes of juxtaposing the domestic and the foreign while holding the tension between them in the produced text. Taking the example of the commonplace yoga pose (*āsana*) of *chaturaṇga daṇḍāsana* (plank pose), I argue that the rhetoric of authenticity previously discussed is a thin veil for strategic translations that occur even in the minutiae of practice. I show that while translation is a useful analytic, it also underestimates the impact of domestic interests in the development process of transnational religion as predominantly white yoga teachers become stewards for Indic tradition.

Chaturaṇga daṇḍāsana is one of the most common contemporary postural yoga poses. It is included in the *Sūrya Namaskār*, or sun salutation, both versions A and B, which were first disseminated globally by T. Krishnamacharya and then later by his disciples. In the pose, one aligns the body parallel to the ground with only the balls of the feet and the palms and fingers of the hands touching the earth. Elbows are tucked in, and one hovers the entire length of the body straight, parallel to the earth. In the West, it is often interpreted as a sustained plank pose, and it is both dreaded and exalted for its ability to produce core and arm strength. Recently, I interviewed the globally famous yogi Bija Rivers, who was one of Krishnamacharya's students and founded her own form of *vinyāsa* yoga. When I asked her whether India and Hinduism matter to modern postural yoga, she responded:

> My mission is to bring back prostration culture. We got *chaturaṇga,* but we never made it to the ground. Honestly, that's my thesis, that the rest of the yoga world is on a huge ego detour because we just missed one movement that got lost in translation. I don't think it got lost in translation. I just think it was implied almost like a grammatical thing that native speakers know when something is implied; they don't have to say it. But when it got translated [it was gone]. I don't think Krishnamacharya ever knew that people in the West didn't do prostration practice. I am sure that it never would have occurred to him that anywhere else in the world that people don't do prostration practice. Like somehow the strange conversation that never happened. Pretty much if someone goes to temple, they are going in, they do [prostration]. That is part of the temple ritual, going to temple [and] having *darshan.* So nobody needs to have that necessarily with *Sūrya Namaskār.*[74]

Bija Rivers is actively building a connection between *chaturaṅga dandāsana* and *praṇām* (prostration) in her teaching, workshops, lectures, and writing. She suggests that the correlation between *chaturaṅga* and prostration would have been understood by native speakers. Indians, if told to press the length of their bodies parallel to the earth with toes and palms touching the ground, would understand the movement as similar to, if not a signification of, prostration to the divine. Whether Krishnamacharya actually intended for these two physical postures to imply one another is outside the purview of this inquiry. What is more interesting for this discussion is Bija Rivers's contention that the symbolic implication of *chaturaṅga* as prostration practice was "the strange conversation that never happened." It is not something that was lost in translation but rather an erasure derived from the domestic lack of understanding of the foreign cultural and religious context. It symbolizes a moment of failure in the processes of translation.

In contrast to the Indic context, American yogis have interpreted the posture as a plank, and the majority do not encode it with religious significance. According to Bija Rivers, because of this lack of religious understanding, the yogis of the West are "on a huge ego detour," obsessed with the physicality of yoga. As is well known, postural yoga in the West has become a mode of exercise, much like Pilates; it has even become faddish in a way reminiscent of the aerobics and jazzercise phenomena of the 1980s. Many dedicated practitioners focus solely on *āsana*, or the physical postures of yoga, to the extent that Singleton has suggested reframing yoga in the West as a wholly separate entity, renaming it "transnational anglophone yoga."[75]

Āsana is only a minor character in the long history of yogic philosophy in Indian history. However, it is the primary focus of most yogic activity in the United States, where yoga has become a twenty-seven-billion-dollar fitness industry,[76] far surpassing CrossFit, competitive marathons like Iron Man, and spinning classes like SoulCycle.[77] Representatives of yoga in the West are nearly uniformly thin, fit, low BMI, white, and upper-middle-class women, and many are focused on yoga as a fitness method. The rhetoric of spirituality focused on self-cultivation characterizes only some yogic circles. But, even there, the goal of self-perfection indexes neoliberal ideals that demand the cultivation of improved and self-regulated bodies, as well as minds and spirits.[78] In other yogic environments, even moderate forms of spirituality (let alone prostration practice) are erased, suppressed, and even banned as purveyors of modern postural yoga secularize the practice to become a form of physical exercise.

PROSTRATION VERSUS PLANK: THE "DOMESTICATING PROCESS" OF TRANSLATION

The development of transnational yoga can be interpreted through the theoretical lenses of cultural contact and exchange,[79] globalization,[80] Orientalism,[81] commodification,[82] the portability of practice,[83] neoliberalism,[84] and so on. Here, I want to use the theoretical apparatus of translation to focus on questions of representation in the transnational spread of postural yoga—specifically, processes of domestication of the foreign text. The transmission of yoga practice is the transmission of a signifying text, which beckons the hermeneutical project of deciphering meaning.[85] Lawrence Venuti has argued that "translation is readily seen as investing the foreign-language text with a domestic significance. . . . The foreign text, then, is not so much communicated as inscribed with domestic intelligibilities and interests."[86] As postural yoga has been translated from an Indic context to a global one, it has been translated from the foreign to the domestic; it has been interpreted and altered through domestic "intelligibilities and interests." In the United States, this "domesticating process" has supplied yoga with commonplace colloquialisms such as "downward dog" for *adhomukhaśvānāsana,* "tree pose" for *vṛkṣāsana,* and so on. While there is conversation in the yoga community as to the pros and cons of using these translations in American yoga classes, there is little discussion of the social, cultural, and religious context of Krishnamurti's environs, which were not even included as aspects to be translated.

After all, how could American yogis translate the void of that which was left unsaid, the symbolic significations that were presumed to be readily understood based on the cultural and religious context of an Indic audience? Walter Benjamin famously asserted, "In all language and linguistic creations there remains in addition to what can be conveyed something that cannot be communicated; depending on the context in which it appears, it is something that symbolizes or something symbolized."[87] Employing this analytic of translation practices to the body language of postural yoga, we might consider that the implied prostration was precisely that remainder that could not be communicated. Translated into the American lexicon, the signifier of *chaturaṅga* signified a plank pose without any notion of supplication, humility, or subordination to the divine implied by the motion of placing the full body parallel to the earth. The religious act of prostration was the "something symbolized" that could not be communicated because it was largely foreign to the domestic context, untranslatable within a domestic lexicon.

In the domestic context, American yogis do not inhabit a religious world imbued with the regular practice of prostration. Thus, when they are confronted with the yogic posture of positioning the body suspended parallel to the ground, the lexicon through which the movement was interpreted was that of physical exercise and exertion rather than religious submission. Benjamin suggests that it is the task of the translator to "lovingly and in detail incorporate the original's mode of signification, thus making both the original and the translation recognizable as fragments of a greater language, just as fragments are part of a vessel."[88] If yoga in the West is unrecognizable or a bastardization of its Indic roots, then its translators have failed to render the foreign legible through the domestic lexicon precisely because they are unable to step outside of their own domestic intelligibilities and interests.

Venuti names the task of the translator as the "utopian dream of a common understanding between foreign and domestic cultures."[89] The failure of modern yoga to create this common understanding, to render yoga recognizable to itself, has caused many scholars and practitioners to condemn postural yoga in the West as a dystopian nightmare. In this view, the yoga practiced in the West has been undermined by its predominant focus on physical exercise. Yoga in the West has become predominantly a physical culture and is viewed as a means to attain physical fitness and an attractive physique.

But as Nicholas Campion has recently reminded us, "Utopian and dystopian strands of thought are not entirely separate, but operate together like the interwoven strands of a kind of intellectual DNA. Often a dystopian phase is a necessary precursor to the promised utopian bliss."[90] If the utopian translation of yoga were a situation in which the foreign and domestic forms are rendered recognizable to each other, then the dystopian vision would be the current state, wherein they are unrecognizable. What would need to happen in order to transform the currently unrecognizable into the recognizable, to transform the dystopian into the utopian? Following Bija Rivers, would it be the reinsertion of spirituality and ritual, or simply humility? There are legislative, economic, and cultural reasons why these facets are omitted in the most dominant strains of American postural yoga.[91] Perhaps, then, we must acknowledge that many of the emissaries of American yoga are not acting as translators, endeavoring to bring the foreign and the domestic into legible juxtaposition, but rather as authors.

ARE THE TRANSMITTERS OF AMERICAN YOGA TRANSLATORS OR AUTHORS?

Perhaps prostration was not lost in translation but rather was intentionally omitted. In the broader context of Hinduism and Buddhism practiced by adopters in the West, prostration has been one of the most difficult elements to incorporate. As scholars have documented, members of the SBNR community who engage in Asian religious traditions do so to establish a sense of self-identity wherein their spirituality marks them with distinction.[92] The Western encounter with Indic religions has historically been and continues to be fabricated as a fecund opportunity to construct the self and to find self-affirmation through a foreign context and in contradistinction to the dominant values of the domestic. Because Western engagement with Indic practices revolves so centrally around the construction of the self and self-affirmation, the practice of prostration or the surrender of the self to the divine stands in contradistinction to its very aims. Adopters are drawn to religious exoticism to render the self distinctive, but once they have entered into the practice, it is that very self—that is to say, the egoistic self that seeks distinction—that they are asked to abolish.

Religious exoticism selectively adopts and transforms foreign practices, domesticating them into adopters' domestic lexicons. Oftentimes, practices like prostration that overtly signify the submission of the egoistic self are omitted, while practices that affirm the self are augmented. In this context, American yogis are not acting as translators who attempt to create transparent "pane of glass"–style translations. Prostration practice—not to mention cosmological understandings of Buddhist heavens and hells, Hindu caste restrictions, violent gods and goddesses, and elaborately intricate rules and rituals—are usually omitted from their translations. As demonstrated by significant scholarship on Asian religions in the United States, these features of the foreign tradition are often regarded as "cultural baggage"[93] that will not easily translate into American domestic intelligibilities. Many scholars have shown that both adopters of Asian religions and Asian Americans tend to Protestantize and democratize these traditions to assimilate them into the domestic context.[94]

Imagining translations as transparent "panes of glass" does not take into account the translator's motivations or "the cultural and political hierarchies in the interpreting situation."[95] Understandably, many American translators aim to create a yoga that will be legible and palatable to Americans. This signifies a process of domestification that expands beyond the margins of translation and into the realms of stewardship.[96]

As stewards, they may not aim to represent the foreign faithfully, as a translator would, but rather aim to innovate by branding new formulations, omitting characteristics that would cause discord or discomfort, and augmenting the familiar. Some stewards ascribe to the translators' "utopian dream of a common understanding between foreign and domestic cultures"[97] and attempt to stay close to Indic ideals and traditional forms. But others extract the text from the foreign and encapsulate it within the domestic, to be read and made marketable through a domestic lexicon. In these renditions, all that remains of the foreign is an ephemeral trace, an exotic scent, an air of mystique—just enough oriental musk to create an allure that attracts the novice, who is then comforted by the familiarity of the domestic in their practice of American yoga.

CONCLUSION

This chapter shows how the field of yogic authenticities is a contested space between claims of local and universal knowledge. Grazian's research on the musical form of the blues concludes that "the search for authenticity is an exercise in symbolic production in which participants frequently disagree on what specific kinds of symbols connote or suggest authenticity, and even those who agree on the symbols themselves may share different views on how they might manifest them in the world."[98] Those who ascribe authority to local knowledge base their claims to yogic authenticity on idealized constructions of yoga and Indianness, even if those Indic ideals are translated into domestic understandings of beauty, health, and spirituality. They identify the barometer of authenticity somewhere outside of the self—in a geographic region, a lineage tradition, or a spiritual or yogic leader. While such views may valorize the sacrality of the self, they also tend to uphold more conventional religious values, such as respect for lineage and for persons and places deemed particularly sacrosanct. In contrast, for those who ascribe to the position of yoga as universal knowledge, authenticity is determined by personal intuition and experience. This interpretive community[99] relies on personal perception as the fundamental barometer and thus coincides with what Paul Heelas calls "spiritualities of life," wherein "what matters is delving within oneself to experience the primary source of the sacred."[100] The tension between these two primary interpretive communities echoes the tension between religion and spirituality, between an external versus an internal authority responsible for governing tradition.

In many ways, this chapter documents growing pains as yoga travels from India to become a global practice. We are operating in the context of a major demographic shift, with Asian religious practices becoming popular in the West (albeit often coded as stress relief, exercise, or spirituality) and charismatic Christianity and Catholicism growing exponentially in the global South. Is it merely the unfolding of the globalization process that Christianity's new epicenter may be among Nigerians in Lagos and that yoga's new epicenter may be among whites in California?[101] The primary difference in this analogy is that Western Europe missionized through colonialism to introduce Christianity to the global South, while India is struggling to maintain control over yoga as its primary spiritual export.[102] While there are some who support India's claims of ownership, the interpretive community of yoga practitioners has in large part disassociated yogic authenticity from Indianness and reallocated it to locally constituted ideals. Stanley Fish has convincingly argued that "interpretive communities are made up of those who share interpretive strategies. . . . In other words these strategies exist prior to the act for reading and therefore determine the shape of what is read rather than, as is usually assumed, the other way around."[103] Similarly, the interpretive communities in the yogic field outside of India "share interpretive strategies" that are "determining the shape of what is read." Their anxieties over authenticity are, in fact, debates over the authority of a diverse landscape of stewards multiply engaged in innovative forms of authorship.

Interlude

"White People Are on the Journey of Evolution"

May 23, 2015
    Lightning in a Bottle
    Interview with Niko, a young African American hip-hop musician and DJ

Amanda: What do you think about this crowd here?

Niko: It's definitely diverse. I mean, it's primarily Caucasian people, you know what I mean? Which is cool. But definitely there's shades of all kinds of races, and cultures, and ethnicities present—and it's interesting because this crowd of people seems to really enjoy embracing cultures from abroad, so it's a lot of white people with Indian garments and African head wraps and scarves and stuff, so it's definitely a predominantly white culture identifying with these other areas of the earth, and that's really cool.

Amanda: You think so?

Niko: I think it's dope. It's cool. It's great.

Amanda: Some people might critique that. They might look at it like cultural appropriation or whatever.

Niko: Yeah. I mean, definitely. I mean, I think, look, if you get up in the morning and you have the option of wearing a shirt from The Gap and a pair of jeans and some shoes, you know what I mean?—which we would consider, might think of as the mainstream form of dressing—or you can put on a sari, . . . and you have the option of dressing in an exotic fashion, then, I think, express yourself. If that's what you want to do, let's do it. Cultural misappropriation takes place when the culture is embraced and it's not fully supported, meaning that people, for example, if you take artists who have found critique in hip-hop, artists, say, like Iggy Azalea—I don't know if you are familiar with her. She's been critiqued for cultural misappropriation because she raps, and it's a predominantly Black culture that she is pulling from, but when it comes time to speak up about issues that are really important to Black lives or people being gunned down, those type of people shy away from that because it's publicity that's not good for their career. So that's what I feel like cultural misappropriation is.

But people embracing cultures and being like, "I want to travel to India" and do this—I don't feel like that's cultural misappropriation. I feel like that's just enjoying other cultures. . . . I think the main issue that people have is not that Iggy Azalea exists as an artist but that the mainstream powers that be support that and lift that up so much as opposed to supporting other artists that would shed light on something positive. . . . Is that what we want to choose to represent hip-hop? That's the question. . . . But white, Black, Asian, this and that—these are all titles to define us. But the issues at heart, when I say I'm a Black man, when I say I'm an Asian woman, when I say these things, we're representing the real, tangible places and experiences. So that's the thing about her [Azalea]. There's this whole—there's a lot going on in our country, and for someone who has such a wide voice to not step up and speak up. . . .

White privilege is prevalent. Period. Whether it is at this festival, whether you go to a hip-hop festival—which is predominantly white kids who go to a hip-hop festival. White privilege is something that is boundless, in terms of music genre or whatever. . . . My friend made a comment about the white kids coming here and they're dressing a certain way and identifying with all of this Eastern mysticism and yoga, and it's great—because what would be the other option? You know what I mean? You have to think about it like that. And I think, culturally speaking, white people are on the journey of evolution, of embracing these cultures and getting to the point where they are more aware of what's going on. And they are, but it's a journey, because however many years ago, it was a totally different climate, and you have to realize that it takes time for that. You know what I mean? It takes time for a young white woman to be in a room and to be faced with these issues and embrace it and be like, "It's the truth, I admit to that." And this is how it is. It takes time for that to happen. It's not going to happen overnight.[1]

While we talked, the Favela Bar was churning out a set of deep house music, the pulsating beats creating a party in the midday sun. The cacophony of music and assembled dancers was dwarfed by two immense iron mammoths facing off against each other in a massive art installation. To the right of the Favela Bar was a stage designed as a backcountry front porch that threatened to open up into old-timey banjo riffs and crooning 1920s hillbilly blues. Situated at the nexus of this antique-future scene, surrounded by the blend of hill country blues and EDM, I crawled into a covered wagon for some shade, and there I struck up a conversation with Niko. He told me that this was his first time at LIB and that he had been invited here by his uncle, who was part of a music group performing at the festival. I had seen them perform the night before. It was a live performance of charismatic and participatory spoken word and rap. Audience members had jumped on the stage and performed with the musicians. After I posed an open question about his impressions of the crowd, Niko noted how proliferative white appropriations of nonwhite cultural forms were at LIB. I expected him to condemn them, but instead his reaction was celebratory. He found LIB to be an experiment in consciousness expansion. He recognized that the festival was majority-white, but, from his view, this was one step in the evolutionary journey of white people.

His comments on cultural (mis)appropriation focused on questions of representation and solidarity. The problem lies in structures of white supremacy that enable whites not only to represent nonwhite cultures but also to eclipse nonwhite voices because whites are disproportionately promoted by the mainstream. The problem lies in whites selectively adopting the religion and culture of racialized others without demonstrating solidarity with the struggles of living people of those heritages. It lies in whites who do not use their public platforms to confront violence and oppression against the people who identify within the cultures they embrace. These are the pressing issues, whether the field is hip-hop, sweat lodges, or yoga. What responsibility do those participating in religious exoticism have to the living populations located within the cultures from which they are gaining spiritual inspiration?

Chapter 1 gave a very broad landscape map of the territories of religious exoticism. Chapter 2 focused narrowly on how religious exoticism spurs anxieties over authenticity as practices become increasingly dislocated from their origins. In answer to Niko's questions of solidarity and responsibility, American yogis who privilege local knowledge absolve themselves by citing lineage to and building relations with India and Indian gurus. Those who support notions of universal knowledge feel less responsibility toward the origins of yoga in India because they have reimagined themselves as authorities based on their personal experiences. Neither of these populations acknowledges a responsibility to the contemporary social and political struggles of Indian Americans or Indians as central to their yoga practice. They are far from performing the type of solidarity work that Niko suggests should be demanded of public figures who represent the cultural forms of people of color in the mainstream media.

In his assessment, Niko focused on the twenty-three thousand participants at LIB more than the cultural leaders who occupy mainstream attention to "Eastern mysticism and yoga." These festival participants feel that they are "embracing cultures," not representing them, and that they are "identifying with these other areas of the earth." That exploration sets them on a "journey of evolution" that ultimately begins with a process of self-critique that destabilizes white hegemony. As Niko says, "What would be the other option?" To name it explicitly, the other option would be to go along with the mainstream American view that is complicit in the status quo of white supremacy—to wear clothes from The Gap and live an unexamined life. The exploration and valuation of nonwhite cultures is the first step to a white person being able "to be faced with these issues [like white privilege or #BlackLivesMatter] and embrace it and be like, "It's the truth, I admit to that."'"

Niko's analysis marks a turning point in this book, where I draw his notion that white people "are on the journey of evolution" to the fore. The following two chapters highlight the spiritual work that participants are doing in transformational festivals, focusing particularly on ascetical and mystical modes. In Niko's view, these slow evolutions will be transformative and will result in participants "getting to the point where they are more aware of what's going on." In its first stages, evolution demands the destabilization of the present condition. The pupa must first become something that is not a pupa well before it becomes a butterfly. Inside the chrysalis, the tissue, limbs, and organs of a caterpillar must all be changed and reformed before it is ready to emerge. It is in recognition of this slow evolutionary process that these festivals are called transformational festivals. The transformation is not immediate; one does not simply become a butterfly, no matter how many fairy wings one wears. Instead, it is a gradual process of layered awakenings, mental shifts, aha moments, learning anew, and destabilizing and unlearning that which no longer serves.

In times past, this type of spiritual work was relegated to aficionados, the virtuosi of the world's religious traditions. Whether the ancient *ṛsis* (seers) and medieval yogis of India, the Desert Fathers in the Mediterranean and northern Africa, the medieval Christian mystics of Europe, the Buddhist sages of Tibet, or the Zen masters of Japan, these religious specialists were focused on the transformation of the self. They (or those around them) developed extensive literature recounting and explaining their experiences and practices. Scholars of religion have crafted significant literatures analyzing and contextualizing these processes of self-transformation in the study of asceticism and mysticism.

In what follows, I build on this scholarship to analyze the personal transformations that festival participants are experiencing and cultivating. Ascetic practices, or the denial and disciplining of the self, destabilize conventional understandings of the self in favor of the birthing of a new self. The next chapter investigates how transformational festivals support ascetical acts through geographical dislocation, emotional deconstruction, and bodily and dietary disciplines. These are slow, methodical processes of shaping the self into a new form. In the following chapter, turning the discussion to mysticism, I discuss how these gradual ascetical modes of transformation are complemented by more shocking, wonderous, and overwhelming experiences that arrest participants in altered worlds of existence, framings of reality, and conceptions of self. Transformational festivals are intentionally produced as spaces of wonder, wherein nature, art, psychedelic experience, devotional music, and connection with others intertwine in a cacophony of possibilities. These intersections burst with mystical growth moments, wherein the self is shocked into new formations of being. Both strategies, asceticism and mysticism, produce new selves—and both are hard at work in transformational festivals.

In the ascetic and mystical traditions of India, the goal is freedom, variously imagined. In Buddhist and Hindu traditions, it is freedom from the cycle of birth-life-death-rebirth (*saṃsāra*), alternately conceived as *nirvāṇa* and *mokṣa*, respectively.[2] In the final chapter, I analyze this notion of freedom, which is by far the most commonly iterated experience among transformational festival participants in these fields. Participants encounter affective experiences of freedom in these spaces, whether this freedom is conceived as freedom from work and responsibilities, from social judgments and isolation, or from that which binds us in *saṃsāra*. In conclusion, I evaluate whether Niko is right that these temporary, affective experiences of freedom have an evolutionary impact on festival participants. I question what makes these spaces utopias and—in recognition that they are majority-white spaces—ask, utopias for whom?

3

Deconstructing the Self

At the Limits of Asceticism

Whites engaged in religious exoticism are often depicted as no more than spiritual tourists superficially experimenting in the fields of Indigenous and Indic religions. As such, religious exoticists share the critiques of spiritual tourists, who are often fashioned as objects of ridicule. Tourists are often portrayed nearly as a foreign species that "flocks," "stampedes," and "swarms" to peak destinations: *Turistas vulgaris*.[1] Some studies subtly critique their superficial explorations, ignorance, and lack of cultural acumen.[2] The act of tourism is construed as a form of both neocolonialism[3] and late-capitalist modes of accelerated consumption.[4] Even the act of seeing becomes a consumptive act, which absorbs, cannibalizes, and excretes the other.[5] The field of tourism impact studies focuses on the environmental degradation that comes with excretions of tourism.[6] Consumption and excretion appear to be the primary modes of the tourist.

Are these utopian transformational festivals merely playgrounds for the superficial spiritual explorations of cultural tourists? Those most senior in these fields cannot rightly be considered tourists because many of them have adopted their spiritual proclivities over the course of decades, fully formulating alternative identities aligned with the cultural and religious forms of racialized others. Senior yoga teachers, shamans, meditators, ritual specialists, and transformational space holders have dedicated their lives to the pursuit of their practices. But what of the novices who use these festivals as a break from reality, a respite rife with the potential for spiritual transformation? If we privilege the experiences of tourists rather than their consumptions and excretions, is there anything interesting happening religiously in this form of spiritual tourism? This second question is the primary focus of this chapter and responds to a call to shift attention to the experiential aspects of the traveler.[7]

Of the transformational festivals in this study, Wanderlust festivals embody the ideal of spiritual tourism most acutely. They are hosted in vacation destinations and combine luxury accommodations and stunning natural environments with athletic activity, yoga, self-enhancing workshops, fine dining, and the promise of adventure and experience. They focus on the importance of first-person experience; the festival's motto is "Find Your True North." They are designed to catalyze transformational experience, readied for the participatory tourist engaged in what Paolo Prato and Gianluca Trivero call "body-expanding technologies."[8] As touristic experiences, they can be superficial engagements with yogic spirituality and worldview. As Andrea Jain argues, spirituality (and its appended practice of buying spiritual commodities) is a somewhat empty performance of anticapitalism: "Spirituality, with its countercultural and subversive gestures, is domesticated to the dominant culture, to a neoliberal capitalist rationality."[9] Jain's argument echoes Mark Oppenheimer's perspective on the 1960s counterculture, which he summarized as being more about style, aesthetics, and sharing an "unusual psychological state" than about substantive social reform.[10] Jain suggests that "neoliberal spirituality represents a religious complex through which protest against the reigning socioeconomic and cultural order is simultaneously expressed and contained."[11] Wanderlust festivals fit easily within neoliberal understandings of the importance of self-governance and self-regulation, which dovetail with the ethos of SBNR practices and discourses.[12] Their emphasis on firsthand experience emerges from late-capitalist and particularly neoliberal understandings of the self, a self that is sovereign and autonomous, one that makes choices in a marketplace of goods and then is defined by those choices.

But it is important to recall the extraordinarily broad spectrum of spiritual engagement among SBNR practitioners. In chapter 1, I detailed the gamut of religious exoticists and argued that there is a significant difference between the costuming practice of donning a headdress and a lifelong devotion to Krishna that results in daily sari wearing. Similarly, there are tourists who exhibit mere "gestural subversions," gaining an ego boost from pithy "do good"[13] messages on yoga apparel, but there are also those who engage deeply and attend transformational festivals seeking to alter their very consciousness. These participants are already at the edge of a precipice that is likely to transform their conventional understandings, practices, vocations, and modes of resistance.

In this way, they are on the path of what Robert Stebbins calls "serious leisure," that is to say, "the systematic pursuit of an amateur, hobbyist, or volunteer core activity that people find so substantial, interesting, and fulfilling that, in the typical case, they launch themselves on a (leisure) career centered on acquiring and expressing a combination of its special skills, knowledge, and experience."[14] In fact, many participants at transformational festivals have redesigned their lives to identify with the festival itself or the spiritual practices therein. For example, many Wanderlusters become yoga teachers or pursue work at Wanderlust events. Burning Man veterans identify as Burners and deepen their social relationships year-round in Burner communities. Many Bhakti Fest participants become *kīrtan* singers, vendors, or even Hare Krishnas. This deeper engagement in forms of serious leisure also results in gradual modifications to how they perceive themselves as ethical subjects and how they activate "protest against the reigning socioeconomic and cultural order."

In this chapter and the next, I detail how many SBNR practitioners in my field sites are, in fact, serious in their pursuits and experience transformative awakenings, engaging in a process of what Niko called a gradual "evolution." Their aspirational desire to perfect the self echoes contemporary neoliberal ideals, but it can also be read as a battle for self-mastery, an ascetic ideal that would have been as familiar among Christian monastics as among Indian yogis in the medieval period. Framed this way, SBNR seekers are not only immersed in neoliberal understandings of self but also in ascetic and yogic ideals. The various ascetic forms produced at this confluence challenge Gavin Flood's contention that asceticism and modernity are antithetical.[15] Instead, the intersection of ascetic forms of contemporary yogic spirituality with neoliberal capitalism may suggest a twenty-first-century formulation of a new "spirit of capitalism," echoing the Protestant ethic of the eighteenth century.[16] Before delving deeply into ethnographic data, I argue that both festivals and asceticism can be productive spaces for social engagement.

THE PRODUCTIVE SPACES OF FESTIVAL

In the introduction, I discussed how the Durkheimian school argued that festivals renew and even reinvigorate the very social structures that they parody. Roger Caillois suggests that such bacchanalian festivals went extinct in modernity—with the exception of Carnival, which he mentions only in passing.[17] However, festivals in the Caribbean and Latin America complicate Durkheim and Caillois's understanding of festivals as periodic cathartic release that enable participants to return to social stasis in rejuvenated form.[18] In contrast, festivals can be sites that present alternative social structures that are concealed throughout the year but expressed publicly in the festival. In his discussion of the nineteenth-century elaborate street processions of *cabildo* leaders in Cuba, David Brown argues that it was only outside observers who regarded slaves' royal and military performances during processionals as mere play on their one day of freedom before returning to subservient stasis. He explains that "such displays were also intended to underscore the participants' potent roles as duly constituted . . . year-round authorities."[19] In his view, when marginalized and oppressed groups donned authoritative symbols (scepters, crowns, medals, and so on) in the festival processionals, they not only represented the temporary expressions of "antistructure," but also demonstrated "ongoing alternative structures of authority that publicly assert themselves during the carnival moment."[20]

In fact, festivals must have been productive spaces for subaltern communities because they were sanctioned and prohibited by colonial governments. Between 1880 and 1886, the Spanish colonial government in Cuba actively suppressed the *cabildos de nación* to "prevent consolidation of distinctive African-based group identities."[21] The colonial government put pressure on the *cabildo* ministates that had been central to the festival processionals and encouraged or forced them to bureaucratize and reformulate as civic organizations. State persecution of religious customs of African origin began in earnest with police raids, witch hunts, yellow-press vitriol, and military massacres.[22] In a very different context, the British colonial government displayed similar tactics as it attempted to regulate the quadrennial gathering of Hindu ascetics—the Kumbh Mela—in India. In particular, the colonial government feared the political power of ascetics who gathered at the Kumbh Mela and viewed the festival as a potential forum to foment nationalist fervor and governmental subversion. In response, the British attempted to control the gathering by making it orderly, clean, healthy, and safe, which had the unintended consequence of attracting more pilgrims, making it larger than ever before.[23] As previously discussed, European countries actively extinguished populist festivals between the seventeenth and the mid-nineteenth centuries in efforts to assert a new form of bourgeoise civilization and urban modernity.[24]

But what of the contemporary festivals in this study? Are they vacations? Serious leisure? Revolutionary subversions? Like the Cuban *cabildo* or the Kumbh Mela, there is a revolutionary impulse to transformational festivals like LIB or Burning Man. Evidence for this lies in the political and social critique present in these festivals and in the community's pursuit of permanent lands upon which to build utopian communities. These are also massive gatherings (at their peaks, LIB and Burning Man had twenty-seven thousand and over seventy-eight thousand participants, respectively) that promote play and parody as a form of social critique and include practical workshops directed at social change (on topics ranging from Bitcoin to permaculture). Because of their scale, these festivals have revolutionary potential; participants direct their attention to social and political critique in some years more than others.[25] In a notable parallel to the colonial festivals of India and Cuba, Burning Man has had a tenuous relationship with the US government in the form of the Bureau of Land Management (BLM) for decades. In 2018, the BLM used the justification of an ongoing campaign targeting the opioid epidemic on tribal lands to pull over, persecute, and arrest large numbers of participants on their way to Burning Man for minimal infractions (dim tail lights, trailers touching the white line, and so on).[26] In 2019, Burning Man nearly lost its permit in a dispute with the BLM,[27] and Burning Man recently sued the US Department of the Interior for $18.1 million for what it believes are exponentially increasing and prejudicial permit costs.[28]

There is revolutionary potential at Burning Man and LIB, but there is also a tendency to focus on spiritual transformation as a project engaging the internal self. Yoga programming accentuates this by emphasizing personal evolution as the initiatory nexus of social revolution. Although Burning Man and LIB do not focus explicitly on yoga, they include significant numbers of yoga classes, and participants' search for spiritual transformation often takes on a yogic ideal and ethos. In his research on festivals, Mikail Bakhtin marks the inward turn at the Romantic period, noting, "Unlike the medieval and renaissance grotesque, which was directly related to folk culture and thus belonged to all the people, the Romantic genre acquired a private 'chamber' character. It became, as it were, an individual carnival, marked by a vivid sense of isolation. The carnival spirit was transposed into a subjective, idealistic philosophy."[29]

The romantics developed this inward motion into the discovery of what Bakhtin calls the "interior infinite" and sought to become liberated from "dogmatism, completeness, and limitation."[30] Contemporary transformational festivals encourage participants to look toward this interior infinite to cultivate awareness and conscious evolution. The self is reimagined in its incompleteness and in the rejection of limitation and boundaries. This striving subject has been read by numerous critics as a neoliberal subject,[31] but it is also the striving subject of romanticism and thousands of years of ascetic and mystic religious engagement.

Yoga festivals, in particular, shift the focus from populist social renewal to the inner transformation of the self. They emphasize the cultivation of an ethical self through the physical practices of postural yoga but also through the *yamas* and *niyamas,* the moral ethical codes of Patañjali's *Yoga Sūtras.*[32] At the entry levels of yoga in the United States, novice yogis begin by practicing bodily discipline. However, as they delve deeper into yogic worlds, practitioners complement the bodily practice with mental disciplines and ethical and somatic principles, as Joseph Alter's research among Indian yogis and wrestlers has shown.[33] Yogic ideals begin to penetrate their extrayogic lives and start to bear weight in decisions regarding diet, ecology, political action, and vocation, translated and adapted to the particular affinities and values of modern yoga culture in the West.[34] It is largely for the novice yogi that yoga remains merely exercise, and even conventional forms of physical practice incorporate mental, ethical, and somatic disciplines.

Many contemporary yogis attend yoga classes merely to keep fit. Though that is an act with "ascetical dimensions," it is not an ascetic act by definition, because there is neither "ideology of repeated abstinence" nor a "tradition and linguistic community that legitimate[s] the practice."[35] Those who aim to go deeper into their practice often seek out immersive events as communal spaces through which to practice within a spiritual frame. There they learn more about context, philosophy, soteriology, and practical spiritual tools; they begin to "enact the memory of tradition."[36] This enacting demarcates asceticism from "a secular pursuit, such as health."[37] In these environs, yogis enact the memory of Indic religious traditions, but also the values of SBNR traditions that valorize Indigenous lifeways, vegetarianism, environmentalism, communal and back-to-the-land living, consciousness-expanding drug experiences, sex positivity, artistic creativity, and so on.[38]

During transformational festivals, participants remove themselves from the pressures and obligations of work and family and relocate to an extrasocial environment. Festival programming creates the potential for experiences that foster opportunities for self-cultivation by pushing one beyond the confines of the well-worn and comfortable paths of daily existence. At Bhakti Fest, participants surround themselves with healthy and organic food choices and may experiment with juice fasts, raw or Ayurvedic diets, or vegetarianism. At Wanderlust, yogis push themselves physically through yoga, hiking, running, surfing, slacklining, and so on. Yogic spiritual tourism creates environments that equally enable the exploration of both internal and external worlds. This exploration centers on self-cultivation, deeply intertwined with the crafting of the ethical self through physical practices and exercises in self-discipline.

Transformational festivals bring together an intersecting network of ideas and practices that when viewed aerially forms an *ideological commons*. This does not mean that all participants share a singular doctrine; they may be on opposite sides of a debate, as chapter 2 has shown. But SBNR participants exuberantly come together to share ideas and connection with adjacently like-minded people. They are drawn from different geographical regions, brought together in the collective experiences of and reactions to late-capitalist modernity. Their forms of expression are numerous, but they comprise "symbolic universes," signifying "universes of meaning, of which the individuals and groups inside them are just an expression, defining themselves in terms of the same criteria, the same values and the same interpretation procedures."[39] The festivals then become celebrations of this newfound community. In this way, they differ from medieval festivals, wherein an existing community came together to parody and reject its oppressive authorities. Yet they share the power of the colonial gatherings of the commons, which used the festivals as a space of connectivity to catapult their social platforms and revolutionary ideas across thousands of participants. The next section shows that transformational festivals are also introspective gatherings, focused on cultivating the "interior infinite."

THE ASCETIC FESTIVAL: AN OXYMORON OF SORTS

In the pursuit of religious goals, the novice ascetic must destabilize the conventional sense of self so as to pursue some higher ideal of subjectivity. Gavin Flood writes that in a variety of religious traditions, asceticism entails the eradication of subjectivity. The irony, or what he calls ambiguity, lies in the fact that in order to perform this eradication of subjectivity, ascetics must assert their subjectivity in voluntary acts of will.[40] In other words, the act of emptying the self of conventional subjectivity can be performed only with the tools at hand, namely the willing subject. Similarly, Michel Foucault notes that the Greeks understood asceticism as a battle within the self, the endeavor of the better part of the soul to triumph over the weaker part of the soul.[41] This ambiguity of the self positioned against the self lies at the heart of ascetic practice.

The root of the term *asceticism* derives from the Greek *askein*, "to exercise," and later developed into the idea of training, or *askesis*. Asceticism assumed the ideal of training in self-discipline, particularly manifested in the religious field as religious training. Asceticism and its practice of self-discipline developed richly in the field of religion, boundless in its extremities and myriad in its expressions. But it maintained its relation to the governance and disciplining of physicality and, in several fields, its relation to physical culture and exercise. For the Greek philosophical tradition, physical exercise was intertwined with the exercise of the soul. As Foucault recounts, "The importance of exercise ... was considerably amplified: new exercises were added, and procedures, objectives, and possible variants were defined; their effectiveness was debated; *askēsis* in its different forms (training, meditation, tests of thinking, examination of conscience, control of representations) eventually became a subject matter for teaching and constituted one of the basic instruments used in the direction of souls."[42] The connection between bodily discipline and mastery of the self/soul is a theme throughout Greek literature. It also proliferates in yogic traditions, wherein self-mastery is a crucial foundational step toward liberation.

But while ascetic practice shapes a new self, it also has the power to shape culture, because the ascetic (no matter how reclusive) is socially embedded. Richard Valantasis explains:

> At the center of ascetical activity is a self who, through behavioral changes, seeks to become a different person, *a new self;* to become a different person in new relationships; and to become a different person in a new society that forms *a new culture.* As this new self emerges (in relationship to itself, to others, to society, to the world) it masters the behaviors that enable it at once *to deconstruct the old self and to construct the new. Asceticism, then, constructs both the old and the reformed self and the cultures in which these selves function:* Asceticism asserts the subject of behavioral change and transformation, while constructing and reconstructing the environment in which that subjectivity functions.[43]

Thus, the ascetical project demands the formation of a new self in place of the conventional self, but it is also a utopic vision that similarly aims to construct a new society in the ruins of the old.

The practice of asceticism is an embodied practice of self-awareness, self-regulation, and self-discipline that slowly sculpts the mind, body, and consciousness. As a variety of personal accounts, hagiographies, and monastic manuals attest, this process is lengthy and difficult, and it can be challenged by latent temptations and desires even after decades of practice and deliberation. Famously, the German sociologist Max Weber divided asceticism into inner-worldly and world-rejecting forms: inner-worldly ascetics cultivated self-discipline while remaining engaged in society, while world-rejecting ascetics extricated themselves from society, viewing participation in society as acceptance of social conventions.[44] In his work on American Protestantism, he argued that the Calvinist theology of predestination (the belief that there is a place reserved in heaven only for the good) resulted in Protestants attempting to prove their merits by living frugal, pietistic lives, evidenced through good works. Weber argues that this theology fueled the development of capitalism; the proof of one's meritorious actions was to be found in material and economic success.[45]

SBNR exploration also tends to focus on the importance of good works and practices of inner-worldly asceticism, meaning the adoption of self-disciplining spiritual exercises that one can practice while maintaining familial and societal relationships. Practices range from yoga, meditation, mindfulness, diet restrictions (vegetarianism, juice fasts, raw diets, no alcohol or tobacco, and so on), chanting, rituals, and contemplative nature exploration. But this inner-worldly asceticism also depends on a semblance of karma theory (past actions determine future events) blended with New Thought ideas about the power of thoughts to manifest specific futures (self-narratives determine future events). Both of these theological frames focus on the importance of individual actions and, like Calvinism, are based in a meritocratic system. Except in this framing the effects are immediate instead of heavenly: positive thoughts and actions are rewarded with prosperity, while negative thoughts and actions result in misfortune.

If we abide this soteriology, the SBNR population constitutes a social group—an ideological commons—that desires to be set apart with distinction and is constituted through its socially conditioned and constructed tastes. Pierre Bourdieu famously argued that taste is a classification system that creates group identity and social distinction from nongroup members. Taste also "governs the relationship with objectified capital"[46] and causes "the fields of cultural-goods production . . . to be predisposed to function differentially, as a means of distinction."[47] In other words, the field of production is dependent on taste, which enables taste to be realized by consumption of "cultural goods" that together signify a "system of stylistic features constituting a life-style."[48] In these transformational festivals,

12. Sunset meditation after postural yoga class, Lightning in a Bottle, 2016 (photo by author).

those that identify as SBNR create communities of distinction, bound together through collective expressions of shared ideologies, preferences, and taste. Of course, these tastes operate symbiotically with the field of production, that is to say, capital and goods produced in the commodities market. But the ideological commons is not wholly reduceable to those commodities or the SBNR population's engagement with them. In short, there is more than "do good" slogans on yoga pants, feathers, and body paint happening here: there are ascetics as much as aesthetics at play (see figure 12). The remainder of this chapter begins with an exploration and analysis of the various ascetic forms enacted within transformational festivals and concludes with the question of how such forms might also articulate a new spirit of neoliberal capitalism.

TRANSFORMATIONAL FESTIVALS: THE VARIETIES OF ASCETICAL EXPERIENCE

There are ascetical elements to each of the festivals in this study, but in general, the more explicitly they incorporated yoga, the more traditionally ascetical they were. Bhakti Fest and Shakti Fest were the most traditional in their ascetic inclinations, evidenced by their strict prohibitions against meat, alcohol, and tobacco; they also supplied extensive course offerings in postural yoga, chanting, meditation, and *kīrtan*. Wanderlust festivals also highlighted vegetarian and vegan foods, including significant selections of raw foods and superfoods. The postural yoga at Wanderlust was the most intensive of any at the festivals I studied, and a large portion of participants are yoga teachers with the skills and stamina to take three ninety-minute yoga classes each day and also assist in or observe several others.

LIB was probably the least ascetic of all of the festivals. It intends to be an accessible consciousness-raising festival; until 2015, festival vendors were only allowed to sell vegetarian food. But as one of my interlocutors explained, "It is definitely more drug oriented,"[49] and the drug and rave culture interlaces the festival's many offerings. Psychedelic experiences can destabilize the conventional self, and I discuss them as mystical explorations in the next chapter. Still, even within the indulgent atmosphere of LIB, yoga classes abounded on three different stages; participants experienced the dislocations and difficulties of travel; and the majority were tent-camping, meaning that they were deprived of traditional comforts.

Burning Man has an ambivalent relationship to asceticism. From one angle, Burning Man is a hedonistic party offering a wide variety of indulgences, the antithesis of asceticism. Its ethos is about self-expansion rather than self-restriction—this despite the fact that there are hundreds of yoga classes, organized self-introspections, and meditations organized on the playa. It is hardly vegetarian; there is a great abundance of bacon available on the playa because its combination of salt and protein effectively replenishes dehydrated bodies. But from another angle, it might be considered the most ascetic of these festivals because in the dust of the playa, particularly during a "whiteout" (the famed playa dust storm), the self is stripped bare, rendered raw and vulnerable, in a confrontation with its own subjectivity and mortality. The Black Rock Desert is the most severe of the natural and social environments, and thus the most taxing and destabilizing for the mental, emotional, and physical components of the conventional self.

Part of the reason I argue that these forms of spiritual tourism are grounded in the ethos of asceticism stems from an autoethnographic understanding of self-discipline and denaturalization of the conventional self. During much of the time I spent in yogic festivals, I was forced to curtail and hide my own indulgent and addictive behaviors. Furthermore, the rigorous yoga schedule I kept while attending these festivals was extraordinarily physically taxing and far beyond my conventional exercise routine. These factors combined with the physical exertions demanded for survival, the moderate deprivations of tent-camping, and the destabilization of self-identity that occurs with travel. I also experienced the radical and somewhat dangerous feeling of self-erasure in the blank canvas of Burning Man's Black Rock Desert, both when destabilized in whiteout conditions and in experimenting with radically other identities. In sum, my personal experience revealed that transformational festivals impose an ascetically inspired regiment in a variety of forms.

For many participants, the consciousness-raising potential of the festival is intimately related to its imbrication within ascetic practice—that which has the potential to destabilize conventional understandings of self to bring about self-transformation. Assessments of the ascetic and, thereby, consciousness-raising ethos of a festival are based in ethical values and thus vary by participant. Many participants who are interested in spiritual work and raising their consciousness embrace an ascetic ethos and believe that it positively contributes to the energetic vibrations of the festival. Put simply, a more ascetic ethos positively changes the tenor of one's conversations and interactions within community. For example, Arthur, a midthirties volunteer with dreadlocks at Bhakti Fest, contrasted what he viewed as the ascetic ethos of Bhakti Fest with the indulgences of LIB: "[At LIB,] in the morning instead of like, 'I did the most awesome retreat!' it's like, 'Dude, I was so fucked up last night—where's my smokes? Smoke some hash, man.' And that was kind of when I was like, 'Hm, I'm done.' That is why I like how Bhakti [Fest] just funnels it down another layer. . . . This place spoils you rotten. As much as I love Burning Man, there's pockets of this, but you've got to find them."[50] In Arthur's view, conscious behavior, rooted in asceticism, involves "retreat" and is antithetical to excessive inebriation, cigarette smoking, and beginning the day with drug use (instead of spiritual practice). At Bhakti and Shakti Fests, and at Wanderlust, it is common to witness campers welcoming the dawn with meditation, chanting, and yoga, warming up with superfood smoothies and açai bowls, and greeting each other with calm presence and loving awareness. Breaches of this communal ascetical code are uncommon, and if they do occur, they are discouraged.

GEOGRAPHICAL DISLOCATION, A FIRST STEP TOWARD ASCETICAL PRACTICE

Part of the allure of tourism is the destabilization and confrontation of the self, enacted through engagement with radical others. Ellen Strain writes, "When one's own culture becomes denaturalized through the experience of the wide range of diversity possible among cultures, boundaries of self appear disturbingly diffuse as one tries to separate self from the arbitrarily formed armature of culture."[51] The encounter with other peoples, cultures, and modes of being has the potential to denaturalize and destabilize conventional understandings of the self and reality, calling into question habituated assumptions and understandings of the subject's perspective on the self and its emplacement within culture and geography.

Spiritual tourism at transformational festivals only partially entails an encounter with radically other geographic and cultural environments. Participants may encounter people from other cultures during transit (at airports, in taxis, and so on) and in the days surrounding the festival, during which many participants explore the local region. But once they are on the festival grounds, they become absorbed into the ideological commons and a relatively familiar demographic. Despite the variety of interests and talents among participants, all have dissociated from conventional society and embarked on journeys aimed at raising their consciousness and at self-transformation.

Still, the act of travel involves the separation from family and work responsibilities and their coinciding identity formations. Most famous tales of religious ascetics begin with their leaving the home and embarking on a journey of self-exploration. In Carl Olson's study of Indian asceticism, he writes, "Suffering is also associated with attachment to various kinds of social relationships. By cutting associations with society, the ascetic wanders devoid of possessions, a condition connected to the experience of bliss (*sukham*) because a person is free of all ties."[52] The yogi participants at transformational festivals are not "wandering devoid of all possessions," but they have left the material comforts of home to embark on journeys, accompanied by limited possessions. The act of camping and living out of suitcases often involves a level of minimalism and contributes to quasi-ascetical denials and acts of disciplining the conventional self.

Some arrive at these festivals with little to no provisions, while others come with U-Haul trucks and RVs. At Wanderlust, many participants book rooms in the affiliated five-star hotel, but others tent-camp and must navigate their daily lives without extensive provisions. If the festival provides basic necessities (food for purchase, water, shelter), then provisioning oneself becomes infinitely easier than at Burning Man, where nothing (save coffee and ice at one or two sanctioned outposts) is available for purchase. Still, even at Burning Man, there is mounting concern among the more minimalist participants about the growing number of RV campers, who demand resources and expect comforts on the playa.

However, although excessive luxury tends to be frowned upon at Burning Man, any expenditure can be justified, particularly if it fulfills a greater existential purpose. As Shaw, a thoughtful, middle-aged veteran Burner with a love for opera, explained,

> With this experience [Burning Man] I go truly as minimal as I can in terms of my clothing, my food, my self-care stuff—sunscreen, whatever. I have an exhaustive five-page list. This is what I absolutely need to take care of myself. But beyond that—how superfluous do I want to be? . . . I could make an excellent case for bringing a bowling ball to Burning Man. I could make a great case for it. I love bowling. It's superfluous. It's unexpected. It's an art piece. I could just bring it. It's useless, but there it is. But I think people bring stuff where they can use it as tools for destroying their identity—their common [default] identity. Like for instance, I bought a kilt this year for Burning Man. I don't usually wear kilts. But it was an opportunity for me to destroy that suit and tie life that I have on a daily basis. . . . It could have been anything, but this is what it happened to be this year.[53]

In some sense, the performative self that people exhibit at Burning Man intentionally supplants—and even, in Shaw's terms, "destroys"—the conventional, everyday self. It is not purely ascetical in the sense of minimalism, because frivolity, play, and parody can justify even a bowling ball. But for many, Shaw included, while the bowling ball or the kilt are not significant as material objects, they can be vital if they are endowed with artistic significance or used in the destruction of the conventional self. Most importantly, as articulated by Shaw's "exhaustive five-page list," comfort and survival become a question rather than an ensured security. This aspect of survival, self-reliance, and potential danger tends to destabilize the conventional self and force participants to uncover their internal reserves and resources. Stripping participants bare of standard resources that buttress and define the self in their daily conventional lives opens the door for the rebuilding of the self through the content of the festival.

DECONSTRUCTING THE OLD SELF TO CONSTRUCT THE NEW

Despite their differences, all participants in these transformation festivals are drawn into creative worlds with the space and freedom to cultivate the self. Festivals' production companies and participants curate environments that aim to transport their temporary communities into very different ways of being. At Bhakti and Shakti Fests, Hindu devotional music (*kīrtan*) resounds from multiple stages throughout the day and night. Devotional music saturates the festival and creates a spiritual foundation that aims to purify participants' thoughts and actions, while sanctifying the festival grounds as sacred space. The idea behind this is a traditional Indic notion that as *kīrtan* becomes the soundtrack of participants' thoughts and social exchanges, participants shift their consciousness to align with the *bhakti* tenor of the festival—to "Be in the *bhav*,"[54] the motto of Bhakti Fest. This process decenters conventional modes of behavior and increases the likelihood that participants will act with more awareness and adopt devotional values.[55]

At LIB, participants are introduced into a whimsical world of large-scale art, music, workshops, and classroom spaces, all generated from that which the producers decide is consciousness-raising content. The producers solicit and invite community leaders to share their skills with the LIB community, resulting in workshops on conscious entrepreneurship, permaculture, sound bath experiences, yoga, and so on. Raven, a twenty-year-old wearing colorful harem pants, with her hair done in Havana twists, explained why she thought LIB was different from other festivals: "Consciousness. The consciousness behind everything that goes into creating this festival. It is not just solely about the art that is brought into it or the music. It is about the people behind that and their views about sustainability, love, unity, permaculture—no judgment—all about just that oneness. Though there are people like that who go to Coachella,[56] I wouldn't say that the festival is focused on that. Here, this festival *is* that very thing—*everywhere, every day, every moment*. There are those people who are practicing that, who are getting to know themselves and each other—that conscious mentality."[57]

As participants settle into such environments, they gradually reflect the pace and ethos of their surroundings. In countless interviews, participants recounted how astonished and grateful they were to be in a place where people were so kind and loving toward each other, even at the most basic level. At LIB, Brandi, a midtwenties woman with long curly hair, wearing a black bathing suit, combat boots, and sunglasses, explained, "Everyone is just so nice—like they really care about you—just like outside in our society no one really, like, goes out of their way to see how you are doing—but here people are like—oh, you know, how is your day? It's really cool."[58]

On a gorgeous and temperate blue-sky day in the exquisite French-Canadian ski resort town of Mont Tremblant, Jeanne, a slender, middle-aged mother wearing Lululemon yoga apparel, explained why she came to Wanderlust: "It's healthy living. It's a lot of fun. It's just, to be here in the vibe too. I met one of my yoga teachers [here, and] . . . we said the same thing. It's just something about the—if you believe in that—the energy, the vibe. . . . It's energizing and calming at the same time."[59] At LIB in 2016, I interviewed Harley, a yoga, slackline, and motorcycle enthusiast who at the time was living in his van on his jobsite at an autobody shop. He used similar terms as Jeanne to compare the "vibe" and "positive energy" of LIB in contrast to Electric Daisy Carnival (EDC), one of the largest annual EDM festivals in the United States:

Harley: Last year I went to EDC and it was a lot of fun, but it wasn't the vibe I was looking for. . . . It's very mainstream. I don't want to downplay it by any means, it's a lot of fun. It was just a weird—it was in Las Vegas—so it just kind of had that city vibe to it. . . . It's at a racetrack. This [LIB] feels a lot more free. In a racetrack, you really felt like you were in a stadium, and this feels like there's no boundaries. There's not a wall that says "don't go past here" everywhere you look. It's free, and *you feel free*. . . . I think something like this is focused more on spiritual and inner growth rather than just partying. This is very self-healing, and there's just a lot of positive energy. I feel like EDC is just focused on the partying, on the rave. There's nothing wrong with that. But I definitely appreciate this a lot more because it gives you that balance between the party and just that everybody's super health conscious. All the venues here are—like I've seen a lot of them posting all organic, really, really well-grown, good food. That's impressive. I like to see that. Because when you go to EDC and it's sponsored by like, Bud Light and you can get pizza and hot dogs,[60] . . . it's not like here, where these people come out and these people are putting their all. This is what they've been doing for a really long time, and then they're coming out here to showcase like, "Hey, this is what we've been doing," and to spread that into the world.

Amanda: Do you think people take it in? Or do you think that it's effective?

Harley: I think that people are going to be affected whether they are fully aware that they are being affected or not because people are just so impressionable as humans that even if they may not fully realize they're being affected in a way, they actually are. You can see people eating healthy, and they think to themselves, "Oh man, I brought a bunch of junk food" or something, and then subtly it might make a subtle shift inside their head.[61]

Harley concludes that the festival provides exposure to alternative lifeways, which inevitably has an impact on participants, whether they realize it or not. That same year I interviewed Beth, a young mother and a veteran of the festival scene who had traveled with her husband from their home in Maine and had been commissioned to help build "The Village"[62] at LIB. She explained, "I think it's a little kind of utopia for a weekend. But my hope is that, even for myself, whether there is one speaker that I heard and whose book I go and buy or whose website I go and look up, it's like one person can lead you to a whole new place on your path or support you on the path that you're already on."[63]

Shifting into the festival geography and ethos begins the process of denaturalizing the conventional self as it is juxtaposed against others. It is not only traveling to the festival destination that contributes to this process but also the limitations on material possessions due to being on the move and the stripping of the psychological self through extreme physical and psychological experiences. Travel renders participants more open to new experiences, and the festival ethos promotes social connectivity and openness to others. The festival encourages participants becoming more porous selves, and recent psychological research into Burning Man suggests that this occurs as participants consider themselves more connected to others as a result of the festival experience.[64]

Destabilized in their self-understanding and open to new experiences, participants encounter the festival offerings, impactful, multisensory spaces that can cultivate a sense of stimulation overload. This is true whether participants are receiving yogic training at Wanderlust, becoming immersed in *kīrtan* or workshops at Bhakti Fest, or staring awe inspired at towering art structures at Burning Man. For many, the familiar-unfamiliar generated in the cacophony of the festival feels like a homecoming that simultaneously destabilizes and denaturalizes conventional conceptions of the self and reality.

EMOTIONAL DECONSTRUCTION

The practice of yoga seamlessly blends with the therapeutic as teachers and students alike designate yoga practice as a time for self-inquiry, cleansing, rejuvenation, and healing. In the yogic spaces of transformational festivals, attendees are invited to delve deeply into their inner selves to acknowledge and excavate negative patterns of thought, emotions, and behavior. Routinely, teachers congratulate students for coming to their mats and dedicating special time for themselves and for their practice. In their view, yoga practice is the first step in the journey of self-cultivation and, ultimately, self-realization. As discussed previously, yoga teachers in the festival circuit are more likely to blend the physical, postural practice with its philosophical and spiritual underpinnings. They incorporate psychological strategies of behavioral analysis with yogic philosophical ideas to guide students in the gradual process of identifying and eliminating that which is not the ultimate self. For example, at Wanderlust Great Lake Taupo in 2017, Tobias Day, a passionate surfer and famous yoga teacher, closed his class as follows:

> Receive light. Literally feel like there is a field of light coming down through your body and into your hands, because there is. Bring it to your heart, and allow your heart to get wider and broader. Bring the hands on the forehead and drop the head, and I want us to get clear again of those stories, the negative thought mood that we find ourselves in. You know we have them. Really be honest with yourself. Just let it go right here, right now. I am enough. I am worthy. And these people around me are worthy, and we do not have to be in competition. We can really build a beautiful world together. You know why? Because yoga really fundamentally asks us one question, and that question is, "Who am I?" And we are not those thoughts, we are the underlying love, and peace, and connection. And sometimes those thoughts unplug us from that source, but not now.[65]

He then brought the class to climax by inviting participants to put their hands on their neighbor's heart, breathing together, while a live band played the Beatles' song "Let It Be." He created a powerful exchange, and emotions ran high. Tears rolled down students' faces as they came together in shared catharsis and human connection.

This kind of therapeutic spiritual work courses through festivals in a variety of forms, but most explicitly in yoga classes and workshops focused on emotional healing. These workshops guide participants through introspective exercises aimed at locating and addressing moments of trauma through emotional release. Partner sessions, journaling, and meditative introspection draw exuberant release and tearful recollections from participants. Kailash, an Indian American yoga teacher who teaches at Bhakti and Shakti Fests and Wanderlust festivals, often uses emotional release techniques in her teaching. Her classes can be shocking to observe as she guides participants from cradling themselves to releasing cathartic screams. She explains:

> I suggest just trying emotional release techniques because it really works, at least in the temporary moment when you're going through something so [*screams*] "I can't wrap my head around it." For me, and for the people that

I have gotten testimonials from, it's been like a huge shift. Anytime something comes up, instead of going to, trying to fix it, it's like, "Oh! Ok, I'm just going to [*screams*] express it out and have a moment of clarity," and come back to, "Oh my god, I'm not going to die. I'm going to be ok." And it's a sobering technique really. That's what I—we all—when we go into that phase of overly mental processing and that anxiety, I call that when you're not sober. You know when you come back to your core and you find that sobriety, you can feel it. It's like, "Oh my god, here I am. Wow, I was far away from myself." You come back to yourself. It's a sobriety. It's like, "Ok I'm here again. Wow, I got wound up!" You know, there it was. So I think it's just coming back to ourselves again and again, that's what I'm teaching people.[66]

Such strategies of cathartic release help participants to recognize and confront complex emotions and to work through feelings of anxiety, depression, and unworthiness. Many teachers also guide participants into introspective practices that aim to connect them with their core self and to confront the layers of trauma concealing that self.

At Shakti Fest in 2015, I was partnered with Josh—a thirty-year-old bohemian man with shoulder-length hair and kind eyes—during a workshop on masculinity and femininity lead by Breath Arrow, a leader and coach in the men's spiritual growth movement. Over the course of three hours, Breath Arrow led the group through a series of emotional contact exercises wherein we were instructed to vocally confront our parents, past partners, and experiences of emotional pain and pleasure—and to share those experiences verbally with our partner. In speaking of his father, Josh broke down sobbing uncontrollably, choking out his words as he recounted feelings of childhood unworthiness and his current feelings of terror that he would become just like his father. Breath Arrow instructed partners to hold space for emotional release, and so Josh and I sat knee to knee among dozens of other assembled couples, and I held him while he sobbed, and my own eyes welled with tears of empathy at his visible emotional pain. Throughout the workshop, participants sobbed, screamed, and collapsed as they followed instructions to viscerally confront their emotional pain and pleasure. After the workshop, we all emerged from the tent emotionally raw and with reddened eyes, holding each other in our collective experience of emotional catharsis; we then parted ways and proceeded on to the next workshop or yoga class. At these festivals, it was common to witness participants experience intense emotional breakthroughs as they peeled away layers of their psyche in the practice of doing this spiritual work. In conversations, participants often expressed that they were feeling emotionally "raw" or "drained" after a particularly "intense" cathartic release in workshops, breathwork, and yoga classes.

Jeremiah Silver's breathwork workshops were a constant at Bhakti and Shakti Fests wherein hundreds of people filled the geodesic domed space of the temple with "guardians" dressed in white prepared to receive them. Silver introduced the sessions by encouraging participants to drop into their heart centers and recognize that "there is an expansion of conscious awareness, and we are all a part [of it]" and that "we have been brought here to do some work together," and to "feel love, for this gift, for our ability to be together, for the ability to create and grow and blossom into our heart."[67] He warned participants that in "this work" they may be "introduced to the place inside of yourself that is pure love" and told them to "release something that no longer serves you in this space." He explained that this is a practice of *prāṇāyāma* (breathwork) that may lead to *mokṣa* (liberation). When he began the breathwork, he played an "alchemy" of shaman songs, bird songs, drum beats, and flutes and led participants through a series of breath exercises interlaced through a guided meditation. Responses varied, but throughout the breathwork practice participants released energy through ecstatic laughs, cries, wails, sobs, and screams. Afterward, participants were drawn back into reality and then released into the festival.

In 2015, Joseph, an army veteran of the war in Iraq, had an intense emotional experience at Silver's breathwork at Shakti Fest. In his words,

> I went to that [breathwork] workshop yesterday. It was pretty intense. These kind of types of workshops that are—they are very intensive—and me not being very experienced in this kind of community or having any of this sort of exercise. At one point it was a little scary for me because it just invoked so much that I felt really vulnerable and out of control, so at one point, I caught myself, you know, because I was so focused on breathing, I caught myself—and it wasn't even really the energy in the room. It could have been because you could kind of hear the weirdness that was going on, . . . but I found myself thinking about my mother for some reason and kind of crying. . . . I was ready to walk out of there, but then I was like, no, I am going to stick through it. But it ended up being really cool. . . . What happened was, I think I had this weird—obviously I don't have any memories of me as an infant, but for some reason, when I thought about my mother, I thought of the way she was holding me as an infant, and I thought about the way she was looking at me—the way she still looks at me now. So it was really weird, and I got that feeling. . . . It was my mom and how she looked in '82. It was pretty powerful. I've never—I've done some *prāṇāyāma,* but it was more geared toward my population—vets—so it wasn't as intensive. . . . . There was this weird body high with it too. . . . It felt like I dropped ecstasy because there was this euphoric feeling too. . . . I don't think that I've cried so much in over ten years maybe.[68]

As Joseph recounted the experience, he was concerned that he was expected to rejoin the festival with calm and equanimity, despite having experienced such an intense emotional release. He felt like this was a somewhat dangerous practice, and he thought there should be trained counselors on hand to help participants process the emotions brought out by the experience. He recounted his own experience and how it had triggered latent PTSD from his time in the military and said that there were probably other veterans or trauma survivors who participated in the workshop and could have really intense experiences. He explained, "I'm taught to always be on guard and not be so vulnerable. When something catches me off guard—I don't like speaking broadly, but at least for me, I don't like feeling vulnerable. And I think that is what yoga does."[69] For many participants, Jeremiah Silver's breathwork workshops were similarly intense, cathartic, and potentially emotionally destabilizing.

Programming at transformational festivals can contribute to the destabilization of the conventional sense of self through yoga and emotionally intense workshops, but it is also complemented by participants' engagements in the magical realism of the festival. The magical realism of the festival has the propensity to spark wonder, as will be discussed in the next chapter, but it also is intended to destabilize conventional reality. Unusual people and things abound, and uncommon experiences frequently occur. At Burning Man, one might be just as likely to encounter a troupe of alien-clad participants making a pilgrimage to a massive art installation of their alien leader as to encounter someone costumed as the pope. The festival creates a protected world where anything seems possible and the boundaries of conventional reality are bent and broken. Participants are encouraged to push those boundaries and to open themselves to consciousness-expanding experiences, which can sometimes lead to destabilizing and even frightening experiences.

At Burning Man, the harsh environmental conditions can quickly strip away all other social interests and force participants to confront their own humanity at its most basic levels. For example, my very first day at Burning Man was consumed by dealing with an allergic reaction to the alkalinity of the playa dust that resulted in head-to-toe hives and swelling (several people told me that this is not an uncommon reaction). For several hours, I sat in the shade, drank fluids, took Benadryl, and applied cold compresses vigorously, all the while praying not to be medivacked off the playa. Others end up in med tents being treated for dehydration-related illnesses or injury. Aside from the precarities of staying alive, whiteout dust storms can last from a few minutes to a few hours; during those disorienting storms, survival and psychological and emotional well-being, become foremost concerns.[70] The following story illustrates one such event.

Many Burners choose to get married on the playa because of the magical environment and because their chosen family—their Burner family—will be there. Burning Man has created infrastructure for this common desire, and Calliope, the Black Rock City wedding planner, refers many couples to the Black Rock Bakery for wedding cakes. In the months preceding the 2018 festival, a bride named Karin reached out to me (in my role as the bakery's camp leader) with detailed plans to cocreate an elaborate multitiered wedding cake with candied flame decorations and a cake-topper figurine of the Man that she had purchased online for seventy-five dollars. From the outset, I was apprehensive about this bride and her intricately laid plans, knowing the unpredictability of the playa and fearing that her extravagant vision would end in disappointment.

On the day of the wedding, there was a severe whiteout. Though Karin and her fiancé were scheduled to arrive at the bakery at 9 am, they were several hours late. They arrived just as we were closing to escape the afternoon heat. Her fiancé found me in the bakery and told me that Karin was emotionally unwell and so disillusioned that she was about to cancel the wedding. He led me to a corner of the front room where Karin, a beautiful woman in her midthirties, sat on the floor with her head on her knees, hands over her face, sobbing uncontrollably. She was wearing what had once been perfect makeup and a fancy white Western outfit consisting of a G-string bikini and chaps.

As I knelt beside her, she began spitting words through her desolation and tears, wailing in exasperation that it was so dusty on her wedding day. She cried out about the wretched unfairness that the weather had been clear for the few days prior and now, today, on her wedding day, it was a complete whiteout. Admittedly, she was right. It *had* been remarkably clear for the past few days, and on that day, we were experiencing consistent and fairly extreme whiteout conditions. But her intense emotional dishevelment as a result of predictably dusty conditions at Burning Man seemed poignantly ridiculous to outside observers, myself included. As her perfect vision confronted imperfect reality, Karin was emotionally paralyzed and could not raise herself from the corner of the floor. Instead, she sat sobbing, pitiful in her emotional unraveling, thoroughly unable to cope.

At this point, I would ideally write about how Karin successfully triumphed over her situation—and to a limited extent, she did. She mustered her internal strength, and we began to bake. We laughed and talked and had a few drinks in the afternoon heat, and she decided to keep her wedding plans despite the whiteout. But around 2 pm, I was exhausted, and I left her alone to continue work on her wedding cake. When Marcus, our lead pastry chef, came in at 4 pm, Karin was still there, working diligently, but once again she was in tears. With a full crew scheduled to produce hundreds of eclairs and vegan marshmallows, every baking station was accounted for, and he asked her to leave the bakery. She left with her unfinished cake.

Karin's sad story illustrates that although Burning Man is an elaborate playground, it also demands one to come to terms with one's own bodily needs and psychological limitations. In the language of veteran Burner and community philosopher Caveat Magister,

> If you go to Burning Man spaces, there will be times when you will be absolutely miserable—desperately, frighteningly miserable—and that's okay.... It's a sign that you are really engaging with your applied existentialism. It's a sign that you really are present with us. It might even be a sign that you are growing as a person, right in front of our eyes. It's an experience that we have all been through, and will go through again, because this is not utopia—not even close.[71] But it is a chance to be honest with ourselves and others, and to grow, and it turns out that's really important, even when it's miserable. Maybe especially when it's miserable.[72]

In this sense, Burning Man can cultivate an ascetical attitude, both in a practical and a metaphysical sense. Participants must consider what material goods are actually necessary for their survival—water, goggles, dust mask—and prepare to face the consequences of ill-preparedness. But aside from the dust, the unpredictability of the playa demands that participants learn to relinquish their attachments to conventional expectations. Attachments to plans, scheduled meetings, others' behavior, and even one's own sense of self tend to be upset by the unpredictability involved in their collision with an exceptional number of possibilities. As the well-known saying goes, "Don't bring *anything* to Burning Man that you aren't prepared to lose."

BODILY DISCIPLINE

Wanderlust festivals focus on deconstructing the self through emotionally intense psychological work and on gaining introspection into one's inner core through yoga practice and demanding physical exertion. As noted earlier, Tobias Day explained at Wanderlust Great Lake Taupo in 2017 how the primary aim of yoga is to address the question, "Who am I?" Yoga invites the deconstruction of the self, a process which can be painful, disconcerting, and destabilizing. As the celebrated yoga instructor Helena Blake explained during her yoga class at Wanderlust Squaw Valley in 2014,

> Every day when we practice yoga, it's a cleansing process. The by-product is that we get stronger, more flexible. But I'm sure many of you in this room have had an experience of yoga where you're practicing, all is fine, life is great. Get to the end of the class, teacher plays a song or says a word or recites a poem, and you're in a fetal position, crying, for seemingly no reason at all—and you get this release of energy out of your body. When you release the tension, it connects you to your vulnerability. You begin to hear again, but not through your ears, through your heart.[73]

It is from this emotional and psychological work that the commonplace trope of someone sobbing and having a "meltdown" on the yoga mat emerges.

During the transformational festivals I attended, participants collectively engaged in physically intense yoga classes, where instructors guided them to a point of mental stillness through the exhaustion of repetitive movements and the intensity of sustaining difficult postures. In a ballet-inspired yoga class at the top of the mountain at Wanderlust Squaw Valley in 2014, Cherry Hughes, a lithe ballerina, blended yoga poses with the repetitive pulsing of short motions intended to build lean muscles of ballerinas. She inspired us with demands of "up, up, up, up" as we drew from our reserves of strength to persevere through the strenuous regimen. And Asha Savi Kaur, in her *kundalini* yoga class at Wanderlust Squaw Valley that same year, had the room of one hundred yogis rolling into plow pose (*halāsana*) repeatedly and rapidly, in unison. The sequence involved beginning in corpse pose (*śavāsana*), then swiftly lifting the legs high into the air for a shoulder stand, and then placing both feet extended back behind the head. With this motion, the body is folded, with back and buttocks raised, arms extended downward, and toes planted firmly above the head. Participants were instructed to rock in and out of plow pose vigorously, dozens of times, which created a lightness of being as blood rushed to and from the head. Such practice also demands considerable core strength and clarity of focus to keep the physical motion sustained and controlled.

There are countless examples of similar moments, wherein the yoga at Wanderlust festivals was so intense as to demand complete attention on the physical body and focused precision of the mind to be able to complete the classes. At Wanderlust Mont Tremblant in 2014, Jordan

Light's class on yogic flying (aerial yoga and inversions) brought together some of the most serious and skilled yogis in practice, many of whom were yoga teachers eager to accelerate their already advanced skills. Also at Wanderlust Mont Tremblant, I found myself dripping with sweat and physically exhausted in the exuberant Lena Bryant's intense and demanding yoga class. In contrast, the young woman on the mat next to me easily and repeatedly increased the difficulty level by practicing the challenging eight-angle pose (*aṣṭāvakrāsana*), wherein the practitioner extends the legs to one side so that they are hovering parallel to the floor while using arm and core strength to hold the body several inches above the mat in a modified form of suspended plank pose (*chaturaṅga*). During a break, I asked her how she had gotten so advanced in her practice. She told me that she had intentionally moved into a building with a yoga studio across the street and attends the 6 am class every day before she goes to work. On most days, after she gets home, she also attends a *yin* yoga class (a slower and meditative class that many yogis view as relaxing). At Wanderlust Oahu, I left one of Dakota Lemon's classes when I was unable to keep up with the speed and difficulty of the poses. Muscles trembling and a bit ashamed for having left, I revisited the program in the hallway and saw that the class was marked as advanced, meaning that it was a class sought after by aficionados and teachers.

Yoga is an ascetical practice. While the Western expansion of yoga and its subsequent commodification has distracted significantly from its religious forms, its current focus on physicality actually expands its roots as bodily discipline. Many modern yogis practice to purify their minds and bodies in service of physical and spiritual perfection. Even the secular practice of modern postural yoga requires extraordinary discipline, such as waking early every morning to attend a ninety-minute yoga class at 6 am before work and then another upon returning home in the evening. It takes hours of dedicated practice and perseverance to learn to "fly" in aerial poses like Jordan Light can. These are no small feats, and they require significant commitment and self-discipline. Practitioners accentuate this bodily discipline through dietary restrictions, denial of pleasures, and the regimentation of time, each of which draws on ascetic legacies in the religious field.

Even for seasoned yoga practitioners, the number of daily yoga classes taken during the course of a festival is above and beyond the standard rhythm of American yogic practice (only 6 percent of yogis attend yoga classes five or more times per week).[74] At Wanderlust,

13. Yogic discipline, Wanderlust, Stratton, VT, 2018 (photo by Chris Eckhart, copyright Wanderlust).

Bhakti Fest, and Shakti Fest, the demand is so high that participants are limited to only three yoga classes per day. To circumvent this, some attend additional classes as observers or teacher assistants, and many follow along, performing poses with the class but from the sidelines, as unofficial participants. Three challenging ninety-minute yoga classes with some of the most advanced global yoga instructors is an intense physical commitment. In terms of the caliber of yoga, the physical culture of Wanderlust yoga classes was often the most advanced, geared toward yogic aficionados and teachers. The yogic bodies that surrounded me in these classes were lithe, toned, strong, and practiced. Inversions were commonplace. Long holds and demands for repetitions passed without a hiccup for many of the astute practitioners present. Their practice at Wanderlust festivals revealed significant hours spent on their mat—in studios and in private—sculpting and disciplining their bodies into a yogic aesthetic and ascetic ideal (see figure 13).

Many yoga classes at these festivals were situated at the nexus of health and spirituality, and based in the conviction of the interdependence of both. Discussions of diet and bodily health intertwined with discussions of raising awareness, of consciousness, and of recognizing the presence of beauty, nature, love, or spirit. At this nexus, the yoga class is an opportunity to stop time, check in, and adjust one's habitual behaviors. Helena Blake began her detox yoga class at Wanderlust Oahu as follows:

> So the question here is: How has your health been? Is where you're at in your life today, have you been really consistent and focused and making sure you're nourishing and nurturing yourself every single day? That you're committed to your yoga, your meditation, your prayer, and your diet as nonnegotiables so that your life can be more sustainable? Or because of circumstance, because of maybe some trauma that's going on, you've been a little off the wagon? Maybe eating foods that are convenient or *filled* with sugars and other substances? Maybe you're drinking a little bit more than normal, smoking cigarettes, pot? Taking recreational drugs, pharmaceutical drugs? Just where are you at? Without any judgment attached to it, just a check-in. How's your health? And is there anything that you're doing that you know is contributing to a lack of balance?[75]

In this view, yoga is a critical tool to detoxify the body from the negative influences of convenient foods, sugar, alcohol, cigarettes, marijuana, and recreational and pharmaceutical drugs. It is to be accompanied by meditation, prayer, and diet—the "nonnegotiables" of a yogic ascetic practice of bodily discipline. Kailash explained a yogic lifestyle as follows:

> There's all sorts of things. There's detoxing the body, mind, and the spirit. And then there's rejuvenating the mind, body, and spirit. And then there's a realignment that happens. So we're using all of these things—so yes, meditation for sure. The cleansing techniques would even include things like doing neti pot[76] every day. You know, it actually is known to clear out the mind. Also, then using an oil in the nose. There's all of these things that flush out the congestion that can be in the body. So it's using a little bit of, in Ayurveda it's called *panchakarma,* so the five deep detoxes of the body. And you don't have to go hardcore, you know. So that's how I teach it. It's like, we do a little bit at a time throughout our lifestyle instead of doing these harsh [*makes groaning, choking noise*] which can be—what is it called?—imbalancing within itself. So yeah, with yoga we do some *āsana,* but really it's more the practices, *prāṇāyām.*[77]

Kailash expresses a very Indic (if vague) understanding of the expansive nature of a yogic lifestyle, foundational to which are ascetic practices of cleansing and purifying the body and mind.

Importantly, in Indic yoga, these practices are imbued with moral significance. Consumptive habits have either positive or negative effects that influence emotional well-being, mental clarity, physical health, and moral composition. Transformational festivals focused on yoga usually include multiple opportunities to take classes in Ayurveda, which views the body and mind as comprised of the qualities (*guṇas*) of *sattva, rajas,* and *tamas*. In short, *sattvic* qualities are yogic in nature, and they are defined by coolness, purity, and the color white. *Rajasic* qualities are active in nature, and they are defined by heat, energy, and the color red. *Tamasic* qualities are inert in nature, and they are defined by lethargy, heaviness, and the color black. Foods, practices, and behaviors can be classified within these three qualities. For example, meat and alcohol are *tamasic,* and thus ingestion of those substances causes lethargy and inertia. Curry or pizza are *rajasic* foods that provide energy but detract from bodily purity. *Ghī* (clarified butter) and yogurt are *sattvic* foods that are suited to purifying the body in preparation for training in yoga. That which is ingested is manifested in both the mind and the body, internally and externally. In yogic philosophy, you are, quite literally, what you eat.

DIETARY DISCIPLINES

Yogic dietary disciplines overlap with "white class privileged moral logics of 'green' justice"[78] and what Crawford has termed "healthism," the individualization of health as a moral duty.[79] Read through a Foucaultian lens, health-consciousness has become a form of governmentality, wherein taking personal responsibility for health promotion "becomes viewed as a moral enterprise related to issues of self-control, self-knowledge, and self-improvement."[80] Kate Cairns and Josée Johnston argue that such practices exacerbate existing social divides, even when applied across neoliberal subjects: "The logic of health as personal responsibility reaffirms the boundary work of white middle-class populations, able to adopt 'healthy lifestyle' practices, working to distance themselves from unhealthy Others, . . . and often serving to justify their own privilege."[81]

There is an extensive literature on the topic of nutrition, health, and food justice, but spatial constraints prevent a full consideration of this subject herein. However, the discussion of dietary regimes is an important point at which to reference the significance of what Kimberlé Crenshaw famously termed "intersectionality," how political and social identities such as race, gender, class, and other individualized characteristics overlap and intersect.[82] Ideations of neoliberal notions of the choice of a "healthy lifestyle" are the privilege not only of elite whites but also of the middle and upper classes, for whom food scarcity is a distant notion instead of a visceral reality. Research has shown that the slender body is deeply associated with whiteness, but it is also associated with the middle-class, female, heterosexual body.[83] While this book focuses particularly on whiteness, my intention is not to occlude other forms of social and political identity that also have significant bearing on this field, such as class or gender. The health-conscious, vegetarian, and organic foods that are celebrated particularly at Wanderlust and Bhakti and Shakti Fests are raced, classed, and gendered offerings. *White Utopias* argues that religious exoticism is a primary reason that these fields remain predominantly white, but that should not obfuscate the fact that health, wellness, and opportunities for self-care are luxuries afforded disproportionately across racial and class divisions. Social station and economic privilege awards participants adequate nutrition, access to health care, and free time for exercise and self-care. Yet participants commend themselves for making conscious choices in support of wellness and use those decisions as entrance criterion to forming distinctive spiritual communities. This embodied neoliberalism is so complete that participants view themselves as exercising freedom of choice in the market of consumable goods—without seeing how their freedom is an effect of their social station and an expression of economic privilege.[84]

Food preferences can also be tools to create social distinction and to forge communal identity. For example, during my first year at Shakti Fest, I met Rain while hanging out toward the back of the crowd at one of the *kīrtan* stages. He was a handsome man in his late thirties with shoulder-length hair and an affable smile. While we talked, he offered me some of his kale chips, to which I made a joking comment and wrinkled my face, questioning whether kale chips would taste good or not. He chided me, mocking what he presumed to be my equation of green foods with unpleasant taste. I felt ashamed and took a kale chip as he extended the bag to me. But our camaraderie had dissipated, with both of us recognizing that, despite our initial connection, my reaction to his offer had wedged a division between us.

The division of subcultures over something as trivial as a preference for kale chips may seem absurd, but as Bourdieu has argued, communities exemplify their values through taste and create subcultures through those identifications.[85] Food preferences are often based in ethical convictions, and thus food is a significant means of creating divisions between social and religious groups. Dietary restrictions and prohibitions are also a fundamental means of forming religious identities: we are those who don't eat shellfish, we are those who don't drink alcohol, and so on. My handsome bohemian flirtation was of the kale-chip-eating spiritual subculture, and I was an outsider, and presumably not very advanced in my yogic and spiritual work.

However, after three or four years of adapting to my field sites, I began to eat kale chips, and not only kale chips but also kale smoothies, kale juice, kale salads, and even homemade kale pesto.[86] In other words, I began to adopt some aspects of the ascetic ethos of the yogic festival gradually through diet. At Bhakti Fest in 2015, Ryan, a devotionally oriented yogi, explained that this is a common process of acclimation and that even the less ascetic festivals and yoga classes were useful tools to help outsiders slowly acclimate to a more ascetic ethos. In his words, "Some people will even [come a]cross that [at LIB] and they get turned onto this [Bhakti Fest] and they are like, 'Yeah, these are the people that I want to be with.' Hopefully that is happening and the whole yoga community is doing that. Even the straight-up classes, . . . they're turning people on. . . . Just like the roommate who is like, 'Why don't you try these kale chips?' And they are like, 'Oh that's awesome,' and they put down their Doritos, and like, little by little."[87] Self-mastery occurs as a gradual process, "little by little," diminishing the power of human desires for unhealthy indulgences.[88]

Ryan suggests that yogic dietary habits become normalized and adopted over time until nonyogic choices, such as eating meat or smoking cigarettes, become unthinkable. Acculturated yogis I spoke with, who had long since adopted these "yogic" dietary conventions (kale smoothies, kombucha, and so on), derided festivals that moved away from these yogic principles of asceticism. For example, some yogis thought that the alcohol supplied during the night events at Wanderlust detracted from the "energetic level" of the festival and chose to go to bed early on those nights. I interviewed several participants who were disappointed and even disillusioned when LIB began hosting food vendors who sold meat products. Yoga teachers at these festivals also provided mimetic models for ascetic behavior, whether Helena Blake's "plant-based diet" and strict 10 pm bedtime or Tobias Day's diet of "high *prāṇa* whole foods"[89] and extensive athleticism. There was also a sense of communal surveillance that demanded these ascetical yogic behaviors and, importantly, envisioned them as indices of morality.

CONCLUSION

At the transformational festivals in this study, participants encountered a wide variety of experiential opportunities that had the potential to destabilize the conventional self. Festivals involved long-distance travel, limited or different personal possessions, weather extremities, extraordinary stimulation, emotional release, self-examination, physical exertion, dietary restrictions, and so on. In isolation, any one of these factors might contribute to the destabilization of or even a rupture with the conventional self, but these festival worlds create an onslaught of all of these factors combined.

Importantly, if a significant rupture occurs, it happens within the context of the festival, wherein participants are surrounded by copious amounts of diverse therapeutic and spiritual tools with which to fill the void. They are also surrounded by a community and a sense of tribe, which reminds them that they are with others who are weathering similarly disruptive experiences. The festival is crafted as a supportive and safe environment wherein participants can be more emotionally and physically vulnerable and therefore more open to new ideas and connections with others. Ideally, once the conventional self is destabilized, the bare, emotionally raw, and vulnerable self is lovingly encapsulated within a sense of communal belonging and exposed to limitless possibilities for its reconstruction with content intended to promote consciousness expansion.

Within this broad transformational field, the yoga class, in particular, provided a means to draw practitioners into a receptive state wherein teachers could then influence them to adopt a distinct set of values or practices. At a Founder's Speakeasy at Wanderlust Squaw Valley in 2014, Helena Blake described the unique space of festival yoga as follows: "What an incredible opportunity to be able to activate all this energy. . . . We create this environment where people are happy and healthy and inspired and excited and motivated, and you get them to this super ecstatic place, and they're all looking to make a difference, and at that moment they'll do anything."[90] Although Blake is describing the importance of convincing yogis to commit to humanitarian activism, her premise is that transformational festivals make people particularly malleable and acquiescent to new ideas. This is especially true when they become somatically receptive while listening to spiritual sermons during yoga classes.

When participants practice intense amounts of yoga at a festival, they become more receptive—physically, emotionally, and mentally. There is an atmosphere of openness to new ideas, and many practice yoga with a journal resting at the ready beside their mat. Some practitioners make journal notes because they are yoga teachers aiming to learn new sequences. Others make notes for inspiration and spiritual growth. Still others journal for therapeutic aims, seeking to work through emotional trauma. Moments of cathartic release open a void, which is then filled with the multifarious contents of the festival, including various forms of religious exoticism (yoga, meditation, rituals, drum circles, ceremonies, shaman-led visualizations, and so on). The festival is aimed not only at destabilizing conventional notions of self and reality but also at replacing those conventional notions with a new sensibility and supporting those new sensibilities with a new community, a tribe.

On the last day of Burning Man in 2019, I ran into my friend Nomad on the way back from the porta-potties. During our conversation, he offered me a bottle of hard alcohol that he had been gifted. He explained that he wanted to "gift it" because he doesn't drink and neither do any of his friends at Burning Man (most of whom were with Camp Mystic, one of the more spiritual villages). The unspoken statement in such an offer was the assertion that alcohol consumption, unlike psychedelics, is a low-frequency, spiritually detrimental pastime that deadens rather than heightens the senses. In my sensitivity, I tried to interpret this gift as a generous gesture, though I noted that it subconsciously classified me as a low-frequency (non-ascetic, non-spiritually advanced) person. Admittedly, this is a far cry from the Burning Man experiences of many Burners. One can easily chart the week in a series of drunken, debaucherous, and hedonistic experiences—and there is nothing wrong with that. But my friend Nomad finds his spiritual community at Burning Man, and he has radically changed his life because of navigating psychedelic explorations and whiteout conditions there. In the course of his four years of burning, he has gone from a suit-and-tie-wearing, entrepreneurial carnivore to a nondrinking, vegetarian, globe-trekking artist who has earned his yoga teacher certification.

Nomad is an excellent example to keep in mind as we circle back to Weber's theories about how Protestant proclivities toward inner-worldly asceticism aid in the furtherance of capitalism. One could argue that these ascetic notions of the endlessly perfectible self generate infinite markets for insatiable desires. Furthermore, the perfected self must be proven, and this is accomplished by socially demonstrating sculpted bodies, aesthetic comportment, and conscious behavior. Embodied individuals exhibit their perfected, ascetic selves, demonstrating that they have effectively selected the best spiritual tools and products from the market to further their personalized evolution of consciousness. In this way, these subcultures symbiotically create both new consumers and new markets. However, in contrast to Weber's Protestant ethic, there is significantly less emphasis on the importance of bridled sexuality, worldly engagement, and the sober performance of rational labor in "a calling." Here, it is not external material prosperity that provides evidence of one's good standing in God's grace. Instead, the evidence of prosperity is internalized; the performance of the ascetic self becomes the ideal. This results in a somewhat incongruous blending of an ascetic ideal of self-mastery and the psychological anxieties produced within Calvinist theologies of predestination, wherein that mastery must be proven, recognized, and displayed for others.

But that too is only part of the story. In yoga, and in the transformational scene more generally, there is also a world-rejecting asceticism. Some participants become so enchanted by these alternative lifestyles that they become full-time practitioners of self-cultivation: modern, world-rejecting ascetics. Some become fully engaged in festival worlds—building art, becoming vendors or producers, or creating new identities defined by the liminality of festival space. Others become yoga teachers or *kīrtan* artists. A noticeably significant percentage of the population attempts to live sustainably, off the grid. Others become global nomads, trekking constantly in search of peak experiences and spiritual evolution. In essence, these modern world-rejecting ascetics attempt to diminish their engagement with neoliberal capitalist society and choose spiritually engaged lives over material gain. People like Nomad and Luke, discussed in appendix 2, come to mind. Of course, despite their imagined escapes, they are never fully disconnected from neoliberal capitalism—but one could argue that no contemporary human can be. As a dear friend and world-renouncing ascetic in India once told me, "Everyone wakes up hungry in the morning." But their lives are defined by critique, and they attempt to distance themselves from neoliberal capitalist values in favor of alternative structures of authority and identity constituted by alternative systems of ethical values. Transformational festivals create forums for exposure that introduce and immerse participants, even touristic ones, in uniquely modern forms of asceticism expressed in both inner-worldly and world-rejecting forms. And, turning to the topic of the next chapter, they can also provide catalysts for mystical experience, defined as an encounter with the sublime resulting in affective experiences of reverence, awe, and wonder.

Interlude

Sculpting Bodies and Minds

Iyengar went on to popularize yoga in America as some kind of gymnastic effort, and then Lululemon got hold of it and turned it into fashion and body dysmorphia—you know, people hating their bodies and working out—and it just played into the whole fitness, fashion, cosmetic, body dysmorphic illness of America, and this is not what yoga is.

—Henry Stevenson, yoga class, Lightning in a Bottle, May 27, 2016

In the West, the aspirational yogic ideal often materializes in the conflation of physical beauty with spiritual advancement. This conflation leads to yoga teachers occupying a mimetic role for students, wherein they are under pressure to represent perfected bodies as reflections of their advanced yogic spirituality.[1] At transformational festivals, despite the ubiquitous rhetoric of self-love and acceptance, I experienced shame for not conforming to idealized beauty conventions—among Burners, LIB partiers, *bhaktas,* and yogis. For perspective, in the genre of autoethnography, I include here my most tragic and vulnerable moment in the field, as recounted in my field notes:

Wanderlust, Great Lake Taupo, New Zealand
Friday, February 3, 2017

After the international flight from Los Angeles to Auckland, the drive from the airport was longer than I expected, about four hours. I arrived at the hotel, which was less of a luxury resort than I expected, and it was about ten minutes north of Great Lake Taupo. I think I was imagining a fancy five-star resort right on the shores of a massive volcanic lake—check your expectations. Instead, it was a small, cozy, cottage-style resort with a small pool. It was a bit convoluted to get back to the camping area, but everyone was kind, helpful, and welcoming. There was absolutely no parking, but they said that I could just double-park and haul my things over to the camping area. I did, only about one hundred meters, but up and down hills, and I was still jet-lagged. When I got to the boutique camping, there were about eight lotus tents. No one was there to check me in, so I just picked one and put my things inside. I went back to the car and parked across the road as directed and then walked the quarter mile back to camp and went straight back to the tent to flop on the bed. The insides of the tent were nice, but not nearly as nice as the pictures. There was a double bed air mattress, a duvet, and two pillows. The promised end table was there, but it was a crate with a board on top of it.

I found the promised showers, but they were converted porta-potties with a spout at the top for water. It was hot for about five minutes and then turned ice cold. At $190/night, this was a bit more roughing it than I had imagined—especially since I later found out that the hotel rooms were $185/night. Though I shouldn't complain—I booked late, and that is the price for not being local. I was happy that I wasn't beginning to set up a tent.

I was pretty jetlagged, puffy, and developing a sty. I went out to check out the festival—the population was sparse, not even enough to call it a crowd—one or two people milling about here and there. Some people eating from the various food trucks, but mostly people just walking around and checking things out. I went over to Shelby Michaels's yoga class, which had about sixty people in it, and took the opportunity to watch and to charge my phone.

Around 5 pm, I decided to take a little nap to see if my sty would go away. About halfway in, around 6 pm, someone began to unzip and "knock" at my tent. Kirstin introduced herself as the coordinator of the glamping and wanted to change the batteries of my lights and take one away (I had two). I got up groggily and began to talk with her. She apologized that I was napping. I told her that I had just flown in from LA that morning, and she excitedly told me that she had just sold her house in New Zealand and was moving to LA. As we began talking, I realized that my right eye was nearly swollen shut, and I became immediately self-conscious to be so ugly when she was so beautiful and fresh—yoga pants, tank top, fashionable hat with a feather in it, long wavy locks of dark hair, and impeccable skin and make up. She was beautiful, and here I was looking and feeling like complete ass. I tried to kindly get rid of her as nicely as possible. She went on about how she had sent an email regarding the accommodations but that she was sorry that it was sent quite late. (Later on, I checked and found that I had received it just that morning.)

After she left, I lay down for a little bit again, but by then it was 6:30 pm, and there was something starting soon—music of some kind—maybe the opening act for the Wanderlust Spectacular. I tried to freshen up, but my eye was really bothering me. My right eye was nearly completely swollen—not fully shut, but bad enough that anyone looking at me would immediately think that something was the matter. I went to the main food truck area, hiding in my sunglasses, and found a tea-tincture truck. There was a woman with an Indian print sundress and long curly/wavy hair with perfect skin and perfect teeth who greeted me with a big smile. I asked her if she had any green tea, thinking that it would take down the swelling if I put a green tea bag on my eye. She said no but offered me detox tea or a digestive tea—reminding me that all immune troubles begin in the gut. I took the detox tea and asked her for a tea bag. After a bit of communication troubles, she kindly gave me one wrapped in a napkin for free. I looked around a bit at the beautiful yogis in their assorted expensive yoga pants, with beautiful skin and long flowing hair, and decided to retreat back into my tent. I put the tea bag on my eye for about twenty minutes, trying to get the swelling to go down. It did some, but it didn't look good for the future. I went out for a bit to listen to the music, but there really wasn't any "work" that I was going to get done. It was just a crowd of beautiful white women dancing around. There were some moms with their children—Wanderlusts in New Zealand and Australia seem to be very family friendly. I ate an amazing vegetarian beet patty burger—New Zealand/Australian style with everything but the kitchen sink on it. Awesome . . .

Around happy hour time, Rue Boheme [a bar/dancing stage] lit up with some fabulous DJs really pumping up the crowd. I went over there to see what was going on, and it was absolutely packed. This was the Wanderlust welcome party. I made my way through the crowd over to one of the bars, where they had nonalcoholic sodas and Pino Grigio. I asked if there was a cost, and he said no, but I needed to get a chip. He pulled out a bark chip and told me that a woman with dark hair and a green shirt had a satchel full of them and she was passing them out. If I wanted a drink, I had to find her. I looked around at the sixty to one hundred yogis around me packed into a very small dance floor space and decided that I didn't care enough. I stood around for a while, but everyone was partying and seemed to know each other. I know that isn't the case and that many of them are just there with a friend or two and are meeting people, but with my face and my jet lag, I didn't have the energy to work the happy hour scene. Eventually, I went over to the Om Kombucha bar, where they were giving away free glasses of kombucha—lavender or ginger. I tried the lavender, and it was really good, but also a bit like drinking something rotten—or like skunked beer. The yogis seemed to be loving it though. I saw that there were two small trays that had once had free hors d'oeuvres on them—their small size seemed almost ridiculous for the size of the crowd. It seemed like a typical bar scene, but mostly full of yogically dressed women in flowing whatever over their designer yoga pants—fancy sunglasses—dancing together—some dancing wildly. DJ killing it. Still, I wasn't really feeling it.

At 7:30 pm, the crowd moved from Rue Boheme over to the Greatest Place, and DJ Sai began warming up the crowd for the upcoming Wanderlust Spectacular. . . . By 10 pm, the big, loud extravaganza ended, and after that it was relatively quiet. I reasoned that if I went to bed early and sober, maybe my eye would be better off in the morning. I snuck outside to the parking lot and smoked a cigarette—not another cigarette in sight. I felt furtive, and disfigured, and really done with the yoga and festival scene altogether. I thought about how I really didn't need to be here, and how my research budget was overdrawn, and how New Zealand isn't as gorgeous as

I thought it would be, and how the festival wasn't as cool as I thought it would be—and how if I saw another gorgeous woman in yoga pants and all of the materialistic apparel that goes along with modern yoga ("All who wander are not lost" t-shirt, fancy mālā beads worn for fashion, flat-brimmed hat that says "Just Be" and so on), I would scream. My ankle that I sprained a month ago was swollen and painful from the jet lag. I felt broken.

I went back to my tent and crashed, hoping that my bad attitude was just jet lag and it would be over in the morning. It wasn't. I woke up, and my eye was swollen worse than it had been the day before. I went to the tea lady again, and she gave me another tea bag. She also filled up my water bottle with tea, and I went to the parking lot to press the hot bottle against my eye, praying for the swelling to go down. I smoked another furtive cigarette and checked my email. I went into the hotel bathroom, where there was a long line of yoga-pantsed, beautiful women waiting for the toilet. I kept my sunglasses on for as long as I could, but eventually it was ridiculous. So I took them off and then felt completely dirty and self-conscious and ashamed. I looked around at all of the lean, tanned, tall, beautiful women with their long locks, perfect manicures, mālā beads, and small gold jewelry—a tiny lotus on a long gold chain—etc., and just felt like I wanted to crawl into a hole. I went over to the mirror to look at my eye. I couldn't see anything on the rim of the eye, but then when I pulled down my under-eyelid there was a huge puss-filled pimple-like thing about a quarter centimeter down. Awesome. I peed and washed the cigarette off of my hands and then went back to my tent to try to become a little more human.

By 8:30 am, the crowd was a little bigger, and there were dozens of people milling about at the various vendors and food trucks. Some things were just being set up still. I finished my tea while I looked around a bit and then filled up my jug with the alkaline water (that guy is at every festival). I felt like I looked like crap, and to some extent, I felt like crap because I couldn't seem to get my mind away from my eye. My eye was swollen, but so was my face, and my hands, and my feet, and my ankle. It was very difficult to get my mind away from that reality when it was so present on my face. And certainly, I couldn't imagine taking any interviews with my face looking so gross. I felt guilty about that, but I really didn't want to have to explain to one of these beautiful, pure, spirulina-drinking yogis that my face was swollen ridiculously because I had been totally stressed, and not doing yoga, and letting my immune system run down. It was also a personal wake-up call to check my own health—too many cigarettes, too much alcohol, too little self-care. In my day-to-day life, it is easy to slide into these bad behaviors, and then it was such a striking contrast when faced with the pure-living, beautiful yogis of New Zealand, who looked like they just walked off of a commercial for a beach.

I went back to my tent to soak my eye some more and change clothes to get ready for the day. Somehow, with a few liters of water, a large detox tea, and thirty minutes of warm compresses, the swelling went down to a reasonable size, and I felt nearly human again. By 10 am, I started the day. I went out to find some food. . . . I settled on an açai bowl from the Raw Organics vendor, a bit grumpy because I really wanted to put something of substance in my belly—to settle my stomach and ground myself after the long flight, etc. But it was not to be. Surprisingly, it turned out the açai bowl was absolutely amazing. It was like a frozen smoothie, but in a bowl, with banana slices, raisins, coconut, açai chips, apple slices, and a little yogurt. I could feel the antioxidants working, and my swelling began to come down some. A little caffeine in the coffee and another liter of water and I was almost back to my regular self—that is, except for the feeling that there was a small pebble on the inside of my right eye. Ugh.

In hindsight, this passage is amusing—and ridiculous. I had tried to squeeze in this festival during a quarter of university teaching, and my immune system had crashed. But why did I feel so awful? Reading the words I was using—"broken," "bad behaviors," "dirty," "self-conscious," "furtive," "disfigured," "ashamed"—I realize that I had assimilated a commonplace notion that proliferates in yogic circles that external bodily deficiencies are evidence of internal impurity. Such a philosophy is deeply intertwined with the marketing and control of women's bodies in the West. But this is merely a compounding factor of impulses already present in Indic yogic traditions. In India, physical beauty has a long tradition of being associated with spiritual prowess. Fat is commonly seen as a nonascetic result of indulgence, acne a result of impure diet, and illness a result of negative karma accrued through negative actions.

Like models, bodybuilders, and dancers, professional yogis in the West inhabit aspirational bodies that perform an aesthetic ideal. Maintaining this aesthetic ideal demands ascetic practice. A fashion model who eats only kale salads is dieting, but a yogi eats kale salads with metaphysical purpose, ensconced within a religious context that imbues such choices with moral value and a soteriological goal. Although the conceptual nuance of that yogically informed soteriological goal is often lost in translation, the demand to purify one's moral character, emotions, mental state, and physical body through ascetical behaviors remains.[2]

This implied relationality between external and internal composition is buttressed by a broader theme, which shares resonances with more mainline forms of metaphysical religion and even diffusions of Christian prosperity gospel. It stems from theories of abundance, rooted in New Thought, that have been popularized in self-help works like *The Secret*.[3] In such a worldview, put simply, thoughts become reality. *The Secret* tells readers, "Your life right now is a reflection of your past thoughts."[4] If only readers would become aware of and actualize the power of the law of attraction, they would draw in that which they desire most: "When you become aware of this great law, then you become aware of how incredibly powerful you are, to be able to THINK your life into existence."[5] This notion places significant emphasis on the power of positive thinking as a means to transform personal reality. In such a view, negative life circumstances are the result of negative thought patterns. The onus for negative life circumstances is placed squarely on the shoulders of individuals, who have the power to change their life conditions by changing their thought patterns. Such a view can be extraordinarily empowering in that it provides individuals with the confidence that they have the power to change their lives.

However, it can be devastating for those dealing with systems larger than themselves that negatively impact their life conditions. For example, those confronting institutional systems of oppression and racism that increase the difficulty of reaching their fullest potential are told that the fault for their circumstance resides in themselves, instead of in oppressive social systems. It can have devastating consequences for those struggling with mental health issues, who are told by their transformational communities that their struggles can be resolved with the power of positive thinking.[6] *The Secret* tells readers, "Decide what you want to be, do, and have, think the thoughts of it, emit the frequency, and your vision will become your life."[7] Thus, if one suffers from depression or anxiety, it is the result of lack of self-mastery. In a community imbricated with such a philosophy, negative speech is often regarded as detrimental to both the individual and the community because it is believed to be a self-fulfilling prophecy. As *The Secret* tells readers, "Thoughts become things!"[8] Expressions of self-doubt, depression, and negative emotions are considered dangerous for those expressing the negative emotion and also potentially damaging to others who would come in contact with them. According to *The Secret,* "If you are complaining, the law of attraction will powerfully bring into your life more situations for you to complain about. If you are listening to someone else complain and focusing on that, sympathizing with them, agreeing with them, in that moment, you are attracting more situations to yourself to complain about."[9]

Over drinks on Christmas Day at Canter's Jewish deli in downtown Los Angeles in 2015, Sloane, a veteran Burner and builder in the community, told me that when he was suffering a prolonged period of depression, he had been deeply hurt that his Burner friends of several decades really weren't there to support him in his time of crisis. It wasn't only that they were absent but that they had actively avoided him because they had felt that his negative energy was "toxic." This social shunning sunk him deeper into depression and caused him to question both the quality of his friendships in the Burner community and his identity as a Burner.[10] It is likely that his feelings of social isolation were partially rooted in his depression. But it is also likely that those who abide by the transformational ideals of *The Secret* would distance themselves from someone who is processing and expressing negative emotions. In their view, sympathizing and engaging with someone else's suffering would attract suffering into their own lives.

This form of magical thinking results in a social pathology in which the powerful survive by separating themselves from the weak. Individuals are in full control of themselves and their destinies. Faults and failures are the result of negative thought patterns derived from weakness and lack of self-mastery. Anything can be achieved if one manifests it through the power of positive thinking and affirmations. Failure is also manifested by negative thinking and faulty affirmations. Such a philosophy buttresses neoliberal conceptions of a society comprised of autonomous and self-governing individuals who are fully responsible for their own well-being and survival.

This view sounds extreme in its purest form, likely because it echoes logics found in Ayn Randian objectivism or a Nietzschean celebration of the "will to power."[11] But it is rampant in variously diluted forms in SBNR communities. It informs the yogi who writes affirmations on a slip of paper and slides them underneath her mat during her practice. It informs the commonplace practice of setting an intention before starting an activity. It informs the artist who believes in manifesting financial abundance through sheer will, faith, and positive affirmations and thus goes deeply into debt for Burning Man projects.[12] It informed my thinking that my unsightly sty was a result of my "bad behaviors," as a result of which I felt "ashamed," "disfigured," and "broken." Each of these examples is founded on the belief in the law of attraction: thought manifests into reality. In this worldview, the external is a direct result of the internal. By extension, there is the commonplace, though not often consciously expressed, presumption that beautiful people are more spiritually advanced. This presumption pressures those who would like to be regarded with the positive attributes of being spiritually advanced, yogic, or conscious to discipline themselves through ascetic practice in order to cultivate both internal and external beauty.

4

Wonder, Awe, and Peak Experiences

Approaching Mystical Territories

I ate some LSD, then started yoga, then India, then this [Burning Man].
—Laughlin, Burning Man, 2017

The bicyclists following the art cars in pilgrimage through the parched void was the most magnificent display of the word *church*—italicized—back to its real meaning, you know?—that I've ever witnessed. Like, it brings me almost to tears to try to fit it in my head—a fucking act of reverence. As spirituality wanes, experience is the new face, and we are refugees from the mundane. Burning Man, by being such a brilliant assemblage of reality constructs, forces you—gobsmacks you—into, I think, experiencing something finally commensurate to your capacity for wonder. I mean, it is in the act of wonder that we get off with God, right? And that's fucking awesome, right? So that's Burning Man so far.
—Jason Silva, Burning Man, 2018

With this chapter, I invite readers to shift from analyzing deliberate ascetic practices performed in pursuit of self-transformation to considering self-transformation that is unexpectedly catalyzed through encounters with the sublime. Historically, encounters with external presences (often envisioned as supernatural) were most commonly characterized as mystical experiences. Since the Age of Enlightenment, they have often been discussed through the lens of the sublime, "A complex feeling of intense satisfaction, uplift, or elevation, felt before an object or event that is considered to be awe-inspiring."[1] From the philosophy of aesthetics in the writings of Kant, Hegel, Schopenhauer, and Nietzsche to the present-day psychoanalysis inspired by Freud, Lacan, and Kristeva, the notion of the sublime has captured philosophers of aesthetic contemplation. Shifting away from a purely religious frame, encounters with the sublime became a secularized confrontation with that which is comprehended as larger than the self, a comprehension that reduces the self into a state of awe.

This process of reducing the self, or what Bruce Malina calls "self-shrinkage," is the "dissociation and elimination of the social self, with its identity, roles, statuses, skills and attributes, from individual self-awareness. What is left (apart from the case of successful suicide), is the self as a living psychophysical entity, conscious or unconscious."[2] Self-shrinkage involves the separation of the essence of self from personal identification with social relations, ego, particularity, skills, and so on. As discussed in the previous chapter, it can be achieved through the practice of asceticism, particularly bodily discipline that concentrates the mind into an egoless self. But self-shrinkage can also occur in the encounter with any expanse that reduces human self-perception to that of a mere speck in a vast galaxy. The resulting experience of wonder dissociates the individual from social and egoistic attachments and reduces the self to a confrontation with its essence.

In the academic fields of phenomenology, Indian philosophy, and mysticism, there are cannons of primary and secondary sources that aim to parse the particularities and distinctions between various forms of "mystical" experience. This chapter disengages from this phenomenological query into the nature of paranormal experiences, and the subsequent debate between a sui generis or ascriptive interpretative framing of its cause. That is to say, I am not interested in whether the experience is real or imagined.[3] Instead, I am interested in the social conditions through which the doorway to wonder is opened, which enables the individual to dissociate from the entrapments of the mundane and to experience alternative expressions of reality.

Participants journey to these festivals for their potentially transformative value, to open the possibility of extraordinary experiences. In this way, there is an element of escape in their journeys. But escape implies a lack of productivity, a flight of fancy with no ultimate significance besides reprieve and release. Some critics have used this notion of escape as a means to discount this field of religious belief and practice as politically impotent escapism. Slavoj Žižek confronts Western Buddhism as the ultimate counterpoint to Western Marxism, describing it as a religious practice that presents itself as the remedy for the "stressful tension of the capitalist dynamics" while enabling participants to fully participate in exploitative capitalist systems.[4] Žižek contrasts this, what we might name *inner-worldly escapism*,[5] with the "desperate escape into old traditions,"[6] a reference to seeking solace in conventional religions. Max Weber attempted to distinguish both inner-worldly and world-rejecting asceticism from what he saw as a similar "flight from the world" inherent in mysticism. He argued that the ascetic is a "warrior in behalf of God" and that his "opposition to the world" is felt as he becomes a "repeated victor over ever new temptations which he is bound to combat actively, time and again."[7] In opposition, he characterized the mystic, notably typified in the religious exemplars of "Asiatic religions," as one engaged in the activity of contemplation, which can only succeed in quietude and the "extrusion of all everyday mundane interests."[8]

I argue, in contrast to these positions, that the mystical encounter can initiate personal transformation and provoke social engagement. Those who turn inward eventually return to face outward, and when they do, they are differently socially engaged because of their inward journeys. The turn inward may be critiqued as flight, escape, and ultimately depoliticized action, but the history of revolutionary mystics reveals that the social impact of this turn can be far from impotent. Mystics have been some of the most influential religious and social reformers—consider, for example, Confucius, Siddhartha Gautama (the Buddha), Jalaluddin Rumi, and Rabia Basri. Radical mystics like Hildegaard von Bingen, Jeanne d'Arc (Joan of Arc), Milarepa, Mirabai, and Anandamayi Ma have been extraordinarily influential catalysts for social change. Few mystics are complete recluses, and even those who are can be socially influential since stories of their feats travel beyond the confines of their isolation. Mystics who return to society after inwardly transformative experiences routinely challenge conventional authorities and power structures. Asceticism and mysticism, though they may be practiced in isolation, are inherently social acts.

At transformational festivals, participants are called away from the mundane into spaces of wonder, awe, amazement, and overwhelm. They confront magical surrealism and are bombarded with stimuli that aim to alter conventional conceptions of reality. On the yoga mat, participants may aim to produce the experience of mental stillness by following Patañjali's famed yogic prescription of *citta-vṛtti-nirodhaḥ*, the cessation of the turning of the mind. Others may focus on cultivating an experience of harmonious flow, creating fluid movements with their bodies and rhythmic breathing.[9] A variety of interactive, participatory, experiential spaces create doorways into wonder. Even a fleeting mystical encounter has the potential to spark wonder and to revision previously held conceptions of one's reality and purpose. In her work on the intentional construction of the affect of wonder in Hindu temples in Bangalore, Tulasi Srinivas argues, "What wonder does in the world is important. This is no mere escapism; escapism suggests a removal from reality, a lack of responsibility. Rather, wonder suggests the hope and possibility of an alternate reality, a better future more conducive to joy and care. It celebrates a dexterous opportunism."[10] This chapter focuses on such moments of wonder, wherein practitioners confront the self, the cosmos, and the vicissitudes in between through visceral and spiritually overwhelming—wonderous—experiences.

MYSTICISM IN MODERNITY

Modernity has increasingly few social institutions that buttress and support mystical experience. Nonnormative fluctuations of the mind, such as fits, temporary paralysis, hearing voices, and seeing visions are usually perceived as mental or physical illness. Sufferers are regarded as victims or patients, and the underlying view is that such tribulations are problems that need a solution, usually in the form of psychotropic medications. People afflicted with these experiences are no longer viewed as specially touched or gifted, but as unwell. The medicalization of such mental fluctuations has resulted in the flourishing of the mental institution and the pharmaceutical industry alongside capitalism and industrialization in the past two hundred years.[11] The long history of mystical experience that preceded the industrial revolution was in some ways cruel to persons experiencing these unique realities (witches were burned at the stake, for example), but in other ways, that history was more tender and accommodating of a spectrum of mental difference.

In contrast to the current paradigm, exemplary mystics and lay religious figures across a large gamut of cultures have sought out unconventional, heightened experiences as opportunities to communicate with the suprahuman, however it may be conceived, whether characterized as talking to God,[12] listening to the spirits,[13] or being overcome by supernatural entities. Religions fostered the belief in the existence of real presences that were unexplainable and perceptible only in particular circumstances, and sometimes only by specially gifted people. High science, such as imaginary math or quantum physics, also seems to be much more tolerant of the unknown and unexplainable and, in a sense, reverent of the mysteries of the universe. Those who imagine themselves as modern and scientific (the "buffered self")[14] hold some of the most conservative views when they presume that reality is always perceptible, logical, and interpretable through intellectual reason.

In contrast, the modern mystic cultivates an enchanted, "porous self"[15] that is receptive to wonder. In advocating for an anthropology of wonder, Srinivas equates the extraordinary affect of wonder with Rudolph Otto's famed description of the feeling of the "'numinous' . . . which encompassed, in alphabetical order, awe, bewilderment, curiosity, confusion, dread, ecstasy, excitement, fear, marvel, perplexity, reverence, supplication, and surprise. It is also a return to passion, as something not to be discredited as lacking reason, as in the Cartesian view, but to be embraced as an interaction with the inexplicable divine."[16] Passion, wonder, and the numinous are affective sentiments that turn toward emotionally evocative, overwhelming, intimate, and immanent experiences of presence(s) or void.

The multifarious experiences of paranormal, supernatural, or otherwise mystical events that participants might encounter at festivals may resemble Santerían "copresences," a more Christocentric ideal, or anything in the spectrum between. The famed German theologian Meister Eckhart contended that the novice mystic must become as an empty vessel, a self fully eviscerated so that it may be filled with the transcendent presence of Christ.[17] Arthur Schopenhauer argued that the experience of the sublime occurs in the conscious and forcible breaking away from the will, by the conscious transcendence of the will.[18] The point is not that one interpretation is more correct than the other, but rather that the study of mystical experience must be flexible and receptive to multiple notions of overwhelming encounters and the disruptions of the conventional self that bind them together.

Such experiences and interpretations are never fully separate from systems of knowledge and power that are embedded in particular social and historical circumstances. Michel de Certeau's work invites us to consider how paranormal or supernatural experiences are deeply embedded within and even constructed through particularly situated epistemological frames. In his view, it is no coincidence that the "heresy" of unconventional expressions of the sacred flourished at the margins of society;[19] for example, witches lived on the outskirts of towns.[20] Even extricated from society, social values shape both the expressions of mystical experience and the ideological frames used to interpret it. Events interpreted as supernatural give voice to latent and subconscious desires and values in the one who experiences but also in those who interpret accounts of those experiences.[21]

Transformational festivals privilege—and in many cases assume—that mystical experiences are possible, and even probable. Such events seek to cultivate an enchanted world, one confronted by increasingly open, porous, and vulnerable selves that are receptive to an unseen realm of spirits and powers.[22] Many participants are prone to magical thinking, reading meaning into circumstance and presumable coincidences.[23] Commonplace experiences are infused with magic and meaning; every event and action is symbolically legible. For participants looking for direction, floating through the spiritual cacophony of the festival brings them to precisely the experiences they need.[24] Many of my interlocutors felt that invisible forces guided them through the festival, presenting signs, encounters, and experiences to augment their spiritual growth.

Participants are bombarded with opportunities to encounter and nurture threshold experiences of wonder. These environments have been curated by festival producers (or, in the case of Burning Man, Burning Man Project),[25] who locate the festivals in stunning natural spaces and complement them with music, workshops, opportunities for play and connection, and interactive art installations. The environments are meant to displace, to shock, to surprise, to invoke wonder, and to transport participants into alternate realities that are playful, transcendent, and surreal. Whether it is the immensity of massive interactive art and the stark desert expanse of the playa at Burning Man, the awe-inspiring stage production at LIB, the breathtaking natural environments of Wanderlust, or the rapturous collective chanting of Bhakti Fest, the space of the festival draws participants into wonderous worlds, both cultivated and raw.

By committing to attending, participants extract themselves from their everyday routinized behaviors and push themselves psychologically to experience unknown mental and physical spaces. There are multiple facets of the festival that encourage this process of distancing the conventional self from the essential self, and these create opportunities to question the stability, fixity, and reality of "the indexical I"[26]—that is to say, the conventional, egoistic self. It is this first step away from conventional reality that enables some festivals to warrant the title of transformational festivals. The adjective *transformational* signals this process, whereby the setting is staged for the possibility that conventional understandings of the self and reality, and their relationship, will be challenged and potentially displaced.

This chapter considers experiences of wonder encountered through nature, art, psychedelics, devotional music (*kīrtan*), and connection with others during transformational festivals. Each of these frames generates the potential for an experience of the sublime that introduces participants into multiply conceived realities larger than themselves. In each section, I embrace the dissonance between how these spaces create openings for self-transformation and how they can also reproduce white viscosity. Arun Saldanha uses the materialist term *viscosity* to explain the ways in which the "attractive forces" between whites create a "surface tension" that makes such spaces less penetrable by nonwhites. In the sciences, the term *viscosity* is applied to refer to the "inherent resistance to flow (kinetic dimension) and to perforation (dynamic tension)."[27] In his research on psytrance beach parties in Goa, India, Saldanha writes, "Viscosity explains why music, ways of dancing, clothing, architecture, the beach, stereotypes, the psychohistories of colonialism, the distribution of light and money power together make white bodies stick and exclude others. Viscosity is about how an aggregate of bodies holds together, how relatively fast or slow they are, and how they collectively shape the aggregate."[28]

This chapter embarks on a journey into the wonderous worlds of transformational festivals and highlights participants' personal accounts of mystical experiences. However, I keep Saldanha's notion of white viscosity as a subterranean theme of analysis. This speaks to the overarching questions of this book: Wonderous for whom? Utopian for whom? These wonderous spaces hold the potential for mystical experiences, but they are also socially, politically, and historically situated territories. They are not flat; they are not blank canvases. As a result, unless participants in these wonderous spaces actively work to make them inclusive, they will default into spaces of white viscosity with thick, rather than porous, boundaries.

NATURE

Beatific natural environments shock the system into heightened awareness. Festival participants are encouraged to purposefully acknowledge sunrises and sunsets, to walk barefoot through forests, to hike mountain streams, and to lounge in flowering meadows—to draw their

14. Nature church, Wanderlust, Squaw Valley, CA, 2019 (photo by Ali Kaukas, copyright Wanderlust).

attention to the extraordinary beauty of the natural world. Joshua Tree, the home of Bhakti and Shakti Fests, is revered as ancient and sacred land. The stark beauty of the Black Rock Desert arrests even the most callous of Burners. Wanderlusts are held adjacent to brilliant turquoise rip curls in Oahu, Hawaii; white-hot sulfur rivers in Great Lake Taupo, New Zealand; and lush, dense pine forests and stark mountains in Mont Tremblant, Quebec. Festivals bring participants into direct contact with nature and encourage them to acknowledge natural splendor—and their place in it—with intention (see figure 14).

Countless times, informants told me that being immersed in nature was a catalyst for their spiritual experiences at transformational festivals. In my "Yoga and Festival Cultures" survey, 93 percent of respondents stated that nature is a primary source of spiritual inspiration, putting it ahead of all religious traditions.[29] For many participants, the act of communing with sacralized nature supplants institutional religion. As Lorelai, a middle-aged, blonde meditation practitioner, explained to me at Bhakti Fest: "I go to church now. Nature is my church. That is how I communicate. I have had a relationship with God from the get-go. . . . I always had that inner knowing anyways—connectedness. I am just one of those people who always was connected.

I've had awakenings, but I've always had a relationship with God. . . . Even just a beautiful sunset, I would be like, 'I know I'm alright.' I always had that cosmic connection."[30] Lorelai is deeply committed to her relationship with God, her "inner knowing," and her "cosmic connection." She has had "awakenings" and practices her religion independently in the church of nature.

In 2016, at Lightning in a Bottle, I made my way up the steep path to the Meditation Lookout to participate in a ritual led by Mila Volkov, a priestess of Slavic Siberian shamanism. Dressed in white robes and a traditional Siberian headdress, Volkov spoke in Russian (assisted by a translator) as she guided the sixty assembled participants in a visionary meditation, wherein we traveled to the sacred waters of Lake Baikal through our breathwork, accompanied by drums, bells, and Tuvan throat singing. The meditation interlaced deep reverence for the spirits of the earth with powerful invocations imploring them to help the ritual participants release personal obstacles and set themselves free. An excerpt from this powerful ritual is worthy of quotation in full:

> Sit down with our spines straight. Right now, special music is playing, and this music will help us travel. . . . Make an inhale, exhale, and close your eyes. And right now, we will be appealing to spirits. Bring your hands up. Open up your palms facing the sun. Feel your breathing, and feel how the wind is blowing on you. This place is greeting you, and we are greeting the spirits. Inside of our mind, let's appeal to the spirits of this place, all the great spirits of this place. Help us in this ritual. Give us power to come to a place of power. All the spirits of the earth, . . . we are appealing to you, and we are asking you: give us the power and resilience in this traveling. Oh, the spirit of fire, you burn away all fears, all doubts. Burn them on my path. Oh, the spirit of water, give me flexibility. Give me the state of going forward always to be like a mountain river. I will always be aiming to go forward. Wind. You're ruling over air and forests. You're blowing on me, and you carry my desires and dreams, and I'm asking you, bring to realization my dream. And right now, lower your hands onto your heart, and let's appeal for help to the great shamans. Feel the connection with all the shamans of the world. And I'm appealing to my teacher, . . . I'm appealing for help. Give me power. Allow me to be your channel and to guide these souls to a place of power to realize their visions.
>
> And feel the beating of your heart. And start breathing in and out deeply. Feel very deep in your body. There are obstacles. See your path, and see what kind of obstacles you have on your path—maybe there are fears, maybe there are doubts, maybe there are illnesses, maybe the past is holding you, maybe you don't have faith, maybe you have doubts. And right now, make a decision for yourself to be completely totally devoted to this practice, to let go, to let go and allow yourself to come to the place of power, to trust the

spirits. Feel where in your body you have blockages and tension, and right now start to breathe actively as you help yourself to free from blockages. Sharp exhalations from your nose or through your mouth. Exhale! Exhale! Exhale! Exhale! You can help yourself with the hands. Help yourself with the hands. You can make the breathing exhalation with a sound. . . . You are taking out the pain from your heart. You free yourself from the heaviness, from whatever is holding you back from going to a place of power. Exhale! Exhale! Exhale! I am making efforts. I free myself from illnesses, from fears, from lack of belief in myself. I exhale the pain. It burns up. I get rid of doubt. I want to come to a place of power. I have to free myself![31]

Volkov is emblematic of the current Siberian neoshamanistic revival. Her message resonates with the desire of LIB participants for enchantment through Indigenous ritual, viewed as intimately connected to the veneration of earth spirits. She entreats ritual participants to become cocreators with these spirits of nature and ancestral shamans in order to remove obstacles (fear, doubt, illnesses, the past, lack of faith) and realize their "desires and dreams." The purpose of the ritual is "to come to a place of power" and become "free." By participating in the visionary meditation ritual, participants shift their position from alienated subjects who are "being acted upon" by external forces to agents with control over their destinies and the power to actualize their desires.[32]

Nature religion[33] envisions the natural world as a medium for divine revelation[34] and provides a shared language for transformative experiences.[35] In the nineteenth century, Rousseau initiated what later became a commonplace conviction that one could "truly exist" as "precisely what nature willed" in solitary self-contemplation in nature.[36] For the Romantics, who were inspired by Rousseau and later the American Transcendentalists, only once they had extracted themselves from the corruptions of society were they able to further their projects of self-inquiry and spiritual inspiration.

At the turn of the twentieth century, outdoor excursions like mountaineering, camping, and exploring became popular among white Americans. The once solitary self-explorations of nineteenth-century Romantics and Transcendentalists became group events, sometimes with annual organized adventures of fifty to one hundred American strangers forming a small village for hiking and camping for a month at a time.[37] Evan Berry, a scholar of American religion and environmentalism, explains:

> This insistence on the collective enterprise of nature spirituality represents a major revision of the romantic inheritance. The kind of alienation relieved

by recreational outings was not grounded in a rift between the human individual and the created order but instead among members of a complex, fragmented, and psychologically distressing society. The outdoors provided the appropriate cure for modern alienation, and that cure was the result of both the experiential authenticity of time spent living according to nature's rhythms and the special kind of social cohesion facilitated by the camping life, a kind of togetherness impossible to the routines of workaday society.[38]

Transformational festivals can be read as a continuation of this legacy. They are, in essence, collective camping excursions that build social cohesion and provide opportunities for transformative experiences through communion with nature and extraction from "workaday society." Like their predecessors, they also use the "gypsy lifestyle" to emphasize the central importance of "carefree, unconstrained experiences in American nature spirituality."[39]

In the later twentieth century, the connection that Berry notes between the cultivation of a "gypsy lifestyle" and "carefree" experiences of nature spirituality expanded among the hippie-generation, many of whom got "loose" in the eco-villages and communes of the back-to-the land movement.[40] Today, the commune craze of the counterculture has largely lost momentum, but it continues at the fringes of society in retreat centers like Esalen and Kripalu, on organic farms, and in utopian communities.[41] From exploratory adventures to planned settlements, these utopian environments invite participants into the reformulation of the self by engaging with radically different systems of sociality.

Historically, part of the project of imperialism has been white people conquering the land as their own. European heritage is marked by imperialist and colonial relations to the land, imagined as terra incognita, uncharted territories waiting to be explored, learned, and dominated. As a result, in Anglo-European societies, it is a commonly romanticized notion to pack the bare essentials and set off into the wild. For the white explorer, confrontation with nature becomes a test of strength and will and an opportunity for the development of new avenues for self-awareness. In contrast, through colonization and slavery, the land became resignified with exile, occupation, theft, and bondage for people of color. For many, the notion of setting off into the wild with only the bare essentials conjured emotions of fear, flight, escape, and subterfuge—hardly a romantic vision. Wilderness was also often a space of white violence against people of color, whether by lynching or by starvation. Despite traditional forms of nature religion among Native peoples, settler colonialism has also marked Native land as white property.

As Carolyn Finney writes, "A 'white wilderness' is socially constructed and grounded in race, class, gender, and cultural ideologies (DeLuca and Demo 2001). Whiteness, as a way of knowing, becomes *the* way of understanding our environment.... Racialization and representation are not passive processes; they also have the power to determine who actually participates in environment-related activities and who does not."[42] For multifaceted reasons, the history of white possessivism as it relates to the natural environment remains significant for many people of color who interpret transformational festivals held in remote wildernesses as white exclusive spaces.

ART

Art has long been acknowledged as an effective means of articulating and accessing the sublime. In Ralph Waldo Emerson's words, "Thus is Art, a nature passed through the alembic of man."[43] If nature forms the raw material of human existence, then art can be imagined as the human response to it. Burning Man has been particularly influential in its large-scale artistic productions, many of which aim to inspire, produce awe and feelings of the sacred, and bend the mind away from conventional understandings of reality. Art that debuts at Burning Man also travels to other transformational festivals and, increasingly, into public spaces.[44] Some art projects tower thirty to forty feet above the playa and serve as beacons of the artists' visions, often signifying the whimsical, the magical, and the surreal. Their constant presence reminds Burners throughout the week that they are living in a radically alternative reality and have left the default world behind. Practically, they become geographical markers one can use to find the way home in a dust storm or after a long night; they become touchstones of the familiar-unfamiliar. Traditionally, they are burned one by one at the end of the week, thus transmitting philosophical messages of impermanence and ephemerality. As these artistic geographical markers on the playa are gradually erased, participants can become easily disoriented and forced to contend practically with the realities of locating the self.

Many art pieces also aim to transmit the particular message of the artist, such as love, magic, intimacy, abandonment, global warming, and so on. They also symbolically convey unintended messages to participants that can appear to have profound significance in serendipitous and chance encounters. Festival spaces cultivate openness to suggestion and encounter. This is in part because the immense scale of the festivals ensures that the best-laid plans as to where and when to meet usually fail. As a result, veterans commonly advise novices to wander the festival, open to "saying yes"[45] to unexpected experiences. Releasing control is a major component of the experience, as the phraseology of Halycon's famed Pink Heart camp at Burning Man tells us: "Love more. Fear less. Float more. Steer less."[46] The psychological effects of this rule are that participants are suggestible and are looking for synchronicities, serendipity, and directive signs. As if on demand, Burning Man produces them in abundance. For example, Shaw—the veteran Burner with a penchant for bowling—described his encounter with an art piece:

> I was on the playa and there was ... an eight-sided room with doors that were all identical ... So I walk in the door, and the door closed behind me, and on the reverse side of every door is a tarot card and very elaborate, fully artistically executed with surpassing artistry. Somebody who took the time to make these was a professional and devoted a lot of time and a lot of thought to make these an extraordinary, moving, piece of art—every individual card. And you walk in, and the directions to this piece of art basically said, "You have walked through a specific door; look at that door. Why do you think that you walked through this door instead of any of the other doors?" Not necessarily that it is spooky or surreal or supernatural, but play with it. Indulge the symbolism for a moment. What does the symbolism of this experience tell you? ...
>
> And I looked at it, and I thought, I can understand what this is telling me, and I can relate that to a part of my life. And I can reflect on where I am with this aspect of my life right now. Not that it is predicting the future—it's only a symbol that is telling me. And then—that is where the interesting part of this is—you're going to choose to leave this room, to leave this room eventually. Which symbol are you going to choose to take with you as you leave? And all of the sudden—you didn't have a choice when you walked in, but you have a choice when you are walking out. OK. And you look around and you go, what needs work in my life? And I walked through a particular door, and five minutes later I thought, that wasn't the right door! And I went back in and I thought—*that's* the door I need to leave through. *That* is what the symbols are telling me right now. *That's* what's resonating in my heart. And again, I don't want to put too much supernatural to it, but I do want to honor the idea that there are things that are inexplicable in this world that I cannot possibly explain. And sometimes I find explanations through serendipity, through sheer chance.[47]

This art piece, *Wheel of Fortune*, also traveled to LIB in 2015. There, of the twenty-two possible tarot card doors, I walked in through the door with the tarot card entitled "VII Chariot," upon which was written: "DRIVE YOUR DESTINY."[48] Several years later, I still remember the affective and tactile experience clearly: the dark red glow of the interior of the space, the crystal doorknobs, the artistic imagery on each door, and the air of mystery inside. Depending on one's level of suggestibility, such experiences can be revelatory. For the many who attend transformational festivals in search of inspiration and guidance, such signs become potent signifiers of meaning.

In 2017, the *Tree of Ténéré* art installation at Burning Man brought a magnificent and technologically wonderous tree to the playa.[49] Comprised of twenty-five thousand LED leaves, the towering, four-story tall, lifelike tree offered daytime shade and climbing opportunities at night. It produced an infinity of interactive displays of light that were responsive to human sounds, movements, and, what the creators call, "biorhythms." On cool nights, people piled along the base of the tree, lying on its roots to stare at the shifting color displays articulated by its magnificent leaves. Like many other art installations, the *Tree of Ténéré* became a destination. On Sunday night, after finishing the hard work of build week, I happened upon my new friend Adrian on a neighborhood lane. We had made a light connection earlier during build, and feeling the serendipity of our chance encounter, we decided to walk far across the playa to the *Tree of Ténéré*. As the night exploded around us with art cars, fire artists, and LED lights, we meandered through the bright and dark spaces. At the outset of our journey, the *Tree of Ténéré* was a very distant illuminated marker on the horizon, and on our way there we stopped to climb and explore various art pieces. Once we made it to the tree, we lay beneath the illuminated LED leaves and lost ourselves in the display. Time ceased to matter. We became completely absorbed in experience of the art. It was wonderous.

The next morning, my friend Rodney came by my tent early for a chat with his coffee, as he commonly did. He is a very tall African American man with a dark complexion and short hair and is usually uncostumed, wearing shorts or jeans and a loose button-up short-sleeved shirt. I enjoy his morning rounds when he comes by my tent space, though sometimes he finds me somewhat disheveled, just waking up. That day, however, I roused myself quickly because he was distraught and needed to share. With an animated and incredulous tone, he began to narrate a disturbingly negative experience that had happened to him the night before at the *Tree of Ténéré*. He had heard that the Playa Pops Orchestra was going to be playing a concert at the *Tree of Ténéré*, and he thought that it would be a beautiful way to spend a romantic evening with his wife. They headed out early, brought a picnic and wine, and made it out there in time to secure a great spot right in front. As the orchestra began to play, the *Tree of Ténéré* lit up, and the sun set in that magical Burning Man way. It was wonderous.

But as more people realized that the Pops were playing at the *Tree of Ténéré*, the crowd started to fill in behind them. He was standing next to his wife, who was sitting on her mobility scooter. In time, the crowd began sitting all around him, but he preferred to stand. Someone from the back of the assembled crowd yelled at him, "Hey! Down in front!" Rodney said he ignored him, but the guy, a white guy, kept on, yelling again and again for him to sit down. Rodney hollered back at him that if he wanted to get a better view, then he should have gotten there earlier. He kept standing. The situation escalated. The guy at the back "was pissed," and by Rodney's own account, so was he. He said that it got so heated that they nearly came to blows. Rodney said that just as this guy was getting in his face and it was fairly uncertain that this altercation would end nonviolently, he was very happy to see that there were about "six brothers [African American men]" who were at the tree just kind of "on alert" about the situation. Rodney felt like they were "there to back [him] up" if something bad happened—and that it was "nice to see" and to feel supported in that way on the playa. On previous days, after rough experiences, Rodney had come by to tell me that "there is definitely racism at Burning Man." But he felt that this experience was evidence that Burning Man is "way more diverse this year."[50]

Potentially wonderous experiences are not static. Rodney and I approached the *Tree of Ténéré* on the same night and experienced the same initial affect of wonder. But Rodney's experience of wonder was immediately tempered by what he perceived as a racialized assault. As the white guy got angrier and angrier, Rodney looked through the white crowd to find his "brothers" for support, wondering, "Who here has my back?" This is an entirely different kind of wondering. In this case, Rodney's perception of white viscosity eviscerated his capacity to experience wonder catalyzed by extraordinary art.

PSYCHEDELIC EXPERIENCE

In contrast to the predominantly sober events discussed in the previous chapter, transformational festivals like Burning Man and LIB[51] have developed in tandem with EDM (electronic dance music) and tend to embrace drugs as a means of reaching liberatory altered states of consciousness. Participants at these festivals may eschew the term *drug* because of its negative connotations and instead prefer the terms *entheogens, psyche-*

delics, or *medicine.* But drugs are an important part of the culture of these festivals, and they are often seen as a means to expand consciousness and reconfigure the relationship between self and reality.[52]

Key figures in the 1960s counterculture—like Timothy Leary, Ram Dass (aka Richard Alpert), William Burroughs, Aldous Huxley, and later, Terence McKenna—encouraged a generation to experiment with LSD, psilocybin, mescaline, and DMT (a primary psychotropic element in ayahuasca) to reach higher states of consciousness.[53] In the late 1980s and the 1990s, the emergence of electronic music developed techno-music counterculture, wherein illegal underground raves supported similar consciousness explorations with psychedelics such as MDMA and LSD, in part because they had no liquor licenses. As the millennium turned, there were significant government initiatives launched to curtail and contain underground rave culture and its rampant drug use. In the 2000s, several major busts resulted in a shortage of LSD.[54] At the same time, it became increasingly difficult to procure pure MDMA, and the drug was cut with so many other drugs (resulting in premature deaths) that much of the public lost trust in it. The absence of these staples produced a massive upsurge in the popularity of the psychotropic elements contained within psilocybin (psychedelic or "magic") mushrooms and ayahuasca, including the active ingredients DMT and its less popular cousin, 5-MeO-DMT.[55] Building on Terence McKenna's ethnobotanical evolutionism, many imagined Indigenous medicines to be "a purer prehistorical and psychogeographic beyond [the one] given to the white man."[56]

With the rise in the popularity of ayahuasca, DMT, and DMT-related compounds, participants in psychedelic culture have contextualized their desire to experience drug-induced altered states of consciousness with an interest in Indigenous knowledge. At transformational festivals, many argue that the illegality of this type of Indigenous medicine represents a continuation of the colonial project, whereby Indigenous knowledge has been (and continues to be) suppressed by imperialism (e.g., US drug laws). Some ayahuasca and DMT advocates see their work as resuscitating and spreading this Indigenous medicine as a powerful anticolonial initiative. For example, when the theme of LIB was Indigenous Knowledge in 2016, multiple speaking and workshop platforms were reserved for Indigenous leaders who serve as guides for ayahuasca, DMT, and 5-MeO-DMT experiences.

Many who are experimenting with these chemical compounds are doing so explicitly in the search for mystical experiences. For example,

160 | Wonder, Awe, and Peak Experiences

Caleb took the open-mic stage at Center Camp at Burning Man in 2016 to tell the story of his recent mystical experience with 5-MeO-DMT:

> For the last six or seven years, . . . I've been using it [5-MeO-DMT] as frequently as I can to try and approximate the mystical experience. And I've had one or two major breakthroughs, but what came this morning was far beyond anything I have ever experienced. Because I was high and just in poor judgment, . . . I got the visions of Christ, and I knew it was an impetus to smoke the DMT. So I pick up my pipe, and I loaded it with the DMT, and I put a little bit in because it's fucking scary. . . . I hit the first hit, and it was dreamy, and I was like, "You know, you are just fucking with yourself—you are not doing it right." So I took the capsule, and it was like four or five hits, and I just put the whole lot in there.

His girlfriend cut in at this point to continue the story, explaining that he began screaming—an "insane primal lion roar screaming"—for five to seven solid minutes. Caleb took over again:

> Screaming. I have a vague memory of that as well, and it was absolute fear of death. It was—I was dying. I died in that moment. OK. I have been smoking this DMT for years, and I have had a few breakthrough moments where I have come out of it screaming "I AM, I AM, I AM" and, like, moving in these crazy ways. But this time, this time I fucking died. *There is a large part of my identity that is just dropped away this morning.*
>
> And things are a little different. I close my eyes and press into them a little bit, and I can see DMT visions. That's trippy. That's never happened before. And it's weird shit too—really, really random—like blocks flying through the clouded sky and random figurines walking. It's just like nothing—no relevance, no symbology, no nothing—just really strange aspects of my unconscious mind, I gather. My leg and my posture, all of it better, my energy—I have had such a nice day and a half or two days. . . . I haven't slept, and I am feeling great. I feel amazing. My energy has been profound. And all that I can say that happened is that as the energy was expanding with the massive, massive hit of DMT. I got past the point where my ego could stop it or something. It just kept pushing, and it did, and it kept trying. I was at war with the devil man. I could feel temptation.[57]

Caleb interprets his DMT experience within a Christian mystical framework: a vision of Christ tells him that it is the appropriate time to ingest the drug, and he describes the following trip as being "at war with the devil." While few participants would frame the experience in such explicitly Christian terms, many would have echoed Caleb's belief that he was dying while under the influence of the drug.[58] Brice, a virgin Burner in 2019, recounted that he had had a cataclysmic experience at Burning Man, wherein after seventy-two hours on LSD, he realized he hadn't had any food or water in days. He said he had felt very weak and was still tripping hard, so he had lain down in his tent. There, he had felt his heart slowing to a weak pulse, and reconciled himself mentally to accept what he believed was his impending death.[59] Such encounters with death strip away unnecessary aspects of personal identity and reduce the individual to its primal core of existence. While Brice lay in his tent and resigned himself to die, Caleb contended with the very core of his existence, screaming "I AM, I AM, I AM!"

These kinds of existential experiences can have lasting impacts on a person's psyche. Even if a person fully returns to stasis cognitive patterns, the psychedelic encounter has the potential to destabilize conventional securities of the self and its position in relation to reality. Charting the use of DMT and other psychedelics for shamanic ends, Graham St. John argues that neotribal, psytrance productions aim for a "superliminalized state of *being in transit*—an experimental field of experience optimized by technicians and event-habitués with the aid of psychoactives, including 'entheogens.'"[60] Psychedelics, used as a means to experiment with the boundaries of self and reality, can produce new modes of self-awareness. They also generate new forms of global community (neotribes) and give rise to the figure of the technoshaman, usually a DJ who is "capable of affecting transpersonal states through the application of their technique."[61] Psychedelic, ecstatic "peak experiences"[62] can be the first step in situating conventional reality as only one among many possible realities and destabilizing understandings of the conventional self. Psychedelic drugs have often been conceived as rite-of-passage drugs, and those who have experienced psychedelics often distinguish themselves as a distinct social group. In Ryan Grim's phrasing, "Psychedelic drugs give one a very real feeling that there's some type of intangible divide between those who have turned on and those who haven't."[63]

For many in the counterculture of the 1960s and 1970s, psychedelic experiences became a catalyst for existential searching into "Eastern" religions, which already had millennia of philosophical traditions aimed at revealing the multiple, conditional, and illusory nature of reality. An entire generation of the counterculture blended acid trips and fantasies about Indian mysticism. Ram Dass began his journey in India with a vial of LSD, sharing the drug with *pandits* (sages) and looking for spiritual wisdom. There, he encountered Bhagavan Das, who brought him to meet his guru, Neem Karoli Baba, who ingested a significant amount of LSD (915 micrograms) without apparent effect.[64] Psychedelic exploration and religious exoticism seamlessly overlapped in the 1960s counterculture, and the intersection continues today. During our interview at Shakti Fest, Lorelai explained,

> A lot of what brings people to yoga is altered state.... And if you look at anybody's bio or background, ... a lot of people were drug addicts. Because you are constantly looking for higher consciousness—shifting out of, "I've got to get out of my head. I've got to shift the paradigm." And so drugs are an easy way to do it. Well then, when you find out that you can do this by yourself through meditation or yoga or whatever—and then you are like, "Oh my God, I can do this by myself?" And then that drives you to pursue—like, wow—how far can I go with my own head, with my own chemicals, and with my own consciousness? . . . I think human nature has a desire to shift their consciousness. Altered states, they're blissful, they're fun, exciting—whether it's drugs or *kīrtan* or yoga.[65]

But spiritual tourism in search of peak experiences has also had deleterious effects on the cultures in question. Whether this tourism takes the form of neoshamanic journeys in the Amazon or pilgrimages to the holy cities of India, "oppression, exploitation, and the piracy of valuable traditional knowledge" has accompanied the positive effects of self-transformation and innovative religious experimentation.[66] Indigenous medicines have become hypercommodities in international networks of spiritual seekers, and there are some troubling patterns of white viscosity in these networks, wherein white neoshamans not only represent but also exploit profit and resources from Indigenous cultural worlds.

Some subcommunities within the transformational festival scene have made drug experiences a primary source of transformational experience. Kylie, a young Australian participant at Wanderlust Oahu, derided the four-day Australian music festival Rainbow Serpent as providing an excuse for a three-to-four-day "bender."[67] Many participants spend the duration of the festival in altered states induced by a variety of drugs, often taken in direct succession. Zane, a young tech entrepreneur at Burning Man, recounted how he had kept a "pretty steady" buzz of psilocybin mushrooms throughout the two weeks he had been at Burning Man, which provided the baseline stasis point for the additional psychedelics (mostly LSD and MDMA) that he had ingested periodically. In 2016, my friend Parker was offered and drank a vial of an unknown psychedelic substance at a party early in the Burn and four to five days later, he still had not returned from what his friends characterized as "magical thinking."

Most strikingly, the ubiquity of pharmaceutical drugs at transformational festivals suggests that a significant shift has occurred between the drug use of the countercultural baby boomers and that of today's millennials. In nearly all categories of drug use, baby boomers still rank the highest (in percentage of consumption at age twenty), scoring well above both Gen Xers and millennials in their consumption of alcohol, marijuana, cocaine, stimulants, heroin, sedatives, tranquilizers, hallucinogens, and psychotherapeutics. However, millennials take the lead in one category; they have turned to prescription painkillers as their drug of choice, consuming these drugs at nearly double the rate of both Gen Xers and baby boomers.[68] Sometimes dubbed the Rx generation, millennials are much more likely than previous generations to have access to pharmaceuticals and to misuse them intentionally to seek a high.[69] One of my campmates at Burning Man in 2016 told me that his camping neighbor at Symbiosis Gathering, another transformational festival, spent the entire festival freebasing Percocet that he had crushed and placed in aluminum foil. In 2015 at LIB, I camped next to a group of young millennials who appeared to be amateur chemists, modifying their own personal drug cocktails with assorted vitamin supplements (e.g., Vitamin C to bring out the visuals in LSD) and pharmaceuticals (e.g., Xanax to calm down from LSD-induced anxiety), each mix designed for specific desired results.

Among the festivals I studied, there appears to be an inverse correlation between emphasis on yoga and drug use. In 2015 at LIB, I overheard a young woman say to her friend, "Hang on, let me just do this line of Adderall and I'll come with you to yoga." This somewhat outlandish comment struck a chord in my memory because of its strangeness. In general, the more a festival was focused on yoga, the less drugs were viewed as a primary means for attaining personal awakening. This may be because a strong majority of American yogis get involved in the practice because they believe it is associated with good health: 75 percent of American yogis believe that "yoga is good for you," and 79 percent use yoga to complement other forms of exercise (including running, group sports, weight lifting, and cycling).[70] Today, Wanderlust festivals maximize the intersections between yoga and health consciousness, while festivals like Bhakti and Shakti Fests draw participants from guru devotional communities (including the Hare Krishnas), who use *kīrtan* and *bhakti* yoga as natural means to reach peak experiences and largely eschew habituated drug use.

At LIB in 2016, Henry Stevenson urged participants in his yoga class to choose the long-term positive effects of yoga practice over the limited bliss experiences of drugs:

You can freak out seeing the content of your aberrated, distracted, dysfunctional mind. Mind: mind that is fearful, mind that is contracted, mind that imagines itself to be separate from its own reality. Mind is not separate from consciousness. Mind is not separate from life itself. But because we can think, we sometimes imagine that it has a separate identity of its own, don't we? And you can take the acid or even the marijuana and you can freak out—not MDMA, because it does something else. But you can take LSD and MDMA at the same time. They call it "sugar-coated LSD," and it assures you of a happy experience. Who has done that? [Nearly two-thirds of the two hundred yoga participants raise their hands.][71] Thank you. But did you feel like shit by Wednesday? Yes. Thank you. Thank you. . . .

I want you to make a rule with me now. . . . The deal is that you never take ayahuasca, marijuana, LSD again until you have established a daily actual yoga practice in your life. . . . The hallmark of Krishnamacharya work is there is the right yoga for every person, no matter who the person is, that is your direct embrace of life itself—direct embrace of reality itself—it makes the mind clear. The mind no longer assumes a separate identity from reality, from the power of the cosmos that is arising in the power of each person. Right? Do you hear me? So it's something that must be there in human life. . . . If the body and mind has contracted at all, which it has because of the society that you've been born into, which it has because of the pain of your mother and father—and not to blame anybody, it is just a cultural momentum, a social disorder, a social dysfunction, where you're living like that [contracted] instead of like that [open], where the body and mind are open to reality itself. And reality itself is nothing but a nurturing power.

This is why you're all here at Lightning in a Bottle. You have intuited this fact that life is a nurturing power that you can utterly participate in. But I'm telling you, despite the beauty of music and drugs, it doesn't give you the whole picture. But if you include your actual yoga practice in the context of music and drugs, it will give you something that is *sublime,* that you don't even know about yet. You know about it when the acid is working good or you flip the good ayahuasca journey, then you know about it. But then there's the days that follow. . . . There must be a practice, if there is a tendency to look like that [contracted] instead of like that [open]. And I'm going to give you that practice—and you'll all agree, no more marijuana, LSD, ayahuasca, MDMA until that practice is established in you on a daily basis.[72]

Yoga programming tends to resist the drug-centrism at transformational festivals, and it may be one reason why festivals like LIB include it. In response to two recent deaths at the festival (one of which was drug related), LIB also introduced the "6 Ways of LIB: Celebrate Life, Create Community, Respect Yourself & Others, Actively Participate, Honor The Land, and Be A Citizen."[73] In a revealing parallel, after the tragedies of 1996, when rogue behavior resulted in deaths and injuries in Black Rock City, Larry Harvey crafted the "10 Principles of Burning

Man: Radical Inclusion, Gifting, Decommodification, Radical Self-Reliance, Radical Self-Expression, Communal Effort, Civic Responsibility, Leaving No Trace, Participation, and Immediacy."[74]

Transformational festivals are playgrounds for experimentation with alternative states of consciousness, but they also introduce sustainable practices that participants can use to craft lasting lifeways that extend beyond temporary drug experiences. In his yoga class, Henry Stevenson urged his attendees not to get trapped in the preliminary stages of habituated and nonproductive drug use.[75] For him, drugs are a powerful tool that can open the mind and therapeutically assist in viewing the aberrated mind, but they are an introduction to that spiritual work, not the end in themselves.

DEVOTIONAL MUSIC

At LIB and Burning Man, the use of psychedelics intersects with EDM to create heightened experiences of extreme psychological impact. Participants easily lose themselves in a particular sound journey crafted by a skilled technoshaman DJ at a multimillion-dollar art car or sound stage. Some of these experiences are designed intentionally to carry participants on mystical journeys of inner exploration.[76] At the other end of the spectrum, but with similar results, *kīrtan* performances can bring audiences to tears in ecstatic communion with the divine. Audiences sing along heartily with arms upstretched to God and embrace each other in shared devotional experience. On the last night of Bhakti and Shakti Fests, all of the *kīrtan* musicians from the festival join together in an epic *kīrtan* performance during which they repeat the *māhāmantra* for hours on end. Someone viewing the emotive intensity of the *kīrtans* from the outside would be hard-pressed to distinguish between the devotional fervor at these festivals and that at an evangelical tent revival.

But some activists feel that a festival comprised of predominantly white *kīrtan* artists engages in a problematic representational politics—even if these artists are serious *bhaktas* and their *kīrtan* is heartfelt. In 2018, observers noted that Shakti Fest had no South Asian *kīrtan* artists. Christopher Wallis provoked the devotional community with a social media post asking, "Is Shakti Fest racist for not inviting any South Asian artists to perform? Discuss."[77] The post incited more than three hundred comments, including vitriolic critiques from multiple perspectives. One critic claimed that Shakti Fest "is a deeply offensive and racist 'brown face' minstrel show."[78] In another comment, the same critic explained, "When this festival is directed by white organizers, based on an appropriated art form, in a culture of white privilege, where white people historically oppressed people of color, where POC had their culture misappropriated without compensation, when there are MANY talented [South Asian] musicians and instructors nearby and available? . . . It's no different from producing a Blues festival with no black bandleaders."[79]

In her Decolonizing Bhakti Yoga workshops (one of which she held at Bhakti Fest in 2017), Prajna Vieira uses the example of an all-white powwow or reggae festival to convey a similar message to her audiences. She explains, "It's not that white people can't participate—you can. But when you have events and festivals that present a cultural tradition extracted from its cultural context, exclusively represented by a culturally dominant group, we're just replicating systems of oppression in spiritual communities now. It's time to knock it off."[80]

All-white powwows, reggae festivals, and blues festivals are relatively unthinkable in the US cultural context. Those fields are highly complex, but David Grazian's research reveals the commonplace assumption that "any song performed by a black singer should rightfully be considered a blues song and, consequently, that the blues can only be delivered in an authentic manner by a black artist."[81] How is it that Blackness is often read as an index of authenticity in American blues music but South Asianness is excluded from American *kīrtan* and yoga?

Inside the *bhakti* community, public statements and personal communications calling on Bhakti and Shakti Fest organizers to diversify have largely been ignored.[82] Furthermore, *kīrtan* and yoga communities continue to support the festivals in their current composition, with whites celebrating South Asian devotional forms without South Asian representation. Festival participants' complicity with and support of this formidable white viscosity suggests that there may be something disruptive about the presence of South Asians. Like the minstrel show, whites performing religious exoticism may, in fact, be the primary attraction, creating "a means of exercising white control over explosive cultural forms."[83] The actual presence of representatives of the "exotic" culture in question inherently challenges white presumptions of cultural knowledge and their assertions of authenticity.

Furthermore, despite chanting "Hare Krishna" hundreds of times throughout the duration of Bhakti or Shakti Fests, attending yoga classes, and chanting the Hanuman *chalīsā* (forty prayers to the Hindu god, Hanuman) at sunrise each morning, most participants at Bhakti and

Shakti Fests reject the notion that these activities are a part of either religion or Hinduism. Instead, they turn to universal conceptions of spirituality, which are accessed personally, without intermediary, through direct inward experience. In this sense, these contemporary *bhaktas* are following the paths of mystics, many of whom also eschewed institutional religion in favor of cultivating a direct and experiential relationship with God. Participants privilege anti-institutional mystical experiences as critical components of contemporary spirituality.

At Bhakti Fest, Jake, a yoga teacher, explained to me the difference between yogic and religious conceptions of God:

> I think that what yoga says about God is that God is in your heart. . . . Yoga is about us finding it [God] in our own heart. Because whatever that light was in Christ or in Buddha, we have that same light. How can we not? We're humans. But it's really kind of concealed from conditioning thoughts, you know? Our environment. So really, God at this festival, Bhakti Fest—God in yoga is, it isn't one God. I've never seen it be taught as one God. And that is where religion and yoga are nowhere near the same.[84]

Another informant, William, explained that religious particularity is merely an outward expression of a universal, inward reality. He explained that people come to Bhakti Fest drawn to the inner exploration of consciousness:

> [It's] more subtle, like you're here with the *bhakti*. It's an inner thing. It's beyond all the outer. . . . I'm not interested in becoming a Hindu. There's a whole movement now that has been developing . . . when different religions come together and people become more aware. . . . [The] "your God and my God" sort of thing slowly dissipates if you have some kind of consciousness to you and you can see it. . . . I think that a lot of the people who come here are universally spiritually drawn. . . . I don't think people are so much in the outer anyway, in the statue world.[85]

William dismisses attachments to religious particularity as a project of the past and calls for a new universalism found through the "inner" experience, as opposed to outward identifications and the "statue world" of religion.

Many attend Bhakti and Shakti Fests explicitly to access this inner mystical experience through communal *kīrtan* singing. The famed yoga teacher and *kīrtan* artist Eli Gordon explains, "Divine love. So *bhakti*, the whole intention is to elevate consciousness, is to raise into the divine love—and the word *bhaj*, which is the root of *bhakti*, means to be attached to God. Then we're always intimate. There's never a moment we are not. We sing the mantra again and again and again and again and again and again until that memory comes back, that yearning, the yearning for what is beyond this world but within every part of this world—the highest love."[86] Participants are attracted to *kīrtan* for the affective feelings of chanting in community; they stay in the practice because they believe that chanting has the power to purify and focus the mind on God. As Devanand (Joshua), a Canadian guru devotee at Bhakti Fest, explained,

> The first time that I heard somebody [singing *kīrtan*], like really sat down and opened my eyes and was really attentive to this kind of performing, I was really struck.... I saw this person belting out the most amazing sense of force and energy exuding from his voice. I don't know if I had ever heard anyone sing at that kind of level before.... I was like, OK, that's freedom, and they know something I don't know. I've got to get there, because that just looks like pure joy right there—the expression. In that unbounded expression where there is no sense of self-consciousness of how it sounds and how it is perceived by the audience.
>
> It's just like, here I am. I am a child of the universe, and I am expressing myself because I have to, because it is unthinkable not to let this light out.... I understood at that point that everything is vibration, and through meditation I was coming from a place of peace, but still felt really blocked up in terms of expressing myself. But when I saw this guy, I was beside myself.... I was amazed. And even though it took a long time to actually learn it, learn how to really do it, and gain more insights into what the practice is and what it can be, I just kind of kept showing up. I think with any of these practices that is just kind of what it is, you just keep showing up because you know that it is leading to something beautiful. It is leading to the purification of your consciousness.[87]

The repetitive chanting of the names of God in *kīrtan* has been used for centuries in Hindu *bhakti* practice for the purpose of purification (sanctification) and to concentrate the mind. For Devanand, *kīrtan* became a means of articulating freedom of expression, "pure joy," and the validation of his voice as a "child of the universe." Numerous participants recounted that their hearts had "cracked open" in singing *kīrtan;* they became receptive to the wonder of divine grace through the devotional practice. In this way, *kīrtan* can be a wonderfully transformative practice.

The majority of the Western *kīrtan* scene remains fraught with the representational politics that its high level of white viscosity engenders. However, there are recent initiatives that aim to integrate and create platforms for the significant numbers of talented South Asian *kīrtan* artists. For example, Prasada Festival attempts "to show the festival world more integrity and accountability" by creating a lineup of *kīrtan*

15. *Kīrtan* artists at Prasada Festival, 2018 (photo by Jennifer Mazzucco).

artists and dancers that is more than 50 percent South Asian and people of color (see figure 15).[88] The festival is "deeply devotional"[89] and "committed to supporting devotional arts of India with a focus on honoring source tradition, inclusivity and cultural exchange."[90] Initiated in 2018, Prasada Festival remains more of a devotional concert than a festival, attracting a mere two hundred attendees. The question arises, then: Who is attracted to spaces defined by white viscosity? And for whom does this serve as a deterrent? Likely, it is this economic calculus that transformational festival producers consider when evaluating the potential profitability of their enterprises. This suggests that in the fields of religious exoticism, high levels of white viscosity attract white audiences. In comfortable spaces protected by white hegemony, participants feel free to experience the exuberant joy and wonder of an encounter with their own constructions of the exotic. The presence of flesh-and-blood South Asians disrupts this mystical imaginary of alterity and challenges white claims of cultural authority.

CONNECTION WITH OTHERS

Festivals develop subcommunities where relationship bonds are easily forged, though sometimes these can be as ephemeral as the festival itself.

Attendees often arrive relatively "open" and ready for new experiences and encounters; they talk about the festival space as a "safe space"[91] and about the return to the festival as "coming home."[92] Many find release in the spaces of festival and often talk about being "opened"[93] throughout the course of the festival. Many of the learning opportunities focus on exactly these ideas, from meditation and yoga classes to psychological and therapeutic workshops focused on deepening the connection with the self and others. Classes and workshops often include therapeutic exercises performed with partners (usually strangers) that aim to develop these skills: open-eyed meditations, visualizations, touch-based energy work, massage, and the intentional showering of compliments (e.g., "For the next two minutes, vocalize admiration for your partner").

Personally, I found this to be one of the most difficult aspects of the festival scene when I first entered the field. Festivals are often hot, sweaty spaces, and my first year at Shakti Fest, when Bija Rivers asked me to partner up and stand toe to toe with the man on the mat next to me, to hold his hands and then lean backward into supported standing back bends, I almost left the class when I felt his warm body press into my pelvis. When Michaela Lyon asked us to partner up for a ten-minute open-eyed meditation during a Tantric visualization workshop at Shakti Fest and the woman in front of me started tearing up and then crying steadily, it was everything that I could do to maintain eye contact. Six years later, I still remember her sea-green eyes, the freckles dotting over her nose, and her curly brown hair. I never saw that woman again, but the intensity of this open-eyed meditation seared the contours of her face into my mind as I watched her tears redden her eyes and run rivulets down her cheeks.

In a neo-Tantric workshop at Bhakti Fest, Chloe Lindsay encouraged us to partner with a stranger, and she softly invited, "As you face each other again, let yourselves make soft eye contact *from a place of wonder—a place of curiosity*. Curiosity invites the unfolding of the beloved in form. When I've already decided who you are and what you mean to me, I close the door on the unfolding. . . . But as long as I stay in *wonder,* not only do you and I continue to open and unfold together, but there's a deep, deep piercing. It's the piercing we all long for and are terrified of."[94] She called on us to experience the wonder of connection, of intimacy, of absolute presence with another human, stranger though they may be.

Many novices experience the festival as a gradual process of opening their hearts, minds, and selves. Sasha, a young attendee wearing a crop top and aviator sunglasses, explained that while she wasn't a habitual psychedelic user, trying LSD for the first time at LIB was transformational in her recognition of the similitude of self and other:

> I did [LSD for] my first time at Lightning [in a Bottle] last year, . . . and I did feel like it was a transformation. I already realized that everything was like a projection of yourself—like, just me. If I find something I don't like in somebody, it's just that I don't like that aspect of myself. I just believe that everyone just comes from one thing and we are all just creating this together, and so that one person comes from you, essentially. They are a part of you in some way. And so I was just feeling that and knowing that—that I was creating all of this that I see around me. Like, this is my creation—I am cocreating this with God. And, yeah—I just figured that out more deeply last year on acid.[95]

As mentioned, there is some evidence that festivals are effective in creating this kind of identification of self and other, transitioning the "contracted" into the "open" self. At the majority of transformational festivals I attended, seasoned festival attendees easily participated in intimate partner-work during therapeutic spiritual workshops. Even in common conversation, participants quickly dropped the social pretenses of polite, superficiality when talking to strangers and headed straight for the juice, the marrow. Veteran Burners are particularly accustomed to exchanges that involve openness, connection, and vulnerability with strangers. For example, a large-scale psychological study conducted at Yale University surveyed Burners and found that with each passing day at Burning Man, participants were more likely to perceive themselves to be closer to other human beings, to identify the self and the other as overlapping entities.[96] In fact, there is somewhat of an unwritten rule among Burners that one does not ask others about the basic superficial details of their default lives—marital status, children, geographical location, and especially profession. This simple idea completely reworks conversation and forces participants to ask themselves, What *is* my existence outside of my family, marital status, and professional identity?

When these social markers are destabilized, conversation tends to roam freely from storytelling to feelings. It is also a leveling strategy that flattens economic and social hierarchies when in the mixed company of a festival, where Google executives may be conversing with massage therapists. While not all festival communities abide by this unwritten Burning Man rule, it is generally considered poor social form to consume a conversation with details of one's social station in the outside world. Such talk interrupts the liminal time and space of the festival and minimizes the distance between the conventional and festival worlds.

Instead, festival social interactions can become spaces where conventional social norms can be skipped over and meaningful relationships can be built immediately. As Dahlia, an executive and yoga practitioner in her midthirties, explained to me at Wanderlust in Sunshine Coast, Australia:

> This is a very easy place to meet strangers and hug them and get to know them really quickly. So for people like me who enjoy meeting people and want to operate outside of the social norm of handshakes and just go straight in for the kiss and the cuddle, this is a really great place to be. . . . I think there is . . . a seclusion and an anonymity that allows people to be much freer . . . and be quite childlike. . . . I think the more of it we see and the more access we have to it, it will be more normal for all of us to behave in the way that it is at Burning Man. And that is the way that we *should* behave—embracing human connection, which is exactly what it is about—and the raw connection with nature, like being outside. It's a beautiful thing.[97]

Dahlia mentioned seclusion and anonymity as important reasons for the freedom and easy social intimacies of the festival. There is an ironic sense of safety in becoming raw and vulnerable with strangers; anonymity contributes to the potential for open and intimate communication. Others more practiced in the festival scene get closer with friends than they ever might in the default world. Veterans understand the emotional tumult of the festival and are ready to listen, soothe, embrace, and sit quietly with all types of emotional expressions. Whether they are experiencing panic attacks or crying tears of exuberant joy, participants may find themselves accepted and nurtured, by friends and strangers alike, in extraordinary ways.

CONCLUSION

In 2018, I rode out to watch the Man burn[98] with a crew of newfound friends. As we sat waiting in anticipation, a circle of hundreds of fire artists began spinning coordinated routines in the area surrounding the towering figure of the Man. We talked and laughed as the crowd grew denser around us. This was a cuddling crowd, and soon the fifteen of us were arm over leg, torso on lap, enmeshed in an untidy array of shared human bodies. In time, the Man was lit, and the first flames began to burn. I watched, awed and wonderstruck, as the towering figure was engulfed in massive, sky-searing flames.

As I turned behind me, I noted that Becka was staring wide-eyed and unmoving. She was entirely captivated, and large rivulets of tears streamed down her face. Someone held her, in silent solidarity, letting her release her emotions. Her tears flowed harder and harder. She wasn't sobbing, but she seemed stunned, awe-struck, and her body reacted to the emotion with a vigorous overflow of tears. Her tears became more intense and her eyes continued to widen as she sat in complete overwhelm while the raging fire seared our faces, the intense heat piercing the cool night—rivers of silent tears, unabated, flowing in a safe communal space of love and comfort. After some time, Patrick, a camp leader in the group, asked her if she wanted a break from the intensity, and they left together for a bit. After a bit of reprieve, they returned, her tears having abated, and continued to watch the Man burn. I asked a friend if she was alright, and learned that she was fine but that she was on acid. Later, Becka recounted the experience:

> I was so fucking overwhelmed with emotion. . . . I was confronting long-held fears and insecurities, . . . so I really learned so much [about] how to love myself more and how to give myself the grace I deserve instead of continuing in negative self-talk. . . . It was an insane week of self-growth for me. . . . I was so apprehensive about going in the beginning, but I'm insanely grateful for my experience there. It's so different from your run-of-[the]-mill music festival. It taught me so much about myself and showed me how much strength and love I do have.[99]

Festival producers curate wonderous spaces by locating festivals in extraordinary natural environments and inviting participants to create art, *kīrtan,* rituals, altars, meditation spaces, *maṇḍalas,* yoga practices, and ceremonies wherein participants are confronted with the magnitude of the sacred and sublime throughout the festival. Some festivals cultivate forums that embolden transcendent experiences of God-presence through *bhakti* yoga, *kīrtan,* guided meditations, and chanting. Others cultivate experiences that encourage attendees to awaken to the presence of the inner self through yoga practice, sound immersion, and creative expression (dance, music, literature, and art). At many transformational festivals (but not all), psychedelics are also a potent means by which participants dislocate from their conventional understandings of self to open the "doors of perception."[100]

This destabilization of the conventional self can result in breakthroughs and breakdowns. Some breakthroughs are revelatory events, and some breakdowns are cataclysmic events; both signify a shift in self, the deracination of the mundane, and the transition into new levels of consciousness. While some are hidden within internal experiences, others are apparent to even casual bystanders walking through festivals, are warned about in festival literatures, and prove to be memorable and an integral part of the experience for participants. A recent survey conducted by the Black Rock City Census revealed that nearly 20 percent of people said they "absolutely" had a transformational experience at Burning Man, and more than 75 percent of people said they had at least a "somewhat" transformative experience; 85.6 percent reported that the change was "still persisting."[101] Part of the aim of the transformational festival is to push the boundaries of one's own psyche and physicality and to detach and destabilize conventional understandings of self—all in an effort to cultivate radically transformational experiences.

As the conventional self is destabilized, the creative features of the festival fill the void with the affective experience of wonder. The festival becomes imbued with magic, reenchanting the newly porous self with hope and the possibility for the activation of a new and utopian reality. Participants breathe in the light and breathe out the darkness in numerous yoga classes, workshops, and rituals; they exhale pain and trauma and "come to a place of power" in order to free themselves.[102] In turn, participants describe the festivals as "pressing a reset button," "reminding me of my values," "rejuvenating," having an "amazing vibe," "filled with love," and being spaces of "positive energy." This dialogical process of emptying and filling the self in contact with wonderous presence(s) makes these fields abundant in their capacity to catalyze transformational experience. With that said, this capacity to generate feelings of magic and wonder is socially constructed, and when it reproduces white viscosity it limits the accessibility of such experiences.

Interlude

Producing Wonder / Branding Freedom

Sloane (Slow McCoy), Burning Man, 2017

> I think that there was a point where I came to Burning Man and it was all new and fresh and magical and everything seemed to be fueled by a different kind of spirit, and it kind of overtook me—in the sense that there was some really powerful stuff happening here. I think there was a turning point, where I stopped being a participant and needed to see what was going on behind the scenes. I didn't know there was a behind the scenes. I thought everything was participant driven. I didn't know there was an organization. I didn't know there was all of this background stuff happening. Before, I knew that I thought it was kind of magic. But then kind of once I found out that there's drivers to these things, that it's not really magic, it's just a thing. You know? But literally, I thought there was, and I still do, to some degree. . . .
>
> [One year] I took far too many mushrooms and had this trip where the Man was a devil and it was raining coals on my head, and I freaked out and I ran out of the circle. And it was such a powerfully negative experience that the following year, I didn't want to have anything to do with going to the Man. So I went to the Temple for the Man burn night, which really didn't help me. . . . It did and it didn't. When I got out there, I was by myself, and I was looking back, and . . . the Man burn was late, and it was this kind of Asian—I think it was a David Best Temple—and it had an arch, and it looked like something you might see in Cambodia or whatever, and the moon, the full moon, came up out of the East right through the arches of the Temple and shone on the Man just as they started to set the fireworks off. So here I am going like, wow, this has impeccable timing.

This is more than just a party, right? There's some other shit going on here.

So that kind of reinforced the year before, and then my friend Mickey, God bless her soul, slid up behind me with these warm, soft, comfortable hands and said, "Are you OK?" And I was like, tough guy, "Yeah, I'm OK, whatever." And she was like, "Do you mind if I sit with you?" And I was like, "No." And I was kind of sharing the story of where I was at with her, and she had a radio on. She's on the media team. She was like, "Do you want me to turn the radio off?" And I was like, "No, actually, I want you to leave the radio on." And as it turned out, Daily TV was doing an exposé on Burning Man, and they had a satellite uplink, and the Man started burning, and this and that, and Daily TV wanted to know if the Burning Man organization was going to pull the Man early before they lost their satellite feed, and the organization basically kept putting them off and putting them off and putting them off until it was like two minutes beforehand, and they were like, "No, we're not going to pull the Man—especially, you know, not for Daily TV." . . . So Daily TV then basically had to extend their satellite time, and at that point—within forty-five minutes—I was like, this is a show. This is highly orchestrated theater—which in some way broke the magical spell that I had probably created in my own head about what any of this was. But at the same time . . . when I'm sitting on the couch—back to your question—and I see something that many other people would be like, "Oh my god, that's just the bestest thing in the world!" I'm like, "Remember when I would have thought that was magical?"

In recent years, Burning Man has launched a campaign to distinguish itself from festival culture. Promotional materials, email notices, informational videos, and even the tickets to the event inform participants directly that "Burning Man is not a festival." Part of the rationale behind such an information campaign is to encourage attendees to become participants rather than passive consumers. At a festival, one buys a ticket in exchange for an experience. The ticket is a promise made by the producers that they have curated an experience that the consumer will find worthy of the ticket price. In contrast, a Burning Man ticket makes no such promise. Instead, it only grants the purchaser entry into Black Rock City and access to porta-potties. Burning Man experiences are entirely dependent on the contributions of participants. There are no corporate sponsors, and Burning Man Project operates as a governing body, not as a producer. Any music, food, art, and so on that one experiences at Burning Man is there only because a participant decided to bring it to Black Rock City.

This adamancy on the part of Burning Man's leadership reflects the concern among many veteran Burners that consumer orientation is eclipsing participant orientation among new Burners. In a recent article in the *Burning Man Journal,* Marian Goodell, CEO of Burning Man, called for a "Cultural Course Correcting," arguing that "Burning Man is not a festival" but rather an "invitation to participate" in creating Black Rock City. Decommodification is one of the 10 Principles of Burning Man, but it is increasingly threatened by the ubiquity of neoliberal capitalism that bleeds onto the playa in the form of "convenience culture," like "all inclusive" prepackaged Burning Man experiences and exclusive and expensive "plug and play" camps.[1] There is also an acculturation struggle, with high percentages of first-time participants, or "virgins" (40 percent in 2018), destabilizing the principles of Burning Man that are so deeply respected by veterans. As festival culture has become increasingly popular, its consumer mentality has proliferated, and Burning Man Project at least in its current iteration, is trying to resist.[2]

As the market has increased, brand managers and corporate sponsors have recognized the potential to reach vast captive audiences at festivals. Spirituality, freedom, and individual expression have become branded experiential commodities that the wealthy can purchase with tickets to these exotic playgrounds. Burning Man is struggling to offer a point of resistance to the more mainstream, commodified music festivals like Coachella, but it is a salmon swimming against the current in a powerful river. Every virgin Burner needs to undergo a process of reeducation so that they come to Burning Man expecting to create rather than consume.

But whence did Coachella-style festival culture arise? Contemporary festivals were preceded by 1960s hippie gatherings, Rainbow Tribe gatherings (founded in 1972), and Burning Man (founded in 1986). But there was a paradigm shift in 1991, when Perry Farrell, at the time the lead singer of the alternative band Jane's Addiction, created Lollapalooza. Lollapalooza became one of the first of the new generation of large-scale music festivals, with corporate sponsorships that began targeting "alternative" youth. Farrell had recently been to the Reading Festival in the United Kingdom, and he returned with a vision to create something similar in the United States. It was only supposed to happen once, a grand extravaganza that would be more of an experience than a rock concert. His vision was a grand, carnivalesque event, with political impact, circus performers, and an extraordinary lineup of musical acts. On the first Lollapalooza tour, bands and circus performances were accompanied by the activist organizations Rock the Vote and PETA (People for the Ethical Treatment of Animals). It was such an immense success that Farrell and his partners decided to repeat it more formally the following year, accompanied by the Jim Rose Circus Sideshow. When the partners of the original Lollapalooza split, Paul Tollett went on to cofound Coachella, now one of the highest-grossing music festivals in the United States.[3]

Lollapalooza introduced a new genre that was quickly encroached upon by corporate interests. Woodstock '99, which drew 400,000 people over four days, hosted vendor malls and had dozens of corporate sponsors. Live coverage of the festival was sold as pay-per-view and later on CDs and DVDs. Fires, violence, looting, sexual assault, and allegations of rape sullied the festival. Despite the violence and corporate sponsorship that marked Woodstock '99 as radically different from the original peaceful mass gathering, music festivals continue to be big business. In 2015, Coachella sold 198,000 tickets and had a total gross income of over $84 million,[4] with $704 million in overall economic activity generated by the festival (spending by consumers and businesses).[5] Similarly, in Chicago, Lollapalooza boasted a crowd of 270,000 and had an economic impact of $120 million in 2012.[6] Electronic dance music (EDM) fans have fueled the expansion and corporatization of the once-underground rave culture, with Las Vegas's Electric Daisy Carnival drawing more than 300,000 people and generating $207 million in 2012.[7] "The five biggest festivals (Stagecoach [~$18.5M], Outside Lands [~$19M], Lollapalooza [~$29M], Austin City Limits [~$38M], and Coachella [~$78M]) combined grossed more than $183 million in ticket sales in 2014, not including sponsorships or merchandise, food and alcohol sales."[8]

Performers make more money from festivals than from tours, and many fans see festivals as a bargain because they get to see so many different performers all at once over several days, even if ticket prices range from $185 to $450. Festivals also appeal to the current valuation of experiences over things. The phenomenal spectacles that festivals make possible—from the mass of humanity to outrageous costuming and large-scale art—easily boost one's presence on social media profiles. "In just the first weekend of Coachella 2015, fans posted more than 3.5 million tweets." However, while 75 percent of online social conversations about music festivals are created by attendees aged seventeen to thirty-four, the common assumption that festivals attract only youth is largely incorrect. Only about a quarter of music festival audiences are millennials, aged twenty-six to thirty-five; older age groups (thirty-six to forty-five, forty-six to fifty-five, and fifty-five and up) are tied at approximately 21 percent each.[9]

Festivals have become the Walmarts of the music industry—a one-stop discounted shopping experience—and consumers love the chance to see their favorite artists all in one place. Festivals also promise a wide variety of experiences, born from the multiplicity of offerings and the liminal extrasocial environment. Participants are extracted from their habituated geographies, their work-life commitments, and their place within social conventions. There is also significant downtime in the three to five days and nights of festivals, which means that one is likely to make connections with others in the course of wandering and communal living. Opportunities for connections are also intensified because participants can invent and reinvent themselves in the unfamiliar spaces of festivals. The leisure of the festival combines with the shared purpose of participants to encourage sociality and connection.

Like a wide gamut of leisure activities, festivals are available only to a particular demographic—those who have the means and the ability to take a break from their conventional lives, travel to faraway territories, and afford the ticket price and ancillary costs of attendance. However, the common assumption that these spaces are exclusively for the rich is also largely incorrect. As a point of comparison, the median household income in the United States in 2016 was a record high of $59,039.[10] In the survey that I conducted among yoga festival participants, respondents reported household incomes that were relatively polarized: 22 percent earned between $100,000 and $124,999 annually, while 22 percent earned less than $24,999 annually.[11] At Burning Man in 2017, the most heavily represented personal income bracket was $50,000 to $99,999, making up 30.3 percent of the Black Rock City population. However, Black Rock City also attracts the extraordinarily wealthy (23.5 percent earn $100,000 to $299,999, and 4 percent earn over $300,000 annually).[12] This disparity signifies that there is a cadre of wealthy participants (see figure 16), but there is a concurrent subnetwork of travelers who catch free rides, camp, network, work, and barter in exchange for tickets. This population lives on the open road, working intermittently and as necessary to sustain a minimalist lifestyle and an affinity for festival culture.

Audiences and producers alike have realized that the festival crowd is a powerful force. Sponsors have recognized the potential value of being associated with a popular festival's brand and the benefits of mass

16. Jaguar luxury car in front of a tent at Shakti Fest, 2016 (photo by author).

exposure to crowds of potential consumers. Burning Man Project bans all corporate sponsors and logos, but Lightning in a Bottle and Wanderlust partner with corporate sponsors who align with their visions. At these festivals, participants are surrounded by vendors who promote festival fashion and various health foods and beverages. Companies promoting health-conscious lifestyle choices (including brands such as Kashi, Tulsi, and Brew Dr. Kombucha) are hosted at Wanderlust festivals, and Kashi cereal has even included advertisements for Wanderlust festivals on some of its products. The implication in this dialogical marketing strategy is that those who are health conscious are also interested in the spiritual exploration and wellness promised by the festival. One Kashi cereal box advertisement for Wanderlust reads:

Not All Who Wander Are Lost
 Sometimes it's the journey that matters most. It's a lesson we're reminded of from our friends Jeff Schuyler and Sean—the founders of Wanderlust. Like us, they started with a purpose-driven mission to create community around shared values of mindful living. They fantasized about an event rooted in fun, but full of underlying ideals. A place people could leave feeling better than when they came. And what was once the dream of three college

students in the 1980s has now blossomed into a series of can't-miss festivals, daytime events, and world-class yoga studios. But it's not all downward dogs and just-woke-up-from-savasana buzz. Wanderlust has become a central gathering point for all of us with like-minded values. And we created our GOLEAN foods to power the lifestyle they cultivate. Because while we're all incredible alone, we only get stronger when we join forces. It's a unity that radiates when things #GOTOGETHER.

Wanderlust embraces corporate sponsorships, but only from those corporations whose politics are on message. They have developed partnerships with, among many others, Adidas, Jeep, Subaru, and Toyota (they occasionally raffle off a Prius at festivals). They also support vendors who sell essential oils; Ayurvedic tinctures; spiritual, energetic, and microbusiness jewelry (such as Satya, HiChi, and Puravida, respectively); and of course a wide assortment of festival and yoga apparel, including yoga apparel made from organic cottons and recycled plastics (from famed brands like Spiritual Gangster). Lululemon sponsors their primary communal space, D'Om, where participants can congregate for coffee and tea, shopping, and crafting. The Lululemon products for sale include yoga mats, gear, and high-priced yoga apparel (a yoga bag for $98, yoga pants ranging from $98 to $118, a yoga bra for $48, and a hoodie wrap for $128).

The relationship different transformational festivals have to overt capitalism varies widely. Wanderlust is the friendliest to corporate sponsorships and, relatedly, is the most mainstream of the festivals; its marketing team targets the Sexy, Successful, Spiritual Woman (SSSW), a branch of the Female Lifestyle Empowerment Brand (FLEB).[13] Bhakti and Shakti Fests also collaborate with corporate sponsors, but only with small businesses in the fields of *bhakti,* yoga, Ayurveda, and nutrition. The producers of both festivals target the Lifestyles of Health and Sustainability (LOHAS) demographic, which consumes natural products that are ethically produced. As of 2008, LOHAS was a more than $290 billion market, and it comprised approximately 30 percent of the US consumer market; at the time, projections suggested that it would arc upward toward $490 billion in the next three years.[14] Wellness festivals, like Wanderlust, are growing at about 20 percent annually and comprise a significant part of the $3.7 trillion global wellness market.[15] The Do LaB produces Lightning in a Bottle (and a stage at Coachella) and works with a variety of corporate partners and vendors. LIB envisions itself as a pipeline from Coachella to Burning Man, a middle-ground festival that is more transformation oriented than the mainstream music festival party scene of Coachella but more accessible than the extremities of Burning Man. Bhakti and Shakti Fests, Wanderlusts, and Lightning in a Bottle also produce their own branded merchandise, including water bottles, yoga mats, T-shirts, hoodies, and hats.

There is mounting concern among those who preferred the "countercultural carnivalesque"[16] of early generations of festivals. Many reject the ways in which corporate sponsorship has subsumed the festivals' initial aims of cultural resistance and social critique. Lena Corner, a journalist and critic writing for the *Independent* (UK), explains, "The point was to offer an alternative reality. Now, it's a slick industry. The television rights have been sold, and with that have come price rises, mass audiences and corporate domination—the antithesis of everything they stood for."[17] This is particularly true of the genre of large-scale music festivals, which have overt corporate sponsorships and feature massive food and beverage corporations that provide fast-fare sustenance and libations. In contrast, at transformational festivals, food and beverage tends to be offered by small businesses, food trucks, and juice bars; corporate sponsorship is usually subtle and understated. But perhaps even more nefariously, the corporate sponsors at these festivals situate their products as moral imperatives, vital spiritual tools, and signifiers of the new conscious consumer.

In contrast, Burning Man Project is a nonprofit organization, and it is explicitly anticapitalist. Though the rule is often broken, the display of logos is discouraged on the playa (whether on RVs, cars, rental vehicles, tents, or clothing). Many Burners parody logos by altering them to convey alternative messages. More strictly enforced is the fact that nothing is for sale on the playa (save for coffee at Center Camp and ice at Artica and Ice Caps). Burning Man's principle of Decommodification reads, "In order to preserve the spirit of gifting, our community seeks to create social environments that are unmediated by commercial sponsorships, transactions, or advertising. We stand ready to protect our culture from such exploitation. We resist the substitution of consumption for participatory experience."[18] Still, despite Burning Man's critique of consumerism, Rachel Bowditch, performance artist and scholar, concludes that it "functions as an attempt to escape the commodity and the reigns of the global empire of exchange, yet inevitably fails."[19] While participants may wander the streets of Black Rock City enmeshed in a cashless gift economy, the cost of tickets and building elaborate buildings, art, and experiences in the lead-up to Burning Man reveals the ambiguity of the capitalism-free utopian ideal. Instead, Bowditch argues that Burning

Man is a "theater of consumption, a temporary enclave that represents a lively, expressive and creative model for consumption."[20]

The ambiguous relationship to consumption and capitalism has taken center stage at Burning Man in recent years. There is no money exchanged for goods or services on the playa, but "plug and play" camps are becoming more frequent.[21] There are rumors of elaborate sixteen-thousand-dollar-a-ticket dinners hosted by Silicon Valley elites, and private jets arrive and depart in style from the Black Rock City Airport.[22] There are also quiet side deals that contradict the anticapitalist spirit of Burning Man. For example, in 2017, on the night of the Man burn, I was with a group of friends looking for a place to settle with a good view. I spied my friend Pebbles's art car right up front, and all six of us raced over, climbed the stairs, and settled down among the comfy pillows happily, ecstatic in our luck. As I looked around for Pebbles, a camp leader informed us that he had rented Pebbles's art car for the night and it was reserved for his camp members only; we were unceremoniously asked to leave. Several years later, Pebbles begrudgingly sold a different art car for fifteen thousand dollars in order to make ends meet.[23] Off the playa, in the preliminary preparations for Burning Man, there are extensive and expensive collaborative projects that are well funded, artists hired to create art, costumes purchased, survival supplies secured, and so on. None of these people or festivals can be fully extricated from neoliberal capitalism, but they should not be reduced solely to it either, because their social entanglements, soteriological goals, and human expressions are infinitely more complex.

5

The Cathartic Freedom of Transformational Festivals

Neoliberal Escapes and Entrapments

In classical Greek thought, the "ascetic" that enabled one to make oneself into an ethical subject was an integral part—down to its very form—of the practice of a virtuous life, which was also the life of a "free" man in the full, positive and political sense of the word.

—Michel Foucault, *The History of Sexuality*

Freedom and equality can only be enjoyed in the intoxication of madness and . . . the greatest desire rises to its highest pitch when it approaches close to danger and relishes in voluptuous, sweet-anxious sensations.

—Johann Wolfgang von Goethe, *On Roman Carnival*

This chapter is written in the tension between the two different notions of freedom with which it begins, as expressed by Foucault and Goethe. Writing on ancient Greek asceticism, Foucault motions to ascetic practice as the means to attain ultimate freedom: the freedom from vices and from the constraints of desires enables the freedom of the ethical subject. In contrast, in his work on Roman carnival, Goethe writes that not only freedom but also equality occurs in the "intoxication of madness" of the carnival, when "desire rises to its highest pitch" in its nearness to "danger" and "sweet-anxious sensations." Transformational festivals attempt to straddle these two access points of freedom; they are both ascetic and ecstatic, focused on both self-cultivation and wild abandon, fostering both control and release.

I conclude with this chapter because, above all, the most common emotion expressed by my interlocutors was that of freedom; the majority understood transformational festivals as spaces of freedom.[1] However, freedom is one of the most overused and polyvalent terms in the United States, so it is the aim of this chapter to unravel the precise underlying meanings that participants were referring to in expressing their ecstasy at their newfound freedoms in festival environments. Chapters 3 and 4 revealed that festivals constitute a radical rupture from familiar geographies and the routines of the mundane. Festivals transported participants into uncharted territories wherein they could experiment with their boundaries of self and conventional conceptions of reality. Some experimented through drugs, sexuality, and interpersonal connections. Others experimented through rituals, ceremonies, and communion with nature. Others experimented through yoga, sound baths, meditation, diet, and ecstatic *kīrtan*. Whatever the modality, the continuity was in the theme of radical rupture of the conventional self. It was in the peeling away of the layers of social normativity that participants experienced that which they described as freedom.

In Paul Heelas's work on what he calls the "spiritualities of life," freedom is a key word, which operates "hand in glove" with the cultivation of the singularity of the subjective life, an expansive understanding of the holistic self that is crafted through the harmonization and balance of mind, body, and spirit. He explains:

> One cannot live one's unique life if one has to conform to an established order. By definition, established orders specify roles, duties, and obligations which apply to categories of people, not the person *per se*. To conform means being the same as at least some others. To live "out" one's unique life, to be "true to oneself", means finding the freedom, the autonomy, to be oneself, to become oneself, to "turn" into oneself, to live one's life to the full. Hence the importance attached to activities which enable participants to experience a sense of liberation. Not permanent liberation—for that is *very* rarely promised—but enough freedom from the conformist authority of established orders to enable participants to listen to their "inner voice" or "true self" to live their own lives; to exercise *self-responsibility*.[2]

These moments of liberation may arise on a yoga mat, in the joy of a barefoot hike, from the catharsis of a women's circle, in the exuberance felt while ecstatic dancing, drumming, or chanting, or in the stillness of meditation. Such moments interrupt the mundane stasis of daily living, the life spent in bondage to established systems, hierarchies, and habituated ways of living.

The affective experience of freedom is intimately intertwined with that of bondage in late-capitalist modernity. Festival participants represent a relatively privileged demographic group, one that is largely triumphant within the current neoliberal economic system and situated at the top of racialized hierarchies. But even these communities of elite whites cannot escape increasingly restrictive regulatory forms that stifle "the freedom of the expressive self to live 'out' its own life by exercising experimentation."[3] In their influential book *Empire,* Michael Hardt and Antonio Negri argue that global and supernational alliances have ushered in a new form of empire, one that places increasing demands on citizens.[4] Paul Heelas warns that the increasing industrialization and instrumentalization of human relationships is rendering humanity increasingly "antlike" and "boring" in its vacuous pursuit of capitalist utility. He writes, "The possibility of becoming institutionalized aside, one never values freedom so much as when one is in prison. Analogously, one never values 'human' aspects of life—time to ponder, the opportunity to *be* oneself, the possibility of living as a free spirit—so much as when one feels oneself *under* the systems of capitalistic or quasi-capitalistic modernity; the experiences of engulfment, of invasion; the sense of the doors clanking shut to exclude 'life.'"[5]

But within what systems are these social elites imprisoned to the extent that they experience such radical feelings of freedom once extricated from them? Furthermore, if spiritualities of life promise only a temporary experience of freedom, then is this why they appeal to those who benefit most from current social structures? Is this why those for whom the existing systems are particularly oppressive are more inclined to look for more permanent solutions for freedom, namely social justice or promises of eternal reward in heaven?

These are the central questions I will address in this chapter, but first I will articulate some of the different catalysts for feelings of freedom and reveal how that freedom can have deeply cathartic properties. Through the festival, participants are extracted from the confines of conventional social realities and transported into utopian environments. They find themselves suddenly encompassed by extraordinary natural beauty and confronted with the dissolution of both daily responsibilities and social norms of behavior. The vacuity of social conventions opens a space to perform the self, extracted from its customary confines. The emptiness opens a creative space for refashioning the self in dialogue with a new vision of utopia. The first effect of this absence-presence is most often articulated as feelings of freedom.

The latter sections of the chapter focus on the tension between ascetic and carnivalesque conceptions of freedom. I argue that the ascetic form tends to align with neoliberal notions of self-governance and the freedom of the ethical subject. In contrast, the carnivalesque is defined by the equalizing power of intoxication, what Durkheim termed "collective effervescence," but it is inherently temporary, a fleeting affective feeling of unity. Transformational festivals are "moments in and out of time," generating what Victor Turner calls *communitas,* the "recognition (in symbol if not always in language) of a generalized social bond that has ceased to be and has simultaneously yet to be fragmented into a multiplicity of structural ties."[6] In his seminal work, Turner shows that the values of communitas that sacralize spontaneity, immediacy, and collective existence are "strikingly present" in the discourse and practices of those who represent the counterculture (the "beat generation," "hippies," and those who "opt out").[7] As liminal spaces, transformational festivals create the experience of communitas across an ideological commons, building collective will to form new utopias.

Critics argue that neither the ascetical mode nor this temporary affective experience of communitas is directed outward at lasting social change. The ascetic form is inherently individualistic, and although it might produce social change if everyone had the means to do it, it does not address social structures that produce and reproduce inequalities. The carnivalesque addresses the inequalities by creating effervescent spaces of unity and equality, but it is temporary. One cannot remain in the heightened state of collective intoxication, whether taken figuratively or literally; the experience is too intense to sustain.

While the feeling of communitas is fleeting, it is transformative and builds closer identifications between the self and the other, feelings of human connection. By bringing diverse communities into connection—physical, emotional, and spiritual—there is an opportunity to bridge social boundaries. That bridging becomes a practice when repeated, which shapes patterns of behavior. In contrast, the practice of yoga, as it is replicated today, may in fact reinforce individualistic thinking and neoliberal notions of investing in the self as a project of self-regulation and self-governance. In its inward focus, it leads to an identification with the individual, not with society. Yoga practice was explicitly designed by religious virtuosi who were revolutionizing their bodies and minds in an attempt to gain special powers (*siddhis*). Contemporary yogic messaging depends on the expansive logic that social revolution is dependent on personal evolution, only multiplied.

Festivals provide all participants the affective experience of freedom from the enclosures of modernity. In the wild and affirming nexus of possibility, many feel limitless and empowered by the absence of social judgment. Exercising the freedom of time and personal space away from work and family responsibilities, participants are brought together in feelings of community, solidarity, and connectivity with like-minded people. This communitas generates feelings of freedom from isolation, loneliness, and depression. Many yogis interpret freedom both through the lenses of traditional yogic philosophies and through the context of psychological, therapeutic language. In the following sections, I discuss each of these freedoms in turn.

FREEDOM FROM THE ENCLOSURES OF MODERNITY

What do producers and participants feel that they need to escape from? Why is a new utopia necessary? Certainly, not everyone feels the malaise, the ennui, or the disenchantments of modernity. Many people are content with the system as it is, particularly those who benefit from it most. But social critics such as Henry David Thoreau, Karl Marx, and Franz Kafka have been sounding the bells of alarm for centuries, arguing that modern industrial capitalist modes of production are not the panacea that many presume them to be. They warn of a grave, unforeseen danger that threatens all life and has plunged humanity into a state of what anthropologist Anna Tsing has more recently termed precarity: the condition of living in an unstable world shaped by vulnerability and indeterminacy.[8] Every religious cosmology needs a crisis to which it offers a solution.[9] For SBNR communities, it is this precarity, this crisis of modernity (imbued with neoliberal capitalism, environmental catastrophe, and the fragmentation of the commons), to which it offers its utopian vision as a solution.

In 1854, contemplating life, spirituality, and society in solitude on the banks of Walden Pond, Thoreau penned the following famous lines:

> I sometimes wonder that we can be so frivolous, I may almost say, as to attend to the gross but somewhat foreign form of servitude called Negro Slavery; there are so many keen and subtle masters that enslave both North and South. It is hard to have a Southern overseer; it is worse to have a Northern one; but worst of all when you are the slave-driver of yourself. . . . Public

opinion is a weak tyrant compared with our own private opinion. What a man thinks of himself, that it is which determines, or rather indicates, his fate. . . . *The mass of men lead lives of quiet desperation.*[10]

Thoreau was an abolitionist, and this passage reflects his critique of human enslavement. But he also uses the notion of slavery to reveal the enslaving systems of capitalism, industrialization, and above all the way in which one becomes "the slave and prisoner of his own opinion of himself." Thoreau imagined an alternate vision of the purposeful individual, a human being who was self-emancipated and therefore powerful, immortal, and divine. For him, this is the true nature of the human condition, but we do not recognize it because we are ensnared within multiple forms of bondage. These multiple registers of enslavement—physical, economic, and psychological—are what reduce humanity to "lives of quiet desperation."

There are many other theorists who have similarly warned of the potential for mental enslavement outside of overt systems of human bondage. Feuerbach and Nietzsche critiqued religion as an inhibitor of human potential. Marx and scholars in his legacy, including the neo-Marxists of the Frankfurt School, critiqued industrialization and capitalism as producing modern forms of alienation.[11] Though their solutions differ, the notion that individuals are stifled, exploited, and bound within economic and psychological structures that limit their potential for greatness resonates all the same. Among the postmodernists, from Walter Benjamin to Jean Baudrillard, there has been an articulated subterranean fear that modernity has ushered in an age of mechanical reproduction in which life itself becomes a copy, an imitation, a mere simulation.[12] Broadly speaking, postmodern thinking has challenged the existence of any fixed center that can be experienced. It is an infinite regress wherein each signifier conjures another signifier and there is no origin point to rest easy upon. Such theories question reality itself; they contend that that which is presumed to be real is in actuality the result of perception, a perception shaped by socially conditioned responses.

One might argue that these are lofty theoretical ideas that have little impact in the everyday lives of people. But these notions lend easily to the assortment of media representations that have directed popular attention to nefarious forces that are writing the script behind the scenes, programming human perception as a means to control. At the transformational festivals I studied, such theories were proliferate, but the identity of the "they" that controlled and limited the dystopian society varied. It was alternately crafted as government, politicians, schools, corporations, marketing, Western medicine, or media. Generally, proponents referred to multifaceted modes of indoctrination by which modern subjects are influenced by systems beyond their control. Conspiracy theories abounded, substantiated by a distrust in "the establishment" inherited from the 1960s counterculture and a New Age propensity toward conspiratorial thinking.[13] Among contemporary yogis, these theories were also compounded by modern renditions of Advaita Vedanta, particularly the philosophical contention that the world is *māyā* (illusion) and the ultimate goal is to break free from that deception. In popular (mis)understanding, the forces behind *māyā* become agentive and there is a notion that "they" are controlling and limiting humans without our knowledge and that our goal must be to shake ourselves awake, recognize systems of control and limitation, and break free from their shackles. In the ashes of that limiting world, a utopian society can be erected wherein humans will be encouraged to be expressive, limitless, powerful, and creative.

In popular culture, these ideas are ubiquitous, particularly in science fiction; one might think, for example, of the plots of classics like *1984, Brave New World, The Fountainhead,* or even *The Hunger Games*.[14] In the first *Matrix* film, the main character, Neo, hides his computer disks in a copy of Jean Baudrillard's seminal book on the postmodern concepts of hyperreality and simulation, *Simulacra and Simulation*. He follows a white rabbit (a reference to the surreal world that Alice experiences in Wonderland) and eventually is faced with a choice between waking up and seeing the world as it really is or staying asleep and enjoying the simulation of the Matrix. When Neo asks Morpheus, "What is the Matrix?" Morpheus responds:

> *Morpheus:* It is the world that has been pulled over your eyes to blind you from the truth.
>
> *Neo:* What truth?
>
> *Morpheus:* That you are a slave, Neo. Like everyone else, Neo, you were born into bondage, born into a prison that you cannot smell, or taste, or touch. A prison for your mind.[15]

In the film, the Matrix can be read as a thinly veiled critique of capitalism wherein humans are used like batteries for their productive value. The *Matrix* trilogy has made more than half a billion dollars ($594.2 million total franchise gross domestic) in the United States. Obviously, audiences resonated with the notion that our lives are mechanized for the benefit of invisible, malicious forces—the belief that the world is somehow less real than we believe and that if only we could wake up, we would see the system manipulating us and find the means to destroy it. In *The Matrix,* no one quite knew the cause of the dissatisfaction, the malaise, the ennui, the anger, but everyone knew that something wasn't right. The protagonists nurtured a dream that life could be different and somehow more fulfilling, that there must be a way to live outside the Matrix that would make one feel more alive, more authentic—and less like a Duracell battery.

Similarly, the producers of transformational festivals intend to unveil and reject the false narratives of smallness and subordination that, they argue, confine us. The producers of LIB provide an experiential sensorium through talks, workshops, and platforms that catalyze ecstatic and wondrous experiences, wherein one of the primary messages is freedom and liberation. In this view, part of the spiritual work of the transformational festival is to identify that mythology, locate its source, deconstruct it, and supplant it with a new vision of limitlessness, power, creativity, and freedom. When I asked Lia, a young midtwenties woman at Lightning in a Bottle wearing feather earrings and a headwrap, the simple question "How is your day so far?" she responded with, "Good. [*Sighs.*] It's like being Alice down the rabbit hole. . . . It's not like your average day in reality. . . . Everything is set up in a way that everything is actually an experience. . . . LIB is a blend of intellectual growth and experiential growth."[16]

One of the primary messages that emerged from LIB's Temple of Consciousness in 2016 was a multifaceted approach to unlearning false programming and the idea that we have been conditioned to believe that we are small when in fact we are powerful. Crystal Dawn, one of the producers of the Temple of Consciousness, spoke in these terms about her vision:

> [I wanted to] lift my spirit, to break out, to be free, to feel strong and powerful—the feelings that I knew inside of me that I had, everything that I knew inside of me that I had, that somehow I couldn't quite get to. I couldn't quite land. I'd find myself vacillating in and out, in and out. I'd have these moments, often at events like this, where I would feel my spirit soaring, and I would feel myself so huge, and then all of a sudden I would get back to the "real" world, and all of a sudden I would feel myself like *uuughh,* and then before I knew it I would be suicidal, wanting to leave the planet. . . . So I'm trying to figure out: Why am I getting sucked down? Whose ideas are sucking me down? Because they're not mine. They're not my ideas. Because I remember when I was a little girl. When I was a little girl, I was *powerful.* I was *a force.* Do you remember when you were little? Do you remember it? Can you remember that far back, before you watched TV, before you got

17. Dystopian tattoo on the back of a yogi at Bhakti Fest, 2013 (photo by author).

indoctrinated with the message that they blasted into you? Do you remember who you were? Do you? Did you remember this weekend? [*Pauses for cheers.*] A little bit? Come on. [*Pauses.*] *Live it! Live it!* . . . In all my years of trying to elevate my soul and trying to break out of the bullshit that I could never get out of, I couldn't figure it out. . . . We are born into a world that has shrunk us so small that we have forgotten who we are. We have completely forgotten. In my research for how I wanted the Temple [of Consciousness] to go this year, and the journey I wanted to take you on . . . [my research] was unraveling us from the coil of the code that they have drilled into our heads from the time when we were little children. . . . You must do your own research. You must unravel it for yourself. You must begin to unravel it. . . . We know everything inside of us, that we are super, *super* powerful—powerful beyond belief, but we're locked in a matrix that doesn't tell us we're powerful and that isn't good for us. . . . I like the crazy people. I talk to homeless people. I talk to everyone, and I get major downloads from those people, because those are the people that already know that the matrix doesn't work—so they are already outside of the matrix.[17]

The conspiracy theories that were supported by the Temple of Consciousness in 2016 created tension within the LIB community and among their leadership team. Particularly controversial was the heavily attended presentation by David "Avocado" Wolfe, one of the leading flat-Earth theorists at the Temple of Consciousness.[18] Still, there is broad consensus that part of the "inner work" of the transformational festival is to "unravel" false narratives that suppress and confine the individual spirit. To experience a radical rebirth, to create a new utopia, participants must recognize their dystopian environs and locate the oppressive narratives within which they are bound (see figure 17). The experience of shedding these narratives can generate a lightness of being that participants articulate as freedom.

FREEDOM FROM JUDGMENT

For marginalized groups (people of color, gays, queers, and to a lesser extent, women), transformational festivals provide a radical freedom from everyday structures of oppression. Individuals who are accustomed to societal surveillance, racism, and judgment can find the freedom of invisibility in the sea of creative expression and inclusivity of the festival environment. (Note, this is more true of some festivals than others.) At Burning Man in 2018, Julius Anderson, a founder of the People of Color camp, spoke at Center Stage. He explained that, though a person of color, he was often overlooked on the playa because people with horns or rainbow glitter captured more attention. His skin pigmentation became less of an object of white gaze because there were simply so many other unusual people for that gaze to be directed toward. In his words, "I felt invisible here.... In the outside world, I felt a certain kind of surveillance and a sense of self-surveillance.... Here, the dust erases all of us.... I felt a sense of sadness in the realization of the pressure I'd been living under for so long [in the default world]."[19]

Anderson established the POC camp in 2013 to create a space for catharsis to help nonwhites navigate these territories. He explained, "The racism is not here. It's the racism you feel outside that you end up processing here."[20] The sudden freedom from judgment and racism is liberating, but the lightness of being that percolates in its absence reveals the gravity of daily encounters of oppression and entrapment in the default world. For Anderson, creating the POC camp was a vital part of his gift to help his fellow Burners of color to find a place of solidarity and community to process this revelatory experience of freedom from racism.

I interviewed Xavier during a hot and dusty afternoon in the shelter of Center Camp at Burning Man. Xavier, a Puerto Rican man in his midthirties, sat in the shade with his boyfriend, the two trading long sips from their Camelback. We talked about what makes Burning Man feel different, reflecting on our exuberant feelings of freedom and possibility that seemed to percolate right under the surface of daily activity during Burning Man:

> *Xavier:* Yes. That's exactly why I came. And I feel free! I mean, I was telling him [his boyfriend]. I was riding my bike today, and I was telling him, "I don't know why, but I feel free *just to be*—*just to be*—that's it. I'm not expecting anything from anyone. *Just to be.*" You know? And living in that.
>
> *Amanda:* Yeah. There is something in the—I feel lighter. It seems silly to say, but—
>
> *Xavier:* It's true! It's true! And you know what I told him, I said, "Dan, the way that we feel today and yesterday—when we leave here, we can't forget that feeling!"[21]

This feeling of freedom means different things to different people. For Xavier, a gay Puerto Rican man, it was very important to feel like he was in a unique space of nonjudgment and acceptance, free "just to be" whomever and however he wanted to be.

Becka framed her experience at her first Burning Man as an empowering feeling of being a self-reliant, independent woman without the need for the protection or support of a male partner. She explained,

> [Burning Man] showed me how much strength and courage I 'DO' have and it meant everything! I felt so much personal power for the first time in my life! I feel like, especially as women, we're kind of conditioned to feel like we need a masculine presence to . . . excel or survive, or god forbid, find happiness in this world?! And that's simply not true. . . . I remember . . . feeling that moment of peace and clarity and happiness, but in a way that was only connected to me. No one else. It was an overwhelming feeling of 'being free'![22]

This temporary freedom from judgment may disproportionately impact nondominant populations, but it can be seen as impacting all of humanity if one subscribes to one of the aforementioned critiques of the various oppressive systems in which we are all enmeshed. During our interview at LIB, Lia spoke emotionally about how these festivals were trying to sustain something that the external, default world attempts to extinguish. She framed the modern world as comprised of "evil" and "outdated systems" that attempt to "slaughter" and prevent humanity from "evolving" into "higher states of consciousness." Her strongly worded phrasing speaks volumes:

> There seems to be a really rebellious nature to the festival—trying to keep something alive that the rest of the world might be trying to slaughter in a way—not purposely trying to slaughter, but there's a sense of trying to preserve something. . . . A lot of the speakers talk about how we're so limited by what we're being told, and part of our spiritual ascension of humanity is evolving into these higher states of consciousness. So the governments, the systems that we're believing, fighting over what religion is right, and what government, what politician is right, is just like this outdated system that doesn't serve a function anymore, and there's so much evil in the world, and so much good at the same time. And there should be enough for everybody. So like, it's sustainability, and it's health. . . . I feel like there's a lot of trying to dissolve the myth.[23]

In such a view, systems of government, politics, and religion are all social constructs that create divisiveness. To this list, many participants would add race, gender, and class as further social divisions that detract from humanity's ability to come together in unity. There is a tension in these transformational festivals wherein unique identities are both supported and celebrated, but social differences are also minimized in favor of building an ideological commons. The risk in the latter is that these predominantly able-bodied, economically comfortable, white communities frequently perpetuate pablum maxims like "We are all one" and the famed "I don't see color," both of which obfuscate the lived realities of oppression and compound feelings of erasure that are often experienced by marginalized groups.[24]

FREEDOM FROM RESPONSIBILITIES

There is no more quintessentially American value than the ideal of freedom. But if freedom is sewn into the fabric of America, then why are so many Americans escaping to the desert, to ancient and desolate lakebeds, to enchanted forests, and to a variety of other faraway, idyllic locations in an effort to experience freedom? Flight from bondage (real or perceived) is a privilege. Many people desire freedom, but only some have the means to actualize it. The demographic that attends transformational festivals largely represents this fact: they are mostly white, upper-class, urban professionals. But this also presents an interesting irony. These are the people who are dominant in the system, those who have been included within the social contract since the inception of the nation.[25] As members of the demographic possessing the highest social capital, these should be the Americans most likely to experience freedom in their daily lives.

But even these privileged classes are searching for an experience of freedom denied to them. Most are confined by the responsibilities of work and family, the mundanity of waiting at traffic lights and in grocery store lines, and the capitalist demand to make money to sustain lifestyles that require more money. At Wanderlust, many of my interviewees viewed the festival as a spiritual reprieve replete with opportunities to experience nature and escape from the burdens of daily living. There were also disproportionate numbers of single, professional women who had traveled to the festivals alone as a means to relax and recalibrate from their taxing work schedules. Wanderlust festivals in particular were largely retreats where professional women could challenge themselves physically, learn yogic techniques and philosophies, relax in arrestingly beautiful natural settings, and celebrate community and life with outstanding musical performances, healthy and delicious foods, and a bit of wine or kombucha.

Many of the women I interacted with were professionals who were taking a reprieve from their busy schedules, taking "time out" for themselves to "center" and "reset." Hailey was a successful finance executive who worked in the main corporate office of a national health-care firm in Melbourne. As she was lounging on the grass at Wanderlust Sunshine Coast in Australia, I asked her about whether her professional life was stressful. She replied:

> It [my job] *can* be [stressful] if I let it. Yeah. Absolutely. Yeah. And I was just thinking, actually, coming from Monday, Tuesday, Wednesday at work and

yesterday at work to here today—the difference in the energy just alone is just phenomenal. The thankful people—people just helping each other up and saying "thank you" to strangers and having conversations with perfect strangers that are very, very kind people is completely, is huge in my face [very apparent] just sitting here this afternoon. Coming from my work, it's sometimes just dog eat dog. To see this kind of kindness is just beautiful. Yeah. It is real.[26]

After what she called "a really hard start to the week," Hailey had decided on a whim to fly from Melbourne to the Sunshine Coast for Wanderlust. She spent the first day lounging, talking to people, and enjoying the food and music; the next day she had a full schedule of yoga planned.

Similarly, Deirdre had abruptly fled to Wanderlust Mont Tremblant in Quebec after her most recent job as a production assistant in the fast-paced film industry. She described her last six to seven weeks on location as extraordinarily hectic and demanding. We met while eating at adjacent tables, both alone. We decided to eat together, and over dinner she related to me how the job had completely exhausted her mental, physical, and emotional capacity. After the meal she was off to the Wanderlust-sponsored nighttime wine and sailing cruise, and she was delighted to be on her own adventure before her next project started. At Wanderlust Oahu, I struck up a conversation with Catherine, a single woman who was sitting at the bar with a drink, listening to the music. She was alone and seemed to be having a good time. She told me that she was an administrative assistant and a photographer and held a very stressful job in Los Angeles. She was single and routinely decided to treat herself with adventurous trips whenever she had a break from work. Toward the end of the festival, we exchanged Instagram handles; in the time since we met in 2014, she has posted hundreds of images from yoga adventures around the world.

The outstanding number of professional women who seek solace in daily yoga practice and in the escapism of yogic retreats may suggest that there are underrecognized pressures unique to professional women in the contemporary workplace. It is significant that women in large numbers feel exhausted and entrapped within the professional workplace and that they seek out yoga and transformational festivals in hopes of restoring themselves. They attend these festivals, often alone, to find themselves, recalibrate and return to their bodies, remind themselves to be healthy, recenter their values, and find joy and wonder and freedom despite their professional obligations (see figure 18).

18. Yoga retreat, Wanderlust, Mount Tremblant, 2018 (photo by Chris Eckhart, copyright Wanderlust).

FREEDOM FROM ISOLATION

Some festival participants I spoke with recounted how their modern lives are plagued by feelings of isolation. It is fascinating that this was the case even among the successful participants with high degrees of social capital. Bacchus, a business owner and entrepreneur, explained, "I've lived in this neighborhood [his Burning Man neighborhood] for *one day,* and I have more meaningful relationships with everyone in this neighborhood than I have in my neighborhood in LA where I've been [for nine years], or I know New Yorkers, and they actually *have* neighborhoods, and they say the same thing!"[27] At LIB, Lia, a professional actor and dancer, explained,

> You definitely feel a sense of community [at LIB]. You feel like you have that village, that tribe feeling. So it just feels so good. . . . [It] is just, like, a very cozy feeling. It's a sense of something bigger than yourself, some sort of tradition. . . . We're so isolated in the way cities are set up now. Everyone has their unit. We're so isolated, and then everyone comes together for an event or a concert, to go to work, and we're in a building with other people, but ultimately we're pretty isolated—like *actual* living. Go to the store, pick your food, take it home. [LIB is] a return to how things might have been before cars and technology, phones. It's like a return to that. . . . It's kind of like a utopia.[28]

Detached from the isolating, compartmentalization of modern life in urban environments, festivals create opportunities for visceral experiences of community.

Participants at each of the festivals in this study used the term *community* incessantly to describe the utopias they were building. Those focused on yoga spoke in broad terms about the community of yoga practitioners as a whole. At the start of one of his breathwork workshops at Shakti Fest, Jeremiah Silver explained how everyone present is a part of a family, and when we see each other with our yoga mats strapped to our backs, even in the airport, "we know we are of the same tribe."[29] Invited speakers and participants alike iterated frequently the concept that there is a consciousness evolution happening on the planet and that all who were present were cocreators of a new utopic reality.

The opportunity for real, affective, human connection is part of the radical freedom of the festival space. Zane, a leader of a Burning Man theme camp, explained it this way: "About 50 percent of people go to parties to meet people and *connect*. That is what people are doing at Burning Man. Connecting. And that is what the festival is about, because in the default world we go on autopilot and it is difficult to build moments of connection and freedom—radical freedom. That's what Burning Man boils down to."[30]

The break from isolation and the relocation into wild and effervescent spaces creates opportunities to connect intimately with oneself and others. The intensity of the festival and participants' dislocation from social ties and boundaries enables them to connect at a level of intimacy that they do not often experience in their daily lives. One witnesses this in the commonplace occurrences of intimate conversations with strangers, long hugs, snuggling, cuddle puddles, and in some cases increased sexual affection. Moments of intense connection are highly valued in these communities, and they can translate into deep and lasting friendships or poignant and memorable, yet ultimately ephemeral, intimacies.

Many of these festivals create lasting communities beyond the temporal confines of the actual events—for example, the Burning Man Regional Network, Burners without Borders, and Wanderlust yoga studios. But some participants open themselves up so radically that they don't want to entertain those relationships in the default world. Dusty, a builder at Burning Man who spends approximately six weeks each year on the playa, explained,

> I know quite a few people out here. We come out and meet. I don't know what they do in real life. . . . I don't want them to know what I do. . . . I see

some people once in a while [in the default world], but I don't seek them out.... This is just the moment in time. You have to remember those moments. You have to enjoy the person while it is [while Burning Man is happening].... What I do is, when I meet people here, I enjoy them for the moment. I know that I will probably never see them again, so I have to be with them and reveal to them the person I am and talk to them—to hold that and love them as my friend and then go from there. That's it. That was it. I really love you, and I think you're great. I hope you have a great life.[31]

YOGIC FREEDOM, SPIRITUALITY, AND NEOLIBERALISM

The sense of freedom expressed heretofore has been an ephemeral ideal of freedom. It is the temporary escape from bondage, whether in the spontaneous wonder of a sunset bike ride, the temporary release from work and family responsibilities, or the immediacy of human connections supported by the ethos of the festival. But for some, these temporary releases uncover a taste for a completely alternative way of living in the world, a taste so tantalizing that participants recalibrate their lives to more closely mirror the utopian ideal of ultimate freedom. The practice of yoga has long been used as a practical method for attaining freedom that operates within a variety of systematized philosophical frames. In his translation of Patañjali's *Yoga Sūtras*, Edwin Bryant explains, "In early Sanskrit texts Yoga referred to a form of rigorous discipline and concentration for attaining the direct perception of the *ātman* [essential self] and gaining liberation that was appropriated and tailored by different traditions according to their metaphysical understanding of the self, rather than a distinct school."[32] Similarly, in the modern context, postural yoga has been adopted as a practical method that has been "appropriated and tailored" to conform to the cosmological understandings of various metaphysical traditions. In the yogic sense, freedom is less of a fleeting experience and more of a long-term goal of spiritual liberation.

Mark Bentley, one of the leaders of Wanderlust, thought about yoga practice as fulfilling both soteriological goals and a need for community engagement, calling it a new form of "secular church." During a well-attended Wanderlust Speakeasy at Wanderlust Squaw Valley in 2014, he explained,

> We do live in a world where some of the other classic touch points for community, such as churches and other things like that, are lower in attendance. And I think in a lot of ways yoga is filling that need for a secular church, if you will, for a certain kind of person. And it brings people together,

and it also serves a spiritual purpose for many. So yeah, I see it continuing to go up, and . . . it's just our goal to be a part of that. We don't see ourselves necessarily as one of the people contributing to that trend, but we're also in the process of reflecting an existing societal trend, and we're really just trying to foster it along.[33]

Bentley recognizes that Wanderlust is tapping into a growing market. Many people are becoming increasingly disenchanted by religion, and he is correct in noting the decline in liberal Protestant and even "mainline" Protestant churches.[34] Many millennials were not raised within religious communities as children; they are the most common age group to choose "none" on surveys that question their religious affiliation.[35] These populations comprise the increasing numbers of religiously disengaged people who are nevertheless looking for opportunities to feel supported within a like-minded community, to explore and develop the spiritual self, and to connect with a sense of something larger than themselves.

Yogic spaces iterate the importance of community frequently, and many yogis form communities through the practice of yoga. But the practice is ultimately about the individual's relationship with her own body, mind, and spirit. Yoga teachers active in this environment use language that reflects this mission. They affirm the inner beauty of their students and congratulate them for taking this time to focus on themselves. They encourage students to invest in themselves and their spiritual journeys, and they teach pragmatic tools to help participants minimize and discard the effects of egoism, judgment, and self-criticism and instead foster equanimity, compassion, love, and the recognition of the essence of self (spirit, soul, energy) within oneself and others. These are yogic goals recoded in the language of spirituality, and yoga teachers situate them as a process of self-cultivation determined by individual choices—and as such they hold easy resonance with neoliberal ideals of the self and agency.

Wanderlust is perhaps best characterized as an enchanted secular worldview (a "secular church") that coalesces easily with neoliberal notions of self-care. What follows are just a few samples of the therapeutic language used by the most popular yoga instructors at Wanderlust festivals:

Helena Blake (Wanderlust Squaw Valley, 2014)
   You are not your stories, or these bodies. You are not the roles you play. You are not mother or father, husband or wife, not son or daughter, not lover or artist, perpetrator or drunk, you're none of these things. Although all of them are an aspect of your experience, they do not define, but they add

a unique and interesting color to your palette of being. What we are is light and essence. What we are is magnificence and magic. What we are is love. Be that love. Be that love. . . . So we practice *āsana* to release the tension, so that we can sit, so that we can remember who we are and allow for that authentic self to resonate through us, so that that's the essence that speaks and creates, illuminates. We practice *āsana* so we can come home. Close your eyes and remember who you are. . . . It's real. And life is *here*. And it is *magnificent*. And it is *yours*. Let go completely of anything you're carrying that's not love. Surrender into the earth loss and heartbreak. Surrender disappointment and disillusionment. May all of these energies be transformed. Let everything go. And rest.[36]

Katie Kurtz (Wanderlust Oahu, 2014)
Now we're in the new moon time, and it's the time of new beginnings. *So let's all really contemplate and reflect on what it is that you are calling into your life right now.* The way of newness, the way of origins. *What old form needs to dissolve so that a new one can be born?*[37]

DJ Akash (Wanderlust Squaw Valley, 2014)
So yoga works from the outside in. *If you think about a piece of bamboo that had a lot of crusty dirt on the inside, right. Imagine a hollow tube of bamboo, and inside it's kind of dirty. So we can hit the bamboo from the outside. That's kind of how* āsana *is. When we twist, we bend, we fold, we jump up and down, we do lots of* vinyāsas, *and it shakes the bamboo, and then the dirt becomes loose and starts to fall out.* So *āsana* is an amazing tool. Sound vibration, *mantra*, works from the inside. It's like *prānāyāma, mantra,* those are the more subtle practices that we have in our lineage of yoga that can clear the tube from the inside out. . . . *It purifies our thoughts, purifies our hearts, and it has this way of dissolving self-doubt, fear, judgment. All these things that crowd and cover the true nature of who we really are.* And when that starts to dissolve, then we reveal the diamond, the diamond in the lotus, the diamond quality of our highest self. Like our true beauty, our true deepest compassion for other beings, our most incredible joy, our brilliance gets revealed.[38]

Zachary Ellis (Wanderlust Squaw Valley, 2014)
Let's just take a moment to be grateful, grateful to be here in this space with all of this *prāna* surrounding us, and friends, and like-minded individuals. Just soak in this presence of all of this beauty that is all around us right now. The fascinating thing that is really helpful to remember is that *whatever you are experiencing in terms of that beauty is actually just a reflection of you. The beauty is you.* And when we are in a nice environment, we are reminded of what is in us already.[39]

Although these yoga instructors have different rhetorical styles, there is remarkable consistency in their messages.[40] In these excerpts, there is the sense that one's true self—which is understood as love, the highest self, or beauty—is encumbered or clouded by negative emotions, habits, addictions, mental patterns, self-doubt, fear, judgment, and ego. The goal of the yoga practice is to stop, to take the time to be grateful and witness beauty in a natural environment, to cultivate awareness to identify these negative patterns, and to choose to release them.

In the *Yoga Sūtras,* the ideal self is the self that is unencumbered by egoism, judgment, emotions, attachments, ignorance, aversion, and delusion. In Samkhya, the philosophical system that codifies the experiential practice of yoga, the essence of self is *puruṣa,* the eternal and internal consciousness. Ultimate freedom occurs when one isolates pure consciousness from its embroilment with the internal workings of the mind as well as the external senses of the body: "Yoga claims to provide a system by which the practitioner can directly realize his or her *puruṣa,* the soul or innermost conscious self, through mental practices."[41] Freedom, ultimate freedom, is the extrication of the internal essence of self (*puruṣa* [consciousness]) from the bondage of ignorance and attachments that binds it to *prakṛti* (matter). Most yogis in these fields articulate this message as letting go of that which does not serve the higher purpose, as sculpting the self, as chiseling away negative thoughts, patterns, emotions, and actions to reveal pure consciousness.

Wanderlust supports this philosophy by encouraging participants to "find their true north" through the Wanderlust experience. Bhakti and Shakti Fests call participants to "Be in the *Bhav,*" meaning that one should align one's inner self with the spirit of the divine. LIB encourages participants to uncover social programming and to find their inner power. Burning Man calls for Immediacy in its "10 Principles," describing it as "the most important touchstone of value in our culture," wherein *"we seek to overcome barriers that stand between us and a recognition of our inner selves,* the reality of those around us, participation in society, and contact with a natural world exceeding human powers."[42] In each of these cultural maxims, there is an aim to recognize and recalibrate the essence of self. There is also the unstated but present idea that this goal has not yet been fully accomplished.

There is an important analytical resonance with neoliberal constructions of the self and agency that is reflected in the ways in which the self is positioned in these discourses. The neoliberal subject is an autonomous self that is, as Ilana Gershon summarizes, "always faced with one's self as a project that must be consciously steered through various possible alliances and obstacles. This is a self that is produced through an engagement with a market, that is, neoliberal markets require participants to be reflexive managers of their abilities and alliances."[43] The self described as such is incomplete as it is. In fact, this is a defining feature of what Paul Heelas terms "spiritualities of life," wherein SBNR practitioners are advised to "be yourself, only better, as perfect as possible: when the strong tendency, in inner-life circles, is for the search for the 'better' to occur within the activities which emphasize expressivist-cum-human values."[44]

At Shakti Fest in 2015, the famed yoga teacher Kailash explained the way in which this kind of thinking can put pressure on participants in the yoga community:

> In the yoga community, ... it is *sooo loving*. ... We walk around and we are all just living for our purpose, and it's just like everything is so flowy and nice and sweet. ... I have been in this community for twenty-two years now. .... So from that we've seen that there are amazing, positive things that can happen in this community, but then the negative side is that we go on this fix of like, "I need to fix it," "I need to fix it," "I'm not this and that," "I need to be more light," "I need to be more this," "I need to be more that." So I am here to tell us all, including myself, that we have everything we need right here, right in front of us.[45]

She is issuing a corrective because in yogic fields the focus on self-cultivation has produced a nearly unattainable image of spiritual and bodily perfection that reveals the extent to which yoga has become one more facet in the ensnarement of the neoliberal subject.

The yoga worlds of transformational festival environments are filled with beautiful people—striking, physically beautiful people—who are invested in expressing themselves as living their bliss. They present as filled with joyful, exuberant beauty—and the majority of them are scantily clad, revealing toned, active, able, yogic bodies. Part of the reason behind this is structural—if you live an active lifestyle, subsist on green juice smoothies and kale salads, practice yoga and meditation, and refrain from detrimental substances, the bodily results are likely to be pretty good. But, in addition to this embodiment of structural privilege, there is an underlying cultural premise that spiritual development is revealed through outer beauty and wellness. Acne, fat, bloodshot eyes, sties, warts, split ends, dandruff, eczema, allergies, and so on become messages from the body signifying not only a physical sickness but a soul sickness. Thus, the drive to perfect the inner self becomes deeply intertwined with the drive to perfect the outer self. Furthermore, one might imagine that people born with bodies that society considers beautiful may be more attracted to yoga as a practice that allows them to be conspicuous about their unearned privilege while simultaneously disavowing that privilege.[46]

At Wanderlust, participants better themselves by finding their "true north," uncovering their spirit, shedding that which does not serve, developing sustainability, and transforming themselves through yoga, *prāṇāyāma, mantra* recitation, healthy eating, and peak experiences. Wanderlust festival organizers and the yoga instructors they hire become a team of experts ready to sell products, courses, information, and experiences that will help students gain perfected selves. Ilana Gershon notes that "the neoliberal perspective creates a new status for the expert—the expert becomes someone with the unique reflexive role of explaining to other autonomous entities how to manage themselves more successfully."[47] Much of Wanderlust's programming and marketing *is* teaching participants how to manage themselves more successfully by making healthier and more sustainable purchases, designating time for self-care, and regulating reactivity, emotions, and ego.

The irony is that these participants, overcome with feelings of material entrapment in neoliberal social and economic systems, take flight to the spiritualities of festival in search of reprieve. There, they experience temporary freedom, but the very endeavor of flight and the pursuit of perfecting the self is recaptured by the logic of neoliberalism. They are brought into yet another market engaging in techniques of self-perfection. The neoliberal subject engages economically in the market in an endless pursuit of self-care that, as Foucault argues, is ultimately about governmental control of the self-disciplining and self-regulating subject.[48] Self-care, like other aspects of leisure, health, and fitness, is dependent on class and race privilege and defined by structural inequities.

Wendy Brown argues convincingly that this emphasis on self-care negatively impacts the strength of the commons: "Citizenship, reduced to self-care, is divested of any orientation toward the common, thereby undermining an already weak investment in *active citizenry* and an already thin concept of a *public good* from a liberal democratic table of values."[49] Spirituality, in general, is heavily invested in the business of self-care; therapies abound that help presumed autonomous individuals navigate the stresses and challenges of daily life. As the self becomes a "valuable asset"[50] that must be cultivated and maintained through self-care, the throngs of yoga instructors and the hundreds of other entrepreneurs in the markets of spirituality not only benefit from but also reinforce the ideals of neoliberalism. When combined with the drive of capitalism, the market cultivates feelings of dissatisfaction with the self *as it is,* which then demands that subjects seek out means to perfect the self and become better citizens (and consumers).

BUILDING THE COMMONS THROUGH COMMUNITAS

In contrast, Goethe's interpretation of the Roman carnival, cited at the beginning of this chapter, suggests that both freedom and equality stem from the collective emotions expressed through the festival—the "intoxication," the "danger," and the "sweet-anxious sensations." Instead of the individual pursuits of the neoliberal yogi, the Dionysian, bacchanalian festival collective comes together to share in communitas, an affective experience of unity that flattens social hierarchies and draws society together. Collective revelry in the rapturous emotions of *kīrtan*, the communal fluidity of a sunrise dance party, a cuddle puddle in the chill space, the sweating crews passing drills and hoisting lumber during build week and strike, the collectively expressed wonder during ecstatic dance, or awe in response to massive art or fire explosions—these are the experiences of communitas that bring together a commons. It is not only the intoxicated moments that create freedom and equality; these emotions are also felt in the shared experiences of common humanity.

On the last night of Burning Man, it is in the reverential silence of death and loss that the community binds together as a shared commons. Unlike any other event at Burning Man, the Temple burn is absolutely silent. Even the art cars are silenced. Nearly the entire population of Black Rock City surrounds the Temple, creating a wide circle of tens of thousands of seated people. In 2016, as the first flames began to lick the sides of the Temple, people started shushing those who were talking in the crowd. Everyone then stood in silence and watched as the flames grew fiercer and, in time, encompassed the Temple (see figure 19). Fire whirls composed of flame and ash shot from the blaze, looking like flaming tornados sucked into the dark night. Some people began weeping in the striking silence. The woman next to me had tears rolling down her face. A voice called out, "I am glad to be alive!" and those surrounding him cheered. Voices began to call out: "We love you, Miley!" "I love you, Dad!" A group of people next to me started singing "Amazing Grace" softly, and then a short repertoire of other spiritual and folk songs. One man with an operatic voice began to sing "Con te partirò (Time to Say Goodbye)," Andrea Bocelli's signature song. Once it was a low fire, Rangers (Burning Man officials) allowed people to get closer; some participants retreated into the desert night, while others rushed toward the smoldering embers.

19. The Galaxia temple goes up in flames at Burning Man 2018 (photo by Scott London).

The Temple at Burning Man is a somber space of mourning and remembrance, wherein participants place memorials to mark actual or metaphorical deaths. As such, the burning of the Temple becomes an important space of release and closure. It commemorates deeply personal losses and the release of profoundly intimate patterns of behavior, including sexual and physical abuse and neglect by parents, lovers, and friends. It also memorializes communal losses, celebrity deaths, and the victims of mass shootings. At the Burn after Robin Williams committed suicide, there was a massive photo of him hanging at the entrance of the Temple. At the Burn after the Orlando Pulse nightclub shooting in 2015, photos and biographies of each victim lined the walls of the Temple. For a community without an external religious axis, the Temple is the grounding center.

Throughout the week, Burners come to the Temple to leave notes, paraphernalia, letters, signs, photos, altars, and ashes in commemoration of someone they have lost or something they would like to release. Shaw explained how he uses the Temple for its metaphorical functions of release: "I have a safe environment in which I can sacrifice things, in which I can pay homage to things that I must let go—in which I can mourn parts of my life that are no longer relevant to me.... I can mourn parts of me that are not here anymore—[parts] that I thought, 'This is me!' But it is not anymore.... I can look at that part of me and say, 'I lay you to rest, and I am going to let you go.'"[51]

For other Burners, the Temple provides a space to cope with severe loss. In 2016, Xavier came to Burning Man for the explicit purpose of using the Temple as a sacred space to release his mother from her ailing physical body. He explained,

> I had heard about Burning Man for many years.... I thought it was amazing, and here I am where my mother has early-onset Alzheimer's and so, [*chokes up with tears*] ... so now she is at the final stages, and so it is pretty, pretty tough, and so when I decided to come here, I decided that this is what I want to do. I want to—even before this, like during the process—I've always felt drawn to spirituality—just felt it. I don't know how to explain it. It is just drawing me in and—anyways—with this happening and the questions in your mind, you start to question your spirituality and things—you know, all of those things. Anyway, so now that she is sort of at the final stage where she is not eating, and this is where, ... give or take, we were saying, one to two months, she's going to go. And so I thought about this Temple, and I thought, ... I want to write her a letter in a way that I am able to explain to her because she can no longer hear me or see me. She is trapped in that body.... So I blew up a picture of her, and so I have it.... But the letter that I want to write is almost a letter to her. It is sort of a peace offering to the universe.[52]

We cried together when he narrated the story of his mother's illness and his role in caring for her in the final stages of life. The conversation was intense. It was intimate, though we were strangers with different sociocultural and ethnic identities. It was ephemeral. It was exactly Burning Man. Xavier's family would have a funeral for his mother in Puerto Rico, but his offering at the Temple was his own personal way to make his peace. On the night of the Temple burn, this microcosmic experience of bridging difference through shared human experience of death and loss creates a commons that is amplified by the thousands of participants who mourn collectively.

The day after I spoke with Xavier, I happened to be close to the Temple during a dust storm when I saw a 1960s Cadillac Deville drive up and stop alongside it. When Clark Coleman, a renowned artist behind many Burning Man temples, got out of the car, I asked him how he came to his visions for the temples. Cryptically, he explained,

> No vision. I just build it. No vision. I never had a vision. None. I mean really. It's just mechanical—it's just really mechanical. There is no vision or bullshit

in it. . . . I will answer it for you as sort of straightforward as I can. I was talking to someone earlier this morning who was asking me that—"How is your relationship to the cosmos and the powerful forces?" And I said to him, . . . realtors find the most powerful points in terms of the earth, and they sell those to fucking people. The most powerful place, the most spiritual, powerful place is where the earth is hurt. . . . You want to find the holy, sacred places, you go into West Oakland or inner-city Detroit. Where people are the most hurt is where you will find the most powerful places. Those are the power points of the earth, not Mount Shasta and Mount Whitney and Mount Lassen, [but] inner-city Oakland.[53]

Whether Coleman denied that the Temple is a spiritually powerful place out of modesty or cynicism, many Burners do believe it to be a sacred place. Perhaps Coleman was directing my attention to the suffering of inner-city America to signify that the collective mourning and reverence for the pain of others should be expanded to places "where the earth is hurt," beyond the utopian confines of the playa. What would society look like if we expanded these feelings of empathy and solidarity to those spaces, and not only experienced them at the Temple burn in Black Rock City? How would my actions change if I felt the same empathy with those places "where people are most hurt" as I did when I shared Xavier's pain over the loss of his mother? The Temple burn is an exercise in building a commons through the shared human experience of suffering. The recognition of shared human experience builds a commons activated by the practice of bridging across sociocultural and ethnic boundaries.

CONCLUSION

Field notes, Burning Man, 2017

As a cool breeze begins to temper the blasting heat of the afternoon, the wind whips, and pastels begin to sweep across the blue sky. The thoroughfares bustle with a livelier hum; excitement for the night is building. On top of RVs, balconies, and art cars, groups of people stand at attention, facing west as the last glimmer of the sun slips behind the Black Rock mountain range. Cacophonous howls echo across the playa, haunting the coursing wind as groups of people raise their arms and howl at the setting sun. The howls echo through the wind in a lingering, caressing melody. I strip off my shirt, tousle my hair free, hop on my bike, and ride into the deep playa. It is my favorite part of the day; in earnest, it is my favorite part of the year. As I speed past people, the cool breeze ushers me along and rewards me for a hard day's work. I zoom through the surreal landscape, and nearly everyone I pass smiles and acknowledges me. Perhaps they smile in recognition of my own ecstatic smile that stretches across my face and the uncontainable giggles that escape my lips—effervescent joy in this perfect moment. Truly expressed emotions are contagious. The light is amazing. The mountains flame in hues of pinks. Anticipation. The moon rises. The mountains turn purple. The clouds hover, exposing a bouquet of pinks, while a final glint of sunlight holds onto a yellow cloud, retaining the last moments of the day. Art cars and villages begin to light up; music pumps through the expanding capillaries of the city. LED lights begin to punctuate the dusky horizon. In the distance, there is music and excitement. The night will begin soon. The breeze drops even cooler, and I ride, rocket fast, then coasting, both alone and together, reveling in my joy, feeling absolutely and utterly free.

Freedom is a polyvalent concept. In Isaiah Berlin's famous iteration, it has both positive and negative valences: negative freedom, meaning freedom from external obstacles to liberty, and positive freedom, meaning that one has the freedom of self-determination, the ability to control one's own destiny and interests.[54] Both valences of freedom are exhibited in festival contexts. Negative freedom manifests in the expressions of freedom from the enclosures of modernity, judgment, responsibilities, and isolation. Positive freedom arises from the ascetic discipline of the ethical subject through yoga and in the communitas created in the shared human experience of the commons. Festival cultures offer momentary reprieves that can introduce ineffable and unusual experiences of an alternative, utopian reality, windows into how social relations might be constructed otherwise.

Participants explained repeatedly that transformational festivals had changed their lives, sometimes in radical ways. Their descriptions included the subtle changes of developing more life balance, patience, sanity, calm, quietude, mental clarity, compassion, and empathy. Some made practical life choices, like buying and consuming organic foods, considering social justice and fair trade in purchases, volunteering in their local community, and changing vocations in order to participate in alternative economies that operate symbiotically with their changing values. Sloane quit the business of installing home security systems because he didn't want his livelihood to be based in the production of fear. Nomad resigned from his company to travel constantly as a global vagabond, spiritual explorer, and artist.

Yoga practice, in particular, initiated new ethical introspection. For example, Jonathan was a butcher who, when I interviewed him at Bhakti Fest, was questioning how to reconcile his livelihood slaughtering animals with his developing yogic ethics of nonviolence. During our interview at Shakti Fest, Melissa told me that she quit her job as a prison guard several years into her yoga practice because she found herself questioning the righteousness of violence within the carceral system. Today, she is training to become a yoga teacher and working as a special education aide for elementary school children. Emerson, whom I interviewed at Wanderlust Squaw Valley, was a corporate manager who had taken a yoga teacher training program and then convinced her boss to let her offer yoga classes at lunchtime in the corporate office park. The festivals overflowed with yoga teachers, musicians, artists, healers, massage therapists, and small-business owners who had aligned their income-generating projects to complement their yogic sensibilities.

Furthermore, yoga teachers at these festivals invited their students to unify divergent aspects of their lives and to live according to a yogic ethic. Wanderlust similarly encourages participants to make verifiable lifestyle changes based in conscious consumerism. The festival organizers recognize that attendees are fully enmeshed within a capitalist system but encourage them to make conscious choices, namely buying holistic, organic, lifestyle brands that the festival organizers deem to be ethical and in line with progressivist values. In this case, freedom does not derive from dropping out or destabilizing capitalism but rather comes from taking responsibility for one's ethical commitments and building a sustainable and utopian vision of society through personal action.[55]

Outside of yoga practice, many festival participants used the educational resources available at festivals to find tools to build collective solutions to social ills and set up creative networks to fuel their passions. When I asked Beth, a middle-aged woman at LIB, how the scene had changed over the years, she explained,

> We're all collectively raising our consciousness. . . . I've been going to quite a bit of talks in the Temple [of Consciousness]. People are really taking action. They're masterminding and taking action and implementing change. And you can just see it on a pretty big scale. It's fucking awesome. And then [it's] inspiring these twenty-year-olds, young twenty-year-olds, who are hopefully having their minds blown and take this energy and inspiration, for all of us, and go home. That's where the real magic happens, not just here. Hopefully it's all being filtered out into our communities.[56]

This hope echoes Clark Coleman's sentiments that the sacred places that require attention are the places where people and the earth are hurt. And there are ways in which festival-generated initiatives are impacting communities positively: Wanderlust hosts beach cleanups, Burners without Borders works on disaster relief and civic engagement, and LIB hosts workshops in practical skills—like permaculture, building gray water systems, and survivalism—encouraging participants to apply their knowledge beyond the festival grounds. In summer 2020, Burning Man, Lightning in a Bottle, Bhakti Fest, and some yoga teachers and cultural leaders in this study issued statements in support of Black Lives Matter. Some marched in the streets; others were silent. A Yoga Alliance Facebook post supporting Black Lives Matter erupted into nearly four hundred comments, including discussions of spiritual bypassing and white advocacy for All Lives Matter.[57] Some whites in these fields used this pivotal moment to continue their anti-racism work, while others began to confront their racialized positionality for the first time ever. Despite their attempts to build the world anew, these utopias are inevitably embroiled in American racism and it is yet to be seen whether our society will collectively evolve toward meaningful, enduring, and sustained social justice. As Dominique Debucquoy-Dodley, a mixed race media staff member at Burning Man Project wrote, "Black Rock City is still a city in the United States. . . .Burning Man is not separate from or immune to the world around us."[58]

The transformational festivals in this study provide extraordinary opportunities to build the social and to create unlikely solidarities across social boundaries. But the more homogenous and internally focused yogic festivals tend to further neoliberal ideals of self-discipline and self-care in service of governance. Because of their white homogeneity, the communitas advanced in these environments becomes a gated commons, reifying rather than dissolving social boundaries. In contrast, at the more diverse festivals, there is considerable emphasis on building on the shared experience of mutual recognition of the human condition by bridging ties between unlike persons. A wide variety of art, music, and workshops—as well as an emphasis on creativity, performance, and parody—creates a platform for unexpected encounters that destabilize conventional patterns of thinking and match unlikely compatriots in a shared commons.

The experience of a shared commons extricated from the multiple bondages of everyday life in neoliberal modernity results in temporary affective feelings of freedom. Regardless of social station, the festival participants I spoke with celebrated the freedom generated in these environments. However, one might hypothesize that these temporary feelings may be particularly appealing to those who are only minimally "unfree" in their everyday lives. Disenfranchised populations subordinated under oppressive structures of inequity may not find similar solace in the temporary relief of an affective experience of freedom. For those populations, "freedom work"[59] is focused less on creating a spiritual experience of freedom that occurs *outside* of conventional reality and more on achieving freedom from racialized and economic structures of bondage *within* society. Whether transformational festivals engage in freedom work depends on the extent to which, in Beth's words, the "real magic" of "taking action" is "being filtered out into our communities."

Conclusion

Since its founding, the United States has been home to a wide variety of religious sects that sought to carve out space for their own utopian visions. The territory itself was colonized as a result of the utopian ideals of both the Pilgrims, who settled Plymouth Colony in 1620, and the Puritans, who established their "Bible Commonwealth" in Massachusetts in 1630.[1] From the Shakers in the eighteenth century to the Mormons in the nineteenth century, American religious pluralism has fostered the founding of new religious sects and communities, bound together by a shared conception of how society might be constructed otherwise.

The anthropologist Roy Rappaport argues that imagining alternative worlds is an important first step in the disruption of existing social orders, even if they do not construct fully formed alternative societies:

> No actual society is utopian. It may, therefore, be difficult to any society's members not to imagine orders in at least some respects preferable to those under which they do live and labor. If they can conceive of better orders, how are their actions to be kept in sufficient conformity to the prevailing order for that order to persist? The conception of the possible is always in some degree the enemy of the actual. As such it may be a first step toward the disruption of prevailing social and conceptual orders, whatever they may be, without necessarily being a first step toward their improvement or replacement by orders more acceptable to those subject to them.[2]

Thus, the success or failure of a utopia is somewhat less revealing than the critique of the status quo and the suggested alternatives that reside at its nucleus. This critique serves as the generative nexus for any potential utopia and reveals much about the society from which it arises.

That is to say, utopias are envisioned in contradistinction to the perception of existing reality (*topia*). Karl Mannheim explains that, for this reason, we must recognize that utopias operate in a dialectical relationship to the existing order of things:

> In this sense, the relationship between utopia and the existing order turns out to be a "dialectical" one. By this is meant that every age allows to arise (in differently located social groups) those ideas and values in which are contained in condensed form the unrealized and unfulfilled tendencies which represent the needs of each age. These intellectual elements then become the explosive material for bursting the limits of the existing order. The existing order gives birth to utopias which in turn break the bonds of the existing order, leaving it free to develop in the direction of the next order of existence.[3]

Mannheim concludes that, given this dialectical relationship, "the key to the intelligibility of utopias is the structural situation of that social stratum which at any given time espouses them."[4] What are the characteristics of life for white, upper- and upper-middle class, educated, liberal, SBNR populations in neoliberal, late-capitalist modernity that have given rise to their supposed utopian antithesis in the form of these transformational festivals? In short, what is the problem that festivals aim to fix?

There is no easy answer here, but if we listen to participants and how they articulate the festival, then taking the inverse of that might lead to some suggestions as to the substance of the existing reality (*topia*), to which the festival becomes the solution (*utopia*). To begin, most fundamentally, participants described the festivals as safe and protected spaces where they felt "at home" (see figure 20). This feeling of being at home within a supportive community directly related to subsequent feelings of openness, connection with others, joy, and freedom. The inverse of this would be an unsafe and precarious space in which one feels not at home or, in other words, displaced—a society in which one feels isolated, disconnected from others, confined (unfree), and as a result, unhappy.

These are characteristics that numerous anthropologists and social commentators have noted as defining features of globalized modernity under neoliberalism. Displacement, social isolation, and (un)happiness have been major sites of investigation among scholars of anthropology, sociology, and psychology, as well as popular cultural critics in the past twenty to thirty years. In the previous chapter, I noted Anna Tsing's

20. Yoga class with "HOME" sign, Lightning in a Bottle, 2016 (photo by author).

notion that precarity defines the modern condition. She defines precarity as the "condition of being vulnerable to others" and living with unpredictability, indeterminacy, and flux in an unstable world in which we are "thrown into unplanned and shifting assemblages."[5] This is a ubiquitous condition in the current context of globalization, wherein, without stable structures of community, even the question of survival has become a reality for much of the world's population.

In her study of wonder, Tulasi Srinivas writes that her informants "perform everyday ritual not only to engage modernity but to disrupt it in productive ways and create new ways of worlding."[6] She shows how, in the rapidly fluctuating economic landscape of Bangalore, adaptation and wonder have become critical apparatuses with which to combat the everyday realities of precarity under neoliberalism. Under such conditions, both magic and wonder "undermine the disenchantment and uncertainties of a precarious modernity."[7] In his seminal study of modern magic among southern Italians, Ernesto de Martino asserts that while precarity, uncertainty, and pressures surely generate the impulse to rely on magic, the impulse is specifically driven by the psychological fear of "the risk that the individual presence itself gets lost as a center for decision and choice."⁸ He concludes, "The experience of being-acted-upon is the risk of crisis from which this horizon offers arrest and configuration."⁹ Considering the multifaceted unseen forces of neoliberalism, capitalism, and globalization and the ubiquitous modern phenomenon of precarity, it is no surprise that the "being-acted-upon" populations addressed in this study similarly turn to the magical and the wonderous in their quest to reenvision their worlds and enchant their environs.

Speaking in particular of the American context, Tsing explains how "a wild new cosmopolitanism has inflected what it means to be an American: a jostling of unassimilated fragments of cultural agendas and political causes from around the world. . . . American precarity—living in ruins—is in this unstructured multiplicity, the uncongealed confusion. No longer a melting pot, we live with unrecognizable others. . . . This cacophony is the feel of precarious living for both white and colored Americans—with repercussions around the world."¹⁰ This analysis, however, raises a more interesting and fraught question. If precarity is related to confrontation with unrecognizable and unknown others operating in unstructured multiplicity, then is safety related to homogeneity? What makes participants feel like these utopian environments are safe spaces? Is it their ethnic and cultural homogeneity? Thus far, I have argued that transformational festivals bring together an ideological commons, united in mutual experiences of and reactions to late-capitalist modernity. I have also argued that the collective experience of shared humanity through communitas has a unique capacity to bridge across spaces commonly characterized by white viscosity—the stickiness of whiteness.

But does diversity make us feel less safe and more uncomfortable? And if so, are participants' feelings that they have "come home" to "safe" environments related to the white viscosity of these transformational festivals? In 2000, the renowned sociologist Robert Putnam released a large-scale longitudinal study on diversity in which he concluded that, in more diverse communities, people tend to "distrust their neighbors, regardless of the color of their skin, to withdraw even from close friends, to expect the worst from their community and its leaders, to volunteer less, give less to charity and work on community projects less often, to register to vote less, to agitate for social reform more but have less faith that they can actually make a difference, and to huddle unhappily in front of the television."¹¹ In short, Putnam quips, "diversity brings out the turtle in all of us."¹² Certainly, this sociological finding is highly concerning in a globalized world that is increasingly dependent on diversity as a central component of modern living.

Furthermore, it is likely that participants in yogic and transformational festival worlds would be outraged to think that some of their feelings of safety, security, and coming "home" in festival environments are directly related to the affluent, educated, urban, liberal, and ethnically white homogeneity of the festival demographics. I would imagine that if this was suggested to them, the majority of participants at Burning Man and LIB would immediately point to the roughly 23 percent of festival participants who identify as nonwhite. In their second breath, they would point out the extreme diversity of appearances (created through elaborate costuming), not to mention the range of ages, political affiliations, geographical origins of participants, genders, and sexual identities represented at the festivals. And they would have a point, but there are other important factors that increase homogeneity, such as the expense of tickets (class), the white majority (ethnicity), and the general adherence to Burning Man and LIB principles (ideology). For participants at Wanderlust festivals and Bhakti and Shakti Fests, emotionally based objections would surely be at the ready, but there would be much less evidence to support them. The fact is that these festivals are largely homogenous environments, and it is likely that this political, ideological, cultural, and ethnic homogeneity contributes to participants' feelings of safety, protection, and the resulting openness to others and affective feelings of freedom.

But if we set aside the racial and cultural homogeneity of these spaces, the sense of a shared ideological commons also minimizes diversity and thus engenders feelings of safety, openness, connection with others, and freedom. Perhaps it is the ideological commons that generates the utopian feeling of coming home to a community of like-minded people. This second valence is of course what is vigorously celebrated by these communities, touted in their promotional literature, and echoed in the sentiments of participants. Putnam's study also reveals that "diversity and solidarity are negatively correlated,"[13] meaning that where there is a decrease in diversity there will be an increase in social solidarity. Applying Putnam's analysis to this demographic, it would appear that festival participants, and in particular the yogis, exhibit a high level of *bonding* social capital (ties to people who are *like* you in some important way) and a low level of *bridging* social capital (ties to people who are *unlike* you in some important way).[14] As I have argued, the bonding social capital exhibited in these fields results in an ideological commons.

The bridging social capital occurs particularly in emotional experiences that solidify empathic feelings of shared commons, like the Temple burn, as discussed in the previous chapter. But an ideological commons can also default into a gated commons that, intentionally or unintentionally, solidifies ethnic boundaries. Thus, while the ideological commons generates feelings of "coming home" and "freedom," it may also contribute to the populations' homogeneity.

In these fields of collected strangers, demonstrating belonging within the ideological commons becomes a critical means to signify group membership. Importantly, Putnam's research revealed that increased diversity within a community resulted in increased distrust of others, regardless of ethnicity.[15] That is to say that in diverse neighborhoods in the United States, high diversity correlated not only to people distrusting their neighbors who were ethnically *different* from themselves but also to them distrusting their neighbors who identified as having the *same* ethnicity as they did. In short, "diversity seems to trigger *not* ingroup/out-group division, but anomie or social isolation."[16] Thus, it would be logical that less diverse environments would trigger increased feelings of collective purpose and social connection. Likewise, communities successfully cultivating such feelings may exhibit homogenizing tendencies, both demographically and ideologically.

Within the ideological commons, self-presentation becomes a vital signifier of the bodily expression of one's ideals, ethics, and values. For example, during my first week of build at Burning Man, Athena—who had blonde waist length braided hair extensions and was dressed in high platform buckled leather boots, fishnet stockings, booty shorts, and a bustier—asked me if I was preparing to leave the playa for the default world because of the mundane way that I was dressed (regular shorts, sheer blouse, and boots). In her view, expressed in her scornful comment, my plain attire signified allegiance with the default world, not the ideals of Black Rock City. A vignette from Dug Claxton, an African American veteran Burner, illustrates how this emphasis on self-presentation as an expression of membership in the ideological commons can also reinforce white viscosity:

> Back in 1999, I came [to Burning Man], and I had the best time! In 2000, I came, and it was a completely different experience. I think people were a lot more standoffish, and the reason I attribute to that is in 1999 I had dreadlocks and in 2000 I did not. And I think there is a friendly, hippie, bohemian negro idea that gets attached to having dreadlocks. I think when my hair looked like every other "scary black person" the white Americans are used

to seeing in their movies and TV shows, people kept their distance. There were other reasons for it, but I didn't come back until 2009, when I had dreads again.[17]

This is a powerful sentiment, and a suggestive one. It may also explain the extraordinary ubiquity of fashion homogeneity in transformational festival spaces. For example, nearly all Wanderlust participants wear yoga pants (Lululemon even sponsors the on-site festival store), nearly all Bhakti and Shakti Fest participants adorn themselves in something Indic or don some form of bohemian-hippie gear, and nearly all Burners (though it is much harder to make generalizations about a group of over seventy-five thousand people) have a particular style. Burning Man routinely parodies itself; in 2004, *Piss Clear,* self-identified as "Black Rock City's favorite alternative newspaper," caricatured this phenomenon with a full-page display wherein a male and a female present "How to dress like a Burner." In this ironic ad, the woman wears furry leg warmers, hot pants, body paint, a furry vest, and a bindi, and the man wears a kilt, an open vest, bracelets, and a cowboy hat with devil horns.[18] In efforts to signal in-group membership and ideological solidarity, transformational festival participants perform cultural ideals through fashion, which signifies their inclusion. Historically, fashion (and the demand for homogeneity) has frequently played a central role in utopian communities; distinctive dress signifies both communal distinction and belonging, as well as moral values and social regulation.[19]

But fashion is only one layer of this signaling of social inclusion. At each festival, there are social norms that define one as an ideological insider, and a breach of those norms can result in social exclusion. For example, eating meat or expressing an overtly atheistic worldview at Bhakti or Shakti Fest, drinking a Diet Coke or smoking cigarettes at Wanderlust, or dressing conservatively (in default world attire) or asking someone's default world profession upon first meeting at Burning Man would all be examples of social breaches in each of those contexts. In the more yogic spaces, expressing overt negativity or anger can be a sign that one has not fully acculturated to the ideological commons or, in insider terms, that one has not effectively done their "spiritual work." As mentioned previously, Sloane, a veteran Burner, told me how he felt like the Burner community completely abandoned him when he was going through a period of clinical depression; many of those he thought were his friends regarded his depression as toxic and potentially contagious negative energy.[20]

The extent to which humans, when extracted from their social mores, systems, and confines, recreate those very social conventions to which they are accustomed—even when presented with radical freedom to do otherwise—is a great irony. As Arun Saldanha writes of the "freaks" in Goa, India "The freaks did feel free. But they felt free *as whites*. Hence, the freaks weren't exactly free from white modernity, but had, being white themselves, understood its potentials. The paradox was that they used the potentials to re-create a smaller replica of the society they thought they had abandoned."[21] Although participants in transformational festivals are transported to extrasocial environments, they bring their learned socialized behaviors with them. Though they may try to reject them or at least suspend them, a lifetime of habitus is not so easily undone.

In 2018, when I mentioned that I was planning to attend Burning Man to an acquaintance, she replied that she never wanted to attend because she was "afraid of becoming trapped in someone else's idea of freedom."[22] Isaiah Berlin's concern with the potential authoritarian aspects of positive freedom can be observed in the regulatory behaviors demanded by populations adhering to utopian visions. Nicholas Campion's research warns of the dangers of a "utopia of the willing," which determines that "the unwilling must be coerced" if the intention is to transform all of society.[23] He argues that elitism inheres within utopias, meaning that at their foundation they privilege adherents who oppose others who must be converted, initiating a process that can merge dangerously with totalitarianism and fascism, creating social utopias wherein "nobody can refuse to be free."[24]

Transformational festivals are defined by the notion that participants are interested in the process of transforming their identities into embodiments of their collectively agreed-upon values. There are various notions of what these collective values may be, but from my research, I might list the values of transforming the self into one who is open, loving, kind, receptive, self-aware, conscious, healthy, blissful, creative, empathic, balanced, energetic, intuitive, and teachable.[25] Participants of any ethnic and gender identity who appear to embody and perform these values are openly accepted in these communities, which pride themselves on inclusivity. However, this search for an ideological commons impacts ethnic diversity in its homogenizing tendencies, demanding outward signifiers of social inclusion.

Is this the reason that transformational festivals, and SBNR communities more generally, are such an overwhelmingly white phenomenon? Yes, in part. But there may be other factors, including the fact that many people of color are located in more secure religious and cultural centers that are less comfortable with spiritual bricolage and religious exoticism. For example, African American Baptists and Mexican American Catholics may have more religious and cultural hurdles to overcome with their churches, pastors, priests, family, and friends should they be interested in participating in yoga, meditation, or religious rituals outside of their home faith. These populations may also find solace and support within strong communal, cultural, and religious networks and thus may be less likely to look for spiritual fulfillment outside of those networks. Or perhaps it is the emptiness, vacuity, and violence inherent in the category of whiteness that leads white people to search for existential meaning outside of their families and histories. Whiteness itself signifies a loss of ancestry: the absorption and assimilation of the Irish, German, Scottish, French, Italian, Swedish, Dutch, and so on, into a noncategory constructed only to dominate systems of racial hierarchy and oppression. Though such queries fall beyond the purview of this study, I look forward to research that future scholars will contribute to these important topics. From my research, I have learned that many people of color feel less comfortable than whites with religious exoticism and the cultural and religious stereotyping that often accompanies it. The Indigenous people and Asian Americans I spoke with often explained that they felt exotified and essentialized when confronted with white (mis)conceptions and commodification of their cultures in these fields.

The optics of these largely white communities are also a self-fulfilling stereotype. The more transformational festivals depict themselves and are depicted as playgrounds of religious exoticism primarily for elite white populations, the more they are perceived as such—as exclusive environments unwelcoming to racialized others. The more yoga is depicted as the exclusive domain of lithe, toned, wealthy, white women, the more it becomes exclusionary to those who do not conform to that stereotype. Increasingly, there are movements, particularly within postural yoga, that attempt to reframe the optics, discourses, and representations of yoga into an inclusive understanding of the practice.[26] There are also popular movements that attempt to "Take Back Yoga" and recapture the practice by relocating it with Indian (often Hindu) authorities.[27] However, these voices remain in the minority and have not yet upset the industry paradigm of yoga as a practice for slender, refined, graceful, able-bodied, white women.

Furthermore, even the framing of religious exoticism raises interesting questions. At the outset of this project, I asked how and why particular religious ideas and practices were consistently grouped together in the New Age bookstores of my youth and in these utopian visions of spiritual transformation and conscious community. What are the foundational logics and the institutional structures that create their presumed coherence? In other words, what makes these amalgamated groupings of disparate, ideologically and geographically distinct religious formations make sense together? And to whom does it make sense?

The field of resources presented as available and efficacious tools on the path of spiritual awakening draws from a specific set of ideas. Those ideas are related to preconceived notions of the premodern, as discussed in chapter 1. In the quest for alternatives to Western modernity, these populations gravitate toward religious forms that are reimagined as ancient wisdom. Indigenous and Indic religious forms and practices are repositioned around Romantic Orientalist ideals. The noble savage and the oriental monk[28] become what British anthropologist E. B. Tylor calls "survivals," echoes of the past enacted in the present.[29] Religious exoticists articulate, extract, and appropriate these forms as utopian possibilities for their visions of alternative countermodernities. But their methods unwittingly reify historical paradigms that may sit uncomfortably with representatives of these very active and modern traditions, whom they unwittingly render as passive archaic artifacts to be recovered and brought into modernity by agentive white outsiders.

The practical social dynamics of religious exoticism thwart the conviction of nearly every participant in these religious fields that they aim to be inclusive. These fields are largely radically democratic: anyone with passion and vision can lead yoga, workshops, drum circles, sound immersions, meditations, or chanting. In these varied contexts, participants surround themselves with spiritual practices drawn from Indic and Indigenous traditions, which are imagined as unbounded and anti-institutional and extracted from their cultural contexts of hierarchies and restrictions. The spiritual worlds of participants are quintessentially experiential. Knowledge is shared. There are no institutionally appointed, hierarchically defined priests and shamans here; there are no limits to consciousness expansion.

But, enacted in the context of white supremacy, this expansive and universalistic ethos ends up denying the authority of nonwhite voices to represent the traditions of their heritage. It also enables whites to hold a space of representation under the logic of white possessivism. It is this pretense of possession that enacts violence, above and beyond the mundanities of everyday cultural exchange. Once again invoking the politics of friendship, sharing culture is an integral and vibrant aspect of cosmopolitan living in a globalized world. But a dominant group usurping, controlling, possessing, and exploiting a historically subordinated culture is another matter. Friendship speaks to shared entanglements, mutually beneficial exchange, lack of control, and openness to the unknown. In a friendship between two radically different subjects, there would be mutual representation, benefit, and solidarity.

A lack of this politics of friendship results in the perseveration on authenticity and authority, as discussed in the micro-level discussion of yoga in chapter 2. One side of the field argues that universal knowledge is based in personal experience and should be shared in egalitarian forms. In contrast, local knowledge traditionalists look to more Indic forms of yogic transmission; they may travel to India or follow a spiritual guru, a yoga teacher, or a specific lineage and build their practice in that channel of authority and imagined authenticity. The tension between these two poles signifies the fraught politics of representation that continue to enmesh yoga practice in the United States. The irony lies in the fact that both of these positions exclude Indians and are largely monopolized by white women.[30] American yogis celebrate a romantic imaginary of yoga's Indic roots while simultaneously erasing living Indians from the practice and dissemination of yoga in the United States. They also operate relatively detached from the current politicized yogic revolution occurring in India.

This strange condition leaves Indian Americans in somewhat of an odd position, as transnational subjects who can see the sharp differences between these contextualized interpretations of yoga as it travels globally and is instrumentalized for different purposes. Many have emotional responses to witnessing their own erasure. These visceral responses echo the gravity of that which Indigenous peoples experience when whites possess their native lands and establish themselves as ritual experts and shamans of Native religious ways. Other people of color may not be emotionally distraught over these somewhat commonplace effects of white possessivism, but they may be enough of a deterrent to dissuade them from engaging in these practices and identifying with these populations. For to do so would demand the reimagining of the self as the exotified other and subsequently enacting an exotification of the self, which together create an uncomfortable relation of simultaneous self-effacement and doubling.

In the previous chapter, I argued that transformational festivals have a unique opportunity to bring diverse communities into spaces of empathic connection, wherein there is a possibility to bridge sociocultural and ethnic boundaries. I suggested that bridging boundaries requires practice, and that practice, repeated over time, shapes patterns of behavior. Diversity may not be comfortable, protected, or safe, but it is the most productive collective space through which to foster creativity, innovation, and problem-solving for the future of humanity.[31] It may not always feel like coming home. It may even produce discomfort. As Robin DiAngelo writes, "The racial status quo is comfortable for white people, and we will not move forward in race relations if we remain comfortable. The key to moving forward is what we do with our discomfort."[32] In the ascetic and mystical practices in these temporary utopias, participants are already engaged in sustained exercises that defy conventional boundaries and experiment with discomfort—mental, emotional, and physical. These are populations practiced at confronting the limits of their endurance, at finding their inner grit. They are also skillful at building solidarities among strangers and cultivating affective feelings of communitas in shared human experience. If their utopian visions are to become plausible countermodernities, they will need to apply those carefully honed skills to building solidarities outside of their current predominantly white populations.

APPENDIX ONE

@Instagram Data for Public Figures Cited

YOGA TEACHER (PSEUD.)	NUMBER OF FOLLOWERS ON INSTAGRAM
Abby Hills	49.4K
Asha Savi Kaur	51.1K
Bill Canter*	7.7K
DJ Akash	119K
DJ Sai	35.4K
Eli Gordon	5.6K
Heather Hancock	10.1K
Helena Blake	103K
Henry Stevenson	16.5K
Kailash	21.2K
Jordan Light	62.6K
Bija Rivers	109K
Katie Kurtz	37.3K
Lena Bryant	155K
Prem Das*	14.6K
Shakti Devi*	14.6K
Shelby Michaels	134K
Dakota Lemon	29.7K

Tobias Day	29.2K
Zachary Ellis	29.7K
Zara Thomas*	3.5K

WORKSHOP LEADER (PSEUD.)	NUMBER OF FOLLOWERS ON INSTAGRAM
Asher Grayson	3K
Chloe Lindsay	1.8K
Breath Arrow	5.7K
Jeremiah Silver	2.8K
Michaela Lyon	1.1K

TRANSFORMATIONAL FESTIVAL	NUMBER OF FOLLOWERS ON INSTAGRAM
Bhakti and Shakti Fests	26.5K
Wanderlust	357K
Lightning in a Bottle	134K
Burning Man**	992K

*Yoga studio
**Note, Burning Man Project dissociates itself from the category of festival

APPENDIX TWO

Methodology

My multisited fieldwork telescopes on three different genres of festivals, each representing a particular kind of spiritual, transformational engagement and a distinctive vision of utopia: (1) Bhakti and Shakti Fests, (2) Wanderlusts, and (3) Lightning in a Bottle (LIB) and Burning Man. There are numerous other festivals that I could have included but did not because I needed to create some sense of a boundary to my field for theoretical and practical reasons. However, similar conclusions might be drawn about large-scale transformational festivals outside of the periphery of this study, such as Symbiosis, Lucidity, Electric Forest, Sonic Bloom, Faerieworlds, Bali Spirit Festival, and Rainbow Serpent Festival, as well as smaller festivals dedicated specifically to yoga, such as Hanuman Festival, Ascend Festival, Telluride Yoga Festival, Dirty South Yoga Festival, and Love Yoga Fest Cape Cod.

In effort to think more deeply about the intents and purposes of festivals and to note the differences between ethnocultural festivals and transformational festivals, I also conducted fifty-two days of ethnographic research at other festivals during this research period. These included the ethnocultural festivals of Noche de Altares and Día de los Muertos in Santa Ana and Los Angeles, California; and Holi festivals in Spanish Fork, Utah, between 2013 and 2015. My research on these festivals comprised one node of the work of an interdisciplinary team of scholars studying public religious festivals in relation to themes of immigration, globalization, and political and civic culture. In 2013 and 2019, I also conducted ethnographic research at the largest religious festival on earth, the Kumbh Mela in Prayagraj (Allahabad), India.

I selected the transformational festivals focused on in this study by using snowball methodology and following participants into their spheres of influence. I first attended Bhakti Fest in 2011, then followed participants to Shakti Fest, then to Wanderlust and LIB, and then to Burning Man. Prior to moving to

California and seeing a flyer for Bhakti Fest in 2011, I had not really encountered any of these festivals, save for Burning Man. I had seen a book of photography from Burning Man sometime in the early 2000s and had tried to convince one of my artist friends to go, to no avail. I also had a good friend in graduate school (circa 2006) whose statement "Burning Man is my religion" gave me pause.

As an ethnographer, I follow both a "reflexive" qualitative sociological approach[1] and Michael Burowoy's understanding of *extended case method,* which examines how a given social situation is shaped by external forces.[2] I also methodologically support respectful[3] and self-reflexive dialogue between researchers and those that they study. This multisited ethnographic project is IRB approved, and my informants are active participants, dialogue partners, and readers of my research. I also engaged year-round local and global festival communities online using netnographic methods[4] and lived vicariously through the pictures and videos of friends who traveled to festivals I could not attend. My methodology offers *genetic* explanations, meaning that it reveals what a particular situation tells us about the world in which it is imbedded, with a particular eye toward power relations.

Importantly, the festivals central to this study are chosen not because of their similarity but because they represent three different genres of popular transformational festivals. Each festival is a contemporary, active, and changing field, and they are all extraordinarily different from one another. And yet, while conducting this research I was amazed at how consistently I encountered familiar faces from one of the other festivals. And even if we didn't directly intersect, participants told me of their travels in this network of overlapping circuits. This has led me to imagine these fields as ephemeral yet intersecting hyphal knots of the SBNR populace.

For example, Luke, whom I know from my previous research on Mata Amritanandamayi (Amma), to my astonishment crossed over into the majority of these field sites.[5] I first interviewed him on the balcony at Amma's San Ramon ashram in Northern California in 2008. He was intense. He told me about the open-eyed meditation that he had been practicing, and we practiced it together for several minutes while he paused between stories of energetic confluences and paranormal events. He related that he subsisted on a diet of spirulina and lived out of his van most of the year. He never spent too much time in one place on account of police harassment, but he had friends up and down the West Coast and was planning to spend the next few months helping out at his friend's organic farm in Oregon.

In the following years, I saw him at other Amma programs exuberantly dancing around the back of the hall. He would be wearing purple wraparound pants, tied in the front—the ones bohemians and global vagabonds wear in cities like Rishikesh, India, though I am not sure if he ever made it so far afield. I was fascinated by Luke. In some ways, he seemed to represent an entire population of people who were not counted within the system. He existed on the peripheries, not that different from those living in Skid Row or Slab City— except for the fact that there was likely money somewhere in his past, which had fueled his love for self-education and given him a sense of classed financial security, if not actual security. I used to smile when I saw him in various cities, jumping up and down, arms flung wide and dreadlocks spinning as he twirled in his signature dance move. I thought to myself that the world was somehow better with him in it.

At Bhakti Fest in 2014, I approached the main stage of ecstatic dancers during *kīrtan*. People were undulating with the music, twirling, and raising their arms in praise as the *kīrtan* band whipped them into a frenzy with the repeated refrains of "*Oṃ Namaḥ Shivāya*." I joined the crowd of dancers, and as I soaked in the scene of release and devotion, to my right I caught a glimpse of Luke in wraparound pants, twirling in devotional ecstasy. The following year, at LIB, I dropped into the Healing Sanctuary to check it out and catch a bit of shade. There was a raised platform with some large stones and crystals on it. A few people were meditating on pillows; others lounged along the sides of the Bedouin-style tent, resting. It was cool and peaceful inside. There, close to the front of the nature altar, was Luke, sitting in lotus position in closed-eye meditation, wearing nothing but a leather loincloth. Later, home at my computer, I was thinking about including Burning Man in this research project, so I did a search for images of Burning Man to get a feel for the ethos of the festival. Countless images scrolled across my laptop displaying dusty beauties in ancient-futuristic costumes enjoying the vast expanse of the Black Rock Desert. There, among the images, was a circle of ecstatic dancers, and in the center of the image was a sky-clad (naked) man jumping for joy. It was Luke, barefoot and soaked in playa dust and elation. Over the next several years, I saw Luke on several occasions, mostly at Amma's programs in Los Angeles and once with a young bohemian woman and a newborn baby.

I relate this story of Luke as one of several possible entry points to this ephemeral yet connected field. I don't know where Luke lives, or if he in fact has a permanent residence these days. I don't know how he sustained his lifestyle financially; his life seemed grounded neither by geography nor vocation. Instead, he floated in a variety of consciousness circles, operating like so many Venn diagrams, intersecting and overlapping at key junctures, held together by the thread of self-cultivation and spiritual exploration. There are others I might have profiled, such as the beautiful young Australian couple that I met outside of Jeremiah Silver's breathwork workshop at Shakti Fest. Several weeks later, after loading my heavy gear into a truck at LIB and climbing a steep ladder into the seating compartment in the back, I found myself sitting next to them. We exchanged happy greetings of reconnection, and they explained that they had been working at one of the vegan food vendors at Shakti Fest and were at LIB to do the same. Late one night at Burning Man, I ran into Lisa at Inferno, both of us dancing while controlled flames licked the roof of the domed structure. She was dancing on the risers, and we reconnected in a resting moment. I had known her from her leadership roles at Bhakti and Shakti Fests and had shared a chai with her at Amma programs in Los Angeles. Later, while perusing a friend's photographs of Camp Mystic at Burning Man, I saw that she had been there too, in the center of the group shot of forty Burner yogis, right in front, smiling elatedly at the camera.

Yoga teachers also traveled along these intersecting and concentric circuits of spiritual sociality. Helena Blake, Abby Hills, Dakota Lemon, and Tobias Day were at several different Wanderlust festivals. Henry Stevenson was at Bhakti and Shakti Fests and LIB. Zara Thomas was at LIB and Burning Man. Shelby Michaels was at Wanderlust and Burning Man. DJ Akash was at multiple Wanderlust festivals and Bhakti and Shakti Fests. Bija Rivers was at Bhakti and Shakti Fests, Burning Man, and several Wanderlust festivals. Just as with Luke, I don't know where some of these people live, or if they even have permanent addresses. I keep in touch with them over the Internet, through social media, and run into them in the scene. In this sense, the yogic spiritual scene is like many other scenes—such as those built around the Grateful Dead, raves, opera, or comic books. Circling around some nexus of passion, crowds repeat and become familiar. As an ethnographer, I have become close with a select crew of principal informants, many of whom I consider friends. But I am also familiar with a much larger cast of characters whom I recognize out of context because of our repeated interactions. At the periphery, I have connected with hundreds of people through interviews, gatherings, and work shifts; these individuals were memorable, but our paths only intersected once.

My field work is bounded in that I focused on specific festivals, though I could have expanded to dozens of others. My field was broadly multisited; however, each field site was simultaneously constant and shifting, year to year. At any one of these festivals, there were organizers, leaders, and participants who attended regularly. But there were also first-time attendees who never returned, and senior leaders who took a year off or retired. None of these festivals tracks its participants as diligently as Burning Man does; if Burning Man is any barometer, in 2017, 36 percent of attendees were "virgins" (first-time Burners), and a further 19 percent had attended for only one or two years previously.[6] There is a strong community of veteran Burners, and many in that community are concerned about these high numbers of virgins and their impact on the communal enactment of Burning Man principles. This high percentage of novices may be exaggerated at Burning Man because it has become a "bucket list" event for many.

Aside from the transient nature of each festival, the sheer size of the field brought multiple complications to the fore. For example, Burning Man has 80,000 participants, Bhakti Fest has nearly 5,000 participants, and Shakti Fest has 1000 to 1,500 participants. At its height, LIB had around 27,000 participants but now is capped at 20,000. Wanderlust festivals have anywhere from 1,000 to 11,000 participants, depending on location. With these figures, in any given year, my combined fields had an average of approximately 120,000 participants. Then, if one considers the conservative estimate that 30 percent of the field is made up of first-time attendees, then my field increased 30 percent each year. Taking this increase and my nine years in the field, my roster of potential informants was a staggering 1.4 million. This would be like conducting an ethnography of Dallas, Texas. In 1929, when Robert and Helen Lynd conducted their study of Muncie, Indiana, giving it the pseudonym Middletown, the population of the city hovered at a mere thirty thousand people.[7] Thus, my research focuses on a simultaneously bounded, expansive, and ephemeral field, mirroring the contours of SBNR populations.

Some readers may be interested in the practicalities of how one does ethnography in such an expansive and ephemeral field. In closing, I devote attention to this micro-level inquiry. At the most basic level, I tent-camped and relied on public porta-potties. Often on a tight budget, I packed in food and sometimes juice-fasted. I began first with participation; I practiced yoga, wandered the grounds, shared meals, built structures, attended workshops, and sang *kīrtan*. After some early failures, in time I learned how to better navigate festivals in relative comfort: what to pack, when to rest, and when to work. I often rose early and took interviews before the heat of the day. During midday and in the early afternoons, I would look for shaded and air-conditioned spaces in which to participate fully. As I participated throughout the days, I also took field notes and recorded yoga classes, lectures, and workshops. Late in the afternoons and in the evenings, I would look for quieter spaces away from the party where I might find participants relaxing without extensive background noise from the requisite concerts. I became bold and approached participants directly, telling them of my research and asking for an interview. I also prescheduled interviews with famous yoga teachers, festival producers, and workshop leaders, most of which occurred on festival grounds. Because of the transience of these festivals, sometimes my interviews were shorter than they might have been in other environments. But often, my interlocutor and I would become engrossed in conversations that were more open and intense than they might have been elsewhere.

From my previous experiences with guru communities, I had learned that work was a successful means to accessing a field and building relationships. I implemented this strategy at Shakti Fest and at Burning Man. In the former, I served as a part of the *sevā* team; in the latter, I ended up becoming a team leader of the Black Rock Bakery. Showing up for work days for the French Quarter Village—my camp at Burning Man—also enabled me to build sustained relationships with fellow Burners. I also attended concerts, gatherings, and ancillary related events when I was invited by participants or felt that they were important adjacent fields. The relationships I built through this sustained and intense field research are some of the most precious relationships in my life. This is also a much deeper and multifaceted field than that of any ethnographic project I have ever worked on, for which massive data organization systems became essential. Throughout, I encountered more people, interviews, experiences, and intimacies than I could have imagined at the outset. I hope that my interlocutors and friends will recognize themselves and their communities in my words.

At the completion of the first draft of this book, I shared the entire manuscript with key interlocutors in the field and solicited feedback. I also contacted all of the interlocutors I could trace who were quoted in the manuscript and shared those sections with them, as well as the title page, table of contents, and chapter and section summaries. Initially, as per conventional ethnographic standards, I gave pseudonyms to all of the everyday people but maintained actual names for famous and public figures, including the majority of the yoga teachers, ritual specialists, and festival officials referenced in this book. But as I was contacted by yoga teachers, their management teams, and "commercial directors," I realized, and was sharply informed, that even being associated with a book that acknowledges and questions the predominant whiteness of these fields could be damaging to their brands. In response, I decided to go against ethnographic conventions and assign pseudonyms to the famous and public figures quoted in this book—unless they requested to be named. One famous yoga teacher was furious at my focus on whiteness and demanded that her interview content be removed from the manuscript. I chose to honor her wishes.

Several celebrity yoga teachers rejected any acknowledgment of their whiteness, white privilege, practices of white possessivism, or their existence within the structural context of white supremacy. This is understandable because many have built their careers on the foundation of white normativity, which allows them to present themselves as universalistic exemplars, as postracial subjects. Many interpreted my identification of them with the category of whiteness to be a personal assault and an accusation of intentional racism. Some responded with emotional reactions of shock, anger, defensiveness, and denial. Their vitriolic reactions to being mentioned in a study on whiteness echoed many of the responses that Robin DiAngelo explores in her book, *White Fragility*.[8] Because their reactions so closely mirrored DiAngelo's findings, it will be beneficial to readers to quote her definition of white fragility at length here. She writes,

> White people in North America live in a society that is deeply separate and unequal by race, and white people are the beneficiaries of the separation and inequality. As a result, we are insulated from racial stress, at the same time that we come to feel entitled to and deserving of our advantage. Given how seldom we experience racial discomfort in a society we dominate, we haven't had to build our racial stamina. Socialized into a deeply internalized sense of superiority that we either are unaware of or can never admit to ourselves, we become highly fragile in conversations about race. We consider a challenge to our racial worldviews as a challenge to our very identities as good, moral people. Thus, we perceive any attempt to connect us to the system of racism as an unsettling and unfair moral offense. The smallest amount of racial stress is intolerable—the mere suggestion that being white has meaning often triggers a range of defensive responses. These include emotions such as anger, fear, and guilt and behaviors such as argumentation, silence, and withdrawal from the stress-inducing situation. These responses work to reinstate white equilibrium as they repel the challenge, return our racial comfort, and maintain our dominance within the racial hierarchy. I conceptualize this process as *white fragility*. Though white fragility is triggered by discomfort and anxiety, it is born of superiority and entitlement. White fragility is not weakness per se. In fact, it is a powerful means of white racial control and the protection of white advantage.[9]

Several prominent yoga teachers claimed that they were being misrepresented (even when they were sent audio recordings and verbatim transcripts) and listed their degrees, travels abroad, POC teachers, and experiences of persecution as reasons that they should be exempt from classification within the category of whiteness. Through their objections they aimed to distance themselves from the category, implying that their knowledge and experience made them somehow less white. With their protests, they not only wished to suppress critical reflection on the overwhelming whiteness in yoga, transformational festivals, and practices of religious exoticism but also failed to consider how all people—including, as in the focus of this study, white people—are emplaced within racist social structures that privilege whiteness.

Writing about American Jews, the religion scholar Michael Alexander states that the rejection of any association with whiteness can be viewed as the psychological repression of whiteness, a repression which stems from a lack of awareness or an intentional denial of the significance of skin color and complexion as important factors in social relations, emplacement, and mobility in the United States as well as in the world.[10] The rejection by religious exoticists of any association with whiteness was so vehement because these populations believe themselves to be choosing nonwhite spirituality over white religion and thereby contributing to the death of whiteness.[11] But, ironically, with this protesting they demonstrate the strength of white supremacy, both in their denial of their own positionality and unearned power and in the way that their spiritual practices actively usurp people of color as representatives of their own traditions. Their reactions surprised me and were unfortunate, not only because of their unpleasantness but also because, prior to these interactions, I (somewhat naively) believed that these yogis had done this internal social justice work already. Instead, their vitriol poignantly revealed how white fragility suppresses important conversations about racism and white hegemony. It also falsely privileges intent over impact. In the yogic field, it is also likely an effect of the acerbic debates regarding white privilege, cultural appropriation, and postural yoga practice circulating in yogic circles and on the Internet, which also solicited my attention in the course of this research.[12] I followed dozens of yogis and transformational festival groups on blogs and social media to keep abreast of their activities and opinions. Sometimes, this was the most difficult part of the field in that every day there seemed to be a new fiasco, commentary, or critique that was going viral.[13] For years I collected this virtual data and waited for a lull in the storm so that I could draw some semblance of distance needed for a summation. The storm has by no means abated, but it is time for this research to be made public. I hope that this intervention will incite engagement and active discussion in the fields of academia, yoga, and transformational festivals and in SBNR communities, so that they too will see the "WHITES ONLY" sign and question where, how, why, and by whom it has been hung.

FESTIVAL		DAYS IN FIELD
Bhakti Fest		
2011	Joshua Tree, CA (September 9–11)	3
2012	Joshua Tree, CA (September 7–9)	3
2013	Joshua Tree, CA (September 5–8)	4
2014	Joshua Tree, CA (September 6–8)	3
2017	Joshua Tree, CA (September 8)	1
Shakti Fest		
2012	Joshua Tree, CA (May 11–13)	3
2013	Joshua Tree, CA (May 17–19)	3

2014	Joshua Tree, CA (May 15–18)	4
2015	Joshua Tree, CA (May 14–18)	5
2016	Joshua Tree, CA (May 12–15)	3

Wanderlust

2014	Oahu, Hawaii (February 26–March 3)	6
2014	Wanderlust in the City-Los Angeles, Santa Monica (May 10)	1
2014	Squaw Valley, CA (July 16–21)	6
2014	Mount Tremblant, Quebec, Canada (August 20–24)	5
2016	Sunshine Coast, Australia (October 20–23)	4
2017	Great Lake Taupo, New Zealand (February 2–5)	4

Lightning in a Bottle

2014	Bradley, CA (May 22–26)	5
2015	Bradley, CA (May 21–25)	5
2016	Bradley, CA (May 26–30)	5

Burning Man

2016	Black Rock City, NV (August 24–September 7)	15
2017	Black Rock City, NV (August 23–September 4)	13
2018	Black Rock City, NV (August 23–September 4)	13
2019	Black Rock City, NV (August 21–September 4)	15
	Total days spent in primary field sites[14]	**129**

Related Festivals

2012	Tadasana Festival, Santa Monica, CA (April 21)	1
2013	Kumbh Mela, Prayagraj (Allahabad), India (January 31–February 22)	23
2013	Noche de Altares / Día de los Muertos, Santa Ana, CA (November 2)	1
2014	Festival of Colors (Holi), Los Angeles, CA (March 7–8)	2
2014	Festival of Colors (Holi), Spanish Fork, UT (March 28–30)	3
2014	Noche de Altares / Día de los Muertos, Santa Ana, CA (November 1–2)	3
2014	Día de los Muertos, Hollywood, CA (November 2)	1

2015	Festival of Colors (Holi), Los Angeles, CA (March 7)	1
2015	Festival of Colors (Holi), Spanish Fork, UT (March 27–30)	4
2019	Kumbh Mela, Prayagraj (Allahabad), India (January 24–February 6)	14
	Total days spent in related field sites	52

Notes

INTRODUCTION

1. Up until 2018, Bhakti and Shakti Fests were held at the Institute of Mentalphysics, also known as the Joshua Tree Retreat Center. This location is in some sense a very apt place to begin this book. It was founded by Edwin John Dingle, who was born in England in 1881, but became known as Ding Le Mei after his extensive travels in China, India, and Tibet. He then returned to the West, stopping first in New York (in 1927) and then settling in Los Angeles (in 1928), where in time he developed the Science of Mentalphysics, techniques that combined breathing exercises, diet control, exercises, and meditation, all aimed to lead to self-mastery. In 1941, the Institute of Mentalphysics was opened in Yucca Valley, the ancestral land of the Serrano, the Chemehuevi, and the Cahuilla people. Although the formal address is in Yucca Valley, I refer to the retreat center throughout as being located in Joshua Tree, reflecting the festival organizers' usage. In 2018, Bhakti and Shakti Fests changed locations and as of 2020, are held at the Joshua Tree Lake RV and Campground.

2. Eli Gordon [pseud.], Yoga Intensive, audio recording, Bhakti Fest, Joshua Tree, CA, September 8, 2014.

3. The *playa* is the colloquial term used to refer to the vast alkaline dried lake bed in the Black Rock Desert where Black Rock City is established each year.

4. Lopez 2014.

5. I use Indic in the broadest sense to signify religions that originated in India, such as Hinduism, Buddhism, Jainism, Sikhism, and Tantra. While this is my primary focus, there are also East Asian religions peripherally present in these fields, such as Japanese Zen Buddhism.

6. Saldanha 2007, 8.

7. Driscoll and Miller 2019, 18.

8. Corn 2019, 3.

9. Crowley 2011, 7.
10. Certainly, there are exceptions. For example, Burning Man Project has multiple programs actively engaged in creating social change, such as Burners without Borders (www.burnerswithoutborders.org). Inspired by Burning Man, many Burners have started independent initiatives aimed at social change; see, for example, the 1st Saturdays program, run by Jon Halcyon Styn of Pink Heart Burning Man camp (www.johnstyn.com). The yoga world also has points of social activism; see, for example, the support for the 2020 presidential candidate Marianne Williamson, including an August 2012 Speakeasy talk that was sponsored by Wanderlust ("The Art of Aligning Body & Soul," accessed April 1, 2020, www.wanderlust.com/journal/marianne-williamson-carry-yoga), and Seane Corn's organization, Off the Mat and Into the World (www.offthematintotheworld.org). I have also written previously about the rise of global yoga tourism in the form of missionary-inspired service trips; see Lucia 2018.
11. Jenkins 2004, 152, 154.
12. See Foxen 2020; Deslippe 2018; Love 2010; Aubrecht 2017; Goldberg 2015.
13. Jenkins 2004, 151.
14. M. F. Brown 2003. For more on the reasons behind the predominantly white upper-class demographic of the counterculture, see Lemke-Santangelo 2009, 35–58.
15. Cohen 1991, 219.
16. The *mahāmantra* is the central mantra of the Hare Krishnas. It is: "*Hare Krishna, Hare Krishna, Krishna Krishna, Hare Hare, Hare Rama Hare Rama, Rama Rama, Hare Hare.*"
17. Raul 2013. For more on Hendrix's "Axis: Bold as Love," see Henderson 1981, 173–4, 204–5.
18. Aldred 2000, 329.
19. Sharf 1998, 111.
20. Jenkins 2004, 147.
21. Quote from Esalen's website, cited in Jenkins 2004, 198.
22. Todorov 1993, 273.
23. Altglas 2014, 12.
24. Todorov 1993, 264.
25. Todorov 1993, 265.
26. Said 1978.
27. Altglas 2014, 320.
28. Bourdieu 1984, 370.
29. Altglas 2014, 323.
30. Deloria 1998, 170.
31. Altglas 2014, 14.
32. Lipka and Gecewicz 2017.
33. Funk and Smith 2012, 9–10.
34. Funk and Smith 2012, 9–10.
35. Albanese 2007, 13–15.
36. Bender 2010; on "entanglement," see pp. 5–7; on metaphysical "cultures," see pp. 16; and on "mysticism and experience," see pp. 56–118.

37. Schmidt 2003; also cited in Bender 2010, 10.
38. Roof 1999; Bellah et al. 1985; Mercadante 2014; Carrette and King 2005; Fuller 2001; Kripal 2007.
39. Bellah et al. 1985, 221.
40. Ram Dass 1971.
41. Altglas 2014, 326.
42. Federici 2019, 1 (emphasis in the original).
43. Federici 2019, 116.
44. Federici 2019, 110.
45. Federici 2019, 91.
46. DeVaul et al. 2017.
47. Lucia 2014b. In 2014, I created a survey targeted at American yogis that contained thirty-five questions about yoga and festival culture in the United States. The survey received 119 responses, with approximately 31 participants answering all questions. The survey was free and circulated on social media and was shared by several highly visible American yoga practitioners. In this survey, 82 percent of yoga festival attendees self-identified as white. Cross-sectional survey data from the National Health Interview Survey (NHIS) in 2002 revealed similar demographic results, concluding that 85 percent of American yogis are Caucasian. Birdee et al. 2008.
48. United States Census Bureau, "QuickFacts: United States," accessed November 15, 2019, www.census.gov/quickfacts/fact/table/US/IPE120218.
49. Statistical Atlas, "Map of Race and Ethnicity by State in the United States," accessed November 15, 2019, https://statisticalatlas.com/United-States/Race-and-Ethnicity.
50. Lopez 2017.
51. Pew Research Center 2017.
52. Although Benjamin's book came out in 2009, his TedX talk on his research for *Searching for Whitopias* was featured on the *TED Radio Hour* on NPR on November 20, 2015, which is likely the segment wherein I encountered his work.
53. Benjamin 2009, 5.
54. Benjamin 2015.
55. Bender 2010; Albanese 2007; Heelas 2008 and 1996; Fuller 2000; Pike 2004; Oppenheimer 2003; Campion 2016; Carrette and King 2005; Lemke-Santangelo 2009; Kripal 2007.
56. Jain 2015; Singleton 2010; de Michelis 2004; Foxen 2017; Williamson 2010. For discussions of whiteness in modern postural yoga, see Foxen 2020; Aubrecht 2017; Miller 2019; Deslippe 2018; and the work of the UC Berkeley Race and Yoga Working Group and their *Race and Yoga Journal*.
57. Gilmore 2010; Chen 2009; Bowditch 2010.
58. Roszak 1969; Love 2010; Hanegraaf 1998; Partridge 2005; Campion 2016; Oliver 2014; Albanese 2007; Ellwood 1979; C. Jackson 1994; Heelas 1996; Pike 2004; Lachman 2012; Natale 2016.
59. Deloria 1998; Jenkins 2004; M. F. Brown 2003; Huhndorf 2001; Aldred 2000; Smith 1994; Donaldson 1999; Owen 2008.
60. M. F. Brown 2003, 236.

61. Jenkins 2004, 240.
62. Lott 1993, 4.
63. Jenkins 2004, 253.
64. Lott 1993.
65. Root 1996; Young 2010; Ziff 1997; Young and Brunk 2009; Scafidi 2005.
66. Moyer 2015.
67. See, for example, Decolonizing Yoga (www.decolonizingyoga.com, accessed July 9, 2018).
68. Srinivas 2007.
69. Jain and Schulson 2016; McCartney 2017; Chakraborty 2006; Singleton 2010, 98–106.
70. Putcha 2018a; Gandhi and Wolff 2017; Murphy 2014.
71. Ta-Nehisi Coates, "Ta-Nehisi Coates on Words That Don't Belong to Everyone," YouTube, November 7, 2017, https://youtu.be/QO15S3WC9pg. See also Putcha 2018a; and Lopez 2017.
72. Said 1978; Lott 1993; Deloria 1998; Root 1996.
73. Moreton-Robinson 2015, xiii.
74. Moreton-Robinson 2015, xix.
75. Lipsitz 2006.
76. Saldanha 2007, 18.
77. Altglas 2014, 327.
78. Saldanha 2007, 18.
79. Stebbins 2007.
80. McKay 2015, 5.
81. Lang 2009, 3.
82. McKay 2015.
83. McKay 2015, 4.
84. Bennett, Taylor, and Woodward 2014, 11–26.
85. Bennett, Taylor, and Woodward 2014, 1; also cited in McKay 2015, 4.
86. Bennett, Taylor, and Woodward 2014, 18.
87. Albanese 2007; Heelas 1996; Bender 2010; Pike 2004; Butler 1990.
88. Urban 2015, 5–6.
89. Durkheim 1995, 216–22.
90. Caillois 2001, 107.
91. Bakhtin 1984, 147–52.
92. Mukherjee 2009, 121.
93. Mukherjee 2009, 130; Caillois 2001, 127.
94. White 1989. On the internalization of southern Italian magical rituals during the same period, see de Martino 2001, 133–60.
95. "The Bloom, Episode 1: Fundamental Frequencies," web series, accessed April 12, 2019, https://thebloom.tv/portfolio-item/episode-i-fundamental-frequencies.
96. Jason Josephson-Storm has argued that modernity and its corresponding era of disenchantment is a myth and that belief in magic and spirits never truly waned (Josephson-Storm 2017). While this is a provocative thesis, it is not shared among my informants in these fields. Instead, my informants largely

agreed that their lives had become disenchanted, and they employed the tools of religious exoticism to reenchant their worlds. They actively sought out opportunities to create magic and wonder and participated in ritualized action as a means to articulate their presence and agency over their lives and surroundings.

97. Caillois 2001, 107.

98. Bija Rivers [pseud.], interview by author, audio recording, Wanderlust Sunshine Coast, Australia, October 22, 2016.

99. Zahir [pseud.], interview by author, audio recording, Bhakti Fest, Joshua Tree, CA, September 8, 2012.

100. There are formal organizational modes of expansion of Burning Man and Burning Man principles, including hundreds of regional events across the globe (see https://regionals.burningman.org); activist organizations like Burners without Borders aim to spread Burning Man principles and culture (see https://burningman.org/culture/civic-initiatives/burners-without-borders). Concerns about proselytization were raised in community surveys that were conducted in 2017 as a part of Project Citizenship, an attempt to set a "cultural direction" for Burning Man. The concerns were raised in response to discussions about whether camp placement on the playa (a high-value entity) should be evaluated in relation to the applicant's level of "engagement" both on the playa and in society. See "Cultural Direction Setting Update," Burning Man Theme Camp Symposium, March 23, 2019, https://themecampsymposium2019.pathable.co.

101. Lucia 2018.

102. Many of the *kīrtan* musicians at Bhakti and Shakti Fests have an intimate relationship with the Hare Krishnas, those affiliated with the International Society for Krishna Consciousness (ISKCON). ISKCON is a highly proselytizing religion dedicated to the worship of the Hindu god Krishna.

103. For example, in 2016, Burning Man acquired Fly Ranch, a permanent property in Nevada. In 2018, the Los Angeles League of Arts purchased 153 acres of land in California City and holds its spring regional event (BEquinox) there. Numerous regional Burning Man collaborations have purchased land or urban spaces for building their utopian visions. See, for example, Noden and Illutron, permanent spaces established by Nordic Burners. Mathias Gullbrandson, "From Event Production to Year Round Movement," Burning Progeny Conference, Fribourg, Switzerland, November 29–30, 2018.

104. Marian Goodell, conversation with the author, Burning Progeny Conference, Fribourg, Switzerland, November 29, 2018.

105. Mallinson and Singleton 2017.

106. See de Michelis 2004; Singleton 2010; Jain 2014 and 2020; Foxen 2020.

107. Despite the fact that CorePower Yoga is explicitly oriented toward the physical benefits of yoga, it has a very dedicated following and uses spiritual language to describe its intents and effects. For example, its website reads, "The magic happens the minute you roll out your yoga mat" (www.corepoweryoga.com). For more on CorePower Yoga, see Hines 2019.

108. "Long-term commitment to soteriological yoga systems frequently required adherents to learn Sanskrit or other Indian languages in order to

systematically study large bodies of sacred literature and to patiently maintain a committed relationship in an inferior position vis-à-vis a qualified guru for years" (Jain 2015, 65).

109. Mallinson and Singleton 2017, 1.

110. For how this came to be, see White 2014.

111. Albanese 2007, 441–42. See also Foxen 2020.

112. Taves 2009, 28–48. Ann Taves builds upon Durkheim's notion of the sacred, arguing that its fundamental premise is that the sacred refers to things that are "special" and thus "set apart."

113. Bija Rivers [pseud.], interview by author, audio recording, Wanderlust Sunshine Coast, Australia, October 22, 2016.

114. Neither the French Quarter Village nor the Black Rock Bakery have anything to do with yoga. I camped there to remind myself that Burning Man is multifaceted and that many participants are not focused on the methods of yoga or spiritual practice, even if they are committed to the notion of personal and social transformation.

1. ROMANTICIZING THE PREMODERN

1. Sundari Lakshmi [pseud.], Kali *homa*, Shakti Fest, Joshua Tree, CA, May 25, 2014.

2. Sarma 2012.

3. Young and Brunk 2009; Young 2010; Ziff 1997; Kraut 2015.

4. Deloria 1998.

5. Donaldson 1999.

6. Root 1996.

7. Altglas 2014.

8. St. John 2013, 177.

9. Gopis are the cowherdess consorts of the Hindu god Krishna.

10. See Pérez 2016; Kraut 2015; Alexander 2001; Lott 1993. In the field of religion, white appropriations of African American religious forms are less common. However, Christopher Driscoll's research focuses on whites who are disaffected from mainline Protestantism and turn instead to Black esoteric religions, such as the Nation of Gods and Earths, as an alternative religious space. See Driscoll, forthcoming.

11. See, for example, scholarship in the field of Afropessimism arguing that anti-Black racism is distinct from racism directed toward people of color more generally (Douglass, Terrefe, and Wilderson 2018). See also Christopher Driscoll's work on anti-Black racism and the construction of white American religion (Driscoll 2015). Vijay Prashad has written about anti-Black racism in *desi* (Indian) communities and the construction of Asian Americans as "model minorities," who are often contrasted against the perceived failures of African Americans (Prashad 2000,118). For a related critique issued from a spiritual thought-leader and activist, see the work of Layla F. Saad (www.laylafsaad.com/poetry-prose, accessed March 31, 2020).

12. DeVaul et al. 2017.

13. The *playa* is the colloquial term used to refer to the vast alkaline dried lake bed in the Black Rock Desert, where Black Rock City is established each year.

14. Devanand (Joshua) [pseud.], interview by author, audio recording, Bhakti Fest, Joshua Tree, CA, September 7, 2012.

15. Kara [pseud.], interview by author, audio recording, Bhakti Fest, Joshua Tree, CA, September 9, 2012.

16. Susan [pseud.], interview by author, audio recording, Bhakti Fest, Joshua Tree, CA, September 7, 2013.

17. Altglas 2014, 245.

18. Altglas 2014, 213.

19. Esme [pseud.], interview by Jen Aubrecht (research assistant to author), audio recording, Bhakti Fest, Joshua Tree, CA, September, 8, 2012.

20. Huffer [Lucia] 2011.

21. Lucia 2014b.

22. Oppenheimer 2003.

23. Hanegraaff 1998, 302.

24. One of the features of Orientalism is the essentialization of a variety of religious and cultural forms into a Western-imagined creation called *the Orient*. Edward Said argued that this "synchronic essentialism" discursively creates a static, unchanging, timeless, and stable ideal of the Orient (Said 1978, 240). I use the term *benevolent*, drawing on the work of Vijay Prashad, who argues that "the conceptualization of a people as having discrete qualities is an act of racist thought" (Prashad 2000, 4); whether that assessment is positive or negative is a matter of circumstance. In *The Karma of Brown Folk*, Prashad argues that *benevolent racism* is the source from which the model minority myth takes its shape (Prashad 2000, 4). Similarly, when SBNR communities essentialize and equate distinct religious and cultural forms of Asia, they do so out of admiration, not malicious intent. I have called this act *benevolent Orientalism* to recognize the tension between this violence and the fact that it is enacted through admiration and even love.

25. Altglas 2014, 213.

26. Oppenheimer 2003.

27. Brian [pseud.], conversation with author, Shakti Fest, Joshua Tree, CA, May 17–19, 2013.

28. Gopal [pseud.], interview by author, audio recording, Holi, Festival of Colors, Los Angeles, CA, March 8, 2014.

29. Several transformational festivals not included in this study have created partnerships with Indigenous communities worthy of mention. 1Nation Earth Camp was an integral part of Oregon Eclipse 2017 (http://oregoneclipse2017.com/environments/1nation-earth-camp). Members of the Pyramid Lake Paiute Tribe collaborated with Symbiosis to create the Pyramid Eclipse 2012, and Symbiosis collaborated with the Miwok Tribe in 2013 and 2015. Global Eclipse (the new form of Symbiosis) is partnering with the transformational festivals Earthdance and Envision and will be held in Patagonia in 2020 in collaboration with Latinx and Indigenous organizers. Burners without Borders has also

developed a collaborative relationship with the local Pyramid Lake Paiute Tribe that has led to multiple initiatives.

30. Bhakti and Shakti Fests also began with Vedic-inspired *homa* (fire sacrifice) rituals, as described in the ethnographic encounters which begin the introduction and this chapter.

31. Lucia 2014.

32. "Take Back Yoga: Bringing Light to Yoga's Hindu Roots," Hindu American Foundation, accessed March 14, 2017, www.hafsite.org/media/pr/takeyogaback.

33. Mallinson and Singleton 2017.

34. Singleton 2010.

35. Bryant 2009, 5.

36. Lucia 2018.

37. At Bhakti Fest, I took my first lesson in communicating through South American crystal skulls. Crystal skulls are a fascinating example of a modern European invention of religion that claims ancient and Indigenous South American (usually Mayan) roots. Despite this history, many Indigenous peoples in both North and South America and New Age metaphysicals have popularized the power of the skulls and have strong convictions about their antiquity and authenticity. See Laycock 2015; Jenkins 2004, 217–18; and St. John 2012, 140.

38. I attended Ana Forrest's classes in Oahu, HI; Great Lake Taupo, New Zealand; and Squaw Valley, CA. She has also taught at Stratton, VT; Whistler, BC; and Hollywood, CA; among other locations.

39. Forrest 2011, 2 (emphasis in the original).

40. Forrest 2011, 171–72.

41. Forrest 2011, 99.

42. Shelby Michaels [pseud.], yoga class, audio recording, Wanderlust, Great Lake Taupo, New Zealand, February 2–4, 2017.

43. Samhita, "Burning Man and the Indigenous Community," *Feministing*, April 14, 2009, http://feministing.com/2009/04/14/burning_man_and_the_Indigenous. See also St. John 2013, 187.

44. Chen 2009, 28.

45. Matthias, who works for Burning Man Project, gave the example of one artist who wanted to bring a miniature guillotine to the playa and place it behind a curtain with a sign reading "insert finger here." Once a participant had inserted a finger, the artist operating the miniature guillotine would chop it off. The organization decided that while such a project fit within the Burning Man spirit of "fucking with people," it would have been "too gruesome" and harmful to be allowed on the playa. Matthias [pseud.], conversation with author, on Fribourg–Zurich train, Switzerland, Burning Progeny Symposium, December 1, 2018.

46. Kevin [pseud.], conversation with author, Burning Man, Black Rock City, NV, August 27, 2018.

47. Bacchus [pseud.], conversation with author, Burning Man, Black Rock City, NV, August 29, 2018.

48. Bacchus [pseud.], conversation with author, Burning Man, Black Rock City, NV, August 29, 2018.

49. Matthes 2016.
50. Matthes 2016, 349 (emphasis in the original).
51. AB Wire., "Brown University Students Protest White, Non-Hindu Woman Singing Kīrtans on Campus," *American Bazaar,* April 25, 2016, www.americanbazaaronline.com/2016/04/25/brown-university-students-protest-by-white-non-hindu-woman-singing-kīrtans-on-campus410592.
52. James 2018.
53. Sarma 2012.
54. Tully 1995, 11.
55. Markell 2003, 175.
56. Kurien 2007, 215.
57. See, for example, Prachi Patankar's (2014) article in *Jadaliyya,* which called on South Asian American anticultural appropriation yoga activists to focus their attention on more pressing problems, such as caste discrimination and rising tides of Hindutva.
58. James 2018.
59. See, for example, the special issue on "The Doniger Affair" in the *Journal of the American Academy of Religions* 84, no. 2 (June 2016).
60. Appiah 2018a, accessed January 2, 2019, https://www.wsj.com/articles/cultural-borrowing-is-great-the-problem-is-disrespect-1535639194. See also Appiah 2018b.
61. Carrette and King 2005, 5–6.
62. See also Kripal 2008, 487.
63. Roopa Singh has also developed the forum Critical Yoga Studies (www.crityogastudies.wordpress.com). For more on Singh and her activism, see https://yastandards.com/roopa-singh.
64. Roopa Singh, "SAAPYA Unedited," YouTube, July 13, 2013, www.youtube.com/watch?v=9o1d1NbKa3c&t=40s. Also quoted in Sri Louis, "Why We Need the World Yoga Festival," *PostYoga,* May 14, 2018, https://postyoga.wordpress.com/2018/05/14/why-we-need-the-world-yoga-festival.
65. See http://redlightning.org/powerofprayer. This was a highly controversial event. Some celebrated the solidarity that Red Lightning camp was building by protesting at Standing Rock. Others condemned the camp members for unsuitable behavior at Standing Rock and for cultural appropriation. Devaney 2017; Breedlove 2016; Dowd 2016; O'Connor 2016.
66. Ashley Atwell, "Review of Red Lightning Tribe," Facebook, September 4, 2017 (has been deleted). Written communications have been reproduced verbatim.
67. See comments on JacQstar Davies, "Sunrise Burning Man the Day of the Global Drum Prayer," Facebook (video), August 29, 2017, www.facebook.com/jackie.davies.967/videos/1496914413707287.
68. One critic wrote, "Im going to say this as a[n] education Who's teepees are those? Because I see a teepee design in the second picture that belongs to a lakota family and if you are not a family member of that family that has the spiritual rights to those paintings you should get rid of it you do not have the right to take those from that family it is disrespectful if you did not earn the right to paint those teepee . . . if you truly respect Native people and the ways

understand not everyone painted there teepee not everyone has that right and if you can't understand that that hearts [hurts] us Natives to see something sacred sarounded by alcohol and drugs then you are part of the problem why there is separation understand things before you do it your are acting like colonial capitalist . . . please respect our ways don't steal." Josh Swagger, September 9, 2017, comment on Red Lightning, "Let it ripple!" Facebook, August 26, 2017, www.facebook.com/RedLightningTribe/posts/10155540072865275.

69. Melanie St. James, multiple replies to negative reviews of Red Lightning Tribe, Facebook, September 7, 2017 (has been deleted), https://www.facebook.com/pg/RedLightningTribe/reviews/?ref=page_internal.

70. Evelise Elrod, "Chase Iron Eyes Explains the Burning Man Situation," YouTube, September 4, 2017, https://youtu.be/5K_1gYtYh-M.

71. Red Bear [pseud.], interview by author, Burning Man, Black Rock City, NV, September 5, 2018.

72. Lightning in a Bottle, "Festival Guide 2015," 21. Available online at www.behance.net/gallery/56643941/Lightning-in-a-Bottle-Festival-Guide-2015, accessed April 6, 2020.

73. Arthur [pseud.], interview by author, audio recording, Shakti Fest, Joshua Tree, CA, May 16, 2015.

74. Gandhi 2006, 26.

75. Maffesoli 1996, 28.

76. http://festivalfire.com/festivals, accessed July 8, 2018 (emphasis mine).

77. For example, tribal body paint techniques have become widely popular at yoga and transformational festivals. Painting another's body can be a fun and interactive way to make contact and the resulting body art contributes to the festival self as an alternative self and serves as a bridge to connect and identify with others. But body paint designs mimic Indigenous forms of body paint (often Aboriginal and Native American). Indigenous body painting signifies the wearer's relationship to their family group, social position, and ancestors and thus carries deep spiritual significance for Indigenous peoples. When whites adopt these practices without reference to their ancestral contexts, it can be seen as deeply offensive and as a cavalier expression of white privilege.

78. Lemke-Santangelo 2009, 47.

79. Perry 1970, 85.

80. Niman 2011, 32. See also Deloria 1998; Guida 2016; and Schelly 2016.

81. St. John 2013, 179.

82. Niman 2011, 37.

83. Schelly 2016, 41.

84. Smith 1994; Aldred 2000; Donaldson 1999; Carrette and King 2005.

85. M. F. Brown 2003, 225.

86. Jonah Haas, "Reframing the Cultural Appropriation Conversation towards Synergy, Co-learning, and Peace," *Dream Journal,* July 29, 2013, https://blog.lucidityfestival.com/jonahhaas/reframing-the-cultural-appropriation-conversation-towards-synergy-co-learning-and-peace.

87. Rosaldo 1989, 108.

88. The "noble savage" played an important role in European travelogues written from the sixteenth and eighteenth centuries. Explorers used the term

noble savage to refer to the valorization of non-Europeans in continents throughout the world. The imagined unity, purity, simplicity, and ecopiety of the noble savages were positioned in contradistinction to European society and levied in efforts to critique European culture. See Todorov 1993, 270–77.

89. In the course of many casual conversations with South Asians about this book, several people recounted their experiences in yoga studios and retreats. One colleague told me that she attends yoga several times a week but just tries to "block out" the spiritual "*bakwās* (rubbish) that the white teacher is saying." One female interlocutor told me that her yoga teacher repeatedly publicly singled her out throughout a yoga retreat and asked her to represent Indian culture and Hinduism. As a Californian, she felt so uncomfortable, angry, and exhausted by his and the rest of the white yoga retreat participants' racialized gaze that she left the retreat early. Some South Asian yogis are attempting to carve alternative paths into American yoga, for example, the collective South Asian American Perspectives on Yoga in America (aka South Asian American Projects in Yoga). As mentioned earlier in this chapter, the Hindu American Foundation has also campaigned to demarcate yoga as Hindu.

90. Jenkins 2004, 67.
91. M. Brown 2003, 67.
92. Lott 1993, 7.
93. Lott 1993, 248.
94. Crane 2018, 244.
95. Crane 2018, 244.
96. Aristotle, quoted in Gandhi 2006, 28.

INTERLUDE: CULTURAL POSSESSION AND WHITENESS

1. Hall uses a broad conception of language that stretches beyond the strictly linguistic. Language, in this framing, is the method of communicating meaning, whether through words, visual images, sound, body language, facial expressions, or the translation of feelings and ideas into these forms. He writes, "Language, in this sense, is a signifying practice" (Hall 1997, 4–5).
2. Hall 1997, 1.
3. Pérez 2016.
4. Kreps 2009.
5. McKinney 2015.
6. J. Cole, "Fire Squad," track 6 on *2014 Forest Hills Drive*, ByStorm Entertainment, Columbia Records, Dreamville Records, and Roc Nation, 2014.
7. Mavis Gewant, "when i was in india one year, a white kirtan couple came to perform for our group and he said, i am going to sing kirtan, invented by krishna das," Facebook, May 13, 2018, https://www.facebook.com/christopher.wallis.942.
8. For example, the term *kīrtan,* often in the form of *anukīrtan* (or the derivatives *anukṛti, anukarana*), meaning "retelling," and the dialogic form of question-answer riddles are both endemic forms found in ancient Vedic scriptures, including the Upaniṣads and the Brahmaṇas, and in many dramatic forms.

9. Marisa [pseud.], conversation with author, March 22, 2012. Marisa is a friend of a friend; although well-intentioned, she is one of the least knowledgeable yoga instructors that I have met. She was not a part of the transformational festival scene.

10. Jagadguru Ballabh Devacharya, interviewed by author (original conversation in Hindi), Kumbh Mela, [Prayagraj] Allahabad, India, February 4, 2019. Daniela Bevilacqua recounted similar sentiments from her interlocutors while conducting ethnographic research among contemporary sadhus in India for the Haṭha Yoga Project (http://hyp.soas.ac.uk).

11. See, for example, Hindu protests against Sheldon Pollock as the head of the Murty Classical Library; Wendy Doniger's book *The Hindus* (2009); James Laine's book *Shivaji* (2003); Paul Courtright's book *Ganesha* (1985); and more recently, Audrey Truschke's book *Aurangzeb* (2017).

12. Khanduri 2012, 348–64.

13. Jeffrey Goldman (Omkara) [pseud.], interview by author, audio recording, Bhakti Fest, Joshua Tree, CA, September 7, 2014.

14. One example is Susanna Barkataki's (2019) article "But, Do I Really Need to Speak Sanskrit?" in which she implores yogis to situate their practice in Indic culture and argues that contemporary global yogis' refusal to learn at least some Sanskrit is "a racial microaggression." In the article, she situates herself as a rightful inheritor and representative of Indic culture and Sanskrit knowledge—though she misspells the Hindu scripture *Bhagavad-Gītā* as "Baghavad Gita."

15. Bajpai 2019.

16. See also Crawley 2018. Crawley builds on an 1981 interview with Foucault, "Friendship as a Way of Life," first published in the French magazine *Gai Pied*.

17. Gandhi 2006, 19.

18. Geertz 1973, 5.

2. ANXIETIES OVER AUTHENTICITY

1. "*Adopters* are those who were not [born into Asian religious environments] and only later adopted various religio-cultural, behaviors, ideas, material environments, and habits of Asian societies" (Lucia 2014a, 151 [emphasis mine]).

2. Lindholm 2008, 9.

3. Cobb 2014, 2.

4. Cobb 2014, 1.

5. Lindholm 2008, 3.

6. Lindholm 2008, 3.

7. Lindholm 2008, 2.

8. Handler 1986, 3.

9. Trilling 1972, 93 (emphasis in the original).

10. Rappaport 1999, 21.

11. Handler 1986, 4.

12. Handler 1986, 4.

13. Grazian 2003, 11–12.

14. Grazian 2003, 16.

15. Graham 2014.

16. See, for example, Alter 2004; de Michelis 2004; Singleton 2010; Strauss 2005; Jain 2015; and Samuel 2007.
17. Samuel 2007, 178.
18. Samuel 2007, 15–16.
19. Miller 2019, 6.
20. Miller 2019, 16.
21. Miller 2019, 7.
22. Foxen 2020; Aubrecht 2017.
23. Jain 2014.
24. Wildcroft 2018.
25. Romantic Orientalism refers to an intellectual movement in England and Europe that was a reaction against the scientific rationalism of the Enlightenment. Philosophers in this milieu were also concerned about the onslaught of industrialization that accompanied the rapid transition into capitalism and modernity. In response to these domestic concerns, leaders in Romantic Orientalism idealized the East, in particular India and Egypt, as geographical seats of great sacrality and ancient wisdom. Importantly, they tended to follow Orientalist modes of privileging the ancient imaginary of the East while decrying its current conditions and extant, living populations. A strict use of the term usually refers to the adoption of "Oriental" characters in British Romantic literature, as in the works of William Blake, William Wordsworth, Lord Byron, and Samuel Taylor Coleridge. But it can also refer to celebrations of the "Orient" in art, music, and cultural trends, as well as intellectual explorations, such as the famed linguists and Orientalist scholars Sir William Jones and Max Müller, for example.
26. Prajna Vieira, "Decolonizing Bhakti Yoga" workshop, audio recording, Bhakti Fest, Joshua Tree, CA, September 8, 2017. Malhotra's readings were included in the workshop's suggested reading handout.
27. Research on yoga in Asia (outside of India) complicates this white/Indian binary as it reveals that in Japan, Japanese women are emerging as the primary representatives of postural yoga, as are Chinese women (the dominant demographic) in Singapore (see Waghorne 2020). Still, while there are few statistics on global yoga production, white women in the United States and Europe are some of the most visible representatives of modern postural yoga in the world. Patrick McCartney has also commented that in Japan, "yoga is a thing that white people do in some way. It's an instrument to become 'whiter' in a sense" (email communication with author, July 16, 2018). This statement suggests that there is an indexical relationship between yoga and whiteness, which is reproduced as the practice travels globally.
28. Lucia 2018.
29. Kraut 2015.
30. Kraut 2015, 4. Kraut cites the critical dance scholarship of Gottschild 1996; Manning 2004; Murphy 2007; Srinivasan 2011; and Wong 2010 as evidence to this point.
31. On yogic influences on Ruth St. Denis, Martha Graham, Merce Cunningham, and Bill T. Jones, see Aubrecht 2017. On white yogis of the early twentieth century, see Deslippe 2018; on Sri Yogendra, see Alter 2014; and on the Omnnipotent Oom, see Love 2010.

32. Appadurai 1996.
33. Saldanha 2007, 197.
34. Kaivalya Maui: Vinyasakrama Yoga of Krishnamacharya, home page, accessed November 12, 2014, http://kaivalyamaui.blogspot.com/2011/01/about-sri-tk-sribhashyam.html (emphasis mine).
35. Bhakti Yatra 2014 advertisement http://bhaktifest.com/bhakti-yatra-presents-returning-home, accessed November 13, 2014 (has been deleted).
36. Bija Rivers [pseud.], yoga class, audio recording, Bhakti Fest, Joshua Tree, CA, September 8, 2012.
37. Bija Rivers [pseud.], yoga class, audio recording, Wanderlust, Mont Tremblant, QC, August 22, 2014.
38. Graham 2014, 97 (emphasis in the original).
39. Hegel 2004.
40. Eliade 2009.
41. Madonna came out as an Ashtanga yogi on *Oprah* in 1998. "Madonna Talking about Ashtanga: I'm Done with the Gym," Claudiayoga, August 16, 2011, https://claudiayoga.wordpress.com/2011/08/16/madonna-talking-about-ashtanga-im-done-with-the-gym.
42. "Sting Hasn't Missed a Day of Yoga in 20 Years," zmark.ca, October 4, 2019, www.zmark.ca/2017/09/sting-hasn-missed-day-of-yoga-in-20.html.
43. Lauren Grounsell, "EXCLUSIVE: Boxing, Yoga, Martial Arts, and Six Meals a Day: Madonna's Personal Trainer Reveals What It Takes to Keep the Notoriously Ripped Star in Shape . . . And Says She Gets THOSE Guns with Just 2.2 Kilogram Light Weights," DailyMail.com, March 18, 2016, www.dailymail.co.uk/femail/article-3498128/Madonna-s-personal-trainer-Craig-Smith-reveals-stars-workout-secrets-Australian-Rebel-Heart-Tour.html.
44. Tribalizm, "Julia Roberts Talks about Neem Karoli Baba," YouTube, August 15, 2011, https://youtu.be/rYrzMzn4N6I.
45. On Sheldon Pollock see Ramakrishnan, n.d. [2016], Chari 2016; on Wendy Doniger see Burke 2014 and Malhotra 2001.
46. Wendy Doniger, conversation with author, Truro, MA, July 30, 2017.
47. Driscoll and Miller 2019, xxvi.
48. See Putcha 2018a, 2018b, and 2019; and Barkataki 2019.
49. See the work of the Black Burner Project at their website (www.blackburnerproject.com) and Instagram account (@blackburnerproject).
50. The exception to this has been the antitransgender commitments of some lesbians and cis-gender women.
51. Jackson 2015.
52. Moreton-Robinson 2015.
53. Moreton-Robinson 2015, 13.
54. Moreton-Robinson 2015, 191.
55. Smith 1978, 290.
56. Huffer [Lucia] 2011, 395.
57. Heelas 2008, 40.
58. Michael Blaine [pseud.], interview by author, audio recording, Bhakti Fest, Joshua Tree, CA, September 9, 2012.
59. Prashad 2000, 4.

60. Asher Grayson [pseud.], interview by author, audio recording, Shakti Fest, Joshua Tree, CA, May 19, 2013.

61. Baudrillard 1994, 12–14.

62. Singleton 2010, 5.

63. Jordan Light [pseud.], yoga class, audio recording, wanderlust, Mont Tremblant, QC, August 22, 2014.

64. See, for example, the work of Matthew Remski, who has been an active critic of the figure of the guru. Remski, "The Guru May Actually Hate You, and You May Actually Hate Him," October 21, 2017, http://matthewremski.com/wordpress/guru-may-actually-hate-may-actually-hate.

65. Michael [pseud.], interview by author, audio recording, Bhakti Fest, Joshua Tree, CA, September 7, 2012.

66. Helena Blake [pseud.], Detox Yoga class, audio recording, Wanderlust, Oahu, February 18, 2014 (emphasis mine).

67. Lucas [pseud.], interview by author, audio recording, Bhakti Fest, Joshua Tree, CA, September 7, 2012.

68. Jordan Light [pseud.], Wanderlust Speakeasy, audio recording, Wanderlust Mont Tremblant, QC, August 23, 2014.

69. Heather Hancock [pseud.], History of Yoga class, audio recording, Wanderlust, Squaw Valley, CA, July 18, 2014. As mentioned, Hancock is correct that there are multiple pronunciations of the vocalic ṛ in contemporary parlance, depending on location. For example, in south India, sometimes the Sanskrit vocalic ṛ is pronounced as a "roo," spelled *rū*, as in *Krūshna* and *pitrū*. This would correspond to the formally unorthodox, though common in both premodern and modern south Indian, pronunciation of *Ṛg Veda* as *Rūg* (pronounced *Roog*) *Veda*. I am grateful to Whitney Cox for explaining this south Indian variant of the vocalic ṛ to me. Cox, email communication with author, April 10, 2019.

70. See www.erichschiffmann.com, accessed November 9, 2014.

71. Taylor 1991, 67–68 (emphasis in the original).

72. Taylor 1991, 69.

73. Judith Butler, cited in Derrida 2016, xi.

74. Bija Rivers [pseud.], interview by author, audio recording, Wanderlust, Sunshine Coast, Australia, October 22, 2016.

75. Singleton 2010, 3–24.

76. PTI, "Over 20 Million Americans Practice Yoga Boosting $27 Billion Market," *Economic Times*, June 21, 2015, https://economictimes.indiatimes.com/news/politics-and-nation/over-20-million-americans-practise-yoga-boosting-27-billion-market/articleshow/47757008.cms, accessed November 13, 2019.

77. Kelly 2016.

78. Godrej 2017; Jain 2020.

79. Singleton 2010; de Michelis 2004.

80. Strauss 2005.

81. Singleton 2010; Altglas 2014.

82. Jain 2014.

83. Peter van der Veer, cited in Csordas 2009.

84. Godrej 2017; Jain 2020.
85. Derrida 2016; Ricoeur 2005.
86. Venuti 2000, 468.
87. Walter Benjamin, cited in Venuti 2000, 81–82.
88. Walter Benjamin, cited in Venuti 2000, 81.
89. Venuti 2000, 486.
90. Campion 2016, 26.
91. Brown 2019.
92. Altglas 2014; Lucia 2014a.
93. Nattier 1997, 72–81.
94. See, for example, Lucia 2014a; Cadge 2005; Gleig 2019; Dempsey 2005; Eck 2001; Kurien 2007; Takaki 1998; and Prashad 2000.
95. Venuti 2000, 486.
96. I use the term *stewardship* intentionally for its colonial importance. As Pedro Funari and Tamima Mourad write, "Power relations are at the heart of social life and stewardship is a concept deeply imbedded in power. Steward, from its inception, is someone who *controls, under the orders of a master* or authority, people and things and so stewardship is the office of administration of power on behalf of someone or some political authority. In our case, the authority is empire, the rule by strength, discretionary power: *imperium*" (Funari and Mourad 2016, 44, emphasis in the original).
97. Venuti 2000, 486.
98. Grazian 2003, 22.
99. "Indeed, it is interpretive communities, rather than either the text or the reader, that produce meanings and are responsible for the emergence of formal features" (Fish 1980, 14).
100. Heelas 2008, 5.
101. This is precisely the argument Jeffrey Kripal makes when he suggests that the epicenter of Indian Tantra has shifted from Calcutta [Kolkuta] to Esalen and San Francisco (Kripal 2008, 500–1).
102. Lucia 2018.
103. Fish 1980, 14.

INTERLUDE: "WHITE PEOPLE ARE ON THE JOURNEY OF EVOLUTION"

1. Niko [pseud.], interview by author, audio recording, Lightning in a Bottle, Bradley, CA, May 23, 2015.
2. Like in the philosophies of Christian and Sufi mystics and Hindu *bhaktas*, in some iterations of yoga philosophy the goal can be the experience of divine love (and sometimes knowledge) in union with God.

3. DECONSTRUCTING THE SELF

1. Löfgren 1999, 264.
2. Palmer and Siegler 2017.
3. Williams 2012.

4. Molz 2007.
5. MacCannell 1992; Strain 2003; Root 1996.
6. Picard 1996; Gren and Huijbens 2016; Rojek and Urry 1997.
7. Collins-Kreiner et al. 2010; Norman 2011.
8. Prato and Trivero 1985.
9. Jain 2019.
10. Oppenheimer 2003, 24.
11. Jain 2019.
12. Carrette and King 2005; Jain 2015 and 2020; Godrej 2017.
13. Jain 2019.
14. Stebbins 2007, 5.
15. Flood asserts that asceticism must be performed within the memory of tradition. As a result, he argues that "the general demise of the ascetic self in modernity as both cultural trope and social fact is linked to the demise of traditional cosmologies, to the rise of the human sciences and Enlightenment reason and to the demise of broader religious tradition within the twofold death of 'God' and 'Man'" (Flood 2004, 235).
16. Weber 2001.
17. Caillois 2001, 12.
18. I am grateful to Alex Rocklin for this suggestion, which he gave in response to my presentation of portions of this chapter at the 2018 American Academy of Religion Conference in Denver, Colorado.
19. D. Brown 2003, 43.
20. D. Brown 2003, 43.
21. D. Brown 2003, 56.
22. D. Brown 2003, 57–58.
23. Maclean 2008, 220.
24. White 1989.
25. Bowditch 2010, 148–56.
26. Kane 2018; Burning Man Project 2019. Other large-scale countercultural festivals, such as the Rainbow Gatherings, have been similarly persecuted by the US government (see Niman 2011; and Schelly 2016).
27. Bureau of Land Management, "Final Record of Decision, Special Recreation Permit Approval Moves Burning Man 2019 Forward," accessed November 13, 2019, www.blm.gov/press-release/final-record-decision-special-recreation-permit-approval-moves-burning-man-2019.
28. Cohen 2019.
29. Bakhtin 1984, 37.
30. Bakhtin 1984, 44.
31. Jain 2015; Godrej 2017; Miller 2018; Carrette and King 2005.
32. Bryant 2009.
33. Alter 1992; 2004.
34. I am grateful to Anya Foxen for reminding me, in response to an early draft of this chapter, that Patañjali had very little to say about organics, GMOs, essential oils, sustainability, Toyota Priuses, and so on. Modern American yogis apply their conceptions of yogic ethical ideals to their current circumstances, creating a subculture with values of its own that is only loosely based on any Indic ethical

convictions. We can see this clearly in the extraordinarily low percentage of American yogis who are vegetarians (around 7 percent), despite Patañjali's first *yama* (ethical principle relating to relations with others) of *ahimsa,* or nonviolence.

35. Flood 2004, 1.
36. Flood 2004, 1.
37. Flood 2004, 1.
38. Binkley 2007.
39. Augé 2008, 27.
40. Flood 2004, 2–3.
41. Foucault 1985, 68. To this point, Foucault is summarizing Plato's argument in the *Republic.*
42. Foucault 1985, 74.
43. Valantasis 1998, 547 (emphasis mine).
44. Weber 1991.
45. Weber 2001.
46. Bourdieu 1984, 231.
47. Bourdieu 1984, 233–34.
48. Bourdieu 1984, 230.
49. Joseph [pseud.], interview by author, audio recording, Shakti Fest, Joshua Tree, CA, May 16, 2015.
50. Arthur [pseud.], interview by author, audio recording, Shakti Fest, Joshua Tree, CA, May 16, 2015.
51. Strain 2003, 18.
52. Olson 2015, 41.
53. Shaw [pseud.], interview by author, audio recording, Burning Man, Black Rock City, NV, August 30, 2016.
54. *Bhāv* (Hindi) or *bhāva* (Sanskrit) means emotion or mood, particularly a divine mood of God.
55. At the 2013 Kumbh Mela, D.P. Dubey explained to me that it was very important that the various camps broadcast religious music (*bhajans* and *kīrtan*) twenty-four hours a day to purify and sanctify pilgrims' minds so that there would be less crime at the one-hundred-million-person festival. Dubey, conversation with author, Kumbh Mela, Prayagraj [Allahabad], India, February 2013.
56. Coachella is a large-scale annual music festival held in the Coachella Valley in Southern California. Although the Do LaB (the producers of LIB) host a stage at Coachella, the festival attracts a mainstream audience interested in the music and partying but not spiritual transformation.
57. Raven [pseud.], interview by Larissa Arambula (research assistant to author), audio recording, Lightning in a Bottle, Bradley, CA, May 22, 2015.
58. Brandi [pseud.], interview by Larissa Arambula (research assistant to author), audio recording, Lightning in a Bottle, Bradley, CA, May 22, 2015.
59. Jeanne [pseud.], interview by author, audio recording, Wanderlust, Mont Tremblant, QC, August 23, 2014.
60. EDC was not a part of this study, and I have never attended, but there are aspects of the festival that seem to be responding to this critique in recent years. The 2019 trailer for the festival compiles footage from EDC 2018 and includes images of yoga, fresh-squeezed juice, camping (glamping), and large-

scale art installations. These inclusions make EDC appear to be trading on signifying images that define festivals like LIB and Burning Man as transformational. Insomniac, "EDC Las Vegas 2019 Official Trailer," YouTube, September 24, 2018, https://youtu.be/GKKQuG9baDg.

61. Harley [pseud.], interview by author, audio recording, Lightning in a Bottle, Bradley, CA, May 28, 2016.

62. According to LIB's 2015 Festival Guide, "The Village is a cultural experiment born from the shared aspiration to explore what village life means and how to bring that into a contemporary context. Our intention is to learn by doing and be engaged, individually and collectively, with how to create and sustain a village." LIB Festival Guide 2015, available online at www.behance.net/gallery/56643941/Lightning-in-a-Bottle-Festival-Guide-2015, accessed April 8, 2020.

63. Beth [pseud.], interview by author, audio recording, Lightning in a Bottle, Bradley, CA, May 28, 2016.

64. Yudkin 2018.

65. Tobias Day [pseud.], yoga class, audio recording, Wanderlust, Great Lake Taupo, New Zealand, February 4, 2017.

66. Kailash [pseud.], telephone interview with Anna Beck (research assistant to author), audio recording, June 9, 2015.

67. Jeremiah Silver [pseud.], breathwork workshop, audio recording, Shakti Fest, Joshua Tree, CA, May 15, 2015.

68. Joseph [pseud.], interview by author, audio recording, Shakti Fest, Joshua Tree, CA, May 16, 2015.

69. Joseph [pseud.], interview by author, audio recording, Shakti Fest, Joshua Tree, CA, May 16, 2015.

70. Some years are dustier than others, and for RV campers, whiteouts may be a mere inconvenience. Still, a quick Google search will reveal the millionaire pop star Katy Perry struggling with her Segway in a dust storm, and in 2017, my friend Melinda helped someone in Beyoncé's entourage who was stranded in a dust storm with a flat bike tire.

71. After the Burning Nerds gathering at Burning Man in 2019, Caveat and I had a good conversation about utopia. As an anthropologist, I argued that Burning Man is, in fact, a utopia because such a large majority of participants believe it to be. As a philosopher, Caveat argued that it is not, because in principle it is not designed to be. In so doing, he echoed other leaders in Burning Man Project (see Debucquoy-Dodley 2020). In contrast, drawing on the study of New Religious Movements (NRMs), I understand a utopia as an enacted vision for an ideal society, which does not imply achieved perfection, but in application, inevitably expresses the full gamut of human experience. Caveat Magister, conversation with author, Burning Man, Black Rock City, NV, August 28, 2019.

72. Magister 2019, 83–84.

73. Helena Blake [pseud.], Chakra Balancing Yoga class, audio recording, Wanderlust, Squaw Valley, July 18, 2014.

74. Ipsos Public Affairs, Yoga Alliance, and *Yoga Journal* 2016, 27.

75. Helena Blake [pseud.], Detox Yoga class, audio recording, Wanderlust, Oahu, February 18, 2014.

76. A neti pot is a container designed to flush water through the nasal cavity.

77. Kailash [pseud.], telephone interview with Anna Beck (research assistant to author), audio recording, June 9, 2015.
78. Harper 2016, 142.
79. Crawford 2006.
80. Deborah Lupton, quoted in Cairns and Johnston 2015, 156.
81. Cairns and Johnston 2015, 156.
82. Crenshaw 1989.
83. Cairns and Johnston 2015, 158.
84. Cairns and Johnston 2015, 155.
85. Bourdieu 1984.
86. I should note that despite my conversion to kale, other aspects of an ascetic yogic lifestyle (no alcohol, for example) were much less appealing to me.
87. Ryan [pseud.], interview by author, audio recording, Shakti Fest, Joshua Tree, CA, May 16, 2015.
88. Foucault 1985, 111.
89. Robyn Shanks, "How One of Canada's Renowned Yoga Teachers Stays Blissful," *Chatelaine*, August 20, 2015, www.chatelaine.com/health/wellness/eoin-finn.
90. Helena Blake [pseud.], speaker, Founder's Speakeasy, Wanderlust Squaw Valley, July 2014.

INTERLUDE: SCULPTING BODIES AND MINDS

Epigraph: Henry Stevenson [pseud.], yoga class, audio recording, Lightning in a Bottle, Bradley, CA, May 27, 2016.

1. Lucia 2018.
2. The soteriological goals of yoga are varied. In the Samkhya Yoga tradition, the goal is the recognition of ultimate consciousness (*puruṣa*) through its dissociation with matter, including the mind and the conventional self (*prakṛti*). More Advaita Vedantic interpretations identify the goal as the recognition of the similitude of the essence of self (*ātman*) and the essence of the cosmos (*brahman*). The *Yoga Sūtras* can be read as guiding practitioners to a union with Īśvara (God). Sometimes, these ideals are articulated with these Indic concepts in popular yoga discourses, but more often than not they are translated into idiomatic phrases, wherein yoga becomes the method to "let go of that which does not serve," "find your authentic self," "get down to your core being," or "uncover your true nature." Although these phrases are philosophically superficial in comparison to the depth of the Indic sources, there is a constancy in the idea behind them: there is an ultimate essence of self that must be realized by discerning its difference from its manifestations in conventional reality.
3. Byrne 2006. Paul Heelas notes how such philosophies have been instrumentalized into various forms of "prosperity spirituality," so named after its famed counterpart, the Prosperity Gospel. In the multifarious terrains of prosperity spirituality, a variety of spokespersons claim to provide "'inner-technologies' to enable participants to experience wealth creation and expenditure as the *manifestation* of inner-spirituality." (Heelas 2008, 52 [emphasis in the original]).

4. Byrne 2006, 9.

5. Byrne 2006, 15.

6. In March 2015, Hemalayaa, a prominent yoga teacher, received yogic vitriol after she wrote a blog post questioning the compatibility of yogic practice with Western psychiatry. Hemalayaa suggested that instead of taking antidepressants, yogis should struggle though life stresses and challenges and embrace all emotions as a part of human existence. She commended herself for taking the "high road" of being "natural" (not medicated) despite her emotional struggles. She wrote that her philosophy derived from self-inquiry, beginning with the ideal that "life is meant to be lived fully, emotions and all," and ending with "I dance and laugh a lot, and I am human, I cry and fall too. I move through the tough times and grow and try to evolve so that my soul is not stuck." She concluded with suggestions of practices for "when the shit hits the fan": (1) have a good cry, (2) self-care, (3) go outside, (4) yoga, and (5) know that you are not alone. Granted, Hemalayaa's post was particularly tone-deaf in regard to the realities of living with mental health challenges, but the level of attack that she received from yogis was astounding. Within days, she took the post down and issued a public apology. Hemalayaa, "Shocked about Yoga Teachers on Meds," *Hema Blog,* March 7, 2015, www.hemalayaa.com/shocked-about-yoga-teachers-on-meds.

7. Byrne 2006, 23.

8. Byrne 2006, 9.

9. Byrne 2006, 17.

10. Sloane [pseud.], conversation with author, Los Angeles, CA, December 25, 2016.

11. Nietzsche 1928.

12. In discussing the gift economy at Burning Man, Rachel Bowditch recognizes that Burning Man can be financially perilous, even ruinous, for artists, who invest heavily in creating expensive art pieces that are burned on the playa, transforming into ash, honor, prestige, and social capital (Bowditch 2010, 104).

4. WONDER, AWE, AND PEAK EXPERIENCES

Epigraphs: Laughlin [pseud.], conversation with author, Burning Man, Black Rock City, NV, August 27, 2017. Jason Silva voiceover in Bianca Smith, "Somewhere in Black Rock City: iRobot Burning Man 2018," Vimeo, September 11, 2018, https://vimeo.com/289176572 (emphasis mine).

1. Clewis 2019, 1.

2. Malina 2008, 163.

3. For those interested in this long-standing debate in the study of religion, Ann Taves (2009, 17–21) provides a helpful discussion.

4. Žižek 2001, 12.

5. Žižek 2001, 13.

6. Žižek 2001, 12.

7. Weber 1991, 169.

8. Weber 1991, 168.

9. For example, many practitioners practice the fluid movement practice of *vinyāsa yoga* or flow arts (hooping, aerial, fire dancing, etc.), as mediations buttressed by the notion of "flow" popularized by Mihaly Csikszentmihalyi (1990).

10. T. Srinivas 2018, 212–13.

11. Foucault 2005.

12. Luhrmann 2012.

13. Beliso-De Jesús 2015.

14. Charles Taylor (2007, 38) argues that modern secularism has ushered in a shift in the conception of the self from that of a porous self to that of a buffered self. The buffered self refers to the modern self that "can see itself as invulnerable, as master of the meanings of things for it." This is a "bounded self" that can disengage from everything outside of the mind. In contrast, the premodern period was marked by the conception of self as a porous self, one that was "vulnerable, to spirits, demons, cosmic forces" beyond its control.

15. Taylor 2007, 38.

16. Srinivas 2018, 7. Phenomenologists have been critiqued for their Christocentric perspectives, including the foundational notion that mysticism is mediation between an autonomous subject and an unattainable (transcendent) object. Aisha Beliso-De Jesús's (2015, 78) work on transnational Santería encourages scholars to think instead in terms of "pluralized relationships" and "a complexity of agents" engaged in multiple "entanglements." These, she argues, are more aptly considered as *copresences,* "energies of nature and spirit, divinity and body entangled in diffracted waves of knowledge and power."

17. Amy Hollywood (1995, 146) writes that "Eckhart's understanding of the necessity for detachment is grounded in an Aristotelian epistemology in which the mind's receptiveness depends on its blankness" and shows that Eckhart echoed Marguerite Porete, who self-consciously viewed her mystical practice to be the act of emptying chalice of the self and filling it with Christ.

18. Schopenhauer 2010, 227.

19. De Certeau 2000, 5.

20. Ginzburg 2004.

21. For example, in *The Possession at Loudun,* de Certeau (2000, 100–103) shows how the possession of the seventeenth century Ursuline nuns cannot be analyzed in isolation as an extrasocial mystical experience. Instead, he argues, the "purifying theater" of possession created social realities (good nuns afflicted by evil forces) and was interpreted through epistemological frames that expressed social tensions and fears of the time (atheism).

22. See Taylor 2007, 25–89, particularly 27–41.

23. For example, during our interview at Bhakti Fest, Zakir explained, "We question things that are unfamiliar to us and we go, 'No way, that's an accident. That's coincidence.' We'll throw any type of an excuse in front of the idea that it can't just be mysterious, mystical in nature, that there can't just be psychic power, clairvoyance, the third eye, awakening. Yes, these things are real. . . . If we train our children to use their clairvoyance, to use their intuition, and really practice, and do that often with a lot of young people—allow them to think that they have magic, that they are magic, then it's like, 'Oh, of course.' You know?

Because it is all part of who we are. We are divine beings in a physical form." Zahir [pseud.], interview by author, audio recording, Bhakti Fest, Joshua Tree, CA, September 8, 2012.

24. Emerson [pseud.], interview by author, audio recording, Bhakti Fest, Joshua Tree, CA, September 6, 2012. Many of my interviewees closed their interviews with some version of the sentiment, "Thank you for listening. I probably needed that."

25. Burning Man Project is the LLC behind Burning Man.

26. Flood 2004, 219–22.

27. Saldanha 2007, 51.

28. Saldanha 2007, 50.

29. Lucia 2014b.

30. Lorelai [pseud.], interview by author, audio recording, Shakti Fest, Joshua Tree, CA, May 16, 2015.

31. Mila Volkov [pseud.], audio recording, Lightning in a Bottle, Bradley, CA, May 25–30, 2016.

32. De Martino 2001, 97.

33. Albanese 1990. See also Taylor 2010; and Pike 2018.

34. Fuller 2001, 90.

35. Berry 2015, 141.

36. Quoted in Venkatarmaman 2015, 231.

37. Berry 2015, 135.

38. Berry 2015, 143.

39. Berry 2015, 148.

40. Binkley 2007.

41. Kripal 2007.

42. Finney 2014, 3; Pike 2018, 29. According to a 2009 National Park Service survey, only 7 percent of park visitors were African American and 9 percent were Hispanic. When the visits are restricted to parks that showcase wilderness and outdoor recreation, such as Yosemite National Park, for example, then the figure for African American visitors drops to just 1 percent. Rob Lovitt, "Where Are the People of Color in National Parks?" NBC News, updated August 3, 2011, www.nbcnews.com/id/44008927/ns/travel-news/t/where-are-people-color-national-parks.

43. Ralph Waldo Emerson, quoted in Albanese 2007, 166.

44. See, for example, the installations of Burning Man art in the Bay Area (Hill 2018), the exhibit of Burning Man art at the Smithsonian American Art Museum (*No Spectators: The Art of Burning Man,* https://americanart.si.edu/exhibitions/burning-man), and the Big Art for Small Towns initiative (https://burningman.org/culture/civic-initiatives/big-art-for-small-towns).

45. Shaw [pseud.], interview by author, audio recording, Burning Man, Black Rock City, NV, August 30, 2016. Shaw happened to reiterate this maxim succinctly, but it is prevalent throughout the community, and I have heard it from numerous participants.

46. Styn 2010.

47. Shaw [pseud.], interview by author, audio recording, Burning Man, Black Rock City, NV, August 30, 2016.

48. Wheel of Fortune Tarot Project is an art installation created by Jill Sutherland and Anne Staveley, which first debuted at Burning Man in 2014. "2014 Art Installations: Wheel of Fortune," Burning Man, Historical Archives, accessed March 31, 2019, https://burningman.org/culture/history/brc-history/event-archives/2014-event-archive/2014-art-installations/#WheelofFortune; "Wheel of Fortune Tarot Project: Major Arcana Tarot Deck & Interactive Divination Installation," accessed March 31, 2019, www.woftarot.com.

49. See https://symmetrylabs.com/portfolio/tenere, accessed April 20, 2020.

50. Rodney [pseud.], conversation with author, Burning Man, Black Rock City, NV, August 31, 2018.

51. To these, one could add Electric Forest, Symbiosis, Rainbow Serpent, EDC, Lucidity, Sonic Boom, and so on.

52. Jarnow 2016, 373–74.

53. See, for example, Leary, Metzner, and Alpert 1964; Burroughs 2003; Huxley 2009; T. McKenna and D. McKenna 1975; and McKenna 1992, among others.

54. Grim 2009, 1–17.

55. Grim 2009, 144–45.

56. Saldanha 2007, 17.

57. Caleb and Destiny [pseuds.], Open Mic at Center Stage, audio recording, Burning Man, Black Rock City, NV, September 2, 2016 (emphasis mine).

58. Strassman 2001.

59. Brice [pseud.], conversation with author, Valley Center, CA, September 14, 2019.

60. St. John 2012, 151.

61. St. John 2012, 126–33.

62. Kripal 2008, 495.This term was first popularized by Abraham Maslow and proliferated in experimental spiritual communities in the model of Esalen.

63. Grim 2009, 12–13.

64. Ram Dass 1971, "Environmental Changes," n.p.

65. Lorelai [pseud.], interview by author, audio recording, Shakti Fest, Joshua Tree, CA, May 16, 2015.

66. Beyer 2009, 337.

67. Kylie [pseud.], conversation with author, beach cleanup, Wanderlust, Oahu, March 1, 2014.

68. "Drug Use across the Generations: Comparing the Drug Taking Habits of Millennials, Gen Xers, Baby Boomers, and the Lucky Few," Drugabuse.com, accessed March 31, 2019, www.drugabuse.com/featured/drug-and-alcohol-abuse-across-generations.

69. Millennials have grown up in very different drug environments wherein prescription drug use is common, prescription drug abuse is even more common, and opioid use and abuse has exploded into epidemic proportions. A 2014 Center for Disease Control study showed that nearly one in ten boys aged six to seventeen have been prescribed medication for emotional or behavioral difficulties in the past six months (Howie, Pastor, and Lukacs 2014). Another study reveals that 12.7 percent of persons twelve and older took antidepressant

medication in the past month and that antidepressant use has increased by nearly 65 percent between 1999 and 2014. Antidepressant use has increased by 64.9 percent for both sexes between 1999 and 2014. (See Pratt, Brody, and Gu 2017, figure 4). Further, opioid use has increased to nearly 7 percent of the US population, and patients are increasingly likely to be prescribed opioids stronger than morphine. From 1999–2002 to 2011–2012, the percentage of opioid analgesic users who used an opioid analgesic stronger than morphine increased from 17 percent to 37 percent (Frenk, Porter, and Paulozzi 2015).

70. Ipsos Public Affairs, Yoga Alliance, and *Yoga Journal.* 2016.

71. At Burning Man in 2017, I went out one night with Carmen [pseud.], a beautiful young party girl, yoga instructor, and global trekker, and her crew of friends. Over the course of the night, each of them took two hits of LSD and multiple "moon rocks" of MDMA.

72. Henry Stevenson, audio recording, yoga class, Lightning in a Bottle, Bradley, CA, May 27, 2016 (emphasis mine).

73. Johnson 2019; email communication, received from Lightning in a Bottle (list@thedolab.com), December 21, 2018, 12:45 pm. The message was also reposted on Reddit: "Letter to the LiB Community," December 21, 2018, www.reddit.com/r/LightningInABottle/comments/a8e6dm/letter_to_the_lib_community. The 6 Ways of LIB are also now posted on the festival's website, https://lightninginabottle.org/6ways, accessed April 20, 2020. In addition to circulating these ethical principles, LIB also decided to reduce ticket sales by 25 percent (reducing the number of participants from 27,000 in 2018 to 20,250 in 2019). Some estimates put 2018 attendance at 35,000 or above, significantly violating the 20,000-person attendance cap established in the agreement between the Do LaB (the producers of LIB) and Lake San Antonio county officials.

74. "The 10 Principles of Burning Man," Burning Man, Philosophical Center, accessed December 23, 2018, www.burningman.org/culture/philosophical-center/10-principles.

75. This is a frequently iterated critique. For example, in his famous work on the 1960s counterculture, Theodore Roszak wrote, "For them [the youth of the counterculture], psychic chemistry is no longer a means for exploring the perennial wisdom; it has become an end in itself, a source of boundless lore, study, and esthetic elaboration. It is becoming the whole works" (Roszak 1969, 160).

76. See St. John 2012.

77. Christopher Wallis, "Is Shakti Fest racist for not inviting any South Asian artists to perform? Discuss," Facebook, May 13, 2018, https://www.facebook.com/christopher.wallis.942.

78. Ekabhumi Ellik, comment on Christopher Wallis, "Is Shakti Fest racist for not inviting any South Asian artists to perform? Discuss," Facebook, May 13, 2018, https://www.facebook.com/christopher.wallis.942.

79. Ekabhumi Ellik, comment on Christopher Wallis, "Is Shakti Fest racist for not inviting any South Asian artists to perform? Discuss," Facebook, May 13, 2018, https://www.facebook.com/christopher.wallis.942.

80. Prajna Vieira, phone conversation with author, January 4, 2019.

81. Grazian 2003, 16.

82. Ekabhumi Ellik, "Open Letter to Shakti Fest Organizers," May 18, 2018, www.facebook.com/notes/ekabhumi-ellik/open-letter-to-shakti-fest-organizers/10155596701113063.

83. Lott 1993, 118. See also his discussion of "the seeming counterfeit," 115–39.

84. Jake [pseud.], interview by author, audio recording, Bhakti Fest, Joshua Tree, CA, September 7, 2012.

85. William [pseud.], interview by author, audio recording, Bhakti Fest, Joshua Tree, CA, September 9, 2012.

86. Eli Gordon [pseud.], intensive yoga class, audio recording, Bhakti Fest, Joshua Tree, CA, September 8, 2014.

87. Devanand (Joshua) [pseud.], interview by author, audio recording, Bhakti Fest, Joshua Tree, CA, September 7, 2012.

88. Prajna Vieira, phone conversation with author, January 4, 2019.

89. Prajna Vieira, phone conversation with author, January 4, 2019.

90. "Bhakti Arts Collective Presents: Prasada Festival," accessed April 17, 2019, www.prasada-festival.com.

91. Donovan [pseud.], interview by author, audio recording, Bhakti Fest, September 6, 2012.

92. Many Burners refer to returning to Black Rock City as "coming home." See, for example, Stefan Spins, "Burning Man 2011 Home," YouTube, September 10, 2011, www.youtube.com/watch?v=WQPQn9TLpPY.

93. Katrina [pseud.], interview by Jen Aubrecht (research assistant to author), audio recording, Bhakti Fest, Joshua Tree, CA, September 9, 2012.

94. Chloe Lindsay [pseud.], neo-Tantra sexuality workshop, audio recording, Bhakti Fest, Joshua Tree, CA, 2013 (emphasis mine).

95. Sasha [pseud.], interview with Larissa Arambula (research assistant to author), Lightning in a Bottle, Bradley, CA, May 21, 2015.

96. Yudkin 2018.

97. Dahlia [pseud.], interview by author, audio recording, Wanderlust, Sunshine Coast, Australia, October 20, 2016.

98. On the last Saturday night of Burning Man, the event that gives the festival its name occurs when Burning Man Project sets fire to the Man, the central figurine.

99. Becka [pseud.], Facebook messenger conversation with author, April 17, 2019.

100. Huxley 2009.

101. Thakkar 2016.

102. Mila Volkov [pseud.], audio recording, Lightning in a Bottle, Bradley, CA, May 25–30, 2016.

INTERLUDE: PRODUCING WONDER / BRANDING FREEDOM

Epigraph: Sloane [pseud.], interview by author, audio recording, Burning Man, Black Rock City, NV, August 29, 2019. Mickey and Daily TV are also pseudonyms.

1. Goodell 2019.

2. Many veteran Burners critique the role that Burning Man organizers played in the consumerist expansion of Burning Man in 2012, when it increased ticket sales and exponentially expanded the population of Black Rock City. See "2012 Event Archive," Burning Man, Historical Archives, accessed November 28, 2019, https://burningman.org/culture/history/brc-history/event-archives/2012-2.

3. While I remember much of this Lollapalooza history from my own teenage years, I am grateful to Nori Barajas-Murphy, who was in Perry Farrell's social milieu at the time and helped to fill in some of these details.

4. Waddell 2015.

5. Faughnder 2016.

6. Mayor's Press Office, "Lollapalooza Sells Out," Chicago Office of the Mayor, press release, April 3, 2013, www.cityofchicago.org/city/en/depts/mayor/press_room/press_releases/2013/april_2013/lollapalooza_sellsout.html.

7. Domanick 2012.

8. Trips Reddy, "Six Factors Driving the Massive Growth of Music Festivals," *Umbel,* October 7, 2015, www.umbel.com/blog/entertainment/6-factors-driving-massive-growth-of-music-festivals.

9. Reddy, "Six Factors."

10. US Census, "Income, Poverty and Health Insurance Coverage in the United States: 2016," accessed September 13, 2018, . www.census.gov/newsroom/press-releases/2017/income-povery.html.

11. Lucia 2014b. Of those surveyed, 8.3 percent earned between $25,000 and $49,999, 13.9 percent earned between $50,000 and $74,999, 11.1 percent earned between $75,000 and $99,999, 8.3 percent earned between $125,000 and $149,999, and 13.9 percent earned over $175,000. I designed this survey and circulated it among American yogis on social media sites in fall 2015; it received 119 responses. Eighty-two percent of respondents identified as white (Anglo-European), and 92 percent of respondents identified as female, which roughly reflects the demographics of American yogis.

12. DeVaul et al. 2017.

13. Conroy 2018.

14. Natural Marketing Institute, "Sixth Edition: Understanding the LOHAS Market Report," March 2008, www.lohas.se/wp-content/uploads/2015/07/Understanding-the-LOHAS-Consumer-11_LOHAS_Whole_Foods_Version.pdf.

15. Raphael 2017.

16. Anderton 2015, 201.

17. Lena Corner, cited in Anderton 2015, 200.

18. "The 10 Principles of Burning Man," Burning Man, Philosophical Center, accessed December 23, 2018, www.burningman.org/culture/philosophical-center/10-principles

19. Bowditch 2010, 111.

20. Bowditch 2010, 108.

21. Robinson 2016.

22. Spencer 2015.

23. Pebbles [pseud.], text conversation with author, December 2, 2019.

5. THE CATHARTIC FREEDOM OF TRANSFORMATIONAL FESTIVALS

Epigraphs: Foucault 1985, 77. Johann Wolfgang von Goethe, cited in Crapazano 1986.

1. Echoing this, Saldanha's notes that "freedom is a word used profusely in Goa to describe what tourists come in search of there." He also writes that "conspiracy theory might seem an exaggerated way of looking at the disciplinary regimes keeping young whites in check, but it demonstrates that psychedelics (taking drugs, dancing to electronic music, traveling to India, meeting like-minded people, becoming viral) is indeed a conscious project of reinventing oneself" (Saldanha 2007, 31).

2. Heelas 2008, 38 (emphasis in the original).

3. Heelas 2008, 2.

4. Hardt and Negri 2001.

5. Heelas 2008, 2.

6. Turner 1996, 96.

7. Turner 1996, 112.

8. "Precarity is the condition of being vulnerable to others. Unpredictable encounters transform us; we are not in control, even of ourselves. Unable to rely on a stable structure of community, we are thrown into shifting assemblages, which remake us as well as our others. We can't rely on the status quo; everything is in flux, including our ability to survive. Thinking through precarity changes social analysis. A precarious world is a world without teleology. Indeterminacy, the unplanned nature of time, is frightening, but thinking through precarity makes it evident that indeterminacy also makes life possible" (Tsing 2015, 20).

9. Riesebrodt 2010, 59–60.

10. Thoreau 2018, 4 (emphasis mine).

11. Marx (1990) focused on economic forces and located the source of exploitation within capitalism and the division of labor. Feuerbach (2008) and Nietzsche (2001) both demanded that humans recognize their own power rather than misdirecting that power to an external, imagined supreme being or God. Nietzsche (2007) even characterized this condition as a sickness, which he argued must be identified, treated, and cured in order for the individual to flourish in his ideal state as his highest self, as the *übermensch*. Rousseau's critique located the cause of bondage within Enlightenment notions of progress and the manner in which humans are socialized in immoral ways through social and historical processes (Maguire and Williams 2018, particularly "First Discourse: On the Sciences and the Arts," pp. 39–68).

Max Weber (2001) wrote of the "iron cage" of modernity, while members of the Frankfurt School working in the interwar years in Germany warned of fascism, reactionary socioeconomics, and the impending determinism of capitalism (Arato and Gephardt 1982). Max Horkheimer and Theodore Adorno (2002, 94–136) famously forewarned that when regulated by capitalist markets, human free will (freedom of choice) ultimately ceases to exist and instead becomes dictated by the choices available within the capitalist market. Their assessment is a bleak one, though it is foreshadowing in the sense that it is becoming increasingly difficult to think beyond and outside of capitalism as the dominant force of modern society.

12. Walter Benjamin (2019, 166–95) wrote of the eclipsing of the real and authentic with the encroachment of mechanical modes of reproduction. Jean Baudrillard (1994) argued that modernity has ushered in a form of hyperreality in which existence becomes mere simulation.

13. Ward and Voas 2011.

14. Orwell 1949; Huxley 2013; Rand 2005; Collins 2008.

15. Wachowski et al. 1999.

16. Lia [pseud.], audio recording, Lightning in a Bottle, Bradley, CA, May 28, 2016.

17. Crystal Dawn [pseud.], audio recording, Temple of Consciousness, Lightning in a Bottle, Bradley, CA, May 29, 2016.

18. Dream Rockwell has cited gender discrimination as a primary reason for her departure from the Do LaB, which she cofounded with Josh and Jesse Flemming. However, a statement from the Flemmings' lawyer reads, "The flat-Earth lecture was certainly a part of the Do LaB's decision to no longer hire Ms. Webb [Dream Rockwell] to produce the Temple of Consciousness at LIB, although her lawsuit against the company really cemented that decision. . . . Dream's insistence on, inter alia, advancing the argument that the world is flat as a sound and enlightened theory at LIB required action by the Flemmings to protect the integrity of the event and their organization" (Duwe 2017). See also the Flat Earth Society (www.theflatearthsociety.org and www.tfes.org).

19. Julius Anderson [pseud.], presentation at Center Camp, spoken word stage, and conversation with author, Burning Man, August 28, 2018.

20. Julius Anderson [pseud.], presentation at Center Camp, spoken word stage, and conversation with author, Burning Man, August 28, 2018.

21. Xavier [pseud.], interview by author, audio recording, Burning Man, Black Rock City, NV, August 30, 2016.

22. Becka [pseud.], Facebook messenger conversation with author, April 17, 2019.

23. Lia [pseud.], interview by author, audio recording, Lightning in a Bottle, Bradley, CA, May 28, 2016.

24. See, for example, one yogi's account of how Western Yoga Culture/Community (WYC) espouses "We are all one" rhetoric and thus disabled persons are "covertly discarded or censured." Laura Sharkey, "10-Ways to Rise above Ableism (Even If You Didn't Realize You Needed To)," Off the Mat, Into the World, October 1, 2018, ww.offthematintotheworld.org/blog/ableism.

25. Historically, European immigrants had immediate access to free citizenship, while Natives, African Americans, and Mexicans, who had lived on this land for generations, were systematically denied these rights. See Rana 2010, 13.

26. Hailey [pseud.], interview by author, audio recording, Wanderlust, Sunshine Coast, Australia, October 21, 2016.

27. Lucifer, conversation with author, audio recording, Burning Man, Black Rock City, NV, August 31, 2016.

28. Lia [pseud.], interview by author, audio recording, Lightning in a Bottle, Bradley, CA, May 28, 2016.

29. Jeremiah Silver [pseud.], breathwork workshop, audio recording, Shakti Fest, Joshua Tree, CA, May 15, 2015.

30. Zane [pseud.], conversation with author, Burning Man, Black Rock City, NV, September 3, 2017.

31. Dusty [pseud.], interviewed by author, audio recording, Burning Man, Black Rock City, NV, September 2, 2016.

32. Bryant 2009, xxxi.

33. Mark Bentley [pseud.], speaking at the Wanderlust Speakeasy, audio recording, Wanderlust Squaw Valley, July 2014.

34. Pew Research Center 2015.

35. Funk and Smith 2012.

36. Helena Blake [pseud.], Chakra Balancing Yoga, audio recording, Wanderlust, Squaw Valley, CA, July 18, 2014.

37. Katie Kurtz [pseud.], yoga class, audio recording, Wanderlust, Oahu, HI, March 1, 2014.

38. DJ Akash [pseud.], yoga class, audio recording, Wanderlust, Squaw Valley, CA, July 19, 2014.

39. Zachary Ellis [pseud.], yoga class, audio recording, Wanderlust, Squaw Valley, CA, July 17, 2014.

40. I selected these excerpts somewhat randomly from scores of yoga classes that I have attended at Wanderlust festivals; they represent common discourses and are not cherry-picked or outliers in any sense.

41. Bryant 2009, xlvii.

42. "The 10 Principles of Burning Man," Burning Man, Philosophical Center, accessed December 23, 2018, www.burningman.org/culture/philosophical-center/10-principles (emphasis mine).

43. Gershon 2011, 539.

44. Heelas 2008, 31.

45. Kailash [pseud.], yoga class, audio recording, Shakti Fest, Joshua Tree, CA, May 15, 2015.

46. I am grateful to Nathan McGovern for raising this important critique in response to an earlier draft of this chapter.

47. Gershon 2011, 542.

48. Foucault 1986, 39–68. At Burning Man, *self-care* is a staple vocabulary word on the playa, but it has a completely different valence. In this extreme environment, self-care means don't die; take care of yourself so that you can be self-reliant. Burning Man and LIB also support medical tents and Zendo tents (psychedelic harm reduction, www.zendoproject.org), and LIB hosts DanceSafe (www.dancesafe.org), which offers drug identification services.

49. Brown 2006, 695

50. Altglas 2014, 321.

51. Shaw [pseud.], interview by author, audio recording, Burning Man, Black Rock City, NV, August 30, 2016.

52. Xavier [pseud.], interview by author, audio recording, Burning Man, Black Rock City, NV, August 30, 2016.

53. Clark Coleman [pseud.], interview by author, audio recording, Burning Man, Black Rock City, NV, August 31, 2016.

54. Berlin 1969.

55. In her recent book *Ecopiety,* religion and ecology scholar Sarah McFarland Taylor (2019) critiques this individualistic approach to looming environmental catastrophe, arguing that this "imagined moral economy" based in "tiny acts of voluntary personal piety" distracts from larger structural systems that further ecological destruction on a grand scale.

56. Beth [pseud.], interview by author, audio recording, Lightning in a Bottle, Bradley, CA, May 28, 2016.

57. Yoga Alliance, "Black Lives Matter," Facebook, June 2, 2020, https://www.facebook.com/yogaalliance/.

58. Dominique Debucquoy-Dodley, "Diversity and Radical Inclusion: Black Lives Matter," *Burning Man Journal,* June 2, 2020, https://journal.burningman.org/2020/06/opinion/serious-stuff/diversity-radical-inclusion-black-lives-matter/.

59. I borrow this term from Thelathia "Nikki" Young, who used it in her keynote address, "'I Will Be Who I Will Be': Ethical Projects of Self (Un-)Making in Black Queer Fugitivity," at the University of California, Riverside, inaugural Conference on Queer and Transgender Studies in Religion, held February 22–24, 2019.

CONCLUSION

1. Pitzer 1997, 6.
2. Rappaport 1999, 17–18.
3. Mannheim 1936, 199.
4. Mannheim 1936, 208.
5. Tsing 2015, 20.
6. Srinivas 2018, 212.
7. Srinivas 2018, 212.
8. De Martino 2001, 87.
9. De Martino 2001, 97.
10. Tsing 2015, 98.
11. Putnam 2007, 150–51. See also Jonas 2007.
12. Putnam 2007, 151.
13. Putnam 2007, 142.
14. Putnam 2007, 143.
15. Putnam 2007, 148.
16. Putnam 2007, 149.
17. Thrasher 2015.
18. "How to Dress Like a Burner," *Piss Clear,* issue 25, September, 3, 2004, www.pissclear.org/PDFArchives/PissClear25ext_2004.pdf. Featured in Bowditch 2010, 146.
19. See "Utopia and Fashion," special issue, *Utopian Studies* 28, no. 3 (2017), particularly the articles by Campbell, Galant, and Pollen.
20. Sloane [pseud.], personal communication, Los Angeles, CA, December 25, 2016.
21. Saldanha 2007, 210.

22. Carly [pseud.], conversation with author, Claremont, CA, August 20, 2018.

23. Campion 2016, 27.

24. Campion 2016, 143.

25. These are values culled from my interviews and interactions that seem to be common across these different festivals. Some values, such as self-reliance, may be extraordinarily important to one festival but not to another and thus have not been listed here.

26. See Dianne Bondy Yoga (www.diannebondyyoga.com); Jessamyn Stanley (www.jessamynstanley.com): and Wild Yoga (www.wildyoga.co.uk).

27. See, for example, the Take Back Yoga campaign initiated by the Hindu American Foundation and the nationalization of yoga led by India's prime minister, Narendra Modi, through massive public relations campaigns and national events like the International Yoga Day, June 21, and through his partnership with celebrity yoga guru Baba Ram Dev. See also Gupta and Copeman 2019; Jain 2020; Chakraborty 2006; and Sarbacker 2014.

28. Iwamura 2011.

29. In his seminal work, *Primitive Culture* (1871), English anthropologist and founder of cultural anthropology E. B. Tylor put forward the notion of "survivals" to refer to practices that have lingered longer than they should have under the current episteme. In his words, "These [survivals] are processes, customs, opinions, and so forth, which have been carried on by force of habit into a new state of society different from that in which they had their original home, and they thus remain as proofs and examples of an older condition of culture out of which a newer has been evolved" (Tylor 2016, 16). Survivals are reminders of a bygone era, which will eventually disappear but have not yet. For example, even today it is commonplace to say "bless you" when someone sneezes despite the fact that the general populace no longer believes that the soul escapes the body during the event.

30. In a recent article listing the bios of the "100 Most Influential Yoga Teachers in America," the author included only two Indian American yoga teachers, both female. I mention this not to highlight the author's biases but rather because I believe this is a relatively accurate depiction of the absence of Indian and Indian American influencers in the current field. Shira Atkins, "100 Most Influential Yoga Teachers in America," Sonima, February 8, 2016, www.sonima.com/yoga/100-most-influential-yoga-teachers-in-america-2016.

31. Page 2007.

32. DiAngelo 2018, 14.

APPENDIX 2: METHODOLOGY

1. Bourdieu and Wacquant 1992.

2. Burowoy 1991, 6.

3. Charles Kurzman (1991, 254) notes a division in ethnographic research between "respect" and "silencing" arguments. Respect for subjects allows the concerns of subjects to shape the scholarly issues a study addresses. In contrast, the silencing argument, "namely, that the subjects are systematically silenced by

social forces preventing them from recognizing or discussing their true situation," suggests that the scholar can, and should, apply a relevant frame of analysis even over the potential objections of his or her subjects. My research is *respectful* in that many of my informants are deeply concerned about the whiteness of these fields. However, this work is also *silencing* in that I interrogate questions of whiteness even when they are suppressed or ignored by my informants.

4. Boellstorff et al. 2013.

5. Amma (Mata Amritanandamayi) is a global guru from Kerala, India, who is famous for her massive public *darshan* (blessings) programs, during which she gives hugs to tens of thousands in one continuous sitting. See Lucia 2014a.

6. DeVaul et al. 2017.

7. Lynd and Lynd 1929, 8.

8. DiAngelo 2018.

9. DiAngelo 2018, 1–2.

10. Alexander 2007, 98.

11. Driscoll and Miller 2019, 18.

12. See, for example, reactions to Gandhi and Wolff 2017.

13. Young 2015.

14. This figure includes only the days spent on site at festivals. It does not include innumerous nonfestival yoga classes and *kīrtan* gatherings, off-site build and work days, and events, gatherings, and parties with informants.

References

Albanese, Catherine L. 1990. *Nature Religion in America: From the Algonkian Indians to the New Age.* Chicago: University of Chicago Press.
———. 2007. *A Republic of Mind and Spirit: A Cultural History of American Metaphysical Religion.* New Haven, CT: Yale University Press.
Aldred, Lisa. 2000. "Plastic Shamans and Astroturf Sun Dances: New Age Commercialization of Native American Spirituality." *American Indian Quarterly* 24, no. 3 (summer): 329–52.
Alexander, Michael. 2001. *Jazz Age Jews.* Princeton, NJ: Princeton University Press.
———. 2007. "The Price of Whiteness: Jews, Race, and American Identity (Review)." *American Jewish History* 93, no. 1: 96–99.
Alter, Joseph. 1992. *The Wrestler's Body: Identity and Ideology in North India.* Berkeley, CA: University of California Press.
———. 2004. *Yoga in Modern India: The Body between Science and Philosophy.* Princeton, NJ: Princeton University Press.
———. 2014. "Shri Yogendra: Magic, Modernity, and the Burdens of the Middle-Class Yogi." In *Gurus of Modern Yoga,* edited by Mark Singleton and Ellen Goldberg, 60–79. Oxford: Oxford University Press.
Altglas, Véronique. 2014. *From Yoga to Kabbalah: Religious Exoticism and the Logics of Bricolage.* New York: Oxford University Press.
Anderton, Chris. 2015. "Branding, Sponsorship and the Music Festival." In *The Pop Festival: History, Music, Media, Culture,* edited by George McKay, 199–212. New York: Bloomsbury.
Appadurai, Arjun. 1996. *Modernity at Large: Cultural Dimensions of Globalization.* Minneapolis, MN: University of Minnesota Press.

Appiah, Kwame Anthony. 2018a. "Cultural Borrowing Is Great; The Problem Is Disrespect." *Wall Street Journal,* August 30, 2018. www.wsj.com/articles/cultural-borrowing-is-great-the-problem-is-disrespect-1535639194.

———. 2018b. *The Lies That Bind: Rethinking Identity.* New York: W.W. Norton.

Arato, Andrew, and Eike Gephardt. 1982. *Essential Frankfurt School Reader.* London: Continuum.

Aristotle. 1955. *The Ethics of Aristotle: The Nichomachean Ethics.* Translated by J.A.K. Thomson. New York: Penguin.

Aubrecht, Jennifer. 2017. "Choreographers and Yogis: Untwisting the Politics of Appropriation and Representation in U.S. Concert Dance." PhD diss., University of California, Riverside.

Augé, Marc. 2008. *Non-Places: An Introduction to Supermodernity.* London: Verso.

Bajpai, Namita. 2019. "Teaching Sanskrit Has Nothing to Do with Religion: BHU Prof Firoz Khan amid Student Protests." *New Indian Express,* November 19, 2019. www.newindianexpress.com/nation/2019/nov/19/teaching-sanskrit-has-nothing-to-do-with-religion-bhu-prof-firoz-khan-amid-student-protests-2064051.html.

Bakhtin, Mikail. 1984. *Rabelais and His World.* Bloomington, IN: Indiana University Press.

Barkataki, Susanna. 2019. "But, Do I Really Need to Speak Sanskrit?" July 3, 2019. www.susannabarkataki.com/post/do-i-really-need-to-speak-sanskrit.

Baudrillard, Jean. 1994. *Simulacra and Simulation.* Translated by Sheila Faria Glaser. Ann Arbor, MI: University of Michigan Press.

Beliso-De Jesús, Aisha. 2015. *Electric Santeria: Racial and Sexual Assemblages of Transnational Religion.* New York: Columbia University Press.

Bellah, Robert N., Richard Madsen, William M. Sullivan, Ann Swidler, and Steven M. Tipton. 1985. *Habits of the Heart: Individualism and Commitment in American Life.* Berkeley, CA: University of California Press.

Bender, Courtney. 2010. *The New Metaphysicals: Spirituality and the American Religious Imagination.* Chicago: University of Chicago Press.

Bender, Courtney, and Pamela Klassen, eds. 2010. *After Pluralism: Reimagining Religious Engagement.* New York: Columbia University Press.

Benjamin, Rich. 2009. *Searching for Whitopia: An Improbable Journey to the Heart of White America.* New York: Hachette Books.

———. 2015. "What Is A 'Whitopia'—And What Might It Mean to Live There?" National Public Radio, TED Radio Hour, November 20, 2015. www.npr.org/2015/11/20/455909004/what-is-a-whitopia-and-what-might-it-mean-to-live-there.

Benjamin, Walter. 2000. "The Translators Task." In *The Translation Studies Reader,* edited by Lawrence Venuti, 75–83. New York: Routledge.

———. 2019. *Illuminations.* Translated by Harry Zohn. Edited and with an introduction by Hannah Arendt. Boston: Mariner Books.

Bennett, Andy, Jodie Taylor, and Ian Woodward. 2014. *The Festivalization of Culture.* New York: Ashgate.

Berlin, Isaiah. 1969. *Four Essays on Liberty.* London: Oxford University Press.

Berry, Evan. 2015. *Devoted to Nature: The Religious Roots of American Environmentalism.* Berkeley, CA: University of California Press.
Beyer, Steven V. 2009. *Singing to the Plants: A Guide to Mestizo Shamanism in the Upper Amazon.* Albuquerque, NM: University of New Mexico Press.
Binkley, Sam. 2007. *Getting Loose: Lifestyle Consumption in the 1970s.* Durham, NC: Duke University Press.
Birdee G. S., A. T. Legedza, R. B. Saper, S. M. Bertisch, D. M. Eisenberg, and R. S. Phillips. 2008. "Characteristics of Yoga Users: Results of a National Survey." *J Gen Intern Med* 23, no. 10: 1653–58.
Boellstorff, Tom, Bonnie Nardi, Celia Pearce, and T. L. Taylor. 2013. *Ethnography and Virtual Worlds: A Handbook of Method.* Princeton, NJ: Princeton University Press.
Bourdieu, Pierre. 1984. *Distinction: A Social Critique of the Judgement of Taste.* New York: Routledge.
Bourdieu, Pierre, and Loïc Wacquant. 1992. *An Invitation to Reflexive Sociology.* Chicago: University of Chicago Press.
Bowditch, Rachel. 2010. *On the Edge of Utopia: Performance and Ritual at Burning Man.* Chicago: Seagull Books.
Breedlove, Christopher. 2016. "From Black Rock to Standing Rock." *Burning Man Journal,* December 6, 2016. https://journal.burningman.org/2016/12/global-network/burners-without-borders/from-black-rock-to-standing-rock.
Brown, Candy Guenther. 2019. *Debating Yoga and Mindfulness in Public Schools: Reforming Secular Education or Reestablishing Religion?* Durham, NC: University of North Carolina Press.
Brown, David. 2003. *Santeria Enthroned: Art, Ritual and Innovation in an Afro-Cuban Religion.* Chicago: University of Chicago Press.
Brown, Michael F. 2003. *Who Owns Native Culture?* Cambridge, MA: Harvard University Press.
Brown, Wendy. 2006. "American Nightmare: Neoliberalism, Neoconservativism, and De-Democratization." *Political Theory* 34, no. 6 (December): 690–714.
Bryant, Edwin. 2009. *The Yoga Sūtras of Patañjali: A New Edition, Translation, and Commentary.* New York: North Point Press.
Burke, Jason. 2014. "Outcry as Penguin India Pulps 'Alternative' History of Hindus." *Guardian,* February 13, 2014. www.theguardian.com/world/2014/feb/13/indian-conservatives-penguin-hindus-book.
Burning Man Project. 2019. "BLM Threatens Future of Burning Man with Draft Environmental Impact Statement." *Burning Man Journal,* March 20, 2019. https://journal.burningman.org/2019/03/black-rock-city/leaving-no-trace/blm-threatens-future-of-burning-man-with-draft-environmental-impact-statement.
Burowoy, Michael, ed. 1991. *Ethnography Unbound: Power and Resistance in the Modern Metropolis.* Berkeley, CA: University of California Press.
Burroughs, William. 2003. *Junky: The Definitive Text of "Junk."* New York: Grove Press.
Butler, Jon. 1990. *Awash in a Sea of Faith: Christianizing the American People.* Cambridge, MA: Harvard University Press.
Byrne, Rhonda. 2006. *The Secret.* New York: Simon and Schuster.

Cadge, Wendy. 2005. *Heartwood: The First Generation of Theravada Buddhism in America.* Chicago: University of Chicago Press.

Caillois, Roger. 2001. *Man and the Sacred.* Bloomington, IN: University of Illinois Press.

Cairns, Kate, and Josée Johnston. 2015. "Choosing Health: Embodied Neoliberalism, Postfeminism, and the 'Do-Diet.'" *Theory and Society* 44, no. 2 (March): 153–75.

Campbell, Jane MacRae. 2017. "Dress, Ideology, and Control: The Regulation of Clothing in Early Modern English Utopian Texts, 1516–1656." In "Utopia and Fashion." Special issue, *Utopian Studies* 28, no. 3: 398–437.

Campion, Nicholas. 2016. *The New Age in the Modern West: Counterculture, Utopia and Prophecy from the Late Eighteenth Century to the Present Day.* New York: Bloomsbury Academic.

Carrette, Jeremy, and Richard King. 2005. *$elling Spirituality: The Silent Takeover of Religion.* New York: Routledge.

Chakraborty, Chandrima. 2006. "Ramdev and Somatic Nationalism: Embodying the Nation, Desiring the Global." *Economic and Political Weekly* 41, no. 5 (February 4–10): 387–90.

Chari, Mridula. 2016. "Make in India and Remove Sheldon Pollock from Murty Classical Library, Demand 132 Intellectuals." *Scroll.In,* February 29, 2016. https://scroll.in/article/804323/make-in-india-and-remove-sheldon-pollock-from-murty-classical-library-demand-132-intellectuals.

Chen, Katherine K. 2009. *Enabling Creative Chaos: The Organization behind the Burning Man Event.* Chicago: University of Chicago Press.

Clewis, Robert R., ed. 2019. *The Sublime Reader.* London: Bloomsbury.

Clifford, James, and George E. Marcus, eds. 1986. *Writing Culture: The Poetics and Politics of Ethnography.* Berkeley, CA: University of California Press.

Cobb, Russell, ed. 2014. *The Paradox of Authenticity in a Globalized World.* New York: Palgrave Macmillan.

Cohen, Allen. 1991. "The San Francisco Oracle: A Brief History." *San Francisco Oracle, Facsimile Edition: The Psychedelic Newspaper of the Haight-Ashbury, 1966–1968.* Berkeley, CA: Regent.

Cohen, Colin. 2019. "Burning Man Sues U.S. Government after Getting Charged $18 Million for Permits." *Digital Music News,* December 18, 2019. www.digitalmusicnews.com/2019/12/18/burning-man-sues-government-18-million-permits.

Collins, Suzanne. 2008. *The Hunger Games.* New York: Scholastic.

Collins-Kreiner, Noga, Nurit Kliot, Yoel Mansfeld, and Keren Sagi. 2010. *Christian Tourism to the Holy Land: Pilgrimage during Security Crisis.* New York: Routledge.

Conroy, Casey. 2018. "The 'Sexy, Spiritual, Successful Woman' Ideal—Why It Hurts Us." *Living Now,* May 14, 2018. https://livingnow.com.au/sexy-spiritual-successful-woman-ideal-hurts-us.

Corn, Seane. 2019. *Revolution of the Soul: Awaken to Love through Raw Truth, Radical Healing, and Conscious Action.* Boulder, CO: Sounds True.

Crane, William. 2018. "Cultural Formation and Appropriation in the Era of Merchant Capitalism." *Historical Materialism* 26, no. 2: 242–70.

Crapazano, Vincent. 1986. "Hermes' Dilemma." In *Writing Culture: The Poetics and Politics of Ethnography*, edited by James Clifford and George E. Marcus, 51–76. Berkeley, CA: University of California Press.

Crawford, R. 2006. "Health as a Meaningful Social Practice." *Health: An Interdisciplinary Journal for the Social Study of Health, Illness and Medicine* 10, no. 4: 401–20.

Crawley, Ashon. 2018. "Ghosts." *New Inquiry*, May 29, 2018. https://thenewinquiry.com/ghosts.

Crenshaw, Kimberlé. 1989. "Demarginalizing the Intersection of Race and Sex: A Black Feminist Critique of Antidiscrimination Doctrine, Feminist Theory and Antiracist Politics." *University of Chicago Legal Forum* 1989, no. 1, article 8.

Crowley, Karlyn. 2011. *Feminism's New Age: Gender, Appropriation, and the Afterlife of Essentialism*. Albany, NY: SUNY Press.

Csikszentmihalyi, Mihaly. 1990. *Flow: The Psychology of Optimal Experience*. New York: Harper Collins.

Csordas, Thomas, ed. 2009. *Transnational Transcendence: Essays on Religion and Globalization*. Berkeley, CA: University of California Press.

de Certeau, Michel. 2000. *The Possession at Loudun*. Chicago: University of Chicago Press.

Deloria, Philip J. 1998. *Playing Indian*. New Haven, CT: Yale University Press.

de Martino, Ernesto. 2001. *Magic: A Theory from the South*. Translated by Dorothy Louise Zinn. Chicago: HAU Books.

de Michelis, Elizabeth. 2004. *A History of Modern Yoga: Patanjali and Western Esotericism*. New York: Continuum.

Dempsey, Corinne G. 2005. *The Goddess Lives in Upstate New York*. New York: Oxford University Press.

Derrida, Jacques. 2016. *Of Grammatology*. Translated by Gayatri Spivak. Baltimore, MD: Johns Hopkins University Press.

Deslippe, Philip. 2018. "The Swami Circuit: Mapping the Terrain of Early American Yoga." *Journal of Yoga Studies* 1: 5–44.

Devaney, Jacob. 2017. "On Cultural Appropriation and Transformation at Burning Man." *Huffington Post*, September 5, 2017. www.huffingtonpost.com/entry/cultural-appropriation-and-transformation-at-burning_us_59aed1cae4bobef3378cdb90.

DeVaul, D.L., D. Beaulieu-Prévost, S.M. Heller, and the 2017 Census Lab. 2017. "Black Rock City Census: 2013–2017 Population Analysis." https://s3-us-west-1.amazonaws.com/brccensus.public.reports/2017+Docs/05.22.18+2013-2017+Population+Analysis.pdf.

DiAngelo, Robin. 2018. *White Fragility: Why It's So Hard for White People to Talk about Racism*. Boston: Beacon Press.

Domanick, Andrea. 2012. "Report: 2012 Electric Daisy Carnival Brought in $207 Million to Clark County." *Las Vegas Sun*, October 2, 2012. https://lasvegassun.com/news/2012/oct/02/electric-daisy-carnival-2012-207-million-Clark-Cou/.

Donaldson, Laura E. 1999. "On Medicine Women and White Shame-Ans: New Age Native Americanism and Commodity Fetishism as Pop Culture Feminism." *Signs* 24, no. 3 (Spring): 677–96.

Douglass, Patrice, Selamawit D. Terrefe, and Frank B. Wilderson. 2018. "Afro-Pessmism." *Oxford Bibliographies.* Last modified August 28, 2018. www.oxfordbibliographies.com/view/document/obo-9780190280024/obo-9780190280024-0056.xml.

Dowd, Katie. 2016. "Standing Rock Activists Asking White People to Stop Treating Pipeline Protest like Burning Man." *SF Gate,* November 30, 2016. www.sfgate.com/news/article/Standing-Rock-protest-white-people-Burning-Man-10640250.php.

Driscoll, Christopher. 2015. *White Lies: Race and Uncertainty in the Twilight of American Religion.* New York: Routledge.

———. Forthcoming. *White Devils: Reflections on Race, Religion and Toxic Masculinity.* New York: Bloomsbury.

Driscoll, Christopher, and Monica R. Miller. 2019. *Method as Identity: Manufacturing Distance in the Academic Study of Religion.* Lanham, MD: Rowman and Littlefield.

Durkheim, Emile. 1995. *The Elementary Forms of Religious Life.* Translated by Karen Fields. New York: Free Press.

Duwe, Morena. 2017. "Lucent Dossier's Dream Rockwell Is Still Waging Her Legal Battle over Lightning in a Bottle." *LA Weekly,* July 25, 2017. www.laweekly.com/music/lightning-in-a-bottle-vs-dream-rockwell-the-legal-fight-continues-as-lucent-dossier-experience-hits-the-road-8448365.

Eck, Diana L. 2001. *A New Religious America: How a "Christian Country" Has Become the World's Most Religiously Diverse Nation.* New York: HarperCollins.

Eliade, Mircea. 2009. *The Myth of the Eternal Return: Cosmos and History.* Princeton, NJ: Princeton University Press.

Ellwood, Robert S., Jr. 1979. *Alternative Altars: Unconventional and Eastern Spirituality in America.* Chicago: University of Chicago Press.

Faughnder, Ryan. 2016. "Coachella by the Numbers: A Breakdown of the Festival's $700-million Impact." *LA Times,* April 22, 2016. www.latimes.com/entertainment/envelope/cotown/la-et-ct-coachella-economy-by-the-numbers-20160420-story.html.

Federici, Silvia. 2019. *Re-enchanting the World: Feminism and the Politics of the Commons.* Oakland, CA: PM Press.

Feuerbach, Ludwig. 2008. *The Essence of Christianity.* Translated by George Eliot. Mineola, NY: Dover Publications.

Finney, Carolyn. 2014. *Black Faces, White Spaces: Reimagining the Relationship of African Americans to the Great Outdoors.* Durham, NC: University of North Carolina Press.

Fish, Stanley. 1980. *Is There a Text in This Class? The Authority of Interpretive Communities.* Cambridge, MA: Harvard University Press.

Flood, Gavin. 2004. *The Ascetic Self: Subjectivity, Memory and Tradition.* New York: Cambridge University Press.

Forrest, Ana T. 2011. *Fierce Medicine: Breakthrough Practices to Heal the Body and Ignite the Spirit.* New York: HarperOne.

Foucault, Michel. 1985. *The Use of Pleasure.* Vol. 2 of *The History of Sexuality.* New York: Random House.

———. 1986. *The Care of the Self*. Vol. 3 of *The History of Sexuality*. New York: Random House.

———. 2005. *Madness and Civilization: A History of Insanity in the Age of Reason*. New York: Routledge.

Foxen, Anya. 2017. *Biography of a Yogi: Paramhansa Yogananda and the Origins of Modern Yoga*. New York: Oxford University Press.

———. 2020. *Inhaling Spirit: Harmonialism, Orientalism, and the Western Roots of Modern Yoga*. New York: Oxford University Press.

Fremantle, Francesca, and Chogyam Trungpa, trans. 1975. *The Tibetan Book of the Dead: The Great Liberation through Hearing the Bardo*. Boulder, CO: Shambala.

Frenk, Steven M., Kathryn S. Porter, and Lonard J. Paulozzi. 2015. "Prescription Opioid Analgesic Use among Adults: United States, 1999–2012." NCHS Data Brief No. 189, February 2015. Hyattsville, MD: National Center for Health Statistics. www.cdc.gov/nchs/data/databriefs/db189.pdf.

Fuller, Robert C. 2000. *Stairways to Heaven: Drugs in American Religious History*. Boulder, CO: Westview Press.

———. 2001. *Spiritual, but Not Religious: Understanding Unchurched America*. New York: Oxford University Press.

Funari, Pedro Paulo, and Tamima Orra Mourad. 2016. "Stewards of Empire: Heritage as Colonialist Booty." *Heródoto* 1, no. 1: 37–54.

Funk, Cary, and Greg Smith. 2012 "'Nones' on the Rise: One-in-Five Adults Have No Religious Affiliation." October 9, 2012. Washington, DC: Pew Forum on Religion and Public Life.

Galant, Justyna. 2017. "Fashion Triumphant and the Mechanism of Tautology in Two Nineteenth-Century Dystopias." In "Utopia and Fashion." Special issue, *Utopian Studies* 28, no. 3: 428–50.

Gandhi, Leela. 2006. *Affective Communities: Anticolonial Thought, Fin-de-Siècle Radicalism, and the Politics of Friendship*. Durham, NC: Duke University Press.

Gandhi, Shreena, and Lillie Wolff. 2017. "Yoga and the Roots of Cultural Appropriation." Praxis Center, December 19, 2017. www.kzoo.edu/praxis/yoga.

Geertz, Clifford. 1973. *The Interpretation of Cultures: Selected Essays by Clifford Geertz*. New York: Basic Books.

Gershon, Ilana. 2011. "Neoliberal Agency." *Current Anthropology* 52, no. 4 (August): 537–55.

Gilmore, Lee. 2010. *Theater in a Crowded Fire: Ritual and Spirituality at Burning Man*. Berkeley, CA: University of California Press.

Ginzburg, Carlo. 2004. *Ecstasies: Deciphering the Witches' Sabbath*. Chicago: University of Chicago Press.

Gleig, Ann. 2019. *American Dharma: Buddhism beyond Modernity*. New Haven, CT: Yale University Press.

Godrej, Farah. 2017. "The Neoliberal Yogi and the Politics of Yoga." *Political Theory* 45, no. 6: 772–800.

Goldberg, Michelle. 2015. *The Goddess Pose: The Audacious Life of Indra Devi, the Woman Who Helped Bring Yoga to the West*. New York: Knopf.

Goodell, Marian. 2019. "Cultural Course Correcting: Black Rock City 2019" *Burning Man Journal,* February 9, 2019. https://journal.burningman.org/2019/02/philosophical-center/tenprinciples/cultural-course-correcting.

Gottschild, Brenda Dixon. 1996. *Digging the Africanist Presence in American Performance: Dance and Other Contexts.* Westport, CT: Greenwood Press.

Graham, Laura Christine. 2014. "Ancient, Spiritual, and Indian: Exploring Narratives of Authenticity in Modern Yoga," In *The Paradox of Authenticity in a Globalized World,* edited by Russell Cobb, 85–100. New York: Palgrave Macmillan.

Grazian, David. 2003. *Blue Chicago: The Search for Authenticity in Urban Blues Clubs.* Chicago: University of Chicago Press.

Gren, Martin, and Edward H. Huijbens. 2016. *Tourism and the Anthropocene.* New York: Routledge.

Grim, Ryan. 2009. *This Is Your Country on Drugs: The Secret History of Getting High in America.* Hoboken, NJ: John Wiley & Sons.

Guida, Jeremy. 2016. "Metaphysical Underground: The Underground Press and the Transformation of Metaphysical Religion, 1964–1973." PhD diss., University of California, Riverside.

Gupta, Bhuvi, and Jacob Copeman. 2019. "Awakening Hindu Nationalism through Yoga: Swami Ramdev and the Bharat Swabhiman Movement." *Contemporary South Asia* 27, no. 3: 313–29.

Hall, Stuart, ed. 1997. *Representation: Cultural Representations and Signifying Practices.* London: SAGE.

Handler, Richard. 1986. "Authenticity." *Anthropology Today* 2, no. 1: 2–4.

Hanegraaff, Wouter J. 1998. *New Age Religion and Western Culture: Esotericism in the Mirror of Secular Thought.* Albany, NY: SUNY Press.

Hardt, Michael, and Antonio Negri. 2001. *Empire.* Cambridge, MA: Harvard University Press.

Harper, A. Breeze. 2016. "Doing Veganism Differently." In *Doing Nutrition Differently: Critical Approaches to Diet and Dietary Intervention,* edited by Allison Hayes-Conroy and Jessica Hayes-Conroy, 133–150. New York: Routledge.

Hayes-Conroy, Allison, and Jessica Hayes-Conroy, eds. 2016. *Doing Nutrition Differently: Critical Approaches to Diet and Dietary Intervention.* New York: Routledge.

Heelas, Paul. 1996. *The New Age Movement.* Malden, MA: Blackwell.

———. 2008. *Spiritualities of Life: New Age Romanticism and Consumptive Capitalism.* Malden, MA: Blackwell.

Hegel, G. W. F. 2004. *Philosophy of History,* New York: Dover Publications.

Henderson, David. 1981. *'Scuse Me While I Kiss the Sky: The Life of Jimi Hendrix.* Toronto: Bantam Books.

Hill, Angela. 2018. "Enjoy Burning Man without Leaving the SF Bay Area." *Mercury News,* August 13, 2018. www.mercurynews.com/2018/08/13/enjoy-burning-man-without-leaving-the-sf-bay-area.

Hines, April. 2019. "Should Every American Citizen Be a Yoga Teacher?" *New York Times,* April 6, 2019. www.nytimes.com/2019/04/06/style/corepower-yoga-teacher-training.html.

Hollywood, Amy. 1995. *The Soul as Virgin Wife: Mechthild of Magdeburg, Marguerite Porete, and Meister Eckhart.* Notre Dame, IN: University of Notre Dame Press.

Horkheimer, Max, and Theodore Adorno. 2002. *Dialectic of Enlightenment: Philosophical Fragments.* Stanford, CA: Stanford University Press.

Howie, LaJeana D., Patricia N. Pastor, and Susan Lukacs. 2014. "Use of Medication Prescribed for Emotional or Behavioral Difficulties among Children Aged 6–17 Years in the United States, 2011–2012." NCHS Data Brief No. 148, April 2014. Hyattsville, MD: National Center for Health Statistics. www.cdc.gov/nchs/data/databriefs/db148.pdf.

Huffer [Lucia], Amanda J. 2011. "Hinduism without Religion: Amma's Movement in America." In "Religion in Asia Today." Special issue, *CrossCurrents* 61, no. 3: 374–98.

Huhndorf, Shari M. 2001. *Going Native: Indians in the American Cultural Imagination.* Ithaca, NY: Cornell University Press.

Huxley, Aldous. 2009. *The Doors of Perception and Heaven and Hell.* New York: HarperCollins.

———. 2013. *Brave New World.* New York: Everyman's Library.

Ipsos Public Affairs, Yoga Alliance, and *Yoga Journal.* 2016. "2016 Yoga in America Study." www.yogaalliance.org/2016YogaInAmericaStudy.

Iwamura, Jane. 2011. *Virtual Orientalism: Asian Religions and American Popular Culture.* New York: Oxford University Press.

Jackson, Carl. 1994. *Vedanta for the West.* Bloomington, IN: Indiana University Press.

Jackson, Reagan. 2015. "Vitriol against People of Color Yoga Shows Exactly Why It's Necessary." *Seattle Globalist,* October 15, 2015. www.seattleglobalist.com/2015/10/15/vitriol-against-people-of-color-yoga-shows-exactly-why-its-necessary/42573.

Jain, Andrea. 2014. "Who Is to Say Modern Yoga Practitioners Have It All Wrong? On Hindu Origins and Yogaphobia." *Journal of the American Academy of Religion* 82, no. 2 (June): 427–71.

———. 2015. *Selling Yoga: From Counterculture to Pop Culture.* New York: Oxford University Press.

———. 2019. "Namaste All Day: Containing Dissent in Commercial Spirituality." *Harvard Divinity Bulletin* (Autumn/Winter). https://bulletin.hds.harvard.edu/namaste-all-day.

———. 2020. *Peace, Love, Yoga: The Politics of Global Spirituality.* New York: Oxford University Press.

Jain, Andrea, and Michael Schulson. 2016. "The World's Most Influential Yoga Teacher Is a Homophobic Right-Wing Activist." *Religion Dispatches,* October 4, 2016. http://religiondispatches.org/baba-ramdev.

James, Alexander. 2018. "Campus Yoga Group Disbands over Cultural Appropriation Complaint." *Washington Examiner,* December 13, 2018. www.washingtonexaminer.com/red-alert-politics/campus-yoga-group-disbands-over-cultural-appropriation-complaint.

Jarnow, Jesse. 2016. *Heads: A Biography of Psychedelic America.* New York: Da Capo Press.

Jenkins, Philip. 2004. *Dream Catchers: How Mainstream America Discovered Native Spirituality.* New York: Oxford University Press.

Johnson, Jim. 2019. "After Attendee Deaths, Lightning in a Bottle Festival Ousted from Monterey County Park." *Mercury News,* January 18, 2019. www.mercurynews.com/2019/01/18/lightning-in-a-bottle-ousted-at-lake-san-antonio.

Jonas, Michael. 2007. "The Downside of Diversity." *New York Times,* August 5, 2007. www.nytimes.com/2007/08/05/world/americas/05iht-diversity.1.6986248.html.

Josephson-Storm, Jason Ā. 2017. *The Myth of Disenchantment: Magic, Modernity, and the Birth of the Human Sciences.* Chicago: University of Chicago Press.

Kane, Jennifer. 2018. "Burning Man Threatens to Sue Feds over Traffic Stops." *Reno Gazette Journal,* August 24, 2018. www.rgj.com/story/life/arts/burning-man/2018/08/23/burning-man-threatens-sue-over-traffic-stops/1075780002.

Kelly, Jason. 2016. *Sweat Equity: Inside the New Economy of Mind and Body.* Hoboken, NJ: Bloomberg.

Khanduri, Ritu. 2012. "'Does This Offend You?' Hindu Visuality in the United States." In *Public Hinduisms,* edited by John Zavos, Pralay Kanungo, Deepa S. Reddy, Maya Warrier, and Raymond Brady Williams, 348–64. New Delhi: SAGE.

Kraut, Anthea. 2015. *Choreographing Copyright: Race, Gender, and Intellectual Property Rights in American Dance.* New York: Oxford University Press.

Kreps, Daniel. 2009. "Kanye West Storms the VMAs Stage during Taylor Swift's Speech." *Rolling Stone,* September 14, 2009. www.rollingstone.com/music/music-country/kanye-west-storms-the-vmas-stage-during-taylor-swifts-speech-83468.

Kripal, Jeffrey. 2007. *Esalen: America and the Religion of No Religion.* Chicago: University of Chicago Press.

———. 2008. "The Roar of Awakening: The Eros of Esalen and the Western Transmission of Tantra." In *Hidden Intercourse: Essays on Eros and Sexuality in the History of Western Esotericism,* edited by Wouter J. Hanegraaf and Jeffrey J. Kripal, 479–520. Leiden, Netherlands: Brill.

Kurien, Prema. 2007. *A Place at the Multicultural Table: The Development of an American Hinduism.* Piscataway, NJ: Rutgers University Press.

Kurzman, Charles. 1991. "Convincing Sociologists: Values and Interests in the Sociology of Knowledge." In *Ethnography Unbound: Power and Resistance in the Modern Metropolis,* edited by Michael Burowoy, 250–70. Berkeley, CA: University of California Press.

Lachman, Gary. 2012. *Madame Blavatsky: The Mother of Modern Spirituality.* New York: Penguin.

Lang, Michael. 2009. *The Road to Woodstock.* New York: HarperCollins.

Laycock, Joseph P. 2015. "The Controversial History of the Crystal Skulls: A Case Study in Interpretive Drift." *Material Religion* 11, no. 2: 164–88.

Leary, Timothy, Ralph Metzner, and Richard Alpert. 1964. *The Psychedelic Experience: A Manual Based on the Tibetan Book of the Dead.* New York: University Books.
Lemke-Santangelo, Gretchen. 2009. *Daughters of Aquarius: Women of the Sixties Counterculture.* Lawrence, KS: University of Kansas Press.
Lindholm, Charles. 2008. *Culture and Authenticity,* Malden, MA: Blackwell.
Lipka, Michael, and Claire Gecewicz. 2017. "More Americans Now Say They're Spiritual but Not Religious." September 6, 2017. Washington DC: Pew Research Center.
Lipsitz, George. 2006. *The Possessive Investment in Whiteness: How White People Profit from Identity Politics.* Philadelphia: Temple University Press.
Löfgren, O. 1999. *On Holiday: A History of Vacationing.* Berkeley, CA: University of California Press.
Lopez, German. 2017. "Ta-Nehisi Coates Has an Incredibly Clear Explanation for Why White People Shouldn't Use the N-Word." *Vox,* November 9, 2017. www.vox.com/identities/2017/11/9/16627900/ta-nehisi-coates-n-word.
Lopez, Mark Hugo. 2014. "In 2014, Latinos Will Surpass Whites as Largest Racial/Ethnic Group in California." Pew Research Center, *Fact Tank,* January 24, 2014. http://www.pewresearch.org/fact-tank/2014/01/24/in-2014-latinos-will-surpass-whites-as-largest-racialethnic-group-in-california.
Lott, Eric. 1993. *Love and Theft: Blackface Minstrelsy and the American Working Class.* New York: Oxford University Press.
Love, Robert. 2010. *The Great Oom: The Improbable Birth of Yoga in America.* New York: Viking.
Lucia, Amanda. 2014a. *Reflections of Amma: Devotees in a Global Embrace.* Berkeley, CA: University of California Press.
———. 2014b. "Yoga and Festival Cultures." www.surveymonkey.com/r/festivalyoga.
———. 2018. "Saving Yogis: Spiritual Nationalism and the Proselytizing Missions of Global Yoga." In *Asian Migrations and Global Religion: Studies on Transnational Religious Movements,* edited by Brenda Yeoh and Bernardo Brown, 35–70. Amsterdam: Amsterdam University Press.
Luhrmann, Tanya. 2012. *When God Talks Back: Understanding the American Evangelical Relationship with God.* New York: Random House.
Lynd, Robert S., and Helen Merrell Lynd. 1929. *Middletown: A Study in American Culture.* New York: Harcourt, Brace.
MacCannell, Dean. 1992. *The Ethics of Sightseeing.* Berkeley, CA: University of California Press.
Maclean, Kama. 2008. *Pilgrimage and Power: The Kumbh Mela in Allahabad 1765–1954.* New York: Oxford University Press.
Maffesoli, Michel. 1996. *The Time of the Tribes: The Decline of Individualism in Mass Society.* London: SAGE.
Magister, Caveat. 2019. *The Scene That Became Cities: What Burning Man Philosophy Can Teach Us about Building Better Communities.* Berkeley, CA: North Atlantic Books.

Maguire, Matthew, and David Lay Williams, eds. 2018. *Jean-Jacques Rousseau: Fundamental Political Writings*. Translated by Ian Johnston. Peterborough, Canada: Broadview Press.

Malhotra, Rajiv. 2001. "RISA Lila—Wendy's Child Syndrome." https://rajivmalhotra.com/library/articles/risa-lila-1-wendys-child-syndrome.

Malina, Bruce J. 2008. "Pain, Power, and Personhood: Ascetic Behavior in the Ancient Mediterranean." In *Asceticism*, edited by Vincent Wimbush and Richard Valantasis, 162–77. New York: Oxford University Press.

Mallinson, Sir James, and Mark Singleton. 2017. *Roots of Yoga*. New York: Penguin Classics.

Mannheim, Karl. 1936. *Ideology and Utopia*. New York: Harvest Books.

Manning, Susan. 2004. *Modern Dance, Negro Dance: Race in Motion*. Minneapolis, MN: University of Minnesota Press.

Markell, Patchen. 2003. *Bound by Recognition*. Princeton, NJ: Princeton University Press.

Matthes, Erich Hatala. 2016. "Cultural Appropriation without Cultural Essentialism?" *Social Theory and Practice* 42, no. 2: 343–66.

Marx, Karl. 1990. *Capital*. Vol. 1. New York: Penguin Classics.

McCartney, Patrick. 2017. "Politics beyond the Yoga Mat: Yoga Fundamentalism and the 'Vedic Way of Life.'" *Global Ethnographic*, no. 4 (May).

McKay, George, ed. 2015. *The Pop Festival: History, Music, Media, Culture*. New York: Bloomsbury.

McKenna, Terence. 1992. *The Archaic Revival: Speculations on Psychedelic Mushrooms, the Amazon, Virtual Reality, UFOs, Evolution, Shamanism, the Rebirth of the Goddess, and the End of History*. San Francisco: Harper San Francisco.

McKenna, Terence, and Dennis McKenna. 1975. *The Invisible Landscape: Mind, Hallucinogens, and the I Ching*. New York: Seabury.

McKinney, Kelsey. 2015. "How Beck Beat Beyoncé for Album of the Year." *Vox*, February 9, 2015. www.vox.com/2015/2/9/8005609/beck-beat-beyonce-grammys.

Mercadante, Linda A. 2014. *Belief without Borders: Inside the Minds of the Spiritual but Not Religious*. New York: Oxford University Press.

Miller, Amara. 2019. "Yoga R/Evolution: Deconstructing the 'Authentic' Yoga Body." Ph.D. diss., University of California, Davis.

Miller, Christopher. 2018. "Embodying Transnational Yoga." Ph.D. diss., University of California, Davis.

Molz, Jennie Germann. 2007. *Travel Connections: Tourism, Technology and Togetherness in a Mobile World*. New York: Routledge.

Moreton-Robinson, Aileen. 2015. *The White Possessive: Property, Power, and Indigenous Sovereignty*. Minneapolis, MN: University of Minnesota Press.

Moyer, Justin Wm. 2015. "University Yoga Class Canceled Because of 'Oppression, Cultural Genocide.'" *Washington Post*, November 23, 2015. www.washingtonpost.com/news/morning-mix/wp/2015/11/23/university-yoga-class-canceled-because-of-oppression-cultural-genocide.

Mukherjee, S. Romi. 2009. "Festival, Vacation, War: Roger Caillois and the Politics of Paroxysm." *International Social Science Journal* 185, UNESCO: 119–38.
Murphy, Jacqueline. 2007. *"The People Have Never Stopped Dancing": Native American Modern Dance Histories*. Minneapolis, MN: University of Minnesota Press.
Murphy, Rosalie. 2014. "Why Your Yoga Class Is So White." *The Atlantic,* July 8, 2014. www.theatlantic.com/national/archive/2014/07/why-your-yoga-class-is-so-white/374002.
Natale, Simone. 2016. *Supernatural Entertainments: Victorian Spiritualism and the Rise of Modern Media Culture*. University Park, PA: Pennsylvania State University Press.
Nattier, Jan. 1997. "Buddhism Comes to Main Street." *Wilson Quarterly* 2, no. 2 (Spring): 72–81.
Nietzsche, Friedrich. 1928. *Thus Spake Zarathustra*. New York: Dial Press.
———. 2001. *The Gay Science*. Cambridge: Cambridge University Press.
———. 2007. *On the Genealogy of Morals*. Cambridge: Cambridge University Press.
Niman, Michael. 2011. *People of the Rainbow: A Nomadic Utopia*. 2nd ed. Knoxville, TN: University of Tennessee Press.
Norman, Alex. 2011. *Spiritual Tourism: Travel and Religious Practice in Western Society*. New York: Continuum.
O'Connor, Roisin. 2016. "Standing Rock: North Dakota Access Pipeline Demonstrators Say White People Are 'Treating Protest like Burning Man.'" *Independent,* November 28, 2016. www.independent.co.uk/arts-entertainment/music/news/standing-rock-north-dakota-access-pipeline-burning-man-festival-a7443266.html.
Oliver, Paul. 2014. *Hinduism and the 1960s: The Rise of a Counter-Culture*. New York: Bloomsbury Academic.
Olson, Carl. 2015. *Indian Asceticism: Power, Violence, and Play*. New York: Oxford University Press.
Oppenheimer, Mark. 2003. *Knocking on Heaven's Door: American Religion in the Age of Counterculture*. New Haven, CT: Yale University Press.
Orwell, George. 1949. *1984*. New York: Harcourt.
Owen, Suzanne. 2008. *The Appropriation of Native American Spirituality*. New York: Continuum.
Page, Scott. 2007. *The Difference: How the Power of Diversity Creates Better Groups, Firms, Schools, and Societies*. Princeton, NJ: Princeton University Press.
Palmer, David A., and Elijah Seigler. 2017. *Dream Trippers: Global Daoism and the Predicament of Modern Spirituality*. Chicago: University of Chicago Press.
Partridge, Christopher. 2005. *The Re-enchantment of the West: Alternative Spiritualities, Sacralization, Popular Culture, and Occulture*. New York: T & T Clark.

Patankar, Prachi. 2014. "Ghosts of Yogas Past and Present." *Jadaliyya,* February 26, 2014. www.jadaliyya.com/Details/30281/Ghosts-of-Yogas-Past-and-Present.

Pérez, Elizabeth. 2016. "The Ontology of Twerk: From 'Sexy' Black Movement Style to Afro-Diasporic Sacred Dance." *African and Black Diaspora* 9, no. 1: 16–31.

Perry, Helen Swick. 1970. *The Human Be-In.* New York: Basic Books.

Pew Research Center. 2014. "Religious Landscape Study." Religion and Public Life. www.pewforum.org/religious-landscape-study.

———. 2015. "America's Changing Religious Landscape." Religion and Public Life. www.pewforum.org/2015/05/12/americas-changing-religious-landscape.

———. 2017. "Religious Landscape Study: Spiritual but Not Religious." Religion and Public Life. www.pewforum.org/religious-landscape-study/religious-denomination/spiritual-but-not-religious.

Picard, Michel. 1996. *Bali: Cultural Tourism and Touristic Culture.* Berkeley, CA: University of California Press.

Pike, Sarah. 2004. *New Age and Neopagan Religions in America.* New York: Columbia University Press.

———. 2018. *For the Wild: Ritual and Commitment in Radical Eco-Activism.* Berkeley, CA: University of California Press.

Pitzer, Donald E. 1997. *America's Communal Utopias.* Chapel Hill: University of North Carolina Press.

Pollen, Annebella. 2017. "Utopian Bodies and Anti-fashion Futures: The Dress Theories and Practices of English Interwar Nudists." In "Utopia and Fashion." Special issue, *Utopian Studies* 28, no. 3: 451–81.

Prashad, Vijay. 2000. *The Karma of Brown Folk.* Minneapolis, MN: University of Minnesota Press.

Prato, Paolo, and Gianluca Trivero. 1985. "The Spectacle of Travel." Translated by Iain Chambers. *Australian Journal of Cultural Studies* 3, no. 2 (December): 25–43.

Pratt, Laura A., Debra J. Brody, and Qiuping Gu. 2017. "Antidepressant Use among Persons Aged 12 and Over: United States, 2011–2014." NCHS Data Brief No. 283, August 2017. Hyattsville, MD: National Center for Health Statistics. www.cdc.gov/nchs/data/databriefs/db283.pdf.

Putcha, Rumya. 2018a. "On Yoga, Minstrelsy, and Namaste." *Namaste Nation,* September 17, 2018. http://rumyaputcha.com/namaste.

———. 2018b. "Yoga and the Maintenance of White Womanhood." *Namaste Nation,* March 31, 2018. http://rumyaputcha.com/115-2.

———. 2019. "Necropower and the Cult of White Woman Wellness." *Namaste Nation,* May 18, 2019. http://rumyaputcha.com/insta-influencers-and-the-cult-of-white-woman-wellness.

Putnam, Robert. 2007. "*E Pluribus Unum:* Diversity and Community in the Twenty-First Century." *Scandinavian Political Studies* 30, no. 2 (June): 137–74.

Ram Dass, Baba. 1971. *Be Here Now.* San Cristobal, NM: Lama Foundation.

Ramakrishnan, Ganesh. n.d. "Removal of Sheldon Pollock as Mentor and

Chief Editor of Murty Classical Library." Online petition. *Change.org.* Accessed December 16, 2019. www.change.org/p/mr-n-r-narayana-murthy-and-mr-rohan-narayan-murty-removal-of-prof-sheldon-pollock-as-mentor-and-chief-editor-of-murty-classical-library.

Rana, Aziz. 2010. *The Two Faces of American Freedom.* Cambridge, MA: Harvard University Press.

Rand, Ayn. 2005. *The Fountainhead.* New York: Penguin.

Raphael, Rina. 2017. "Namaste en Masse: Can Wellness Festivals Grow as Big as Coachella?" *Fast Company,* June 30, 2017. www.fastcompany.com/40421458/namaste-en-masse-can-wellness-festivals-grow-as-big-as-coachella.

Rappaport, Roy A. 1999. *Ritual and Religion in the Making of Humanity.* Cambridge: Cambridge University Press.

Raul. 2013. "The Jimi Hendrix Experience 'Bold as Love' Album Cover Artwork." *Feel Numb,* July 2, 2013. www.feelnumb.com/2013/07/02/jimi-hendrix-bold-as-love-albun-cover-artwor.

Ricoeur, Paul. 2005. *The Course of Recognition.* Cambridge, MA: Harvard University Press.

Riesebrodt, Martin. 2010. *The Promise of Salvation: A Theory of Religion.* Chicago: University of Chicago Press.

Robinson, Melia. 2016. "Vandals Just Decimated Burning Man's 'Fancy Camp' Founded by the Son of a Russian Billionaire." *Business Insider,* September 3, 2016. www.businessinsider.com/burning-man-camp-vandalized-2016-9.

Rojek, Chris, and John Urry, eds. 1997. *Touring Cultures: Transformations of Travel and Theory.* New York: Routledge.

Roof, Wade Clark. 1999. *Spiritual Marketplace: Baby Boomers and the Remaking of American Religion.* Princeton, NJ: Princeton University Press.

Root, Deborah. 1996. *Cannibal Culture: Art, Appropriation, and the Commodification of Difference.* New York: Westview Press.

Rosaldo, Renato. 1989. "Imperialist Nostalgia." *Representations,* no. 26 (Spring): 107–22.

Roszak, Theodore. 1969. *The Making of a Counter Culture: Reflections on the Technocratic Society and Its Youthful Opposition.* New York: Anchor Books.

Said, Edward. 1978. *Orientalism.* New York: Vintage.

Saldanha, Arun. 2007. *Psychedelic White: Goa Trance and the Viscosity of Race.* Minneapolis, MN: University of Minnesota Press.

Samuel, Geoffrey. 2007. *The Origins of Yoga and Tantra.* Cambridge: Cambridge University Press.

Sarbacker, Stuart Ray. 2014. "Swami Ramdev: Modern Yoga Revolutionary." In *Gurus of Modern Yoga,* edited by Mark Singleton and Ellen Goldberg, 351–71. New York: Oxford University Press.

Sarma, Deepak. 2012. "White Hindu Converts: Mimicry or Mockery?" *Huffington Post,* November 15, 2012. www.huffingtonpost.com/deepak-sarma/mimicry-or-mockery-white-_b_2131329.html.

Scafidi, Susan. 2005. *Who Owns Culture? Appropriation and Authenticity in American Law.* New Brunswick, NJ: Rutgers University Press.

Schelly, Chelsea. 2016. *Crafting Collectivity: American Rainbow Gatherings and Alternative Forms of Community.* New York: Routledge.
Schmidt, Leigh Eric. 2003. "The Making of Modern Mysticism." *Journal of the American Academy of Religion* 71, no. 2 (June): 273–302.
Schopenhauer, Arthur. 2010. *The World as Will and Representation.* Translated and edited by Judith Norman, Alistair Welchman, and Christopher Janaway. Cambridge: Cambridge University Press.
Sharf, Robert. 1998. "Experience." In *Critical Terms for Religious Studies,* edited by Mark C. Taylor, 94–116. Chicago: University of Chicago Press.
Singleton, Mark. 2010. *Yoga Body: The Origins of Modern Posture Practice.* New York: Oxford University Press.
Smith, Andrea. 1994. "For All Those Who Were Indian in a Former Life." *Cultural Survival Quarterly* 17, no. 4 (Winter): 70–71.
Smith, Jonathan Z. 1978. *Map Is Not Territory: Studies in the History of Religions.* Chicago: University of Chicago Press.
Spencer, Keith A. 2015. "Why the Rich Love Burning Man." *Jacobin,* August 25, 2015. www.jacobinmag.com/2015/08/burning-man-one-percent-silicon-valley-tech.
Srinivas, Krishna Ravi. 2007. "Intellectual Property Rights and Traditional Knowledge: The Case of Yoga." *Economic and Political Weekly* 42, nos. 27/28 (July 14–29): 2866–71.
Srinivas, Tulasi. 2018. *The Cow in the Elevator: An Anthropology of Wonder.* Durham, NC: Duke University Press.
Srinivasan, Priya. 2011. *Sweating Saris: Indian Dance as Transnational Labor.* Philadelphia, PA: Temple University Press.
Stebbins, Robert A. 2007. *Serious Leisure: A Perspective for Our Time.* New Brunswick: Transaction Publishers.
St. John, Graham. 2012. *Global Tribe: Technology, Spirituality and Psytrance.* Sheffield, UK: Equinox.
———. 2013. "Indian Spirit: Amerindians and the Techno-Tribes of Psytrance." In *Tribal Fantasies: Native Americans in the European Imaginary, 1900–2010,* edited by James Mackay and David Stirrip, 173–95. New York: Palgrave Macmillan.
Strain, Ellen. 2003. *Public Places Private Journeys: Ethnography, Entertainment, and the Touristic Gaze.* New Brunswick, NJ: Rutgers University Press.
Strassman, Rick. 2001. *DMT: The Spirit Molecule; A Doctor's Revolutionary Research into the Biology of Near-Death and Mystical Experiences.* Rochester, VT: Park Street Press.
Strauss, Sarah. 2005. *Positioning Yoga: Balancing Acts across Cultures.* New York: Berg.
Styn, John Halcyon. 2010. *Love More. Fear Less. Float More. Steer Less.* John Halcyon Styn.
Takaki, Ronald. 1998. *Strangers from a Different Shore: A History of Asian Americans.* New York: First Back Bay.
Taves, Ann. 2009. *Religious Experience Reconsidered: A Building-Block Approach to the Study of Religion and Other Special Things.* Princeton, NJ: Princeton University Press.

Taylor, Bron. 2010. *Dark Green Religion: Nature Spirituality and the Planetary Future*. Berkeley, CA: University of California Press.
Taylor, Charles. 1991. *The Ethics of Authenticity*. Cambridge, MA: Harvard University Press.
———. 2007. *A Secular Age*. Cambridge, MA: Belknap Press.
Taylor, Sarah McFarland. 2019. *Ecopiety: Green Media and the Dilemma of Environmental Value*. New York: New York University Press.
Thakkar, Mohit. 2016. "Studies Prove That Burning Man Is Truly a Transformational Experience." *Festival Sherpa,* May 17, 2016. www.festivalsherpa.com/studies-prove-that-burning-man-is-truly-a-transformational-experience.
Thoreau, Henry David. 2018. *Walden*. Richmond, VA: Minerva.
Thrasher, Steven. 2015. "Burning Man's Black Campers Explain Why They Are the 1%." *Guardian,* September 27, 2015. www.theguardian.com/culture/2015/sep/27/black-campers-burning-man-explain-why.
Todorov, Tzvetan. 1993. *On Human Diversity: Nationalism, Racism, and Exoticism in French Thought*. Cambridge, MA: Harvard University Press.
Trilling, Lionel. 1972. *Sincerity and Authenticity*. Cambridge, MA: Harvard University Press.
Tsing, Anna Lowenhaupt. 2015. *The Mushroom at the End of the World: On the Possibility of Life in Capitalist Ruins*. Princeton, NJ: Princeton University Press.
Tully, James. 1995. *Strange Multiplicity: Constitutionalism in an Age of Diversity*. Cambridge: Cambridge University Press.
Turner, Victor. 1996. *The Ritual Process: Structure and Anti-structure*. New Brunswick: Aldine Transaction.
Tylor, E. B. 2016. *Primitive Culture*. Vol. 1. Mineola, NY: Dover.
Urban, Hugh. 2015. *Zorba the Buddha: Sex, Spirituality, and Capitalism in the Global Osho Movement*. Berkeley, CA: University of California Press.
Valantasis, Richard. 1998. "A Theory of the Social Function of Asceticism." In *Asceticism,* edited by Vincent Wimbush and Richard Valantasis, 544–52. New York: Oxford University Press.
Venkataraman, Prabhu. 2015. "Romanticism, Nature, and Self-Reflection in Rousseau's Reveries of a Solitary Walker." *Cosmos and History: The Journal of Natural and Social Philosophy* 11, no. 1: 327–41.
Venuti, Lawrence. 2000. "Translation, Community, Utopia." In *The Translation Studies Reader,* edited by Lawrence Venuti, 468–88. New York: Routledge.
Wachowski, Andy, Larry Wachowski, Keanu Reeves, Laurence Fishburne, and Carrie-Anne Moss. 1999. *The Matrix*. Burbank, CA: Warner Home Video.
Waddell, Ray. 2015. "Coachella Earns over $84 Million, Breaks Attendance Records." *Billboard,* July 15, 2015. www.billboard.com/articles/business/6633636/coachella-2015-earnings-84-million-breaks-attendance-records.
Waghorne, Joanne Punzo. 2020. *Singapore, Spirituality, and the Space of the State: Soul of the Little Red Dot*. London: Bloomsbury.
Ward, Charlotte, and David Voas. 2011. "The Emergence of Conspirituality." *Journal of Contemporary Religion* 26, no. 1: 103–21.
Weber, Max. 1991. *The Sociology of Religion*. Boston: Beacon Press.

———. 2001. *The Protestant Ethic and the Spirit of Capitalism.* New York: Routledge.

White, Allon. 1989. "Hysteria and the End of Carnival: Festivity and Bourgeois Neurosis." In *The Violence of Representation: Literature and the History of Violence,* edited by Nancy Armstrong and Leonard Tennenhouse, 157–70. New York: Routledge.

White, David Gordon. 2014. *The Yoga Sūtra of Patañjali: A Biography.* Princeton, NJ: Princeton University Press.

Wildcroft, Theodora. 2018. "Patterns of Authority and Practice Relationships in 'Post-Lineage Yoga.'" PhD diss., Open University.

Williams, William. 2012. *Tourism, Landscape, and the Irish Character: British Travel Writers in Pre-famine Ireland.* Madison, WI: University of Wisconsin Press.

Williamson, Lola. 2010. *Transcendent in America: Hindu-Inspired Meditation Movements as New Religion.* New York: New York University Press.

Wong, Yutian. 2010. *Choreographing Asian America.* Middletown, CT: Wesleyan University Press.

Young, Cathy. 2015. "To the New Culture Cops, Everything Is Appropriation." *Washington Post,* August 21, 2015. www.washingtonpost.com/posteverything/wp/2015/08/21/to-the-new-culture-cops-everything-is-appropriation.

Young, James O. 2010. *Cultural Appropriation and the Arts.* Malden, MA: Wiley Blackwell.

Young, James O., and Conrad G. Brunk, eds. 2009. *The Ethics of Cultural Appropriation.* Malden, MA: Blackwell.

Yudkin, Daniel. 2018. "Prosocial Transformation at Multi-Day Mass Gatherings." Paper presentation, Burning Man and Transformational Event Cultures, University of Fribourg, Fribourg, Switzerland, November 29–30.

Ziff, Bruce. 1997. *Borrowed Power: Essays on Cultural Appropriation.* New Brunswick, NJ: Rutgers University Press.

Žižek, Slavoj. 2001. *On Belief.* New York: Routledge.

Index

African Americans, 38–39, 85, 158, 261n42, 267n25
Albanese, Catherine, 11
Alexander, Michael, 233
alterity, 5, 22, 24, 32–33, 36–37
Altglas, Véronique, 9–10, 12
Appiah, Kwame Anthony, 53
art, 155–157, 182–183; Burning Man, 2, 47, 183, 261n44; and religious exoticism, 8, 38
artists: Burning Man, 47, 143, 155, 157, 183, 246n45, 259n12; and appropriation, 51, 100
asceticism, 102–104, 106–107, 109–115, 184–185, 187; and festivals, 136; yogic, 133
ascetic self, 110–111, 114–116, 126, 134, 136
Ashtanga Yoga. *See* yoga, Ashtanga
authenticity, 70–73, 202, 246n37, 258n2; anxiety over, 62, 69–81, 83–98, 101, 224; and conceptions of East versus West, 81; and experience, 91, 97; performance of, 52, 72; and POC, 17–18, 52, 166; and whiteness, 166; yogic, 70, 73-74, 76–77, 88
authority, 32, 77, 101, 222–224; and authenticity, 71–72, 91, 98; local knowledge as, 77–78, 80, 85; universal knowledge as, 86–88, 91; white claims of, 32, 37, 70, 101
Ayurveda, 26, 130, 181

Bakhtin, Mikhail, 21–22, 108
Baudrillard, Jean, 189–190, 267n12
Beliso de Jesús, Aisha, 260n16
Bellah, Robert, 12
Bender, Courtney, 11
Benjamin, Rich, 15–16
Benjamin, Walter, 94–95, 189, 267n12
Berry, Evan, 153–154
bhaktas, 25, 66, 80–81, 137, 165–167
Bhakti Fest, 13, 25–26, 31, 39, 246n37; apparel, 220; asceticism at, 114–115, 133; "be in the *bhav*," 118, 203; Bhakti Fest Group, 80; Bhakti Yātra, 80; corporate partners of, 181–182; guru devotion at, 42, 79, 163; Hindu devotion at, 16, 25, 39, 42, 106, 246n30; Indigenous acknowledgment, 43; *kīrtan* at, 30, 66, 118, 165–168, 229; and nature, 151, 237; organizers of, 66, 229; religious exoticism at, 20; size of, 230; and South Asians, 15, 66; as spiritual pilgrimage, 25, 167; "tribe," 58–59; vegetarianism at, 110, 132; workshops at, 75, 123, 166, 170; yoga classes at, 25, 69, 78–79, 129; yoga teachers at, 86, 88, 230
bhakti yoga, 13–14, 31, 78–81, 166–168; adoption of, 42, 79; and cultural appropriation, 51; embodied, 79; in India, 44, 66

Black Lives Matter, 212
Bourdieu, Pierre, 9, 112, 132
Bowditch, Rachel, 182, 259n12
breathwork, 26, 122-123, 152, 199
Brown, Michael, 16, 61
Brown, Wendy, 205
Bryant, Edwin, 200
Buddhism, 44, 96, 103, 146, 239n5; and SBNR, 1, 11, 38, 41-42, 44
Burners, 56, 106, 125; Black Burner Project, 83, 252n49; social conventions of, 143, 171-172, 209, 220, 264n92; veteran, 171, 177, 230, 265n2
Burning Man, 195, 199, 220-221, 228-229, 231; art at, 117, 120, 143, 149, 155-157; performance at, 124; asceticism at, 114, 126, 135; Black Rock City Airport, 18; Black Rock City Census, 14, 19, 174; and Bureau of Land Management (BLM), 108; Burners without Borders, 199, 211, 243n100; and capitalism, 117, 177, 182-183; cultural appropriation at, 47-48, 54-56, 247n65; demographics of, 14, 19, 39, 179, 230; environmental conditions of, 124; leaders, 3, 199; and parody, 39, 108, 117, 182, 212, 220; playa, 114, 124-126, 155, 237, 245n13; Playa Pops Orchestra, 157-158; POC, 47, 83, 158, 193; Regional Network, 199; and revisioning society, 13, 24; and SBNR, 39, 43; as spiritual pilgrimage, 24-25; and Standing Rock, 55; Temple, 175-176, 206-209; and transformational experience, 120, 135, 144, 171, 174; and whiteness, 56-58, 66, 218-220; whiteouts at, 114-115, 124-126, 155, 257n70; workshops, 13; yoga at, 25, 28, 69, 108, 230; magic. *See* magic
Burning Man 10 Principles, 47, 165, 182, 193, 203; Decommodification, 182; Gifting, 13, 117, 135, 259n12; Immediacy, 48, 203; Radical Self-Expression, 13, 193; Radical Self-Reliance, 13, 117, 165, 194, 268n48, 270n25
Burning Man camps, 70, 83, 198, 231; Anahasana Village, 56, 70; Camp Mystic, 135, 229; Center Camp, 160, 182, 194; Pink Heart, 156, 240n10; POC camp, 83, 194; Red Lightning, 55-56
Burning Man French Quarter Village, 2, 32, 49, 231, 244n114; Appropriated Dragon, 47-50; Black Rock Bakery, 48-49, 125-126, 231, 244n114; Blind Mistress, 2
Burning Man Project, 47, 149, 176-177, 240n10
Burning Nerds, 257n71

Cahuilla, 44, 239n1
Caillois, Roger, 22, 24, 106-107
camping, 116, 137-138, 153-154; and material possessions, 116, 120, 134
Campion, Nicholas, 95
capitalism, 13, 53, 78, 147, 181, 183, 205, 251n25; and class distinction, 9, 131-132, 196, 214; enslavement to, 189-190, 266n11; and the Protestant ethic, 106, 112, 135. *See also* Protestant ethic
carnivalesque, 23, 107-108, 182, 184, 187
Carrette, Jeremy and Richard King, 53
Coachella, 118, 177-178, 181-182, 256n56
Coates, Ta-Nehisi, 17
colonialism, 57, 67, 84, 107, 154; legacies of, 62-63, 65, 81-82, 150, 159
commons, 13, 205-206, 208-210, 212, 218; gated, 14, 33, 212, 219; and modernity, 188
communitas, 187-188, 206, 210, 212, 217
communities, 21-23, 110, 123, 142, 216-217, 221; affective, 63, 68; ascetic, 87, 109, 115; and the commons, 13, 201, 206, 215; and diversity, 187, 217, 219, 224-225; guru, 43, 231; local, 210-213; permanent, 25, 108, 118, 154, 199, 220; POC, 18-19, 21, 76, 194; religious, 62, 200-201, 214; SBNR, 22, 24, 113, 180; South Asian, 84, 244n11; subaltern, 107; and whiteness, 4, 15-16, 18-19, 85, 195, 222; yogic, 15-16, 25, 199, 204
community: affective feelings of, 58, 168, 198-199; belonging, 7, 21, 199, 207, 218; building, 23, 110, 142; identity, 132; rhetoric of, 10, 199, 201, 218; "tribe," 58, 134-135, 161
connection, 121, 171; communal, 110, 172, 187, 199-200, 219; with divinity, 29, 56, 152; becoming open to, 14, 134, 149, 199, 214, 225; with nature, 10, 172; with others, 13, 24, 150, 169-170, 179; to South Asia, 68, 80; through friendship, 68; to "tribe," 62
consciousness, 88, 106, 118, 135, 173; altered states of, 158-159, 162;

Index | 293

evolution of, 199; expansion of, 101, 109, 124, 134, 223; exploration of, 159, 167; lack of, 40; purification of, 168, 203; raising, 29, 39, 115–116, 118, 129, 211; Temple of. *See* Lightning in a Bottle, Temple of Consciousness
counterculture, 105, 154, 187, 190, 240n14; and drugs, 159, 161; festivals, 20; religious exoticism in the, 6–7, 54, 60
Crawley, Ashon, 250n16
Crenshaw, Kimberlé, 131
cultural appropriation, 17–18, 37–38, 47–57, 63–64, 244n10; and headdresses, 57, 58*fig.*, 105, 152; and identity, 77, 82, 233; and misappropriation, 99–101; online discussion of, 63, 75; and religious conversion, 82; and religious exoticism, 4, 6, 9; and systemic racism, 61, 63–64; and yoga, 75, 77, 82, 91
cultural property rights, 57, 61, 65, 70, 75

de Certeau, Michel, 148
Deloria, Phillip, 9, 36
de Martino, Ernesto, 216
DiAngelo, Robin, 225, 232. *See also* white fragility.
diet, 103, 129–131, 133, 228
diversity, 52, 116, 217–219, 225; in SBNR, 11; of yoga techniques, 29, 78
Doniger, Wendy, 82
Driscoll, Christopher, 5, 83, 244nn10,11
drugs, 24, 114, 158–165; 5-MeO-DMT/DMT, 45, 159–161; ayahuasca, 38, 45, 159, 164, 185; LSD, 144, 159–164, 185; marijuana, 130, 163–164; MDMA, 159, 162, 164, 263n71; opioids, 262n69; pharmaceuticals, 130, 162; psilocybin, 159
Durkheim, Emile, 22, 106–107, 187

earth: connection to, 10, 81; in crisis, 2, 209, 211; consciousness, 13; Native respect for the, 44, 54, 60; as sacred, 2, 61, 209; spirits, 152–153
EDC (Electric Daisy Carnival), 21, 119, 256–257n60, 262n51
EDM (Electronic Dance Music), 21, 100, 158–159, 178; and drugs, 114, 165; festivals, 119; and rave culture, 159, 178
energy, 40, 119, 127, 160, 202; in Ayurveda, 131; elevated, 197, 211; manipulation of, 46, 123, 134, 160; positive, 119, 174; in SBNR metaphysics, 11
Esalen, 154, 254n101, 262n62

Federici, Silvia, 13–14
festival: circuits, 24, 121; processionals, 107; spaces, 24, 136, 155, 170, 199; worlds, 134, 136, 168, 171; yoga, 31, 128
Festival of Colors (Holi), 227, 234
festivals: colonial, 107; countercultural, 20; ethnocultural, 21, 227; and identity groups, 21, 113; medieval, 22–23, 106, 108, 110, 206; in modernity, 23; and religion, 25; as socially productive, 107–108; as social parody, 22; and society, 25; and the state, 21; as temporary reprieve, 22–23, 104, 107
Fish, Stanley, 98
Flat Earth Society, 193, 267n18
Fortune Tarot Project, 262n48
Foucault, Michel, 184, 205, 250n16, 268n48
freedom, 118, 172, 177, 199, 264n1; of the commons, 206, 212, 215, 218–219; from enclosures of modernity, 185; feelings of, 5, 33, 103, 185–188, 194; in Indic religions, 103, 203; from isolation, 198; from judgment, 193; from modernity, 188; negative, 210; neoliberal, 91, 132, 187, 210–211, 266–267n11; positive, 210; radical, 193, 199, 221; religious, 12; from responsibilities, 196; in SBNR rhetoric, 11, 185; temporary, 107, 195, 205, 212; ultimate, 184, 200, 203; and utopia, 221; work, 5, 212–213; in yoga, 200
friendship, 63, 68, 199, 22

Gandhi, Leela, 63, 68. *See also* community, affective
Gershon, Ilana, 205
Godrej, Farah, 253n78, 255n12
Grazian, David, 72–73, 97
gurus, 80, 87–88, 163, 253n64; yoga, 75, 78

Hall, Stuart, 64
health, 131–32, 180, 195, 204–205; yoga for, 13, 44, 129–130
Heelas, Paul, 86, 97, 185–186, 258n3. *See also Spiritualities of Life*
Hindu American Foundation, 44, 70, 249n89, 270n27

Hindu deities, 46; commodification of, 7, 66; homage to, 35, 53, 79–80, 166, 243n102
Hinduism, 1, 39, 44, 96, 239n5; academic study of, 53, 68, 83; appropriation of, 51, 80, 92; as authentic, 79; converts to, 41–42, 51, 53, 82, 167; representation of, 52–53, 66, 249nn89,7; rituals of, 1, 34–35, 41–44, 96; and SBNR, 11, 15, 38, 41, 167, scriptures of, 1, 44, 66, 79, 250n14
Hindu nationalism, 17, 53, 63, 68, 75, 247n57, 250n11
Human Be-In, 60

identity, 136, 164; and authenticity, 71; and experimentation, 115, 117; and festivals, 21, 143; loss of, 160; in multiculturalism, 52; religious, 36; social, 24, 131, 145; transformation of, 221
imperialist nostalgia, 37, 62–63
India, 43, 98, 141, 144, 227; cultural property of, 70, 76, 98, 101; definition of Indic religions/religions of, 239n5; and globalization, 98; holy cities in, 7, 64, 162, 228; modern, 63; pilgrimage to, 79–80; religious exoticism in, 52; representations of, 51, 53, 83, 91; as site of authority, 35, 78–82, 85–87, 101; spiritual searching in, 87, 161; veneration of, 169; white viscosity in, 150, 266n1; yoga in, 17, 44, 70, 82, 102, 270n27
Indian Americans, 15, 54, 67, 101, 224. *See also* South Asians
Indian Hindus: inclusion of, 66; nationalists, 68, 76; views on cultural appropriation, 51–53, 64
Indians, 19, 52, 66–67, 75; and anti-Black racism, 244n11; as authorities, 76, 79–82, 86, 91; cultural property of, 77, 82, 84, 101, 222; exclusion of, 19, 66, 224; representations of, 7, 67, 80–81, 84, 224. *See also* South Asians
Indian yogis, 37, 77, 79, 85, 106, 109
Indigenous, 16–17, 36–38; cultural property of, 9, 58–59, 248n77; knowledge, 43, 45–46, 56–57, 159; land acknowledgement, 43–44; medicine, 159, 162; and religious exoticism, 4, 6, 11–12, 37–38, 57; spiritual practices, 27, 32, 45–46, 109, 153, 223; "we are all indigenous," 46, 56; and white possessivism, 18, 38, 63, 84

Indigenous people, 56; experience of, 17, 19, 37, 222, 224; exploitation of, 9, 57, 104, 162; partnerships with, 159, 245–246n29; solidarity with, 63
International Society for Krishna Consciousness (ISKCON), 7, 163, 166, 240n16, 243n102; and conversion, 42, 51–53, 106

Jain, Andrea, 74, 105
Jenkins, Philip, 5–6, 17
Jois, Pattabhi, 44, 75, 78. *See also* yoga, Ashtanga

kale (and green juice), 2–3, 112, 132–133, 141, 204
kīrtan, 30–31, 53, 80, 118; and altered states, 162, 165; experience of, 150, 173, 185, 206, 231; musicians, 51, 53, 64, 66, 165, 243n102; and SBNR, 41–42, 46; South Asian, 80, 168–169, 249n8, 256n55; as transformational, 118, 120, 167–168; and whiteness, 51, 64, 66, 165–166, 168
Kraut, Anthea, 76, 251n30
Krishnamacharya, 75, 92–94, 164; lineage, 78, 79; students, 44, 92
Kumbh Mela, 107–108, 227, 234–235, 256n55
Kurien, Prema, 52

Lightning in a Bottle, 13, 20, 195, 203; 6 Ways of LIB, 13, 57, 164, 217; apparel, 182; art, 156; and asceticism, 114–115; community, 198; corporate partners, 180; and cultural appropriation, 57, 59, 85, 99, 101–102; demographics, 14, 19, 108, 218, 226; producers, the Do LaB, 43, 149, 181, 191, 263n73; and drug use, 163, 165, 171; and EDM, 158; Indigenous acknowledgement, 43; Indigenous ritual at, 152–153, 159; size of, 108, 230; and societal impact, 108; Temple of Consciousness, 43, 191, 193, 267n18; as transformational, 39, 43, 171; as utopia, 198; vegetarianism at, 133; workshops, 13, 69, 191, 211; yoga at, 25, 69, 108, 163–164; yoga teachers at, 78–79, 230
The Possessive Investment in Whiteness (Lipsitz), 18
local knowledge. *See* yoga, as local knowledge
Lollapalooza, 21, 177–178
Love and Theft (Lott), 17, 63

Maffesoli, Michael, 59
magic, 11, 149, 174–176, 202, 216; enchantment, 174, 216, 242–243n96, 260–261n23; and magical holism, 63; and magical realism, 124; and magical surrealism, 146
Magister, Caveat, 126, 257n71
Mannheim, Karl, 215
mantras, 34–35, 41, 79, 167, 202
Marx, Karl, 146, 188–189, 266n11
Matthes, Erich, 51
meditation, 40; altered states in, 162; classes on, 128; guided, 30–31, 123, 152, 173; *kīrtan*, 168; open-eyed, 170, 228; walking, 42; workshops on, 39, 69
Miller, Amara, 74
modernity: alienation in, 7, 71, 188–189, 251n25, 266n11; alternative, 4; and asceticism, 106, 255n15; and authenticity, 72; corruptions of, 18–19, 41, 70; crises of, 2, 5, 62, 81, 89, 188; and disenchantment, 24, 63, 188, 242–243n96; disruptions of, 216; festivals in, 23, 107; freedom in, 188, 210; hyperreality of, 267n12; late-capitalist, 25, 110, 186, 215, 217; mysticism in, 147; precarity in. *See* precarity; Western. *See* Western modernity
modern postural yoga, 42, 53, 81, 90, 109, 114; and appropriation, 200; and ascetic discipline, 114, 128; authenticating strategies of, 73–75, 86; commodification of, 61; ethical values of, 109; innovation in, 87–88; invention of, 73; origins of, 29, 44, 75; translation of, 92–95; and whiteness, 16, 19, 76, 222
Moreton-Robinson, Aileen, 18. *See also* white possessivism
Murty Classical Library. *See* Pollock, Sheldon
music, 173, 197, 210, 229; and appropriation, 65, 97, 166, 251n25; devotional, 30, 42, 103, 118, 165; and drugs, 164; industry, 179; and ritual, 152; and white viscosity, 150; electronic. *See* EDM (Electronic Dance Music)
music festivals, 20–21, 173, 177–179, 181–182
mystical experiences, 45, 144–145, 147–150, 159–160
mysticism, 11, 102–103, 145–147, 260n16; and mystics, 109, 146, 167

Native American, 41–46, 54–55, 57–58, 60–62; religions, 6–7, 16–17, 41–42, 154; and religious exoticism, 36, 46, 54, 60–62, 248n77; representation of, 57–58; ritual, 12, 38, 42; rituals, 30, 38; spiritual practices, 12, 30, 38, 41–42, 45–46, 61; traditions, 6, 15, 44–45; and white possessivism, 17, 46, 224, 247–248n68. *See also* Indigenous
Native American people, 10; experience of, 54, 85, 224, 247–248n68; exploitation of, 16, 54–55, 57, 85; partnerships with, 43, 54–55, 245–246n29; recognition of, 62; representation of, 57; solidarity with, 54–55, 247n65; whites identifying as, 7, 17, 36
nature, 46, 151–152; attunement with, 24, 46, 154; communion with, 10, 151, 153–154, 172, 185; festivals in, 105, 149–151, 173; as spiritual inspiration, 42, 44, 151; white exploration of, 154
nature religion, 69, 151, 153–154, 229
neoliberalism, 94, 105–106, 136, 200, 215–217; embodied, 23, 109, 131–132, 203–205
New Age, 37, 223; critics of, 42, 61; origins of, 5, 22, 42; and religious exoticism, 9–10, 16, 40
New Thought, 11, 16, 30, 112, 141
Nietzsche, Friedrich, 145, 189, 266n11
"noble savage," 62, 70, 223, 248–249n88
nutrition, 27, 131–132, 181. *See also* diet

Orientalism, 9, 18, 80, 85, 94, 245n24, 251n25
origins, 62, 71, 75, 101, 202. *See also* yoga, Indic origins of

Patañjali's *Yoga Sūtras*. *See Yoga Sūtras*
peak experiences, 136, 161–163, 205
People of Color (POC), 36, 47, 51–54, 84–85, 193; absence of, 5, 15; erasure of, 65; experience of, 19, 155, 219–220, 222, 224; *kīrtan* artists, 169; racism against, 244n11; violence against, 154; camp, 83. *See also* Burning Man camps, POC camp; yoga class, 83. *See also* yoga classes, POC
petit bourgeoisie, 9
Pollock, Sheldon, 82, 250n11
postmodernism, 9–10, 89, 91, 189
postural yoga. *See* modern postural yoga
power: place of, 152–153, 174, 195, 203; of positive thinking, 142–143; relations, 77, 228, 254n96; structures, 64, 83, 85, 146; will to, 143

296 | Index

prāṇāyāma, 123, 205
Prasada Festival, 168–169
Prashad, Vijay, 244n11, 245n24
precarity, 15–16, 188, 215–217, 266n8
producers, 61, 176–177, 179, 181. *See also* festival producers
property: cultural, 17, 37, 53, 55, 75–76; white. *See* white possessivism
Protestant ethic, 106, 112, 135–136
Protestantism, 11, 74, 96, 201, 244n10
Putcha, Rumya, 242nn70,71, 252n48
Putnam, Robert, 217–219
Pyramid Lake Paiute, 245–246n29

Race and Yoga Working Group, UC Berkeley, 241n56
Rainbow Tribe, 60, 177, 255n26
recognition: of common humanity, 33, 68, 171, 187, 209, 212; of the essence of self, 201, 203, 258n2; politics of, 52, 62
religion, 59, 74, 82, 147, 167; Abrahamic, 11; academic study of, 36, 83, 102, 111, 259n3; and authenticity, 72; critique of, 39–41, 146, 167, 189, 195, 201; and identity, 61, 84; and race, 83; and SBNR, 11–12, 39–42, 97, 141, 152, 167
religious exoticism, 4–5, 7–9, 63; and anti-Black racism, 38; and colonialism, 82; and the counterculture, 6, 161; definition of, 8–9; and the journey of "evolution," 33, 99–103; and imperialist nostalgia, 62; and Native Americans, 46, 54, 62; and Orientalism, 9; and POC, 19, 28, 63, 166, 222; practices of, 36, 63, 96, 101, 135, 232; reenchantment through, 37, 223, 243n96; responsibilities of, 101; and romanticism, 8; and SBNR, 11–12, 36–37, 40, 56, 105, 222–223; and self-distinction, 37; and self-transformation, 9, 36; and stereotypes, 52, 62, 73, 85, 150, 222; and transformational festivals, 222; and whiteness, 10, 18–20, 32–33, 63, 104, 233; and white religion, 5, 233; and white viscosity, 169; and white possessivism. *See* white possessivism
representation, 51, 61; and authenticity, 71–73; contestations over, 64–66; and POC erasure, 51, 54; festivals as collective, 21; of Hinduism, 66, 84; of idealized others, 8, 54; and misappropriation, 99–101; and misrepresentation, 56; politics of, 36, 84, 165, 168;
power of, 64; and racialization, 155; and self-determination, 64, 75, 111; solidarity in, 224; in yoga, 17, 74, 77–78, 85, 222, 224; and white possessivism, 36, 52, 223. *See also* white possessivism
Roman Carnival, 184, 206
Romantic Orientalism, 34–63, 81–82, 223, 251n25
Root, Deborah, 18, 36
Rousseau, Jean-Jacques, 70, 153, 266n11

SAAPYA (South Asian American Peoples Yoga Alliance), 54
Said, Edward. *See* Orientalism.
Saldanha, Arun, 4, 18, 77, 150, 221, 266n1
Sāṃkhya Yoga, 44, 258n2
San Francisco Oracle, 7, 60
Sanskrit, 53, 82–83, 250n14
SBNR ("spiritual but not religious"), 5, 10–11, 15–16, 39, 41, 113; communities, 11–12, 15, 31, 42, 56, 96; populations, 10–13, 22, 25, 28, 41, 112; demographics, 15–16; practitioners, 40, 105–106, 110, 204; values, 22, 31, 69–70, 143
The Secret, 141–143
self, 96–97, 109–116, 149, 174, 185–186; Advaita Vedantic, 258n2; and alterity, 37, 46, 54, 96, 224; buffered, 148, 260n14; Christian mystical self, 260n17; conventional, 116–118, 134–135, 148–150, 173–174, 258n2; disciplining, 103; egoistic, 96, 149; essence of, 89, 108, 121–122, 145, 185; ethical, 109–110, 202–203, 266n11; as exotified other, 224; expressive, 186; fragmented, 9, 62; and other, 32, 57, 170–171, 224; perfectible, 93, 135, 205; perfection of, 204–206; porous, 148, 174, 260n14; production of, 8–9, 18, 24, 96, 118; transformation of, 3, 102, 109, 117, 154, 221; vulnerable, 134; yogic, 89, 173, 200, 203, 258n2; neoliberal. *See* self-governance
self–: affirmation, 2, 5, 30, 96, 143; awareness, 68, 111, 145, 154, 161; care, 132, 201, 205, 212, 268n48; critique, 4–5, 37, 102, 201; cultivation, 93, 109–110, 121, 136, 201, 204; determination, 64, 84, 210; discipline, 110–112, 114, 128, 205, 212; doubt, 142, 202–203; improvement, 41, 131; inquiry, 29, 120, 153, 259n6; knowledge, 114,

Index | 297

131; love, 137; realization, 40, 121; shrinkage, 115, 145; transformation, 4–5, 36–37, 115–116, 144, 162; expression, 25, 57, 114; ascetic. *See* ascetic self; authentic. *See* authentic self; *See also* Burning Man 10 Principles, Radical Self-Expression; governance. *See* self-governance; reliance. *See* Burning Man 10 Principles, Radical Self-Reliance

self-governance, 143, 187, 201, 203; autonomous self, 203; self-as-asset, 205; self-control, 131; self-mastery, 106, 111, 133, 136, 142–143, 239n1; self-perfection, 106, 203; self-regulation, 93, 105, 111, 187; self-responsibility, 185; self-surveillance, 194

Serrano, 44, 239n1

settler colonialism, 18, 43, 46, 59, 64, 154

sexuality, *See also* workshops, Tantric

Shakti Fest, 220, 231, 239n1, 243n102; apparel, 182, 220; asceticism at, 114; "be in the *bhav*," 203; corporate partners, 181; demographics, 15, 20, 180; guru devotion at, 163; Hindu devotion at, 25, 35, 39, 42, 80, 115, 118, 166; Indigenous acknowledgement, 43; *kīrtan* at, 165, 167; and nature, 151; organizers, 166, 229; rituals, 1, 34–35, 165–166, 246n30; size of, 230; vegetarianism at, 132; vendors, 229; and whiteness, 66, 165, 218; workshops, 35, 122–123, 170, 199, 229; yoga classes at, 25, 30, 69, 129, 170; yoga teachers at, 46, 78–79, 121, 204, 230

shamans, 16, 104, 152–153, 223–224

Singh, Roopa, 54, 247n63

Singleton, Mark, 88, 93

social capital, 16, 36–37, 198, 218–219, 259n12

society, 111–112, 206, 221; fragmented, 119; neoliberal, 143; precarity in, 215; racialized, 91, 213, 232; rejection of, 116, 149, 153–154, 187; transformation of, 221; and utopia, 209, 211, 214–215

South Asians, 6, 51, 66, 165–166, 169, 247n57, 249n89

spiritual, 24, 31, 151, 153, 161; awakening, 33; bricolage, 2, 12, 43, 222; community, 20, 42, 132–133, 135, 166; evolution, 32, 136; experience, 21, 24, 30, 70, 151, 212; growth, 44, 79, 137, 149, 195, 201; Indians as, 76, 82, 87, 98, 141, 224; knowledge, 22; Natives as, 55; pilgrimage, 24, 80; places, 24; practices, 35, 112, 115, 223, 244n114; property of Natives, 16–17, 247–248n68; practices and religious exoticism, 7, 9, 42, 101; rhetoric, 2, 243n107; and SBNR, 8; seekers, 12–13, 29, 35–36, 41, 56, 162; tools, 45–46, 109, 134–135, 182, 223; tourism, 104–105, 110, 114, 116, 162, 196; transformation, 5, 29, 108, 201, 223, 256n56; values, 30; void, 23–24, 144; wellness, 180; work, 102, 115, 121–122, 133, 165, 220; workshops, 31, 35, 39, 171; yoga, 105, 121, 128, 134, 200, 229–230; "tribe." *See* "tribe"

Spiritualities of Life, 86, 97, 185–186, 204

spirituality, 41, 167, 177, 200, 205, 208; Asian, 98; bricolage, 11; countercultural, 88; entrepreneurs of, 205; erasure of, 93; Indian, 80, 97; institutions of, 12; individualism, 12; neoliberal, 93, 105; Native, 43, 54; and religion, 97; and religious exoticism, 12, 15–17, 32; and self-care, 205; therapeutic, 9; wellness, 86, 129; and whiteness, 4, 233; yogic, 95, 201; universalism in. *See* universalism, spiritual

Srinivas, Tulasi, 147, 216

stereotypes. *See* religious exoticism, stereotypes

St. John, Graham, 37, 161

Take Back Yoga campaign, 44, 70, 222, 270n27

Taylor, Charles, 52, 91, 260n14

Tea and Turbans, 47–48

teepees, 45, 57, 59*fig.*, 247–248n68

Thoreau, Henry David, 188–189

Todorov, Tzvetan, 8, 10, 248–249n88

transformational festivals, 21–22, 155, 157, 159, 184–185, 215; asceticism at, 110, 113, 115–116, 124, 133, 136; and capitalism, 181–182; and the commons, 13, 23, 195, 212, 217, 224–225; connection with others at, 150; drug use at, 162–165, 173; EDM at, 158; extrasociality of, 109, 146, 154, 187, 193, 220; as institutions of SBNR, 11–12, 15, 39, 41; and partnerships with Native and Indigenous people, 245–246n29; producers of, 191; and reenchantment, 24; religious exoticism in, 9, 12, 36–38, 42, 56–57, 222; social engagement and, 108, 212; spiritual growth and, 38, 134, 174, 221; spiritual pilgrimage, 24;

transformational festivals *(continued)*
spiritual practices of, 69; spiritual tourism to, 105, 116; spiritual work at, 102, 191, 193; temporary utopias of, 11, 24; in this study, 14–16, 20, 25, 28, 227–228; and "tribe," 59; and whiteness, 14–16, 19, 196, 217, 221, 232–233; and wonder 103, 149–150; yoga at, 29–31, 77, 109, 127, 149, 197
translation, 12, 91–96, 141, 200, 249n1
Tree of Ténéré, 157–158
"tribe," 33, 54, 57–62, 134–135, 198–199; countercultural use of, 60
Tsing, Anna, 188, 215, 217, 266n8. *See also* precarity
Turner, Victor, 187
Tylor, E. B., 223, 270n29. *See also* survivals

universalism: spiritual, 40, 167, 224, 232; and white dominance, 54, 75–76, 101, 223
universal knowledge. *See* yoga, as universal knowledge
utopia, 58, 68, 95, 97, 188, 200; Burning Man resistance to, 126, 209, 257n71; as "coming home," 217–218; as conscious community, 187, 190, 198–199, 211, 223; and dystopia, 25, 95, 188, 193, 214–215, 221; elitism of, 221; experience of, 120, 186, 210; permanent, 25, 154, 243n103; and religious exoticism, 6, 8, 18–19; and SBNR, 9–10, 174; and settler colonialism, 214; totalitarianism of, 221; transformational festival as, 4, 13, 20, 24, 103–104, 225; and whiteness, 19, 33, 103, 150

Venuti, Lawrence, 94–95
Vinyāsa yoga. *See* yoga, Vinyāsa

Wanderlust, 43, 106, 115–116, 119–120, 201; apparel, 182; asceticism at, 114, 133; community, 172; and corporate partners, 180–181, 205; and enchanted secularism, 39, 42, 151; "find your true north," 105, 203, 205; Great Lake Taupo, 43, 121, 137–140; and health consciousness, 13, 114, 132, 220; Indigenous acknowledgement, 42–43, 45–46, 48; Mont Tremblant, 80, 87, 119, 127–128, 197; and nature, 149, 151; and neoliberalism, 105, 203, 205, 211; Oahu, 69, 127–130, 163, 180, 196–197; offerings, 27, 110; as secular church, 39, 200–201; size of, 230; and social engagement, 199, 205, 211, 240n10; Speakeasy, 200, 251, 266; Spectacular, 138; as spiritual retreat, 9, 24, 196–197; and spiritual tourism, 105; Squaw Valley, 69, 127, 200–202, 211; Sunshine Coast, 43, 139, 172, 196; and whiteness, 14, 218; yoga classes at, 25, 69, 114, 121, 126–129; yoga teachers at, 45, 78–79, 121, 230
Weber, Max, 112, 135, 146, 266n11
Western modernity, 71; religious exoticist critique of, 7, 37, 45–46, 54, 81, 223
White, Allon, 23
white fragility, 232–33
whiteness, 14–18, 166; category of, 222, 232; colonialism and, 62; and cultural erasure, 18, 36, 38; and cultural property, 19, 64–68, 154–155; death of, 5, 233; of festivals in this study, 14–18; and Hare Krishnas, 52–53; and intersectionality, 132; and nature, 154–155; non-Hispanic, 14–15; normativity of, 76–77, 232; and religious exoticism, 10, 36, 38, 51, 54, 63; and SBNR, 5, 20; and settler colonialism, 154–155; in yoga, 69, 76–77, 82–84, 251n27; and privilege. *See* white privilege
white possessivism, 14, 56, 58, 61, 84, 223–224; *See also* whiteness, and cultural possession
white privilege, 51, 84, 91, 100, 166, 248n77
whites, 52–53, 61–63, 166, 221–222, 224–225; as authorities in yoga, 6, 78, 83, 91, 98; *bhaktas*, 1, 36, 51–53, 66, 75–76, 249n7; as cultural authorities, 36, 73, 75–77, 101; evangelicals, 15; "evolution" of, 99–102; scholars, 66, 83; women, 6, 11, 221, 224, 251n27; yoga teachers, 17, 37, 75–76, 83–84, 92; youth, 18, 61, 266n1; neoshamans, 36, 162. *See also* shamans; "playing Indian," 36, 46. *See also* Deloria, Phillip
white supremacy, 15, 65, 91, 102, 233; and overt racism, 58, 85, 158; and POC displacement, 46, 56, 64, 76–77, 83–84, 101, 223; rejection of, 5
white viscosity, 4, 150, 162, 217; POC experience of, 158, 174, 219; white attraction to, 166, 168–169, 217
Whitopias, 15–16, 241n52. *See also* Benjamin, Rich

women, 3, 5, 138–139, 193, 195–197, 220
wonder, 124, 144–148, 150–151, 168–170, 173–174
Woodstock, 20, 178
workshops, 43, 53, 223; Indigenous knowledge, 45; SBNR bricolage, 13, 38; skills-based for social change, 43, 45, 108, 118, 211; Tantric, 25, 170; therapeutic, 105, 121–122, 124, 170, 174; breathwork, 122–124, 229. *See also* breathwork

yoga, 25–30, 127, 129–130, 202, 205, 223–224; Acro, 26–27, Aerial, 128; and altered states, 162–163; and asceticism, 128, 136; Ashtanga, 78, 82, 252n41; and beauty, 137–143, 204, 221; decolonizing, 17; as exercise, 31, 93, 109–110, 127, 137; festivals, 13–14, 44, 109, 133, 179, 227; and the commons, 212 Haṭha, 78; and Hindu nationalism, 63, 76; Indic origins of, 28, 44, 200, 203; invention of, 87–88; "is good for you," 163; lineage claims in, 76, 88, 97; as local knowledge, 75–78, 81–82, 85, 97, 101, 224; neoliberalism in, 13, 187, 204. *See also* neoliberalism; and POC teachers, 234; "post-lineage," 75; programming, 70, 108, 164; and prostration, 92–96; and purity, 130–131; and receptivity, 134; and religious exoticism, 9–11, 17, 45–46, 80–81, 101; and SBNR, 28–30, 39, 44, 70, 167, 222; sermons in, 30, 134; Slackline yoga, 26–27, 119; soteriological, 29; and South Asians, 54, 66, 75, 79, 86, 222; students, 30–31, 70, 78–82, 137, 201; teachers, 30, 77–82, 90, 127–129, 270n30; therapeutic, 120–122, 124; in this study, 25–28; at transformational festivals, 69–70; translation of, 95; as universal knowledge, 44, 86, 91, 97; Vinyāsa, 78–79, 92, 260n9; and whiteness, 17, 74–77, 85, 98, 232; yoga as index for whiteness, 14, 16, 91, 222, 251n27; workshops about, 90; and capitalism. *See* capitalism; community, 76, 91, 94, 133, 166, 199, 201, 204. *See also* "tribe"; POC Yoga class. *See* yoga classes, POC
Yoga and Festival Cultures Survey, 151
yoga apparel, 105, 113, 138–140, 181, 220; and mats, 29–30, 127, 181–182, 199, 243n107
yoga classes, 31, 69, 211; detox, 130; in this study, 69–70, Indigenous invocations in, 45–46; *kīrtan* in, 30; Kundalini, 127; rigorous, 129; POC, 83–84; sermons in, 77, 80, 88, 134, 163, 165; as producing SBNR values, 12, 25, 29–31, 70, 89–90, 134; rhetoric of, 201–202; Yin, 128
yoga practitioners, 29; as an interpretive community, 98; serious, 82; as a "tribe," 199; in the West, 93; and whiteness, 4
yoga studios, 31, 35, 68, 128, 249n89; financial struggle and, 86; as SBNR institutions, 22; as sites for *kīrtan*, 79; Wanderlust, 181
Yoga Sūtras, 109, 200, 203, 255–256n34, 258n2; elevation of the, 29–30, 44, 82

Žižek, Slavoj, 146

Founded in 1893,
UNIVERSITY OF CALIFORNIA PRESS
publishes bold, progressive books and journals
on topics in the arts, humanities, social sciences,
and natural sciences—with a focus on social
justice issues—that inspire thought and action
among readers worldwide.

The UC PRESS FOUNDATION
raises funds to uphold the press's vital role
as an independent, nonprofit publisher, and
receives philanthropic support from a wide
range of individuals and institutions—and from
committed readers like you. To learn more, visit
ucpress.edu/supportus.